Interviews
from
Red Sox Nation

Interviews
from
Red Sox Nation

David Laurila

Maple Street Press
Hingham, Massachusetts

© 2006 David Laurila. All rights reserved.

No portion of this publication may be reproduced in any way, stored in any type of retrieval device, or transmitted by any method or media, electronic or mechanical, including, but not limited to, photocopy, recording, or scanning, without prior permission in writing from the publisher.

Red Sox is a registered trademark of Major League Baseball. All rights reserved.

Maple Street Press LLC is in no way affiliated with Major League Baseball, the Boston Red Sox or their minor league affiliates.

The opinions expressed in the interviews contained in this book are those of the author and the subjects themselves and not necessarily those of Maple Street Press.

Bottom Front Jacket photo and design: Karen Turley
Top Front Jacket photo: Jim McIsaac / Getty Images
Back Jacket photos: © 2006 David Laurila. Reprinted with permission.
Interior design: Judith Littlefield

David Laurila. Interviews from Red Sox Nation
ISBN 0-9777436-1-6

Library of Congress Control Number: 2006928073

All product names and brand names mentioned in this book are trademarks or service marks of their respective companies. Any omission or misuse (of any kind) of service marks or trademarks should not be regarded as intent to infringe upon the property of others. The publisher respects all marks used by companies, manufacturers, and developers as a means to distinguish their products.

Maple Street Press LLC
11 Leavitt Street
Hingham, MA 02043
www.maplestreetpress.com

Printed in the United States of America
06 7 6 5 4 3 2 First Edition

Contents

Acknowledgments

The vast majority of these interviews were done before I was approached about collecting them in book form, so I'm inevitably going to fail to list a few people who deserve to be mentioned. If you fall under this category, please know that your contributions are appreciated, even if the quality of my memory is not.

As most of these interviews first appeared on the Royal Rooters of *redsoxnation.net* Web site, the first people I should thank are Anne Marie Desmaris, Jim Devlin, Corey Fyke, Don Hyslop, Edward Kirkpatrick, Nathaniel Lee, Mark Schofield and Tim Wescott. You all do a great job of running one of the best Red Sox sites on the Web.

Other Web sites and publications have been invaluable to my efforts. I'd like to especially thank Mike Andrews of *soxprospects.com*, Sean Foreman of *baseball-reference.com*, Sean Holtz of *baseball-almanac.com*, David Smith of *retrosheet.org*, and everyone at *Baseball America* and Sons of Sam Horn (*www.sonsofsamhorn.com*).

I'd also like to thank the great PR staffs in Pawtucket, Portland, Wilmington, Greenville and Lowell for their support. This book couldn't have happened without the help of Bill Wanless, Chris Cameron, Jon Goode, John Sadak, Nick Barrale, and Eric Jarinko.

Many others deserve mention for their support, advice, and other contributions. Among them are: Tom Andor, Rob Bradford, Bill Chapman, Devin Clancy, Herb Crehan, Pete Ehmke, Carol, Carl and Erik Fink, Pam Ganley, Glenn Geffner, Leigh Grossman, Joanna Hicks, Shaun Kelly, Rob Leary, Katie Leighton, John Lenger, Steve Lenox, John Manuel, Carolyn Mattson, Bill Nowlin, Cliff Otto, John Palfrey, Mark Rogoff, Gary Roy, Mike Scandura, Steve Sera, Danny Smith, Cecilia Tan, Bill and Kate Turley, the Chris Turley family, Kevin Vahey, Jim Walsh, Dan Williams, and everyone at the 1369 Coffee House in Cambridge, MA.

Most importantly, I would like to thank Karen Turley and Katie Laurila.

Foreword

Bet you didn't know the Red Sox have a connection to Lynyrd Skynyrd.

It's true. Leonard Skinner—the totalitarian high school teacher for whom the Southern band, recently inducted into the Rock and Roll Hall of Fame, was named—threw future Sox left-hander Rick "Too Tall" Jones off his baseball team in the early 1970s.

And did you hear about the time Win Remmerswaal, a Sox reliever briefly in 1979–80, ran out of gas in a rental car on the Massachusetts Turnpike, walked to the next town, rented another car, and drove off, leaving the first car on the side of the road?

You all remember Joe Mooney as the crusty, curmudgeonly groundskeeper who for years ferociously guarded the turf at Fenway Park. But he's also the guy who would retrieve every home run ball hit into the old left-field net by a player with local connections—regardless of what team he played for—and present it to him after the game.

David Laurila has gathered all these stories as part of his interview series on *redsoxnation.net*. These are the types of stories you'll find in these pages, the stories that breathe life into the very concept of Red Sox Nation.

For too many, Red Sox Nation had been a two-dimensional concept of curses, disappointment, defeat, and heartache. But even before the 2004 World Series championship that changed the landscape, David was talking to the Nation's citizens.

Sox players. Sox followers. Media members. Analysts. Team employees. Minor-leaguers. Draft picks. If they had a connection to the Red Sox—even, in the cases of some local professional players, if it was just as a fan during childhood days—David Laurila talked to them.

Their stories illustrated the depth and breadth of Red Sox Nation. And we discovered it actually *was* a nation, composed of people united by their connection to—and, in many cases, love of—the Red Sox.

David's knowledge of the Sox' history and culture, and his skill as an interviewer, give his readers insights into a subject they thought they knew backward and forward. We hear stories we've never heard before, from people we thought had told us all there was to say about the Red Sox.

Like Rick Jones' brush with fame, as related to David by Hall of Fame reporter Peter Gammons. And the zany world of Win Remmerswaal, remembered with exasperated fondness by Pawtucket Red Sox president Mike Tamburro.

There's more. Much more . . . as you'll discover when you turn the pages of *Interviews from Red Sox Nation*.

Enjoy. These are *our* stories. Gathered and told by one of our own.

Art Martone
Sports Editor
The Providence Journal

Introduction

On February 20, 2004, I posted an interview with a pitching prospect named Beau Vaughan on *redsoxnation.net*, a Red Sox message board. Since that time, more than 300 interviews have followed, all with people associated with the game of baseball. In most cases, Boston Red Sox baseball. This is a selection from those interviews, plus 10 more done exclusively for this book.

Players like Curt Schilling, Lou Merloni, and Jonathan Papelbon are included, but Red Sox baseball is more than just the everyday names. It is also young players like Vaughan, Jacoby Ellsbury, and Jon Lester, who are trying to achieve their dreams of some day playing in the major leagues. Others, like Marc Deschenes, Tim Kester, and Colin Young, have spent a number of years in the minor leagues but remain committed to chasing that dream. Red Sox baseball is also players of yesteryear, like Johnny Pesky, Rico Petrocelli, and Bill "Spaceman" Lee. It is former managers, like Butch Hobson and "Walpole Joe" Morgan, and general managers like Dan Duquette and Lou Gorman. It is current members of the baseball operations staff, like Ben Cherington and Jason McLeod, and it is a scout like Ray Fagnant, who covers the Northeast in search of tomorrow's stars. It is minor-league coaches and managers, like Ace Adams and Bruce Crabbe, and those who own and run the teams, like Drew and Joann Weber, and Mike Tamburro. It is the voices of the game like Joe Castiglione and Carl Beane, the Red Sox public address announcer. It is wives and mothers, like Shonda Schilling and Sheila Papelbon, and fans, like 80-year-old Anne Quinn, who has attended almost every game at Fenway Park for more than four decades. It is someone who has worked for the organization for more than 30 years, like Dick Bresciani, and a college student named Kelly Barons, who has captured the heart of Red Sox Nation as a ball attendant. It is the historians and statisticians, like Bill James and Pete Palmer, and Fenway

Park's long-time official scorer, Chaz Scoggins. And, of course, it is the people who write, and have written, about the team, like Bob Ryan, Bob Hohler, and Stewart O'Nan. With this book, and the interviews it contains, I humbly join that last group. I hope you enjoy the stories.

David Laurila
February 20, 2006
Cambridge, Massachusetts

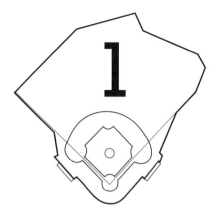

The Players

MICHAEL BOWDEN

MICHAEL BOWDEN WAS SELECTED BY THE RED SOX IN THE 2005 DRAFT AS A SUPPLEMENTAL FIRST-ROUND PICK AS COMPENSATION FOR THE LOSS OF DEREK LOWE TO FREE AGENCY. A 19-YEAR-OLD RIGHT-HANDED PITCHER FROM AURORA, ILLINOIS, BOWDEN SPENT HIS FIRST PROFESSIONAL SEASON IN THE GULF COAST LEAGUE. THIS INTERVIEW TOOK PLACE IN SEPTEMBER 2005.

David Laurila: *You started your professional career in the Gulf Coast League going six scoreless innings in four games. Why didn't you pitch more than that?*

Michael Bowden: I probably overthrew a bit in high school, and my MRI showed a little inflammation. I also had a pretty long break before signing, and the Red Sox had me doing some strengthening before they even let me get on the mound. Then I had two more weeks on the throwing program before I pitched in a game. And even before the MRI, I was told that I wouldn't be going more than two innings at a time. My arm feels good, but I guess they wanted to be cautious.

DL: *Overuse is always a concern when drafting pitchers. How much of a concern do you feel there should be with you?*

MB: I threw a lot of innings, but I was never abused. I'd say I threw over 100 pitches in a game twice . . . maybe three times. The most I ever went in a game was around 115. I think my arm is healthy.

DL: *Your* Baseball America *draft bio said your delivery is a little unorthodox. What were they referring to?*

MB: I've never really had a pitching coach and have always just gone with what feels natural . . . what feels best. Unorthodox seems a bit . . . oh, man, I don't know. I throw over the top, but I guess I'm not smooth. I'm a little herky-jerky, but personally, it's been working. Some people say a few tweaks might increase my velocity. But so far, they haven't changed anything. They're just making a few suggestions and letting me be me.

DL: *You're known for having an excellent curveball. What can you tell us about that?*

MB: I really just started throwing it this year. It's a 12-to-6 . . . a hard, fast-breaking curve. Sometimes I muscle it up too much, trying to throw it too hard. That causes it to break into the dirt, which I'm trying to keep from doing. I'm also trying to tighten it up a little. Still, Goose Gregson, the pitching coordinator here, told me that maybe five guys in the big leagues have a curve like mine. That makes me feel pretty good.

DL: *You didn't throw it before this season?*

MB: I started throwing it going into my senior year. Before that, I threw a slider and change-up.

DL: *Do you still throw a slider?*

MB: I do, although I haven't thrown it down here. I think it's pretty tight, and it has a good break. It's not on a straight plane. I do drop my arm-slot a little with it, but I have a lot of confidence in it and used it as an out pitch before I started throwing the curve. You know, it seems like everyone has been going to the slider the last few years. The curve is becoming kind of a lost art.

DL: *What about your change-up?*

MB: That's been an out pitch for me, too. It's kind of a modified circle-change, and it works well off of my fastball.

DL: *How would you describe your fastball, including velocity?*

MB: I throw it between 91 and 93, and have hit 95. I throw both a two- and a four-seamer, and get a pretty late cut on it.

DL: *Do you see yourself as a starter only, or could you imagine becoming a closer some day? Do you have what people refer to as a "closer's mentality?"*

MB: I've been asked that, and sure . . . I'm up to anything. As for the mentality, oh yeah . . . I'd fit that perfectly. I've always looked at myself as a starter with a closer's mentality.

DL: *Are you aggressive on the mound, thinking, "I can blow this guy away," or are you more cerebral, thinking, "He did this last time, so now I want to..."?*

MB: I'm not a finesse guy, but it's never just blow it by someone. It's all about pitching. Hitting spots is more important, and fortunately I'm usually able to hit them while throwing pretty hard.

DL: *What is your opinion on radar guns?*

MB: They don't really matter to me. Whether you're throwing 80 or 90, an out is an out. I don't ever come off the mound and ask how hard I was throwing.

DL: *You're said to be very athletic. What positions did you play when you weren't pitching, and how much will you miss hitting?*

MB: My senior year, I played everything but second base, catcher, and center field. Wherever they needed me, that's where I played. As for hitting, yeah, I'm going to miss it. I hit .500 with seven home runs, so I've been pretty good with the bat. I'm honored to play for the Red Sox, but I'd have loved going to a National League team so I could still hit.

DL: *Did you grow up rooting for the Cubs, or were you a White Sox fan?*

MB: The Cubs. I'll watch the Sox when they're on, but it's the Cubs for me.

DL: *Any opinions on Steve Bartman?*

MB: Bartman. Man, they beat him up so much. But I don't blame him for what happened. Plus, everybody would have done the same thing. People shouldn't kid themselves by saying they wouldn't reach for a foul ball into the stands.

DL: *Did you play other sports in high school?*

MB: I played football until I was a sophomore but stopped for baseball. I also played basketball—I was a forward—and was the second leading scorer on the team. Our leading scorer was pretty good. He went to Northern Iowa on a full scholarship.

DL: *I read a story about you regarding Mother's Day and a driveway— one that could have impacted your standing in the draft. Tell us about that.*

MB: We live down a gravel road, and it had a lot of potholes. My mom always has us do chores on Sunday, so we decided to fill them. It took all day, and I didn't realize how much work it would be. I was still sore on Tuesday for my next game, and my velocity was way down. That really hurt me a lot, because the scouts didn't know what was up. Fortunately, I had an opportunity to show them more after that game.

DL: *The Red Sox have a reputation for going predominantly after college players. Were you surprised when they drafted you?*

MB: As the season progressed, they showed a lot of interest. They gave me some pretty good hints that they were after me, so no, I wasn't surprised. I told friends that it would probably be the Red Sox. As a matter of fact, there's this Norman Rockwell picture of three Red Sox rookies walking into the clubhouse carrying suitcases. A couple of my friends got me a picture of it, with "Bowden" written on one of the suitcases.

DL: *Did the Cubs have any interest in you?*

MB: I pretty much knew it wouldn't be the Cubs because of where they were drafting. They picked too high in the first round, and then I probably wasn't going to last until their next pick. So no, I knew they weren't going to be taking me.

DL: *In a perfect-case scenario, who do you make your Major League debut against?*

MB: I'm facing the Yankees. That's where it's at.

DL: *You're pitching in the Gulf Coast League, which consists of noon games in the Florida sun with almost no fans. Today, in the last regular season game, you clinched a playoff berth. What was that like?*

MB: It's kind of . . . well, every day it's kind of repetitive down here. But today, with the playoffs on the line, there was a lot of energy on the bench. It was nice to see, because it's always more fun when you're playing for something.

DL: *Two more. Tell us something about yourself that most of us don't know.*

MB: I can sing along to anything, but it's not something I'll do in public. I pretty much have stage fright unless I'm on the mound. I can pitch in front of thousands of people, but I can't give a speech in class.

DL: *Last one: Has it really hit you yet that you're playing professional baseball?*

MB: I think so. But where it will really hit me is once I'm in Fenway Park. I haven't been there yet, but I did get to go into the clubhouse and on the field when the Red Sox were at Wrigley Field. The team brought me down there, and I got to meet a lot of the guys. I talked to Theo for a long time and also met Damon, Millar, Tek, Ortiz . . . and a few others. Ortiz called me a big guy. Man, that was pretty funny, having him say that. It was an awesome experience just to be there.

CLAY BUCHHOLZ

CLAY BUCHHOLZ WAS SELECTED BY THE RED SOX IN THE 2005 DRAFT AS A SUPPLEMENTAL FIRST-ROUND PICK AS COMPENSATION FOR THE LOSS OF PEDRO MARTINEZ TO FREE AGENCY. A RIGHT-HANDED PITCHER FROM LUMBERTON, TEXAS, BUCHHOLZ SPENT HIS FIRST PROFESSIONAL SEASON WITH THE LOWELL SPINNERS. THIS INTERVIEW TOOK PLACE IN JUNE 2005.

David Laurila: *You made your professional debut a few days ago. Tell us how that went.*

Clay Buchholz: It didn't go as well as I'd have liked, but I got through it. I got the first four hitters, but then gave up a couple of hits—one on a broken bat—and hit a batter. It was the first time I've faced hitters in a month, so I wasn't trying to overpower anyone. I was trying to focus on my mechanics but still opened up a little too much and was dragging my arm through the zone. I felt pretty good in the pen but didn't feel the ball jumping out of my hand like I usually do.

DL: *What type of pitcher do you consider yourself?*

CB: I'm a power pitcher. I only hit 92 the other night, but I've topped out as high as 97 this year. I throw a lot of two-seamers, which I like to work back over the plate. I'll also throw four-seamers, mostly trying to get hitters to chase.

DL: *What else do you throw, and next to your fastball, what do you consider your best pitch?*

CB: I throw a curve, slider, and circle-change. My slider is probably my second-best pitch. It has a pretty tight spin and has been an out pitch for me this season.

DL: *Do you throw from over the top, or is your arm-slot more three-quarters?*

CB: I actually throw from two different arm levels. I'm over the top a lot, but I'll drop to more three-quarters for my two-seamers and sliders.

The movement is different from each angle, so I'll come from both with all four of my pitches. I use the lower arm-slot with my two-seamer and slider as an out pitch.

DL: *What adjustments do you think you'll need to make in pro ball?*

CB: The biggest one will be mental. Everybody here can hit, so I need to be mentally tough for every hitter. I'll only be going two or three innings a game here, so that shouldn't be a big challenge, but I'll have to carry it over into next year when I'm going longer.

DL: *How strong-minded are you about pitch selection when you're not on the same page with your catcher?*

CB: I'm confident in what I want to throw, and I'll shake off anything. I take charting and videotaping seriously, and I'm out there with a good idea of what I want to do. I watch how hitters are reacting to a pitch, and I work off of that. The first time through a lineup, you learn a lot.

DL: *Will you work hitters differently the second and third time through the lineup?*

CB: Early in the game, you want to get ahead in the count, and then you can work off the plate a little more for most hitters. If you establish the strike zone, you can make it hard for hitters to lay off tough pitches. You can also get some calls if you've shown the umpire you're throwing consistent strikes.

DL: *What is your demeanor on the mound?*

CB: I get into a serious mode once the game starts. You're not going to find me laughing or cutting up with my teammates. Not that I'll hide in the corner of the dugout after an inning or anything like that. I don't mind guys talking to me. Maybe in a no-hitter . . . then I'll be in the corner by myself!

DL: *How are you at pitching off the stretch and holding runners?*

CB: I'm actually pretty good. Even in high school, I used to be the type that would pick off guys. I'd throw over and take the spring out of their legs. And I'm comfortable out of the stretch. I'll use a slide-step, too, and feel like I don't lose anything with it.

DL: *Can a pitcher learn as much from a catcher as he can from another pitcher?*

CB: I'd say no, because a catcher is a different type of animal. Pitchers and catchers both have to be mentally tough, but it's a different kind of mentally tough. Pitchers are focusing primarily on themselves and the batter; catchers are directing everything. A guy like Jason Varitek knows hitters as well as anyone, especially when it comes to things like what his feet are telling you. But a pitcher who really knows his stuff is probably still better to learn from. He's on the mound, doing the same job you are.

DL: *Along with pitching, you've played a lot of shortstop. Tell us about that.*

CB: Shortstop has always been my home away from home when I'm not on the mound. Had I gone to Texas Tech instead of signing, I was going to both close and play short. I've always had good side-to-side range and get to a lot of balls. I really enjoy the position, but here I'm obviously a pitcher.

DL: Baseball America *said your bat and athleticism would have made you a candidate for the first five rounds as a position player. Could you picture yourself trying to make it as a position player—much like Rick Ankiel is—if you hurt your arm?*

CB: Definitely. I have a good left-handed stroke and love to hit. I led my conference in hitting this past year. I could see myself starting over in the minor leagues as a hitter. And I wouldn't even mind pinch-hitting here, if they'd give me the opportunity. I could at least lay one down. I learned to drag bunt to take advantage of my speed, and I do that pretty well.

DL: *Would you play shortstop, or would any position be fine?*

CB: It definitely wouldn't be behind the plate! I don't like catching. In Little League practice, I broke a finger on a foul tip once. Since then, I've had no interest in being back there.

DL: *Who do you think the most underrated player is on the Red Sox?*

CB: I'd have to go with Kevin Millar. He's been a great clutch hitter, and people should look at what he's done for the organization and have faith in him. I hear people dogging him on the radio, even though he's a good teammate and comes through when it counts.

DL: *How about off the field—what have you been getting into lately?*

CB: I've been teaching myself the guitar. I've always wanted to play but never seemed to have the time with school and baseball practice. I'm still busy with baseball, but I have a guitar with me here in Lowell and practice when I can.

DL: *What else do you do in your spare time?*

CB: I run a lot to keep in shape. I mostly run sprints, anything from 400 meters down. Otherwise, I mostly just hang out.

TIM COX

TIM COX WAS SIGNED BY THE RED SOX AS AN INTERNATIONAL FREE AGENT IN OCTOBER 2004. A NATIVE OF SYDNEY, AUSTRALIA, COX MADE HIS PROFESSIONAL DEBUT IN 2005, PITCHING IN THE GULF COAST LEAGUE BEFORE MAKING TWO APPEARANCES FOR LOWELL LATE IN THE SEASON. THIS INTERVIEW TOOK PLACE IN JANUARY 2006.

David Laurila: *How would you describe yourself as a pitcher?*

Tim Cox: My arm-slot would be high three-quarters, and I tend to pound the strike zone. I also pitch quickly, as in little time between pitches. It's a win–win situation, because it's comfortable for me and upsetting for the hitters. I throw three pitches—fastball, curve, and change. I only throw a four-seam, as I find it has the same movement as my two-seam but with more control. My curveball is my weapon, and I can throw it for an out pitch or for a strike.

DL: *Tell us about the velocity and movement of each your pitches.*

TC: My fastball sits from 85 to 89 mph and gets great movement away from the right-handers and into the lefties. Curveball is 74 to 77 mph, and it's an 11-to-5 o'clock break. My change-up has a typical lefty movement and tends to be similar in speed to my curveball, around the mid-70s. I'm really happy with my change-up at the moment, as I was really only a fast/curve guy prior to coming to the Red Sox. During spring training, the coaches got me working on a change-up and it's come a long way since then.

DL: *If you're facing a hitter you know nothing about, and vice-versa, who has the advantage?*

TC: Good question. I believe the pitcher will always have the advantage, given any situation. He has control of what pitch is coming next and where it will be thrown. Furthermore, he can pitch to the situation at hand. As many coaches in the States have said to me, "A pitcher is always one pitch away from getting out of a jam."

DL: *Following up on that, how much can you learn about a hitter from just one or two at-bats?*

TC: A lot can be learned from one or two at-bats. Obviously, the more you see of him, the better, but paying attention to his stance, swings, body language, and approach can give you an understanding of what type of hitter he is.

DL: *You had Tommy John surgery in May 2003. How has that affected you?*

TC: There's no question it has dramatically affected my physical development as a pitcher. I broke down a couple of months after I'd turned 16 and didn't pitch in a game until I was almost 18. However, I feel I now have returned to the form that I was in prior to being injured, and at the same time learned a lot about the psychological side of pitching.

DL: *Why did you travel to the United States to have Dr. James Andrews perform the surgery, rather than having it done in Australia?*

TC: Dr. Andrews has a well-known reputation for Tommy John surgery and was highly recommended. Although I could have had the surgery done here in Australia, my dad and I felt that with such a specialized procedure, we wanted it done by a surgeon who had performed it several times before. The only bad thing that occurred for me was that I woke up from anaesthetic at 10 o'clock the next morning for a 1:30 p.m. flight to L.A., then a 14-hour flight back to Sydney. I was so heavily bandaged that I looked like I had just survived a war.

DL: *You signed with the Red Sox during the 2004 World Series. What was it like to sign a professional contract with a team that was about to win its first championship in 86 years?*

TC: It's quite funny, in that I was born in the year the last time they were in the World Series (1986), and it had been 86 years since they last won the World Series, so it was quite fitting for me to sign in 2004. Ever since I started playing baseball, it's been my dream to play in America. When the chance came along in 2004, it took me quite a few weeks to really believe that it had occurred. It wasn't until I arrived in spring training in 2005 that I really believed it happened.

DL: *You pitched in the Gulf Coast League last year and then made two appearances with Lowell. How would you assess your first professional season?*

TC: I don't think I could have dreamed of a better start to my professional career. Playing in Australia, you don't get an idea of the competition in the States, so I was unsure of the standard and my place in it. Spring training, I pitched fantastic. I really felt that I belonged there and could compete with the rest of the players. During the first couple of weeks of extended spring, I felt that I didn't perform as well as I would have liked, but as the season approached I bounced back to the level I was at during spring training. I continued this form for the remainder of the season and then earned two appearances in Lowell.

DL: *What was it like playing in Lowell after spending most of the summer in the GCL?*

TC: A totally different and unique experience. Going from five spectators [in the GCL] to 5,000, it's beyond description. You don't get those kinds of crowds down here in Australia. I also found that there was definitely a jump in the ability of the players, especially in the hitters.

DL: *Have you been told where you'll be pitching this season, and is there anything specific you feel you need to improve to have success against a higher level of competition?*

TC: The Red Sox have said that I'll be starting in Lowell—a slight possibility that I may go to Greenville—but I'm preparing mentally for Lowell. As for improvement, continue on perfecting my feel/confidence for my change-up and overall control. A bit more height wouldn't go astray, but that's out of my control.

DL: *Who has most helped you develop as a pitcher, both prior to and since you started your professional career?*

TC: A guy by the name of Ben Sutton was the first coach to really help me with pitching, when I was 13. Ben and I are now great mates and play in the local representative team here in Sydney together. Barry Holland, the pitching coach at the NSW Institute of Sport, then furthered my development as a pitcher from age 16 onwards. Barry played a major role in helping me get back on track after Tommy John surgery. Goose Gregson helped me during the season, especially from extended spring onwards. Not only did he help me with the mechanical side of pitching, but gave me great guidance in the mental side of pitching.

DL: *Certain catchers have a reputation as someone pitchers like throwing to. Was there anyone in Lowell or the GCL who you felt more comfortable with?*

TC: I was fairly comfortable with all the catchers that I threw to. However, if I was ever given the chance to choose, it would always be Patrick Perry. I always felt that we were on the same wavelength with how to set up hitters, etc. Being really good mates with him off the field may have something to do with it, but I first met him during spring training while throwing to him and was really impressed with how he caught.

DL: *How are most people in Australia looking at the upcoming World Baseball Classic?*

TC: Within the baseball community in Australia, the World Baseball Classic is enormous. Everyone thinks it's a great idea and believes it will really take off in the baseball world. As for the rest of Australia, it's not really advertised and with baseball being not a common sport, not many people know about it.

DL: *Do you know many of the players who will be representing your country?*

TC: The final roster hasn't been selected as of yet. Nevertheless, I will know probably 60 to 70 percent of the team. Sydney being the biggest city in Australia, a big portion of the team will be from Sydney so there is a good chance I will know many of the players.

DL: *The Red Sox recently signed Trent Durrington. What can you tell us about him?*

TC: Prior to the recent tournament (the Claxton Shield) that has been held each year in Australia between each state, I had never met Trent Durrington, only heard of him. However, after watching him at the Claxton Shield, I was very impressed with his ability at the plate and defensive skills.

DL: *If you had the talent to play professionally in a sport other than baseball, which would it be—and if it's a team sport, who would you want to play for?*

TC: Golf. I've played it ever since I had enough strength to swing a club. If it were to be a team sport, Australian Rules Football and I'd want to play for the Sydney Swans.

DL: *What are some of your interests outside of the game, and what can you see yourself doing after your baseball career is over?*

TC: I love all sports. Being an Aussie, I love the beach so I'm there quite often. I just recently became a personal trainer. I finished the course in December, and I'm currently instructing gym classes and personal clients with my cousin, who has his own business. I'll continue with this during each off-season when I come back to Australia. After my baseball career is over, I will most likely continue with my personal training, maybe expand into different avenues. Being a personal trainer on a big cruise liner has always interested me and is also a great way to travel and see the world. If for some reason that doesn't work out, I'll go to university to do a business degree. There are many paths I'd like to take. When the time comes, I'll make the decision.

DL: *To close, tell us a few things most Americans don't know about Australia, including a little about your hometown of Sydney.*

TC: Prior to the 21st century, very little was known about Australia from an American point of view. Australia is a very isolated country, compared to the rest of the world. To fly from L.A. to Sydney is a 14-hour flight, and because you cross the International Date Line, you arrive two days later. For instance, if you were to leave on a Thursday in L.A., you will arrive on a Saturday in Sydney. Australia is a very open country, meaning there are vast distances between cities and towns, and nothing in between. This could be due to the fact that 20 million people live in Australia, less than a tenth of the American population.

However, the 2000 Olympics in Sydney have educated not only America, but the rest of the world has learned more about Sydney and Australia. This has occurred through advertising and promotional television/media. We have some of the most spectacular beaches along the coast, and each has its own unique characteristics. There's a great story that I heard about a man who called a hotel in Perth to book a room for the Sydney Olympics. He asked for a room that looked over the Sydney Harbour Bridge, the Opera House, and also Ayres Rock. Unfortunately, Ayres Rock is about 1,500 miles away from the Sydney Harbour Bridge and the Opera House, and Perth is about 2,500 miles from Sydney. It would be similar to me ringing up a hotel in L.A. and asking for a room that looked over Fenway Park and Niagara Falls. So you can understand the disappointment the guy would have received when he was told that those places of interest were nowhere near each other.

MANNY DELCARMEN

MANNY DELCARMEN WAS THE RED SOX' SELECTION IN THE SECOND ROUND OF THE 2000 DRAFT. A NATIVE OF HYDE PARK, MASSACHUSETTS, DELCARMEN MADE HIS BIG LEAGUE DEBUT IN 2005, APPEARING IN 10 GAMES. THIS INTERVIEW TOOK PLACE IN JULY 2004 WHILE DELCARMEN, WHO HAD TOMMY JOHN SURGERY IN MAY 2003, WAS WITH THE SARASOTA RED SOX.

David Laurila: *Your last outing was a scoreless five innings with nine strikeouts. Was it your best game so far this year?*

Manny Delcarmen: Most definitely. All of my pitches were working, and it's the best I've felt since coming back. My last few starts weren't great, so it was nice to finally put everything together. Sometimes, I've thrown well but the numbers weren't there—my coaches would agree with that. This time, it was like clockwork.

DL: *Where are your arm strength and velocity right now?*

MD: They're real good—I think I'm back to 100 percent. As a matter of fact, I might be even stronger. Last year, I was consistently at 93–94 mph and now I'm sitting on 96 and topping out at 98.

DL: *What about command?*

MD: I can't say it's great yet, but I'm making progress. I know there are going to be bumps in the road, but Monday was the first time everything felt like it did, pre-injury.

DL: *Have you spoken to anyone who's had the same procedure?*

MD: Jerome Gamble had it a few years ago—he's pitching in Portland right now. He told me his velocity came back and there haven't been any problems. I also talked to Chad Fox before he went to the Marlins, and he said he came back stronger. It was good to hear those things from guys who went through it.

DL: *Are you on a pitch count?*

MD: I am. They're limiting me to either five innings or 75 pitches. Next season, I should be back to normal, and it will be a big year for me. The second year after surgery is supposed to be telling, and I'll be working hard this winter to make sure I'm ready.

DL: *A good change-up was considered key to your development, and at the time of the injury you were making progress with it. Tell us about that.*

MD: A few years ago, I was told that if I don't find one, they'd send me back to the Instructional League. I worked hard at it—trying different grips—and came up with a pretty good one. It's a circle-change like Pedro's, and it's been an important pitch for me. My curve was good last night, but the last few outings I had poor command of it. That meant I needed a solid change even more.

DL: *Tell us about your curveball.*

MD: It's normally my out pitch, so I'm not sure why I lost it for a few games—maybe I was thinking about it too much.

DL: *What kind of curve do you throw, and do you change speeds on it?*

MD: I throw it around 71–73 for strikes—a 12-to-6 with a big break. I'll also throw one a little harder—about 76—low and out of the zone when I'm ahead in the count. It's not a slider, but I'm looking to get hitters thinking fastball and chase.

DL: *Talk about your evolution from a thrower into a pitcher. Where, and when, did that come?*

MD: Coming out of high school, I knew that location would be important and I'd need to make adjustments. It was a real big step moving up to face professional hitters—everyone in pro ball can play, which isn't the case in high school. My first year in the Gulf Coast League, my mechanics were brutal. Ralph Treuel really helped me with that, and I've received a lot of good instruction at every level. My mechanics were solid by the time I reached Augusta, but my change-up was bad. It's an ongoing process, but I think I'm a pretty fast learner.

DL: *Let's go back to your injury for a moment. Talk about what happened.*

MD: I was throwing a great game, leading 1-0 in the 8th. I gave up a home run that tied it up, and my elbow went numb on the pitch—it was a change-up. I was lifted after that, but not because of my arm. I didn't say anything about it to anyone, and while it felt a little weird for a few days it seemed okay by my next start. I went three innings when suddenly it went numb again, and my velocity dropped from 93 to around 80. I knew that something was obviously wrong.

DL: *Had you had any arm injuries prior to that?*

MD: No, there were never any problems. That was the first time.

DL: *You grew up locally and were the first player from inner-city Boston drafted by the team in more than 30 years. What did that mean to you?*

MD: It was a great feeling. I used to go to Fenway as often as I could when I was younger and always dreamed of playing for the Red Sox. Scouts from other teams would come to the house, and I'd barely listen to them—I'd say that I wanted to play in Boston.

DL: *Tell us about draft day.*

MD: I wasn't even home when the call came. The phone had been ringing off the hook, and I wanted to get out for awhile. I didn't have a cell phone with me, and when I got back several hours later there were all kinds of cars and television cameras outside of the house. My mom came running out when she saw me—she had tears in her eyes—and said that the Sox had taken me. Everyone was really happy, and it meant a lot to the community—especially the Spanish-speaking community.

DL: *Like Pedro Martinez, Manny Ramirez, and David Ortiz, you're of Dominican descent.*

MD: I am. I have family there and in Boston. Pedro is my idol. My father, who played shortstop in the Phillies organization, used to say to me, "Just watch how he pitches." One of my biggest thrills was having Pedro come up to me in spring training and say, "You're Manny, right? You hurt your arm." Having him even know my name was special. I've always loved watching him pitch.

DL: *Tell us about some of the guys you're playing with in Sarasota.*

MD: Charlie Zink is down here now. He's really cool. He reminds me of my buddies from back home. Jon Papelbon is really funny. I can hardly even explain Jon. Nobody else is like him. I get along with everyone down here.

DL: *What do you guys do together when you're not playing?*

MD: We hang out. We play cards, have barbeques. Everyone here has their interests, and it's kind of fun how we're different. I like R & B and rap, but some of the guys listen to country and I'm starting to like it, too. I go home and play George Strait, and people look at me funny and ask what I'm playing!

DL: *Last question: Do you have any superstitions or nicknames?*

MD: Nah, not really. My roomie was calling me "Prince" for about a week because I had sideburns and my hair was a little long in front. That didn't last, though—thankfully.

MARC DESCHENES

MARC DESCHENES WAS OBTAINED BY THE RED SOX AS A MINOR LEAGUE FREE AGENT IN JULY OF 2004. A NATIVE OF DRACUT, MASSACHUSETTS, DESCHENES WAS DRAFTED OUT OF UMASS-LOWELL IN 1995 BY THE CLEVELAND INDIANS. THIS INTERVIEW TOOK PLACE IN JUNE 2005 WHILE DESCHENES WAS WITH THE PORTLAND SEA DOGS.

David Laurila: *You were drafted by the Indians out of UMass-Lowell as a shortstop. What went into the decision to make you a pitcher, and how much experience did you have on the mound at that time?*

Marc Deschenes: The Indians drafted me after my junior year, and I had pitched that season when I wasn't playing short. I had only thrown a handful of innings my freshman and sophomore years—maybe six— but the team asked if I could pitch more that season. Obviously, you'll do anything to help the club, so I ended up logging 79 innings when I wasn't at shortstop. The Indians didn't mention pitching when they took me, but interestingly, the Royals did. Had I lasted another round, they were possibly going to take me as a pitcher.

DL: *When did the Indians decide to put you on the mound?*

MD: It was about three weeks into the following spring training. After I was drafted, I played shortstop that season in the New York-Penn League. But then the next spring, Mark Shapiro, the Indians' GM, approached me and said the organization felt I had more potential as a pitcher. I guess they saw me throwing it 90 mph across the diamond and were more impressed with that than they were with my bat. So I ended up spending three weeks in extended spring training working off the mound, and then they sent me to the South Atlantic League as a pitcher.

DL: *Frank Rodriguez, a top prospect with the Red Sox around the same time, also ended up on the mound instead of at shortstop. Although he pitched in the big leagues, he didn't fulfill his potential and many feel he'd have been better served playing short. Do you ever wonder what might have happened had you remained a shortstop?*

MD: It's funny that you mention that, and it's hard to say. My passion was getting dirty every day at shortstop, and my fantasy was to play there at Fenway Park. But in reality, my bat probably wasn't good enough. My glove and arm may have been, but my bat didn't look like it would be Major League quality. It was a hard decision, because I loved playing short, but it was probably the right choice.

DL: *You've made it as high as Triple A, pitching parts of 2001 and 2002 at that level. How did you find yourself playing in an independent league by the end of 2002, and was it injury-related?*

MD: No, I've actually been injury-free my whole career. I think it was a simple case of not enough need at the time. I started the year as the closer in Double A with the Pirates and did well. The Cubs traded for me and sent me to Triple A but then ended up releasing me when they had to open up a roster spot for Mark Prior. I had workouts with a few teams, including the Sox, but nothing came out of them. I wanted to keep playing, so I hooked up with Nashua in the Atlantic League. It just wasn't the same in independent league ball, though. I pitched there for the rest of the season, but my heart wasn't into it, so I decided not to come back in 2003. But it was a long summer—I had no idea how much I'd miss playing—so in 2004, I decided to go back to Nashua and try to resurrect my career. I pitched well there, and in July the Sox signed me and sent me to Portland.

DL: *You're on a staff with some great arms right now. How does it compare to others you've been on in your 10 years of pro ball?*

MD: I'll tell you, it's unbelievable. It's probably the best starting staff I've seen in the minors. Those guys have a real good idea out there, and their ability to focus and go the extra mile is what makes them special. Pitching is a lot about command and not being afraid, and it's hard to rattle any of them. There's some big league talent there.

DL: *How about yourself? What do you bring to the mound?*

MD: Competitiveness and fastballs. I'm aggressive, and I'll throw my best at you. Ninety percent fastballs is my mentality.

DL: *How would you describe your fastball?*

MD: I throw mostly four-seamers, and while I sit around 90–92, I've topped out at 95 this year. Location is the important thing. I locate in-and-out, up-and-down; change the hitter's eye level. I throw a split and a slider, too, but I'm mostly challenging hitters.

DL: *Has your repertoire or approach evolved over the years?*

MD: I've changed my slider and split grips a little, trying to get different wrinkles. But the only real difference is that I'm smarter now. I've learned to see weaknesses better. I have a better understanding of things like when to climb the ladder, and when to pound lefties away when their sweet spot is down and in.

DL: *Tell us about growing up a Red Sox fan.*

MD: My dad has always been a big fan, as has my grandmother—my mom's mom. She never misses a game! So I grew up a diehard fan, too. I went to my first game when I was eight years old. I remember it was against the A's, and that we had good seats and I brought my glove. I loved infielders like Jody Reed and John Valentin, and emulated them in the backyard. I was just a kid who loved baseball and the Red Sox.

DL: *What was it like watching the Red Sox win last year, and did you think you'd ever live to see it?*

MD: It was unreal. I was at all of the home games in the postseason and watched the others with friends. You know what? After the Yankee series, I believed that we'd win it. Before that, it was hard to imagine. After all these years, you couldn't help but wonder if it might never happen.

DL: *How did this year's spring training compare to others you've experienced?*

MD: It was unbelievable. The whole atmosphere and buzz was amazing. I went to a lot of the big league games while I was in camp and was lucky enough to be in uniform for a few of them. Just being on the field with guys like Manny, Damon, and Tek was an honor.

DL: *You played for Butch Hobson in Nashua. What was that like?*

MD: It was great. He's intense and fiery. His competitiveness is through the roof. He's similar to Todd Claus in that he can't stand to lose, and he puts his players first. He really took to my mentality as a closer, and I enjoyed playing for him.

DL: *Being from Dracut and having attended UMass-Lowell, have you had a chance to attend many Spinners games?*

MD: It's a great park, but because of my own playing schedule I've only had a chance to go to one. Interestingly enough, it was with Ben Cherington in 2003—the year I wasn't playing. I think I want to stay in the game after I'm done playing, so I had been looking into the possibility of an internship with the club. Now that I have my baseball academy, it's hard to say if I'll be pursuing that or not.

DL: *Tell us about your baseball academy.*

MD: It's in Dracut, and it's called the Deschenes Baseball Academy. My partner is Mike Glavine, and we do private lessons, camps, and clinics. He's also the coach of one of my AAU teams. Along with Chris Hall, who's also my agent, I run an AAU team called the Diamond Dawgs. We have 12-, 13-, and 14-year-old divisions, and the 14-year-olds— that's Mike's team—qualified for the nationals this year. The other coaches are Derek Favreau, Joey Robarge, and Tommy Klemm. They all do a great job.

DL: *What qualities and instruction do you emphasize to the kids?*

MD: The biggest is enjoyment and fun. You have to enjoy the fact that you're playing. And respecting the game is big. You listen first, and then do your work. We stress that the individual never comes before the team, and there's a right way to play the game. If you do that and enjoy yourself, your natural ability will come out.

DL: *Once upon a time you were a kid playing ball in Dracut, and for the past decade you've been in pro ball. What has that meant for you and your family?*

MD: The support of my family has been integral. It's hard to do it on your own, and they've been behind me when I've been up and when I've been down. It can be a tough gig in the minor leagues. I've been lucky enough to play near my family for parts of my career, and that's meant a lot to me. I can't say enough about that.

DL: *Last one. You were drafted 10 years ago this month. What do you remember from that time of your life?*

MD: I had the look of an outstanding opportunity. I put some consideration into a senior year at UMass-Lowell, but the chance to play pro ball was too good to pass up. The excitement level was definitely high. Having scouts come to watch you play really makes your dreams kick in. Everybody has dreams and goals, and you wouldn't play if you didn't think you could make it to the top. I still think about it every day. I still hope that I can make it to the Major Leagues and wear a Red Sox uniform.

LENNY DINARDO

LENNY DINARDO WAS ACQUIRED BY THE RED SOX IN 2004 IN THE RULE 5 DRAFT. AS A LEFT-HANDED PITCHER, DINARDO HAS APPEARED IN 32 GAMES FOR THE RED SOX [THROUGH THE 2005 SEASON], AND AS A RIGHT-HANDED GUITAR PLAYER HAS PERFORMED AT THE HOT STOVE COOL MUSIC BENEFIT CONCERT. THIS INTERVIEW TOOK PLACE IN JANUARY 2006.

David Laurila: *You're a musician, as are Bronson Arroyo, Barry Zito and a number of other pitchers. Why do so many of you pick up guitars when you're not on the mound?*

Lenny DiNardo: I guess we have time on our hands and need to find a hobby, but we tend to be more eccentric, too. I can tell you that a lot of pitchers I meet are a little outside of the box—not in their right mind. And just like bands have a front man, we're like the front men of the infield. We're out there in the middle of everything, setting the tempo.

DL: *How similar are pitching and playing the guitar?*

LD: They're very similar. There are 100 styles of both, and the more unique you are, the better your chances of being successful. It's like a lead guitarist, like Joey Santiago of the Pixies. You hear him play, and you know exactly who it is. A lot of other guys are just carbon-copies of someone else. Pitching is the same. A guy like Greg Maddux can throw four different fastballs on the same corner. They'll all move differently, and it's like a work of art how he does it. What he does is a unique, honed craft, just like Santiago.

DL: *Are there any other similarities?*

LD: Sure. Like when you're learning to play the guitar, you reach a point where you get frustrated and want to quit. Some of the chords and changes just seem impossible, so you put it down for a few days. But you come back to it, and pretty soon you find out you can actually do it. It's like learning a new grip on a change-up. At first, they're all going 48 feet but after a while you develop a feel for it, just like you develop a feel for a chord.

DL: *Does playing the guitar affect your arm or fingers?*

LD: Tremendously. I used to get blisters from pitching, but playing the guitar has prevented that because it builds up calluses. It also helps the dexterity and flexibility of my fingers. I remember one Lemonheads song I was learning where I had to actually show my pinky where to go. It didn't feel natural, but with practice I was able to get it in the right place. With the guitar, you're basically training your fingers. When I hold my hand up like this, I can feel where all of my fingers are. Does that make sense? I'm not just throwing the ball—I can divert energy into a finger at a given time. I'm not out there blowing people's doors away, so getting a little extra pressure on a seam can give me better movement and make a big difference.

DL: *I understand that you got one of your guitars from David Wells. Tell us about that.*

LD: Wells has a friend connected with REM and knows Peter Buck. The guitar he helped me to acquire was a black-and-white Rickenbacker similar to the one Buck plays. Wells doesn't actually play himself, but he collects autographed guitars and has some pretty impressive ones.

DL: *How did you get interested in playing the guitar?*

LD: I grew up watching my dad play, sitting on his bed back home. My older brother plays, too, and I attribute much of my taste in music to him. When I was about 11, he played "It's a Shame about Ray," by the Lemonheads, and it kind of went from there. He turned me on to a lot of the stuff I like. My dad listens to some pretty interesting stuff, too—everything from Richard Thompson to Dave Van Ronk to Django Reinhardt.

DL: *Do you have any thoughts on Miles Davis, a jazz guy, going into the Rock and Roll Hall of Fame this year?*

LD: It's not rock and roll, but a lot of Miles' chops are. He influenced a lot of people. As a matter of fact, there's a real chain of influences throughout music, which a lot of people don't realize. For instance, if there wasn't a Bing Crosby or a Louis Armstrong, there wouldn't have been a Jerry Garcia. You listen to people when you're perfecting your runs, and the Grateful Dead took a lot from guys who had their own distinct styles. The Sex Pistols went into the Hall of Fame, too, and I'm way into bands that were influenced by them. The Pixies don't sound like them, but there wouldn't be a Frank Black if it wasn't for the Sex Pistols.

DL: *Hitters have intro songs play over the PA when they come up to hit in their home ballparks. Do you pitch heavy metal guys any differently than country guys?*

LD: No, but that's an interesting thing to think about: Do metal guys have a different approach at the plate than country guys or Latin guys? Nah, I don't think so. Music does say something about the person, but probably not how he hits. I don't think I'd throw Jim Thome fastballs inside because he listens to Garth Brooks instead of Metallica.

DL: *Are you planning to have your own intro song for when you come into games this year?*

LD: Maybe. If I do, I'm thinking of "Where's My Mind?"—either the Pixies' version or the cover version by Nada Surf. The beginning of that song gives me goose bumps, and you want that coming to the mound.

DL: *Besides the Nada Surf, what are some of your other favorite cover songs?*

LD: I heard Steven Malkmus and Pavement do a great live version of Echo and the Bunnymen's "The Killing Moon" once. I'm not sure if they've actually recorded it or not. Another one I like is Calexico's cover of "Alone Again Or," which I believe was originally done by a band called Love.

DL: *How about ones that you don't like?*

LD: I'm not sure who does it, but one that really got to me was a cover of a Don Henley song. I think it's called "The Boys of Summer." Some MTV-type band did it, and it was awful. There are actually a lot of songs out there that people are turning into complete drivel, especially ones from the eighties.

DL: *To close, let's get your opinion of a few bands. Which do you like better: Television or Radiohead?*

LD: I have a biased opinion on that one, because I've been listening to Radiohead since "Pablo Honey." I've only been listening to Television since I was given a copy of "Marquee Moon" about a year ago. I definitely like both, but my history with Radiohead is a lot longer.

DL: *The Jam or Pearl Jam?*

LD: I know they're really mainstream, but I have to say Pearl Jam. I met Pearl Jam guitarist Mike McCready a couple years ago, and it was a big thrill for me. They have a lot of really great songs that a lot of people don't tend to hear about. Some friends of mine have only heard their album *Ten*, but there's a lot more to them. *Ten* came out when I was 11, and there were too many bad hair bands until they and Nirvana hit the scene. Pretty soon, I was stealing my brother's Pearl Jam shirt and wearing hiking boots. I was living in Florida, but I looked like I was from Washington. I was into the whole music scene. As a matter of fact, I guess I'm still into the whole music scene.

JACOBY ELLSBURY

JACOBY ELLSBURY WAS THE RED SOX' SELECTION IN THE FIRST ROUND OF THE 2005 DRAFT. AN OUTFIELDER, ELLSBURY SPENT HIS FIRST PROFESSIONAL SEASON WITH THE LOWELL SPINNERS. THIS INTERVIEW TOOK PLACE IN JULY 2005.

David Laurila: *Give us a scouting report on your offensive game.*

Jacoby Ellsbury: I'd say opposing teams look at me as scrappy and hard to get out. My walks-to-strikeouts ratio has been good, so I'm patient and make pretty good contact. I'm a leadoff hitter, so I want to get on any way I can, be it a hit, walk, hit-by-pitch, or error. I like to try to extend singles into doubles and doubles into triples. I like to use my legs to my advantage.

DL: *From a hitting standpoint, do you feel you do a good job of utilizing your speed?*

JE: I think I do, but I don't focus just on speed. I probably don't bunt as much as a lot of leadoff guys and don't run out of the box like Ichiro. I'm up there to hit, and will even try to run into balls once in awhile. By that I mean drive them. I want to develop some more power and be a well-rounded player. I believe in working on my weaknesses more than my strengths. I do use my speed though, and while I was seldom asked to bunt at Oregon State, at this level I'll probably want to do it more.

DL: *Jerry Remy was recently commenting on a Red Sox telecast that it seems like speed guys are often much better fastball hitters than breaking ball hitters. How do you handle off-speed stuff?*

JE: I think I hit breaking pitches pretty well. I think I'm good at recognizing pitches and keeping my hands and weight back. Some guys tend to get too far out in front, but I can usually stay back pretty well. I trust my hands and will drive the ball the other way.

DL: Baseball America *rated your strike zone judgment third best among college players coming into the draft. Tell us about that part of your game.*

JE: That's always come natural for me. I think you have to be disciplined and trust your eyes, and like I was saying, I'm pretty good at recognizing pitches out of the hand. If something is over the outside corner, I know I can get my bat on it. But if I have less than two strikes, I'd rather wait for a ball I can do more with. A big part of hitting is having the confidence to hit with two strikes.

DL: *Stealing bases is a big part of your game. How big of a lead do you take at first base—is it an aggressive one where you're looking to intimidate or distract the pitcher?*

JE: I definitely want the pitcher to know I'm there. I want him to know that he has to go with fastballs if they're going to throw me out. But do I take a huge lead? Not necessarily. I want my lead to be comfortable so that I'm not limiting myself by having my weight in the wrong direction. Taking too big of a lead is usually not beneficial, and there's a fine line between the right lead and one that's too big. What I want to be is aggressive and force the other team to make plays.

DL: *Do you ever slide head-first?*

JE: Sometimes I do, but not into third or home. I will go head-first into second once in a while, even on a steal. I pretty much make up my mind while I'm running; it's a split-second decision—instinctive. When I was in high school, I hardly ever slid. The infields were hard, and I could usually just go in standing up.

DL: *Does your approach change with an Andy Pettitte on the mound, a pitcher with a great pickoff move?*

JE: Definitely. Like the cliché goes, baseball is a game of inches. You have to give and take a little, depending on the opponent and situation. If a guy has a great move, you need to tip your hat to him and come in a bit. Conversely, if he has a suspect move, you extend.

DL: *If you're leading off an inning, would you rather hit a triple, or hit a single and steal second and third bases on the next two pitches?*

JE: I'd take the triple. Then again, if I'm on first, the next hitter is more likely to get a fastball and the infielders will be moving. So maybe the triple would be more for selfish reasons, and the single better for the hitters. Being on third is the important part, so I guess I'll take either one.

DL: *You're said to be an outstanding defensive player, with good speed and a strong arm. Do you consider the scouting reports pretty accurate?*

JE: I guess so. I think I get pretty good jumps, and I'm willing to sacrifice my body and go hard into the wall if the situation dictates. There's a time for it, though. I don't think the team would be too happy if I was crashing into the wall and risking myself when we were up by 10 runs.

DL: *Having gone from the College World Series to starting your pro career, you've obviously been very keyed-in the last few months. How will you be able to maintain that focus throughout the remainder of the season?*

JE: I've been dreaming of this my whole life, so I don't expect it to be a problem. I think I have a good understanding of what the lifestyle will be. I've talked to some guys who have played minor league ball, and I know there will be some days that I'll be tired. But it won't be anything I can't handle.

DL: *If a day off to recharge your batteries would be beneficial, would you ask for it? Or do you look at it as your responsibility to gut it out and play at less than 100 percent?*

JE: I think that's something that would be more mental than physical, and I could fight through it. A lot of guys are going to be tired, and they aren't going to be asking for time off. So no, I don't think I could ask out of the lineup. That's not my style.

DL: *I understand you wore a Red Sox cap while being interviewed by a scout from another team prior to the draft. What's the story with that?*

JE: I got it when I was playing in the Cape Cod League last summer. I wore it to all of my games at Oregon State last year for good luck. I had no idea I'd end up getting drafting by the Red Sox.

DL: *Were you familiar with Boston's farm system when you were drafted, where the minor league affiliates are?*

JE: I wasn't, but after the draft I started looking. I think I went to *Baseball America's* minor league site to find out where they were. My dad likes to come see me play, so he was doing the same thing. He called to tell me where I'd probably be playing the next few years. He hasn't been out here yet this summer, but he'll be coming later.

DL: *You played summer ball in Alaska a few years ago. What was that like?*

JE: It was a great experience. I played with the Anchorage Glacier Pilots, and it was my second year with a wood bat. Coming out of high school, I played for a semipro team called the Bend Elks, where I was the only guy who wasn't currently playing college ball. I think I made my biggest jump as a ballplayer in that league. I really learned a lot. I think I also made great strides my summer in Alaska.

DL: *Tell us about your name: Jacoby. Is there a story that goes with it?*

JE: My mom saw it on a sign, in Arizona. Seriously. I think it was on an ad for something. It's not a family name, and I don't think she even knew anybody named Jacoby. She just liked the sound of it.

EDITOR'S NOTE: Ellsbury checked with his mother following the interview. The advertiser was a company that sold farm equipment, and the specific ad was for a tractor.

DL: *You've drawn some comparisons to Johnny Damon for your play on the field. But what about off the field: are you an extrovert, and have you ever worn your hair long like his?*

JE: Nah, I'm more laid back than Johnny. Not that I don't like to have a laugh once in a while—I do like to have fun. As for my hair, no, I haven't worn it that long. I actually got it cut a few days ago.

DL: *What are you into off the field?*

JE: I like the outdoors, warm weather, and relaxing with my buddies. I like lake fishing.

DL: *Last one: Tell us something people don't know about you.*

JE: One is that I chased down a deer when I was in high school. Our house is on two acres, and I got a rope from the garage while my brother steered the deer in my direction. Another thing is that I like eating waffles with applesauce. I'm not sure why, but it's something I've always liked. Yeah, I know. It's a little weird.

REID ENGEL

REID ENGEL WAS THE RED SOX' SELECTION IN THE FIFTH ROUND OF THE 2005 DRAFT. A 19-YEAR-OLD OUTFIELDER FROM MONUMENT, COLORADO, ENGEL SPENT HIS FIRST PROFESSIONAL SEASON IN THE GULF COAST LEAGUE. THIS INTERVIEW TOOK PLACE IN AUGUST 2005.

David Laurila: *How would you assess the start of your professional career?*

Reid Engel: I think that signing was the best decision I could have made. I'm learning to play the game better, learning the pro game. I've made a lot of adjustments and still am. A lot of guys have the physical ability, but the mental part is what really matters. In high school, you can get away with just your physical talent, but here you have to be mentally prepared every day. I'm struggling at times but know in my mind that I can compete.

DL: *What went into your decision to sign rather than play college ball?*

RE: I had an awesome opportunity to attend Baylor, and decided to just let the draft unfold and go from there. I figured it would be a good sign if I went in the top five rounds—that I'd be looked at as a prospect and get an opportunity. Six or seven teams said the third, fourth, fifth, or sixth. Had I gone in later rounds, maybe I wasn't ready yet and college would be a better option. I thought, "Hey, whichever way is going to be fine." As it worked out, God wanted me to go in the top five, and I'm happy to be here.

DL: *Which teams showed the most interest going into the draft, and were the Red Sox one of them?*

RE: I actually had a lot of teams interested. I think the only ones that didn't contact me were the Yankees, A's, Blue Jays, and Nationals. I had predraft workouts at Fenway Park and Angels Stadium, so I knew those were two strong possibilities . . . two high opportunities.

DL: *What was it like working out at Fenway Park?*

RE: It was amazing. Just standing there, looking up at the press box and out toward the wall . . . it was one of the best experiences I've ever had. Fortunately, I had gone to the game the night before, which gave me a feel of what it's like to be there. We lost to the Orioles, but the next day David Ortiz hit a walk-off in the afternoon, and then we worked out. It was my first time at Fenway, and it was awesome.

DL: *Your draft bio in* Baseball America *questioned whether you're physically ready for pro ball. What are your thoughts on that?*

RE: I definitely haven't reached my man-strength yet, which is part of what they meant, I guess. But I'm 20 or 25 pounds heavier than what they listed me at—I weigh 185. I don't know why they had that wrong, because it's not like I suddenly bulked up. I felt that I was ready. Still, I'll be doing my due diligence in the off-season to get in better shape and improve my bat speed. I'll be following the program and lifting.

DL: *How will working out improve your bat speed?*

RE: I'll be working on my core, on my rotation. I'll be working on my legs and hips. You want everything in sync, and stronger.

DL: *While you're known more for your speed, you did hit some home runs this year. How much power do you have, and do you feel that you utilize your speed as well as you should?*

RE: I have two home runs down here so far, and think I'll hit my fair share, but I'm not a guy who'll hit a ton. I can run, but I'm more of a back-leg gap-to-gap hitter, not a guy who looks to slap the ball. I try to drive it. I try to let my speed take care of itself, legging doubles into triples, that kind of thing.

DL: *You're hitting in the leadoff position right now. Does that have an impact on your approach?*

RE: I may actually be a little too caught up in that right now. I know what they're looking for, and they'll make suggestions, but I think I'm being a little too tentative. I'm probably thinking too much, trying to get on base rather than just relaxing and being the player they drafted. I need to stick with my approach, which I like to refer to as "aggressiveness under control."

DL: *How would you rate your base-stealing skills, and what do you need to improve in that aspect of your game?*

RE: That's an area where the game is quicker than I am right now, and I need to work on it. I can definitely run, but I need to improve my reads and jumps. I've always been pretty average off the line, building up speed as I go. Here, it won't come as easy, because I'm not running against slow deliveries or catchers with weak arms.

DL: *How would you describe your stance and your swing?*

RE: To be honest, it's been all over the place lately. I've been on my front foot too much, jumping at the ball, wanting to just make contact. I've been pressing. But normally, I'd say I have more of a drive-the-ball swing and a straight-up stance. A straight parallel load-and-go.

DL: *Jason McLeod, the Red Sox' director of scouting, said you're good at hitting the ball where it's pitched. Tell us about that.*

RE: I've always been comfortable going with inside and outside pitches. An interesting thing is that I've struggled with lefties before but am making better contact against them now. I'm staying back better and am getting a lot more confident. I had some success against them early, and it was like, "Gosh, I can hit them." Confidence is really big when it comes to hitting.

DL: *Are there any players you model yourself after, or that you'd compare yourself to?*

RE: I don't model myself after anyone, but I've been compared to a few guys. My hitting coach down here, Cesar Hernandez, said I remind him a little of a young Luis Gonzalez. A few scouts have compared me to Steve Finley and Andy Van Slyke.

DL: *You're a center fielder. Tell us about your defensive game.*

RE: That's another aspect where I've been pressing too much. The outfield has always come easy for me, including getting good reads, but I need to trust myself more. I started doubting myself a little down here, but I'm getting my feet back under me now. I just need to be more relaxed and not put pressure on myself.

DL: *I understand that your dad played college ball. How much has he helped you learn the game?*

RE: He's one of the big reasons I'm here. He played at the University of San Diego in the late seventies and early eighties—he was an outfielder, too—and I've had a bat in my hand since I was a little kid. God blessed me with talent, and he helped me from there.

DL: *Which team did you follow growing up?*

RE: Living in Colorado, I followed the Rockies, but I was more of a Padres guy. My parents are from California, and I was actually born in San Diego, so the Padres are probably in my genes. And the Red Sox have always been up on my list of favorites, too.

DL: *What are some of your interests and hobbies outside of the game?*

RE: I've always enjoyed drawing and go through spurts where I do a lot of that. I've never been that great at imagining stuff and then drawing it, but I can always look at something and draw it. I also play the guitar a bit. I've never had lessons, but I've played for about four years. Mostly alternative rock stuff. Outside of that, I consider myself a strong Christian. I'm all about friends and family, and knowing the Lord outside of the game.

CRAIG HANSEN

CRAIG HANSEN WAS THE SECOND OF TWO RED SOX SELECTIONS IN THE FIRST ROUND OF THE 2005 DRAFT. A RIGHT-HANDED PITCHER FROM GLEN COVE, NEW YORK, HANSEN MADE HIS BIG LEAGUE DEBUT IN SEPTEMBER 2005. THIS INTERVIEW TOOK PLACE IN DECEMBER 2005.

David Laurila: *Dock Ellis, an All-Star pitcher in the 1970s, said that it was all about power—he never thought about setting up hitters or pitching around them. How would you describe your approach?*

Craig Hansen: I'd call myself a power pitcher. Right from a 0-0 count, I go after hitters. I'm not a guy who believes in wasting pitches, throwing the ball off the plate or in the dirt. And while I'll throw to a hitter's weakness if the situation dictates it, I mostly go out and pitch to my own capabilities. What I want to do is get outs as quickly as I can and get the team in the dugout.

DL: *From a pitcher's perspective, what do you consider the hardest pitch to hit in baseball?*

CH: That's hard to say, because different pitchers have different stuff—different movement. It depends on the hitters, too. Some guys have more trouble with a specific pitch, and if their weakness is your strength, that improves your chances. But if I had to name one . . . based on what I've heard, it's probably Wake's knuckleball.

DL: *Do you pitch any differently to a contact hitter than you do to a guy who takes a bigger swing?*

CH: I pretty much go with an aggressive approach against all hitters. At this level, everyone gets their bat on the ball if you don't make a good pitch. Sometimes I'll end up on top, and sometimes I'll end up on the bottom. For the most part, I don't even pay attention to who the hitter is. When I pitched against the Yankees in September, I didn't know I had faced A-Rod, Giambi, and Sheffield until I got back to the clubhouse and somebody told me.

DL: *You gave up a game-tying home run to Melvin Mora last year. Is that something you'll always remember when facing him in the future— or, as you just said, will he be just another hitter?*

CH: I'll always know who hit the first home run against me, but yeah, he'll just be another hitter. It will be another at-bat the next time, and we'll see what happens. Of course, it's important to learn from your mistakes, so you still have to be aware of what pitch someone hit. After that inning, Jason Varitek came up to me on the bench and talked about it. He said that it will happen. He also said we didn't know each other yet—that we'll be more on the same page in time.

DL: *When it comes to pitch selection, it's generally accepted that throwing the wrong pitch with 100 percent confidence is better than throwing the right one with doubt. What if you're thinking fastball and a veteran catcher like Varitek is calling for a slider?*

CH: It's funny, when I was in high school the coach didn't like us shaking off, and we—the pitchers—went and talked to him about that. When you're on the mound, you'll have a certain feeling for what the best pitch is. Sometimes, the catcher will call for something, but you're positive that's what the hitter is looking for. And you're right about needing 100 percent confidence in what you're throwing. If you're second-guessing yourself, it makes a huge difference how the ball comes out of your hand. Tek obviously knows the hitters better than anybody, but he also understands how pitchers think. At first, I didn't want to shake him off—I didn't want to do anything that would look disrespectful. But he told me it's not like that all. It's about working together.

DL: *A well-located 92-mph fastball is usually better than a 94-mph fastball that's out over the plate. How hard is it to harness your command when you need to make a big pitch—and the temptation is to reach back for a little extra instead of hitting your spot?*

CH: There's no doubt that painting the corners is good. Doing the little things is big at this level, and someone like Greg Maddux has been successful by spotting the ball with good movement—not by throwing it by people. I try to throw pretty much the same every time—I rarely take anything off, for instance. However, if I feel like I'm in a good groove, I can get a little extra on a pitch and still spot it well. You don't want to try to really hump it up, though, because you'll definitely lose a little control. You're doing something that's unnatural, so it can change everything in your delivery.

DL: *How would describe the movement on your fastball and slider?*

CH: They say I have a sinking fastball, but I don't really see it, to be honest. I just go with my natural motion, and they claim it moves down. My slider has drop to it—a hard drop. I'd say it moves at a southwest angle. Sometimes, I'll toy with a slower one, but I generally throw it pretty hard.

DL: *A big part of pitching success is the ability to make adjustments, and a lot of guys refine that in the minor leagues. How much harder will your learning curve be if you start the season in Boston rather than in Pawtucket?*

CH: One thing I've learned about this organization is that no matter where you are, someone is working with you. In September, I was rushing toward the plate a little, and Dave Wallace helped me correct that. He and the rest of the coaching staff are good at picking things up, so I think I'll be able to make adjustments when the need arises.

DL: *Where is your change-up right now?*

CH: I throw what's basically a circle-change, which Dave Wallace taught me when I was pitching on the Cape the summer going into my junior year. Right now, I'd say that it's still a work in progress. We're working to make it better, and hopefully by spring training it will be there.

DL: *Could you see yourself going with a split-finger pitch, instead of a change-up, someday?*

CH: I've toyed with it but have never really gotten into it. It can be hard on the arm, too, so it's not a pitch I'm thinking about right now. But I do need to develop a more consistent off-speed pitch, which is why I'm continuing to work on making my change better.

DL: *Intimidation is a big part of pitching, especially for a power pitcher. How much do you feel you need to move guys off the plate—or even knock them down?*

CH: I wouldn't say that's how I go out there, but to a certain extent it's something every pitcher has to do. You can't let hitters be too comfortable in the box, and they understand that. As a pitcher, you have to set the pace—you need to be in control. If you let the hitters get too comfortable, that's when it really starts to hit the fan.

DL: *From a statistical-analysis standpoint, a pitcher who throws 200 good innings is arguably more valuable than one who throws 80. How do you think the Red Sox are assessing your future role, and would you rather start or pitch out of the bullpen?*

CH: I'm not really sure what they'd like. But do you know what? Either is fine with me—I honestly don't have a preference. I just do what they ask, because all that's important to me is that I'm pitching.

DL: *If they decide that your future is as a starter, how much of an adjustment would that be?*

CH: My last appearance in college, I went seven innings and I felt fine, so I could definitely do that without a problem. I've started before, and it's like riding a bicycle, really.

DL: *You went through a little arm-fatigue last year when you were pitching in Portland. Tell us about that.*

CH: I'm really not sure what it was. I was doing my programs and throwing during the break, so I don't think it had anything to do with the time off between my college season and signing. But I've dealt with that in school before, and you just need to take a few days off when it happens. It wasn't a big deal—my arm is fine.

DL: *You'll be going into spring training with a chance to earn a spot on the big league team. How hard will it be to stay disciplined and resist the urge to try to make an early impression—perhaps before you're ready to go all out?*

CH: The best advice I got in September was from Mike Timlin. On my first day, warming up in Tampa Bay, he goes, "Just go out there and don't change a thing—you're here for a reason." The team knows my capabilities, so I just basically plan to go out and do what I always do. Regardless of where you are, in the end it's still baseball.

SHEA HILLENBRAND

SHEA HILLENBRAND WAS TAKEN BY THE RED SOX IN THE 1996 DRAFT AND PLAYED IN BOSTON FROM 2001 UNTIL MAY 2003, WHEN HE WAS TRADED TO ARIZONA. CURRENTLY WITH THE TORONTO BLUE JAYS, HILLENBRAND IS A TWO-TIME AMERICAN LEAGUE ALL-STAR. THIS INTERVIEW TOOK PLACE IN JANUARY 2006.

David Laurila: *You were born in Mesa, Arizona. Is that where you grew up?*

Shea Hillenbrand: I was born there, but we moved to Los Angeles when I was three months old. When I was 14, we moved back to Mesa, and that's where I went to high school.

DL: *You were the Arizona high school soccer player of the year in 1993. Did you consider pursuing a career in professional soccer?*

SH: I was probably better at soccer than baseball, but no, not really. Baseball is huge, and soccer isn't, at least not here in the United States, so I never looked at it as a possible career. I did enjoy playing, though. Of course, back in Arizona and Los Angeles, it was a night-and-day difference from what it's like here. Out there, playing was more or less for fun. Here, sports are like a religion.

DL: *I understand that you almost quit after your first professional season, which was spent in Lowell. Can you share that story with us?*

SH: It wasn't "almost." I did quit. My wife, Jessica, talked me out of it, though. She said she knew I'd regret it someday if I didn't go back. So I did, although I showed up two weeks late for spring training.

DL: *Why were you going to give up baseball?*

SH: It's not the same when you're getting paid to play, and I didn't enjoy all of the politics and business that are involved. I wasn't ready for that. And it can be a tough go, too, with 13-hour bus rides and small paychecks. It's not that I thought it would be any different than it was, because I didn't know what to expect. I hadn't talked to anybody who had played minor league ball. Now, don't get me wrong—I've been lucky to be able to do something I love. Probably 90 percent of the people in the world can't do what they dreamed of growing up. But at the time, I just wasn't sure that it was something I wanted.

DL: *Can you elaborate on that a little?*

SH: Money is why you sign a professional contract, and once you do, everything changes. And while it seems like a contradiction, baseball is a team sport—it's not like tennis or golf—yet it doesn't matter what the team does in the minor leagues. The object is to make the big leagues, so it matters what you do. Most of the guys who sign aren't going to make it, and you're all fighting for that job. And you're not all going to be treated the same, because some of you were drafted higher and got a bigger bonus. When guys in the minors tell you it's all about the team, they're not being honest, because that's not why they're there.

DL: *Someone once said that baseball is an individual game when you're at bat, and the rest of the time it's a team game. What are your thoughts on that?*

SH: Once you reach the Major Leagues, it's never an individual game because you're signed to help the big league team, not yourself. The goal is to win. You always play for the team, whether that means giving yourself up by moving a runner over or helping a teammate with something. And teammates matter. Character is a big reason the Red Sox won two years ago. All that started when I played with the original Dirt Dogs—guys like Trot Nixon and Brian Daubach. It takes more than just talent to win. Look at the Yankees' payroll and tell me how many World Series they've won lately. You don't want to be giving a high-five to a piece of crap because he hit one out—it means more when it's someone you want to play with.

DL: *You were close to Carl Everett and Manny Ramirez, each of whom has been treated, at times, harshly by the media. How often do you think the public perception of players differs from what they're actually like in the clubhouse and away from the game?*

SH: It's not even close. I'd say that probably 90 percent of players are different than how they're perceived. We're human, and people tend to forget that. They don't get to know us, so they can only go by what they see on the field and read in the paper. They see Manny walk into the Green Monster, and think he must be cuckoo. And Carl Everett is a strong-willed person, so people take that to mean he's a bad person. But perceptions aren't always true. As players, we're around each other more than our own families, and we're out there fighting and scrapping, trying to find a way. We're going to war together. Fans don't see what happens when the game is over.

DL: *You were also close to Johnny Pesky when you were here. What did he mean to your career?*

SH: Everything. He was a foundation for me, and it was a privilege to be able to use him as a resource. To have someone like that as a mentor, someone who can say things like, "This is what Ted did," was an honor. He's like an encyclopedia, and you take it for granted until you're not here anymore—until you're not around guys like Johnny, and Yaz, and

Dwight Evans. That's what it's like in Boston. And Johnny actually threatened to quit when I was traded. That meant a lot to me. But baseball is his life, so there's no way I wanted him to do that. I called him and told him not to. I said, "Don't quit, Uncle Johnny."

DL: *You have a reputation as a guy who works hard at what you do. Where does that come from?*

SH: I'm lucky enough to have been blessed with desire and talent, and that's what's helped get me here. And to make it to the big leagues, you need the desire just as much as the talent. You won't find many guys in the big leagues who don't work hard. A lot of people are driven to succeed, and that's not something you can teach. Some guys, if they had a different job—if they worked in an office, instead—they'd be the same way. It's just work ethic. My motto since day one has been that I'm going to get the best out of myself. Someday, I'll sit on my front porch and be gratified because I did that.

DL: *You've played both first base and third base in the big leagues. Do you have a preference?*

SH: I'd rather play one or the other and stay there, because I think you can help a ball club that way. You're not putting a player in the best position to succeed if he's at first base three times a week, third base two times a week, and DH the other two. I love playing defense. When I first came up, people didn't care what I did on D. They told me that if I hit, I'd play. But I've worked hard at it, and I think I can help a team with my glove.

DL: *You actually spent some time as a catcher in the minor leagues before a knee injury moved you back to the infield. Do you ever wonder what might have happened had you remained behind the plate?*

SH: I guess I've thought about it, but we'll never know. But there's no doubt that being able to play anywhere is going to help you stay in the big leagues. I was actually drafted as a shortstop. In the end, because of my bat I think I would have made it regardless of my position.

DL: *Your career numbers are markedly better hitting in the four-hole than anywhere else in the lineup. Why do you think that is?*

SH: I think it's mostly that I've been hitting there more often the last few years, and I'm a better hitter than I used to be. So it's the amount of at-bats I have under my belt, not where I am in the order. Of course, while I can't control where I am, I'm still aware of it. You have to understand strategy and your role on the team. You can't just go up there and hit.

DL: *Who has most helped you improve as a hitter?*

SH: No one person has helped me. I utilize everyone around me, because you always want to listen. Even if someone tells you something off-key, it's going to make you think. You don't want to shut someone off because you don't agree with them. You want to take in all of the information you can and learn from it. I'm not scared to learn, because that's the only way I'm going to get better.

DL: *You've received criticism for not showing great plate discipline in the past. Is this a part of your game that you'd like to improve?*

SH: Watch this year. Things have to happen in order for you to improve, and I've revamped my swing this off-season. I've changed my mechanics, putting myself in a better position to hit, staying on my back side longer so I don't pre-commit as much. If you do that, you're going to recognize pitches better. I'm coiling up on my load better, which is what guys like Ortiz and Manny do. They stay back well, and then explode when the ball reaches the zone.

DL: *You had some pretty big hits in a Red Sox uniform, including a memorable home run off Mariano Rivera. What do you remember about that?*

SH: I felt like Superman when I homered off of Rivera. I felt like that because of the Boston fans. When I'd hit one in Arizona, that wouldn't be the case—it was just a home run. Players feed off of the fans, and the passion at Fenway Park is incredible.

DL: *Prior to the Red Sox trading you in 2003, there was a lot of talk that you'd be dealt. Are trade rumors easier to deal with now that you've gone through them, and are you an old-fashioned guy who would have preferred to play your entire career with one team?*

SH: They're easier, sure. When I left Boston, I took it personally. It was like a divorce, where you're like, "You don't want me?" Now I know better. It's a business where you're a piece of a puzzle, and maybe you fit in, and maybe you don't. But am I an old-fashioned player? I grew up in L.A., man. I never watched baseball. I just do what's in my heart, and I try to be honest.

DL: *There was some controversy when you were dealt, which included a few choice words being said before the trade. What happened?*

SH: I used to do a radio show, on an FM station, once a week, and it happened there. That was around the time Bobby Valentine accused Mike Piazza of being a "faggot," and it had become a big joke on the show. The radio guys were always calling people that. There had been a lot of rumors that I was going to be traded, and I had hit a big home run the night before, so they were joking with me about it and I said, "Trade me now, fag." The problem was, it was taken out of context. If you listened to the show every week, you'd have understood that it wasn't serious and I was talking to the DJs, not Theo. I do regret one thing, though. The statement itself was derogatory toward a certain lifestyle, so I shouldn't have said it. That's one thing I'd take back if I could.

DL: *Have you spoken to Theo since the trade?*

SH: The first time I saw Theo, I went right up to him. I think he was kind of surprised, because he probably had this perception that wasn't true. I told him, "I just want to tell you, man to man, what happened." I told him that it was the situation, not about him at all. He said it was okay, that it wasn't necessary for me to explain. I told him that yes, it was necessary. It meant something to me that he knew the truth. I like Theo, and I knew the trade was because they needed a different piece to their puzzle—they needed a pitcher. It was important that he knew where I was coming from.

DL: *Would you like to play here again?*

SH: I'd love to play here again. There's no better place to play than Boston. As a matter of fact, it's in my blood.

TIM KESTER

TIM KESTER WAS OBTAINED BY THE RED SOX AS A MINOR LEAGUE
FREE AGENT IN APRIL 2003. A RIGHT-HANDED PITCHER, KESTER
WAS DRAFTED IN 1993 BY THE HOUSTON ASTROS AND SPENT THE
2005 SEASON WITH THE PAWTUCKET RED SOX. THIS INTERVIEW
TOOK PLACE IN FEBRUARY 2005.

David Laurila: *You pitched in the Venezuelan winter league this year.
Coming off a season where you were named Pawtucket's pitcher of the
year, why did you choose go down there?*

Tim Kester: I went to Venezuela for a number of reasons. First of all,
I'd heard a lot of good things about how much fun it was to play there,
because the fans love the sport so much. That was true—they really do.
Second of all, I've never been to South America and heard it was a beautiful place, which it really was. And I can now say that I've played professional baseball on four continents. Not many people can say that.
Also, I had it in my contract that I was leaving December 1st, so I knew
I wouldn't get too many innings. And since I didn't get a September
call-up to Boston, money was a little bit of a factor.

DL: *Tell us a little about the experience of playing there.*

TK: Venezuela is a crazy place to play baseball. You see things there you
would never see in a million years in the States. We had a Samba band,
and dancing girls on the dugout and in the outfield bleachers. When
something good happens for the home team, all the fans throw their
beer in the air for five minutes. They buy new beer just to throw in the
air, since it is cheaper than water. One time, we were playing in
Caracas, and I was pitching and accidentally hit Jose Castillo from the
Pirates with the first pitch. He had homered the night before to beat us,
so the whole crowd thought I hit him on purpose (I swear I didn't). In
unison, 15,000 people were chanting something very uncomplimentary
about my mother. Good thing my Spanish is *no bueno.*

    Another crazy thing about Venezuela is that most of the players
carry guns everywhere, and a lot of them play around with them in the
clubhouse and on the bus. Needless to say, that was very unnerving at
times. Our GM actually had a meeting to tell them to stop, because the
Americans were going to freak out and go home.

DL: *Earlier in your career you pitched in both Taiwan and Italy. Do you have a fascination with other countries and their cultures, and do you speak more than one language?*

TK: Yes, I think playing in those countries gave me a different outlook on life in general and on life in the United States. It's one thing to go on vacation somewhere, but it's not the same as living there for an extended period of time and actually working (or playing, in my case) with people who are from those countries. You come to understand that there is more than one way of thinking about the world and about life in general. I still have friends that I talk to from both places.

As for the languages, I dabble in Spanish but would definitely not say I'm fluent. I know enough Chinese to get what I want at a restaurant, or insult an umpire (just kidding).

DL: *Tell us how you ended up in Taiwan and about your experiences pitching there.*

TK: I went to Taiwan because a good friend of mine was over there and doing very well. He recommended me to the team he was on, and they took his advice and signed me. I thought he would be there with me, but at the last second he signed a contract to play in Mexico—so I was on my own on the other side of the world.

Taiwan was where I really started to learn how to pitch, especially under pressure. Over there, if you lose a game there are grumblings of you getting released, and after two in a row they start checking on flights. Not to mention the gambling problems with the Mafia, and not knowing if your teammates were trying to lose a game on purpose. It was very surreal at first, but I got used to it. It made me learn to focus on what I had to do and not worry about anything else.

DL: *How about Italy?*

TK: Italy was the same thing. I had a friend over there who recommended me. I played for a team that had an owner like Steinbrenner. He would sit directly behind home plate, and if a guy got to second base in the first inning he would scream at our manager "*cambio!!!*," which means "change pitchers" in Italian. He wasn't a favorite of the players, but I think that also helped me in a way to deal with pressure.

DL: *Prior to those experiences, you spent seven years in the Astros organization. Turning the clock back to 1993, when you signed your first contract, how did you envision your career? Looking back, could you have imagined where baseball would take you?*

TK: I thought I would move right up the ladder, year after year, until I was pitching in Houston. I guess that's how most kids envision it or they probably wouldn't do it in the first place. I wouldn't have guessed in a million years the path baseball has led me down. Sometimes I look back and I'm amazed at how I've ended up playing in some of these places. I've played in Canada, Mexico, Puerto Rico, Venezuela, Taiwan, Italy, Holland, and just about everywhere in the United States.

DL: *In 1995, you went 12-5, 2.97 as a starter and were a Texas League All-Star. The next season you were moved to the bullpen. Why was that, and how did it impact your career?*

TK: They moved me to the bullpen because Houston was loaded with high-quality arms. I played with guys like Freddy Garcia and Wade Miller, and there just weren't enough rotation spots in Double A. It's funny, because the guy that I flip-flopped spots with was John Halama. He was in the bullpen and did really well, so they wanted to try him as a starter. He did well there, and the rest was history. He got traded for Randy Johnson, and has had a successful Major League career. He is still a really good friend of mine, and I was happy to see the Sox sign him. We'll definitely be hanging out a lot in spring training.

As far as the effect on my career, it was probably pretty big. As a right-hander, I'm not a hard thrower, and my stuff and make-up are more suited to being a starter. Houston was more of a "gun" organization, so the hard throwers were going to have more of an opportunity. That's just the way it was. I was just unlucky that there were so many good pitchers in that organization at the time.

DL: *Tell us about your one game in Triple A Tucson, in 1996.*

TK: You had to ask about that! No, it was a situation where I wasn't really prepared mentally for what I was going to be doing. I was relieving all year in Double A, and they called me up to start a noon game in Phoenix, Arizona. Hell can't be that much hotter than noon in Phoenix in the middle of summer. I was nervous and overanxious, and probably did too much in the bullpen getting ready for the game. The first hitter was about 5' 8" and hit a homer on the first pitch, about 380 feet right down the line. It was all downhill from there. It was just one of those games that can happen once in a while, but it was bad timing that it had to be in my Triple A debut. It really was unfortunate for my career, because I think the Astros labeled me as a Double A guy and I spent the next four years without ever getting called back up.

DL: *How did you end up pitching in an independent league in 2002, and how did you find your way to Portland in 2003?*

TK: I played independent ball in 2002 because, as you can imagine, there aren't that many scouts from MLB teams in Italy or Taiwan scouting free agents. I was an unknown commodity coming back, so I had to prove myself to someone in independent ball. Teams only had reports on me that were over two years old, and probably weren't all that impressive because, like I said, I really got better when I went overseas. Luckily, I led the Atlantic League in ERA and the Sox somehow saw me, or my numbers, and had a little interest. I went to Puerto Rico to play winter ball after that, and maybe they saw me down there. Who knows? They invited me to spring training, unsigned, on a 20-day try-out, which I've never heard of before, but it was the only offer I had, so I took it. I guess I pitched well enough to impress somebody, and they signed me and sent me to Portland.

DL: *How different of a pitcher are you now, compared to 10 years ago— not only in maturity, but in repertoire and velocity?*

TK: Well, obviously I'm more mature, and with maturity comes the mental part of playing this game. This game is so hard mentally that players actually get better with age. If you can keep your body in shape as you age and your brain really learns how to play, you end up with guys like Clemens, Maddux, Schilling, and Bonds. I can do a lot of things now that I couldn't do 10 years ago, like command both sides of the plate and throw my breaking balls for strikes. I've also evolved a little by teaching myself to throw two new pitches and getting rid of one that wasn't very good. I now throw a fastball, curveball, change, and cutter, where I used to throw a fastball, slider, and change. Those two pitches have made all the difference. As for velocity, it's virtually the same except I can maintain my top velocity much longer into a game because of my weight-training and conditioning routine.

DL: *I recently asked Kelly Shoppach this question: If the scouting reports say to throw a certain hitter a curve in a given situation, and your hook is flat that day, what do you go with?*

TK: I try to "unflatten" it as fast as I can. Just kidding. A lot of times, if a hitter doesn't handle the breaking ball that well, he usually doesn't handle even a bad breaking ball that well if it's located correctly. I mean, even good breaking ball hitters don't usually hit good breaking balls that well. It's usually the mistakes they hit hard. I also have other options I can go with, so I might locate a fastball with some sink and try to get a ground ball, or throw a change-up if that's working.

DL: *Shoppach said that as a catcher he has to know which pitchers need comforting and which ones he needs to bear down on. Where do you fit in?*

TK: I probably don't fit in either of those categories. I've been in just about every situation there is with my experience, so I like to think that I don't need much of either. When Shoppach comes to talk to me, the tone of the conversation is similar to one we would have in the clubhouse or in the parking lot. There's really no comforting or yelling. It's usually to give someone in the bullpen time to warm up, or a discussion about what the right pitch might be in the situation we are in. I really don't like too many visits from coaches or catchers because I love working fast, and it kind of breaks my rhythm. Unless they really feel strongly about a pitch, then it's come on out and let's figure this out.

DL: *What's the most interesting or funniest conversation you've had on the mound with a catcher or pitching coach?*

TK: By far the funniest conversation I've ever had on the mound happened in Taiwan. The stadium was full of screaming, crazy, Taiwanese baseball fans. We had a one-run lead in the bottom of the eighth inning with two outs. The bases were loaded, and the other team's three-hole hitter was up. He was a Japanese import and the best hitter on the team. My manager, who doesn't speak a word of English, decided to make a trip to the mound with our interpreter who learned English in school and didn't know any baseball lingo at all. The manager rattled off about a minute of Chinese while I just stood there and pretended to listen. It sounded like Charlie Brown's teacher, or trying to understand a dog barking. When he got done, the interpreter looked at me and said with his thick Asian accent, "Manager says...enemy batter is very strong.... But if you use all your weapons, you may defeat him." I couldn't do anything but laugh, it was so surreal. I just stepped off the mound and said to myself, "Where am I?" Luckily, I used one of my best weapons and got the guy out.

DL: *A lot of Red Sox fans have said that they can now die happy, because the team has finally won the World Series. Could you say the same thing about making it to MLB, even for one game?*

TK: Not really. To say that would mean my whole career would have been a failure if I don't make it up there. I don't see it that way. Is it a major, major goal of mine? Absolutely, but if it doesn't happen, it's not because I didn't give it my best to put myself in the position to get there. A lot of luck is involved, as with anything, and if it happens I will be the happiest guy in the world. But if it doesn't, I will still look back on my career and be happy with the things I've done.

DL: *If you do get a shot, what will it feel like on the mound? At the age of 33, with all you've experienced in life, will you still feel like a nervous 19-year-old out there?*

TK: I have no idea what it will feel like, but I imagine it will feel like pitching on any other mound in the world. If it doesn't, I might be in trouble. When it's over and I'm in the dugout or clubhouse, that's when it will hit me, and I'm sure there will be a feeling of accomplishment and maybe a little redemption. I get nervous pitching in a spring training game with nobody there, but it is the same nervousness I get when I'm in Pawtucket in front of 10,000 people. Hopefully, it will be that same kind of nervousness.

DL: *What comes after baseball, and what do you like to do in your spare time?*

TK: In my spare time, I like to golf and fish, to name just a couple of things. Who knows what comes after baseball? Hopefully, I can find something as fun and fulfilling as taking the mound every fifth day.

GEORGE LOMBARD

GEORGE LOMBARD IS AN OUTFIELDER FOR THE WASHINGTON
NATIONALS. ORIGINALLY DRAFTED BY THE ATLANTA BRAVES IN
1994, LOMBARD HAS SEEN ACTION IN 124 BIG LEAGUE GAMES.
THIS INTERVIEW TOOK PLACE IN APRIL 2005 WHILE HE WAS WITH
THE PAWTUCKET RED SOX.

David Laurila: *Let's start with your family background. Tell us about that.*

George Lombard: I grew up in Atlanta in a biracial family. My dad is from Arlington, Georgia, and worked at GM. I lost my mom in a car accident when I was 10 years old. She was from Weston, Massachusetts, and moved to the South to work on civil rights. She went to Smith College and taught English as a second language at Georgia Tech. She also taught art classes. My parents wanted us to have a well-rounded experience growing up, and we always had foreign exchange students in the house.

DL: *I understand that you used to spend time on Cape Cod.*

GL: My grandfather had a summer house on the Cape, on Wings Neck, in Pocasset. I believe it was built in 1929. We'd go every summer, sometimes for as long as a month. Once I got a little older, my trips became shorter because I was so busy with football and other sports.

DL: *You also have a Harvard connection.*

GL: My grandfather was a dean at the business school there. My great-grandfather was also at Harvard, as were a few other relatives. My sister is about to get a graduate degree there. My brother is a public defender. He went to Colgate and then to law school at George Washington. I play baseball, so I guess I missed that gene!

DL: *I've read that you're married and are starting your own family.*

GL: Yes. My wife and I have been married for about a year and a half, and together for over six. She's Cuban American. We're expecting a baby boy in June, which is really exciting. It's definitely made me relax a little and helped me understand that there's more to life than baseball.

DL: *At the age of 29, do you think much about life after baseball?*

GL: Yes and no. I want to play 10 years in the big leagues, and looking at a guy like Julio Franco, I still have plenty of time! But do I think ahead? Sure. It's a transition you want to make gradually, and I want to be prepared when I'm done with the game. I'm taking some real estate classes now, and getting a degree is something I can always pursue. But there's more to life than school, too. I've traveled all over the world and already experienced a lot. I'll do what's best for my family when the time comes. But for now, I think I still have a good baseball career ahead of me.

DL: *When you signed your first pro contract, you chose baseball over several scholarship offers to play football. Tell us about that decision.*

GL: I was actually going to play both sports in college, but football is what I was most heavily recruited for. I could have gone pretty much anywhere. I was one of the high school all-Americans that were flown to Disney World to announce where we'd be signing letters of intent. Tony Gonzalez was there, Orlando Pace—guys like that. But I got a good offer to play baseball, and decided to go in that direction instead. The fact that I didn't have a lot of money was a factor in my decision to sign, too.

DL: *What was it like as an 18-year-old, playing pro ball?*

GL: It was much different than I expected. There were a lot of guys that you looked at and wondered, "What else would they do if they weren't playing baseball?" And that's pretty much what it was, baseball 24-7. I think we won about 10 out of 60 games that year, in the Gulf Coast League. We had talent—Andruw Jones, Wes Helms, etc.—but we were very young and very, very raw.

DL: *How differently do you approach the game now that you're 11 years older?*

GL: At this stage of my life, I have a better understanding of the way things are. At 18, every scout tells you that you have what it takes. And how would you know any better? I was never really a great player in high school. I had good numbers, but everyone in pro ball had good numbers in high school.

DL: *How have you changed as a player?*

GL: I feel the same, physically. I think I'm smarter. I obviously have more experience. When I was young, I really didn't play enough. I played every sport and didn't focus as much as I could have on baseball. One of the instructors in the Braves organization said to me a few years ago, "George, you've proven you can hit, you just have to stay mentally strong." You can't take away a player's ability, but baseball is such a mental game. A lot of guys have the tools, but you need the right focus to go along with the ability.

DL: *Who has influenced you the most in baseball?*

GL: Leon Roberts is one who made a big impact. He was an outfielder in the Majors for a number of years. One of his claims to fame is that he was on deck when the George Brett "pine tar incident" happened. Anyway, he was coaching in the Braves system early in my career and talked me out of quitting baseball. I was struggling, and felt like I was missing out on the whole college life and would be happier playing football. There was a lot of pressure to do that, too. I was playing in Macon, and as I had turned down a football scholarship to the University of Georgia a few years earlier, it seemed like everyone was trying to talk me into switching sports. I told Leon what I was feeling, and it was one of those things where you say, "Maybe we better grab a pitcher or two of beer, and sit down and talk." We sat down in an Applebee's in Columbus, Georgia, and Leon convinced me to give the game some more time.

DL: *You're best known for your speed. Do you think it's good or bad to be labeled as a certain type of player?*

GL: Jim Rice has told me, "Don't consider yourself just a runner. You have more of a game than that." That said, there are players who stick around because they do one thing very well. Of course, stereotypes have a way of staying with you. I could suddenly lose my speed, and people would probably still say I can run. Or I could start throwing a lot better, and they'd say my arm wasn't very strong.

DL: *Have you had a chance to play in Fenway Park?*

GL: I played in one series at Fenway when I was with the Tigers. I homered in one of the games, which was special because I had family there. It was against Sunny Kim, and the ball hit off the camera in straightaway center and bounced back onto the field. There's an unwritten rule that the trainer will get it for you if it's meaningful, and they brought it to me after the game. I gave it to my grandfather, inscribed, "For the best grandfather ever."

DL: *I'm sure he enjoyed that ball.*

GL: Very much. He'd always show it to people. Even when he got into his nineties and started forgetting things, he'd always remember that. I don't know that baseball was all that important to him, but having his namesake playing in the Major Leagues and "Lombard" on the back of my jersey made him feel proud.

DL: *What's going on in your life right now besides baseball and impending fatherhood?*

GL: My wife and I just bought an old Spanish house in Miami—it was built in 1937—so I've been going to bookstores looking for stuff on that. Along with the baby, that's the main thing.

DL: *Do you read a lot?*

GL: I go through phases where I do and always try to find the time. I mostly read nonfiction and biographies. I'm a big Shaq fan, so my wife just bought me one on him.

DL: *What else do you like to do off the field?*

GL: I love art. I really like fishing and scuba diving. When I was a kid, I wanted to be an oceanographer. I've gone on over fifty dives, including two night dives. One of the cooler places has been the Great Barrier Reef in Australia. It's really a different world when you're in the ocean. It's the natural environment for all the fish swimming by, but for you or me it's crazy—almost like being on the moon. It's an amazing experience and really gives you a whole new perspective on everything.

JED LOWRIE

JED LOWRIE WAS SELECTED BY THE RED SOX IN THE 2005 DRAFT AS A SUPPLEMENTAL FIRST-ROUND PICK AS COMPENSATION FOR THE LOSS OF ORLANDO CABRERA TO FREE AGENCY. A SWITCH-HITTING INFIELDER, LOWRIE SPENT HIS FIRST PROFESSIONAL SEASON WITH THE LOWELL SPINNERS. THIS INTERVIEW TOOK PLACE IN JULY 2005.

David Laurila: *Let's start by getting a scouting report on your offensive game. How would you describe it?*

Jed Lowrie: I'm hitting third here, but I look at myself as more of a two-hole hitter. I can go deep and drive guys in, but I'm just as valuable getting on base and setting the table. Two-hole guys have more power than they used to, and I feel I can do a lot with the bat.

DL: *You're a switch hitter. How do you compare from each side?*

JL: I have more raw pop from the right side and am more consistent from the left. I'm natural from the right, but of course get more left-handed at-bats. Right now, I'm trying as hard as I can to be consistently the same each way. If your swing is the same from each side, you can think the same way up at the plate—you can always be making the same adjustments. The hardest thing about being a switch hitter is keeping both perfect. It takes a lot of swings to get your stroke where you want it to be, and a switch-hitter has to take twice as many to do that.

DL: *Your* Baseball America *draft profile says you have an unorthodox approach at the plate, keeping your hands low with a high leg-kick. It also says you take a big cut for your size. What are your thoughts on those opinions?*

JL: I've always been the same, and it works for me, so I plan to continue doing what I do. Physically, I'm not that big but I think I have good bat speed and good torque. I don't feel that my swing is all that big. You can still get good torque from a compact swing.

DL: *Style-wise, would you compare yourself to Mark Bellhorn?*

JL: Definitely. I've watched him the last two or three years, and I like his game. I know he's slumping now, and he probably Ks a little too much, but he helps produce runs. Strikeouts and home runs are both up in baseball, and I think there's some truth to the idea that a strikeout is no worse than a pop-up. Still, you can put pressure on the defense to make a play if you do make contact. I'll change my approach slightly with two strikes, in order to do that. I don't slap at the ball, though. You can still make hard contact with a shorter swing. But would I have Bellhorn's career if I could? Sure. He's a productive Major League player.

DL: *The* Baseball America *profile also said you were pitched around a lot this year, which caused you to get a little impatient. Do you feel that was a good learning experience for you?*

JL: I think it definitely was. Everything happens for a reason, and sometimes you can lie to yourself during the season. I didn't want to admit that I was trying to do too much, but looking back, John Mayberry and I were the main guys, and I probably was. You have to stay within yourself, and I understand that better now.

DL: *You had a layoff between your college season and the start of your pro career. Do you look at that as bad because you came here a little rusty or good because you got to recharge your batteries a little?*

JL: I'd say it was good for me, because I was pretty beat up at the end of the year. I'm still trying to get back into it, but it's coming. I'll get a lot of at-bats here, and it was good to recharge a little before starting my career.

DL: *You only had 16 stolen bases in three years at Stanford. How would you rate your speed?*

JL: I can run okay; we just didn't run there. The team's approach was to take your chances swinging away, not risk getting caught stealing. If you look my stolen base numbers, they're not good but my success rate was. I feel I have a good grasp on the base paths. Still, I'm excited at the opportunity to work with guys like Luis Alicea to get better. I can learn a lot from someone with his experience.

DL: *In a recent game, the Spinners' broadcasters said you looked good at shortstop and were wondering who played there at Stanford. Who was it, and why were you at second base?*

JL: Chris Minaker was our shortstop. The reason I was given for playing second is that I was way better there than anyone else on the team. The gap would have been bigger had I been at short and Chris at second.

DL: *Do you think you have a better future at second base or at shortstop?*

JL: That's tough to say. I've felt good at short the last several games, but I have spent the last three years at second. Right now, I guess I'm more comfortable at second for that reason, but I can play either position.

DL: *How would you rate your defensive tools?*

JL: I'd say I have an above-average arm; maybe even strong. My first step to balls is pretty good. I can turn a double play. Probably my biggest attribute is that I make all of the routine plays.

DL: *People talk about discipline at the plate, but what about on defense? How hard is it to hold onto a ball rather than making a high-risk throw on a tough chance?*

JL: That's something that comes with experience, and I think I have a good grasp on it. There's an internal clock where you know how much time you have, even when the play isn't in front of you. It's a little tougher if you don't know the speed of the guy—if you've never seen him before—but I think I make those reads pretty well.

DL: *Catchers are looked at as coaches on the field who need to know where everyone is and everything that's going on. Do middle infielders have similar responsibilities?*

JL: We control everything that the pitcher and catcher don't. We're responsible for the signs for all of the infielders and who is covering in every situation. Catchers have more responsibilities, but we have some important ones.

DL: *Do you look at yourself as a team leader, or is your personality more on the quiet side?*

JL: I'm a quieter guy—not very rah-rah—but I'll say what needs to be said. I think I know the game well enough that my opinion is worth something. I'll speak up when I think I should.

DL: *Did you have favorite infielders growing up, guys you looked at as role models?*

JL: Being from the Northwest and seeing a lot of the Mariners, I enjoyed watching Alex Rodriguez. I also like the guy who replaced him when he left town, Carlos Guillen. I liked their style and the way they play. It's funny, because from the stands you can see how hard the game is. On the field, it's always seemed easier to me, because I'm more in control. I have a great appreciation for guys who can make it look easy.

DL: *What do you hope to accomplish in pro ball, and what memories do you think you'll take from the game?*

JL: Those are tough questions. I hope I enjoy the whole experience. After all, what's greater than playing a game for a living? But I think I just need to take it a day at a time and try to get better. I know that's a cliché, but there's a lot of wisdom in having that kind of approach.

DL: *What were your baseball and academic experiences like at Stanford?*

JL: Stanford has a great heritage and history when it comes to baseball and academics, and I got a lot out of both. It's a tough school—very time-consuming when you're balancing baseball with your academics. I haven't graduated yet, but I am ahead of schedule toward a political science degree.

DL: *What are some of your interests off the field?*

JL: I like trying new things. That's one good thing about baseball. There are guys here from all over, and how some of them have fun and go about their day is different from what I'm used to. I think that's cool. A few of the things I'm into are golf, video games, movies, and music. A movie I really liked was *The Thomas Crown Affair.* I like a lot of different kinds of music, everything from rock and punk to country and hip-hop.

DL: *I always find it interesting when guys like both country and hip-hop. Don't you think that's an odd combination?*

JL: You know, it's interesting. A lot of times, they're singing about the same things, they're just using different jargon. The difference isn't really as big as a lot of people think it is.

DL: *Last one: What did you know about the Red Sox minor league organization when you got drafted?*

JL: Not too much, so I went online to find out where the teams are. And a funny thing is, when I was in the Babe Ruth League I played for a team called the Bombers, just like in Greenville. It's definitely great to be here in the organization. Ever since the draft, when I've played video games, I'm always the Red Sox.

CLA MEREDITH

CLA MEREDITH WAS THE RED SOX' SELECTION IN THE SIXTH ROUND OF THE 2004 DRAFT. A RIGHT-HANDED RELIEVER OUT OF VIRGINIA COMMONWEALTH UNIVERSITY, MEREDITH MADE HIS BIG LEAGUE DEBUT IN MAY 2005. THIS INTERVIEW TOOK PLACE IN APRIL 2005 WHILE MEREDITH WAS WITH THE PORTLAND SEA DOGS.

David Laurila: *Let's start with spring training. How did that go for you?*

Cla Meredith: I expected it to be more of a grind than it was. I suppose it did get a little eye washy by the end—too much routine. But getting to throw in both games in Arizona, at the end of camp, was good. That helped put things in perspective, getting to face Major League hitters. Coming into last night's game with the bases loaded seemed a little less daunting.

DL: *A few of your teammates have mentioned that David Murphy and Chris Durbin had good springs. Is there anyone you'd add to that list?*

CM: Probably Conor Brooks. He threw great. And Dustin Pedroia is fun to watch. He's balls out all the time. Jared Sandberg, too. I had never seen him before. This big SOB rolls into camp and starts hitting it 800 feet. That makes you sit up and take notice.

DL: *What did you do in the off-season?*

CM: A lot of conditioning. I lost about 15 to 20 pounds, plus 7 percent of body fat. The club wanted me to get in better shape, and that's what I did. Al Nipper called me fat last year, and while I didn't appreciate that, he was obviously challenging me to improve myself. I did that.

DL: *What did you do besides work out?*

CM: A little golfing and fishing. And I came to Boston for the rookie development camp in January. That was my first trip to Fenway Park, which was a great experience.

DL: *You're the closer here. Are you just a one-inning guy, or can you go more?*

CM: I went as many as five in college, but I expect to be limited to one or two here. That way, hitters won't get to see me twice in any one game. I can use that to my advantage.

DL: *Can you pitch several days in a row—is your arm resilient?*

CM: I just pitched in two, and honestly could go tonight if they wanted. But it's early in the season, and it's probably best to wait until my arm gets stronger. After all, I've only got one arm. Or, to be more accurate, one that I throw with.

DL: *You're a sinkerballer. Do you agree with the theory that sinkerballers are more effective when their arms are tired?*

CM: The velocity isn't there, but yes. My ball dives more when I'm tired. I'm usually between 88 and 91, and my sink is dirtier when I'm around 87 or 88. That said, 91 with good sink is better than 88 with good sink.

DL: *What do you throw besides a sinker?*

CM: I'll throw a change and a slider, but it's 80 to 85 percent sinking fastballs. That's my bread and butter, and it's no secret to the hitters.

DL: *You throw with a three-quarter arm slot. Tell us about that.*

CM: That's how I've always been. I actually didn't pitch much in high school—I played a lot of infield and even caught. I really started pitching at Virginia Commonwealth. And I'll give hitters different looks, too. Sometimes I'll go almost submarine, and on rare occasions I'll even come over the top. Not very often, though.

DL: *Do you attack right-handed and left-handed batters the same way?*

CM: I'll throw sliders to righties and more changes to lefties. But mostly I pitch them the same, keeping the ball down.

DL: *Do you ever go upstairs to change a hitter's eye angle?*

CM: Maybe 1 percent of the time. I pretty much live on the knees and shoe tops.

DL: *Are scouting reports important to you, or are you out there pitching to your own strengths?*

CM: I don't look at them, or even who's coming up. For the most part, I don't care who's at the plate. They have to beat what I have, and that's what I'm going with.

DL: *People say you have a closer's mentality. How would you explain that?*

CM: Off the field, I'm relaxed and easygoing. I'm very loose and love to joke around. But I feel bulletproof on the mound. I feel untouchable, like I can beat the crap out of everyone on the field. And I have no fear of pressure. I love nut-cutting time.

DL: *Many people feel closers need a good strikeouts-to-innings-pitched ratio. As a sinkerball pitcher, what are your thoughts on that?*

CM: I don't try for strikeouts. On an 0-2 count, I will to some extent, but what's important is to get outs—not blow people away. I'm not a big attention guy, either. Stars get it, but I've never been in the limelight. I'm kind of the secret that nobody knows about, and that's okay. Deep inside, I know I'll get to the bigs some day. That's what matters to me.

DL: *Are you a guy who can talk baseball all day, or do you like to get away from the game when you're not playing?*

CM: Back home, guys want to talk about it. They want to hear the stories. I understand that, but I want to get away from the game sometimes. I never tell anyone that I play professional baseball. If I go out for a drink and start talking to a girl, I don't want her to look at me as "Cla, the ballplayer."

DL: *Brian Marshall, who also pitches in the Red Sox system, was your teammate at Virginia Commonwealth. What can you tell us about him?*

CM: I was a year behind Brian, and we split time as the closer there. He's a great guy. He's smart, and wouldn't hurt a fly. Brian has a twin brother in Double A with the Cubs, too. I have nothing but good things to say about him.

DL: *You played for a former Major Leaguer, Johnny Grubb, in high school. Tell us about that.*

CM: He had gone to school there. Meadowbrook [Virginia] isn't what you'd call a high-profile powerhouse, and it's impressive that he came back to coach. There's not a better guy on earth than Johnny Grubb.

DL: *You're known as Cla. Have you had any other nicknames over the years?*

CM: Some guys have called me "Clayboy," or "Bubba." A couple of guys here have learned my given name is Olise, so I'm hearing that a little. I'm not sure if I should be admitting that though.

DL: *Sure you should. Can you tell us a good story that we can close with? As you're a fun-loving guy, I'm sure you have a few.*

CM: Sure, but most of them I better not tell you! My roomie in college, Jason, and I pulled a few stunts—but I'll plead the fifth on those. I will tell you that I was late to camp once this spring. I was in Miami to see a . . . let's just say, "friend," and being the genius that I am, I timed the drive back all wrong. There was a lot of traffic, and with a late start I knew it would be tough to get there on time. And then, to make matters worse, 30 miles into the trip I realized I was low on gas. You have to drive through the Everglades to get from Miami to Ft. Myers, and there aren't many gas stations. I decided I better backtrack rather than push my luck, which meant I rolled into camp pretty late. I had some explaining to do when I got there. What can I say? I won't do it again, and only I would be that much of an idiot.

EDITOR'S NOTE: Meredith was traded, along with Josh Bard, to the San Diego Padres on May 1, 2006 in exchange for Doug Mirabelli.

LOU MERLONI

LOU MERLONI PLAYED FOR THE RED SOX FROM 1998 TO 2003. A NATIVE OF FRAMINGHAM, MASSACHUSETTS, "FRAMINGHAM LOU" WAS THE RED SOX' SELECTION IN THE 10TH ROUND OF THE 1993 DRAFT AND CURRENTLY PLAYS FOR THE CLEVELAND INDIANS. THIS INTERVIEW TOOK PLACE IN JANUARY 2006.

David Laurila: *You're about to go into your 14th year of professional baseball. Who are some of the people most responsible for you being where you are today?*

Lou Merloni: My parents, definitely. Starting from when I was a young age, they're the ones who got me here. Once I got to pro ball, it was guys like DeMarlo Hale, Al Nipper, and Rico Petrocelli. I played under DeMarlo for three years in the minor leagues, and Rico was my hitting coach for two. They're just so good at what they do, and they were always there for me. They're the ones who really helped me create the good work habits I needed to make it to the big leagues.

DL: *What are your earliest memories of Fenway Park?*

LM: My dad used to take me when the Yankees were in town, so I'd say it was him saying, "Make sure you stay close to me" all the time. It can get a little crazy when New York is here, so he didn't want me wandering away. I also remember people booing Reggie Jackson. But do you know what I liked as much as anything? I used to enjoy just watching big leaguers playing catch on the field before the game.

DL: *Did you have a favorite player growing up?*

LM: It was probably Wade Boggs. Watching him hit was something else, because he was always under control. No pitcher ever dictated what he did when he was at the plate. As a matter of fact, the first time I got to choose a number in the big leagues I asked for his. When I first got called up I wore number 50, because you'll take anything they throw on your back, but the next spring training they asked what I wanted. I was actually surprised that number 26 was available and kind of wondered if it was all right for me to take it—it almost seemed like it should have been retired—but that's what I did.

DL: *Do you have a most memorable moment from your Little League career in Framingham?*

LM: I remember being 10 years old and us winning the World Series of our town. I came up in the last inning of a tie game and hit a line drive off the third baseman's glove. He threw the ball away into right field, and the right fielder made a bad throw to third. There was a play at the plate, and I was safe to end the game and give us the championship. It was a typical Little League play, but pretty exciting.

DL: *I recall you reaching on a swinging bunt prior to a game-winning home run a few years ago. Does that sound familiar?*

LM: I think that must have been when we played the make-up game in Philadelphia on September 1st in 2003. That was the time Manny took himself out of the lineup and in the ninth inning went up to Grady and told him he could pinch hit. Grady said no, that if he couldn't play earlier, he wasn't going to use him then. He sent me up instead, with the bases loaded, and everyone was wondering why it was me when Manny was available in the dugout. We were behind by a few runs, and I remember getting jammed and reaching on a little roller down the third base line. Trot then hit a grand slam, which won it for us. That was a huge game.

DL: *The summer before you turned pro, you won the batting title in the Cape Cod League. Was that something that told you, "I'm good enough to make it"?*

LM: You know—it was. The Red Sox had drafted me after my junior year, but not until the 36th round. I had been thinking I would go higher, so that was a tough time for me, confidence-wise. I wasn't going to sign after being taken that late, and it was a no-brainer that I'd go back to school for my senior year, so it was huge for my confidence to know I had just played against the top guys in the country, on the Cape, and accomplished what I did. That's really been the rallying cry for my whole career, being told I'm too small, I can't do this, I can't do that. Being told I'm not good enough has been the driving force behind everything I've done in the game.

DL: *Were you surprised that the Red Sox drafted you again the following season, this time in the 10th round?*

LM: I knew they were still interested, so not really. The year before, when I told the Red Sox scout that I'd be going back to school instead of signing, he said, "I thought you wanted to play pro ball." That was kind of hard for me to hear, but they changed scouts and I was dealing with Buzz Bowers and Ray Fagnant a year later when I signed. Both of them are great guys.

DL: *Were you hoping it would be the Red Sox?*

LM: As a senior, you don't really care who the team is, what the round is, or how much money they're offering. It wouldn't have mattered if it was the 60th round, because I knew what I could do and all I wanted was a chance. Was I glad it was the Red Sox? Sure. I mostly just wanted to play, but who wouldn't want it to be his hometown team?

DL: *Do you ever wonder how your career might have gone had you been drafted by someone else?*

LM: I have. Some guys definitely itch to come home some day. Another thing is that you'll play against guys in Double A, and they're with the Expos or another low-budget team, and they're going to get a chance quicker than you will. Some teams will have a second baseman go down in June, and they'll promote a younger player, often because they can't afford to acquire someone else. Others, like the Red Sox, will often pick up a veteran to replace him. Of course, coming up through the Red Sox system made me better, because there were great coaches and ballparks to play in.

DL: *How did you get your first opportunity?*

LM: You need luck in this game, too—not just talent—and I got a look because Jeff Frye blew out his knee in spring training. While I didn't make the team out of camp, I got the call in May because I had made an impression earlier. Had Frye not gotten hurt, I probably get 10 at-bats in camp and don't get a chance to show them I can do the job.

DL: *What is it like playing against the Red Sox?*

LM: Two years ago in Cleveland was the first time. It was against Pedro, who I wanted to face because I have so much respect for him. And, as it worked out, I played all three games when we went to Boston because Casey Blake was hurt. It was kind of an interesting experience, because I'd get on base and there I'd be, talking to Kevin Millar. I have a lot of good friends on the team, and we'd be ragging each other from the bench. Pedro slapped me on the butt with his glove once when I grounded out and was on my way back to the dugout. Of course, he had just gotten me out, so I didn't necessarily like it too much at the time.

DL: *What is it like playing against the Yankees?*

LM: It's definitely not the same going into Yankee Stadium as a member of the Indians or Angels. When you're with the Red Sox, you actually feel the hatred when you play there and I'm sure it's the same for them at Fenway. There's no doubt it's great to have been a part of that rivalry.

DL: *You went back and forth between Boston and Pawtucket a number of times. How hard was it to remain focused when you'd go back down?*

LM: I was actually talking to Kevin Youkilis about that not too long ago. I suppose there were nights where, deep down, I'd struggle and wonder what I was doing down there. But your job is to be a good soldier and look at it as a chance to play every day and be ready for when you go back up. I never really felt like I was going down because I wasn't doing the job. It always seemed like the circumstances dictated that we needed another pitcher, or maybe we needed to open up a roster spot and I was the only one with options left. I remember Jimy Williams saying to me once, "I can't tell you to work on anything down there. Just keep doing what you do, and you'll be back."

DL: *Which managers have you most enjoyed playing for?*

LM: Jimy was definitely one of my favorites. When I came up as a rookie, he talked to me a lot. He was patient and a good baseball guy. It's too bad it worked out badly for him here, because he's a good manager. Grady Little is another guy I enjoyed playing for. He was the bench coach before becoming manager, so I knew him pretty well. It didn't work out for him either, but you have to give him a lot of credit for what he did here. And he was willing to stand up and take the bullet when it came time to make decisions, too. He went with what he believed rather than taking the easy way out. A lot of guys are afraid to do that.

DL: *Who are some of the best teammates you've had?*

LM: When I think of teammates, Jason Varitek is the ultimate. He leads by example, and when he's not playing he's on the top step of the dugout. And he's not looking into the stands—he's studying the game, looking for an edge. He's honestly out there to just win, which isn't something you can say about everyone. Someone else that comes to mind is Tony Clark. Anyone who has played with him will tell you he's a special person.

DL: *The Red Sox front office went through some upheaval this off-season. Do players really care about what happens in the front office, or do they mostly just focus on what happens on the field?*

LM: They do care, because it can have a direct affect on your career. You can have a good relationship with the general manager or a bad one. To be honest, I was happy when Dan Duquette left because my career under him wasn't the best in the world. When Theo came in, he brought a different attitude and personality, and I know it affected people when he left. Having him come back is the best thing that could have happened for the Red Sox.

DL: *Tell us about your decision to play in Japan in 2000.*

LM: For me, it was a no-brainer. He didn't push me out, but Dan Duquette said that if I stayed, it would probably be more of the same— I'd be a part-time player and there would be no guarantees I'd be in Boston all year. He said it was a good opportunity for me, which didn't exactly make me feel wanted. I had a year and a half in the big leagues at the time, so I looked at Japan as a chance to play every day and make more money. When I came back, a year later, I'd be a free agent and could hopefully find the right situation.

DL: *How would you describe your experience in Japan, and why did you come back to the Red Sox less than a year later?*

LM: Culturally I loved it, but the toughest part of the day was going to the ballpark. I could go two-for-two, but then get pinch hit for in the fifth inning. I didn't understand the culture of the game, and just never felt comfortable there. I started to pursue coming back, and when John Valentin hurt his knee I was able to return and help the team.

DL: *You were a replacement player in 1995. What impact has that had on your career?*

LM: Fortunately, the effect has been minimal. All in all, it's a situation where the sides are a little hard-headed. I had one year of minor league ball, and the boss says to play or go home. Basically, I wasn't a million-dollar player, so I was expendable to them. They didn't care what happened to us, so we paid the price by not being allowed in the union. I never made a cent out of it, either—I walked out when it was time to actually play. That was a long time ago, too, and we're still not allowed in. Like I said, I think they're being a little hard-headed, but there's not much I can do about it.

DL: *How differently do you look at the game now, compared to when you broke in, especially from a business standpoint?*

LM: It doesn't take long to realize that it's a business. You come to understand that it's not personal when decisions are made; it's just the way things are. It does bother me how the media often deals with things, saying why someone is bad and what he can't do instead of what he can. And they're often critical when someone gets a big contract, but it's something you had to work for. For your first three years, you're told what you're going to get, then when you're arbitration-eligible that starts to turn. It's all time and money. This is a business both ways, not just from one side.

DL: *Going back to 2003, what was it like playing in San Diego, and what was it like being traded back to Boston?*

LM: That first year with another team was kind of a tough experience. I left a lot of good friends in Boston, and I definitely watched their box scores. Or the Red Sox would be on TV in the clubhouse, and if someone picked up the remote it would be, "Hey, leave that on." It was such a crazy and resilient team, too, with all those come-from-behind wins. When I got traded back here, in August, it was great. It was just as we were getting ready for a series with the Yankees, so there I was, right back into the chaos. It was, "Here we go again. Bring 'em on!"

DL: *Let's close with one of the biggest moments of your career: Your first at-bat in Fenway Park.*

LM: We were on the road when I got called up, and I got my first hit in Minnesota, off of Mike Morgan. John Valentin was a little banged up, so I knew I'd be playing in the first game when we got home. Because there were a few days for them to prepare—to get tickets and make plans—I had a lot of friends and family at the game. And, as fate would have it, it was my parents' 33rd wedding anniversary. I had always told them they'd come to my first game in a limo if I made it to the big leagues, so I hired them one. My first at-bat was against Jose Rosado, who I had actually faced in my first big league at-bat the week before. Tek and Mike Benjamin were on base, and I hit a 3-2 pitch for a home run. Man, that seems like 30 years ago. And I still get chills when I think about it. I probably always will.

RANDY NEWSOM

RANDY NEWSOM WAS SIGNED BY THE RED SOX AS A NON-DRAFTED
FREE AGENT IN 2004. A RIGHT-HANDED PITCHER OUT OF TUFTS
UNIVERSITY, NEWSOM SAW TIME IN LOWELL, GREENVILLE, AND
WILMINGTON LAST SEASON. THIS INTERVIEW TOOK PLACE IN MAY
2005.

David Laurila: *You're currently in extended spring training in Ft. Myers.
Explain what that is, including what the daily regimen is like.*

Randy Newsom: Extended spring training is like the movie Groundhog
Day. Seriously. Every day, we wake up real early (6:15 or so), get to the
park and lift—at least most of us do—then eat breakfast and then have
a two-hour practice. After that, we have lunch and then we play who-
ever we are supposed to play that day. The next day, we do it all over
again. Every once in a while, Karen, the cafeteria lady, will surprise us
with Belgian waffles at breakfast, but other than that—same thing,
every day. It's just spring training for an extra two months. Some people will tell you it's rough, but honestly it's a great chance to work on a
lot of things.

DL: *How do the games differ from what we see during the regular season?*

RN: EXS games are real laid-back because records aren't kept, there is
no official scorer, and if a pitcher throws too many pitches, they just cut
the inning before it's over—that sort of deal. It's also a random mix of
players, as you have some making their pro debuts, some minor league
vets waiting to get a full season assignment, and even some rehab guys
from various levels. But there is a still a lot of talent on the field, and one
team wins and one loses, so it works for me.

DL: *Who are the coaches and instructors, and who do you work with the
most?*

RN: The Red Sox are great at this because there are so many coaches
and instructors down here. We have had as many as nine here at one
time. There are five coaches down here full-time, two pitching coaches, two hitting coaches, and Ralph Treuel, who is the director/manager

of the whole "extended" thing. I work with Ralph and the two pitching coaches, Goose Gregson and Walter Miranda. They all bring different things to the table, so it works out well.

DL: *You signed with the Red Sox as a non-drafted free agent. Tell us how that came to be.*

RN: The draft was rough. I had heard so many things, and coming from a Division III school it's always a crapshoot. The Dodgers had told me I might go as high as the 15th round or so, and I had heard from some other teams around that spot too, so I expected to go that first day. I had some good workouts before the draft, so I thought it was a done deal. Luckily for me, I was able to pitch at Fenway in front of some Red Sox people in the New England College All-Star Game, and I threw pretty well. So after the draft didn't go my way, the Red Sox gave me a call and offered me a job. That was an incredible day for me. I couldn't have been happier that it was the Sox. I have always felt that I can compete at any level, and all I've ever asked for is a chance—and the Sox gave it to me.

DL: *You grew up in Cincinnati. How did you end up at Tufts, and what did you study there?*

RN: How did I end up at Tufts? I asked myself that question for the first three weeks I was there. I ended up at Tufts because the people there are incredible. They contacted me, recruited me even when I was taking my visits to some bigger Division I schools, and then, after some things fell through, they convinced me that a great school in a great city with the opportunity to play both baseball and football was the way to go. Absolutely no regrets on that. In my opinion, Tufts University is the best college experience going. As for the studying, I ended up majoring in economics with a minor in history. My whole college career, I was planning on law school so I took an interesting choice of classes and every once in a while I would go to them.

DL: *What was your baseball experience like at Tufts, and has anyone from the school played in the Major Leagues?*

RN: Tufts was awesome. I had an incredible group of teammates, and being at the Division III level, no one really has the egos that I think bigger programs have. I would come back from the New England Collegiate

Baseball League [NECBL] or the Cape and it would be refreshing just to be able to play with a bunch of guys who are doing it because they love competition and baseball. Plus, we were good. It's a lot of fun to win 70 percent of your games. And also, those guys knew how to party. It might be a smart school and all, but our drinking team had a baseball problem if you know what I mean. No one from Tufts has made it to the bigs . . . yet.

DL: *How would you describe yourself as a pitcher? Are you primarily a starter or reliever, and what do you throw?*

RN: Exclusively a reliever these days. When I first started pitching as a junior in high school, I was a closer and I always end up coming back to that role. Even at Tufts, I would sometimes close the Friday game, then start one of the Saturday games. I love coming in with the game on the line, so reliever suits me fine. They have me throwing from a sidearm angle now, so I am definitely suited more for the bullpen. I have been using a sinker with a change and Frisbee-slider lately. My game is based on movement, and I try to get as many ground balls as possible.

DL: *I'm assuming you were a Reds fan growing up. Has going to school in the Boston area and signing with the Red Sox changed that?*

RN: First, I love the Reds and their fans, and Cincinnati is a great base-ball town—top five no doubt, but come on . . . Boston. These people are contagious with their enthusiasm. I used to tell my friends in college who were from Boston I wasn't so much rooting for the team as the fans. The Boston fans are incredible. Ever since I went to my first game at Fenway—that was the stadium I saw in my big league dreams. Walking out wearing that uniform and throwing where the Joe Cronins, Ted Williamses, and Yazes have played...you can't dream much bigger.

DL: *What's better: Skyline chili, or New England clam chowder?*

RN: Wow, what an incredibly tough question. I can't believe you know about the power that is Skyline chili . . . The people in Cincy are going to kill me for saying this, but I have to go with the real New England clam chowder. We're talking in a bread bowl at Faneuil Hall. I really do love Skyline and the Reds, but I used to skip classes at Tufts and take the T in just to have chowder for lunch.

DL: *What are you into when you're not playing baseball?*

RN: You know, a little of this, a little of that. I have no attention span but always have to be active, so I do a whole lot of different things. I have a list of 100 things I want to do in my life, and I only have seven done, so I still have some things to focus on. In the off-season, I worked on a political campaign, worked for a computer software company, and visited my girlfriend who was abroad in France, so my interests have an interesting range. As for now, there is a lot of down-time during Extended, so you have to try to keep busy. One hour, I might be playing online poker, sometimes I will read a book. I am trying to write a novel, although it's pretty rough right now. I like all the guys down here, so we usually go out to eat or see a movie or something.

DL: *How did you find out that you'd be going to Cooperstown to pitch in the Hall of Fame game, and what was your reaction?*

RN: Ralph came up to me in the middle of BP one day and said, "News, I never thought I would say this to you, but you're headed to Cooperstown." Once he explained why, I was actually kind of surprised. Being in Extended, and being kind of the anti-prospect (the opposite of what people consider prospects to be), I was pretty floored. I really appreciated the Sox allowing me this honor.

DL: *Last one: Who are your favorite players in the Red Sox system? Major Leaguers don't count—only minor league guys.*

RN: Wow, put me on the spot. Honestly, I am biased because my favorite players also happen to be players that I know are genuinely good people. I am pretty close to Bryan Pritz and Mike Leonard, so I really pull hard for them. Squirrely [Pritz] is a lot of fun to watch. I knew if he got a chance, he could do some damage and so far this year he has. Phil Seibel is about as good a person as you can meet, and when he gets healthy I think he is going to have a good big league career. I also really like Mike Lockwood at Triple A—he's a good guy, and I like the way he plays. I am big fan of some of the Venezuelan players, too—Jesus Garcia and Jimmy James. As for watching, I tried to watch as many of Portland's games as possible during spring training because that team is stacked. Their starting pitching is great, they have some serious bats up, and they are almost all good guys. If I had to pick some sleepers in the system, I don't think enough people know about Durbin yet, but I think he will be a solid Major Leaguer down the line. As for pitchers, I like watching Andrew Dobies and Beau Vaughan. Completely different styles, but they both seem to have a good feel for what they are doing. I am easy because I basically like everyone, and the Red Sox have a bunch of players who are also good people.

Jonathan Papelbon

Jonathan Papelbon was the Red Sox' selection in the fourth round of the 2003 draft. A right-handed pitcher, Papelbon made his big league debut in 2005, appearing in 17 games. This interview took place in July 2004 while Papelbon was with the Sarasota Red Sox.

David Laurila: *Let's start with something important. You won a cow-milking contest in Lowell last summer. Tell us about that.*

Jonathan Papelbon: It was on the field before a game, and they asked if any of us knew how to milk a cow. I didn't, but because I came there from Mississippi they thought I could. I remember asking, "What do I do?" and they told me: "Just yank on them!"

DL: *And you ended up winning.*

JP: Yes—my teammates told me I had to. We were playing the Yankees, and they said, "Whatever you do, you have to win!" That tells you a little something about the rivalry. I know one thing: I sure got a lot of ribbing about it afterwards!

DL: *You pitched at Mississippi State but were utilized there as a reliever. Here, you're excelling as a starter. Tell us about that transition and which you prefer, starting or relieving.*

JP: Definitely starting. I enjoyed relieving in college, but don't think I got as much out of my talent as I could have.

DL: *Why did you work out of the pen?*

JP: The coach wanted me to relieve. We had a few good starters but nobody to use as a closer. It made sense for the team.

DL: *I understand that you threw fastballs and sliders in college but have since expanded your repertoire. Tell us about that.*

JP: Starting has allowed me to utilize more pitches, and I've really made leaps and bounds—especially this year. Al Nipper, my pitching coach, deserves a lot of credit for that. There's no possible way I could be doing what I am without his help. It's incredible what I've learned from him about approach and getting hitters out.

DL: *What are you throwing now?*

JP: A fastball, obviously. That's what I have the best command of. And a curve, but it's not an out pitch for me. Plus, Nipper taught me a change-up with a split-finger grip—it's not a splitter, though—that's really helped. My control of it is slowly getting better, and I'm even throwing it a lot on 3-2 counts.

DL: *What about the slider?*

JP: I'm actually not throwing it anymore, because it's easier to throw my curve for strikes. I have, however, started working on a cutter. That's Nipper again, who's really helping turn me from a thrower into a pitcher. Some day, I'll look back and say that I couldn't have made it without him.

DL: *Matt Murton, one of your teammates, says that you like to attack hitters and "bury them." Do you think that's an accurate description?*

JP: Definitely. Nipper talks about the difference between pitching and throwing, but attacking hitters doesn't mean just raring back and throwing it over the middle. I want to throw strikes early in the count and do it with all of my pitches. I want to challenge every guy in the lineup, and I want to go at least six or seven innings and give my team a chance to win.

DL: *Are there any pitchers you model yourself after?*

JP: My idol has always been Roger Clemens. Our styles are similar, and I actually liked him even before I started pitching. He's such a bulldog. His work ethic is unbelievable. That's something I've tried to borrow from him. I've always thought that if you had equal talent with someone, and wanted to beat him, outworking him was the way to do it. I'm hoping to implement Clemens' workout program in the off-season.

DL: *You and he also have similar builds.*

JP: You know, it's funny, because Juan Cedeno calls me "little Roger." He thinks I look like him, and I guess a few other people do, too. Juan is my roomie down here.

DL: *As you're transitioning from the pen to the rotation this year, are your innings being limited?*

JP: I don't think so. I've thrown as many as 100 pitches in a game, and still felt good. I've stuck to my workouts and have always kept my legs strong. There have been no transition problems so far.

DL: *I understand that you have brothers playing college baseball. I'm guessing that you come from an athletic family?*

JP: Sure. My mother played on LSU's first fast-pitch softball team. She was a pitcher. My younger brothers—they're twins—are playing at North Florida. Dusty Rhodes is the manager down there.

DL: *Did you play other sports growing up?*

JP: I played everything. I actually got recruited more for football than baseball. I was a combination tight end/wide receiver and briefly considered going to Central Florida to play football. Getting a chance to play baseball at Mississippi State was a great opportunity, though, and it was really a pretty easy choice. Baseball is huge there. It's been voted the number one place to watch college baseball. There are over 10,000 fans there for the games.

DL: *What was it like getting drafted last year and playing in Lowell?*

JP: It was fantastic. I couldn't believe how many people were there for every game. And that's just the way I want it. I don't want to play for a team where the fans don't care and don't lose sleep over who wins and loses.

DL: *They certainly care in Red Sox Nation. Have you been to Fenway Park?*

JP: I was there last year when I was with the Spinners. The whole team was invited, and it was really cool thinking about all the tradition. The seats were a little rough, though.

DL: *How so?*

JP: Hey, I'm 6' 4", and the seats weren't built for a guy my size. I thought about it, and told myself: "Man, Fenway is great, but I don't want to go back to watch. I want to go back to play!"

DL: *What were your thoughts on being drafted by the Red Sox in 2003?*

JP: It was kind of weird, to be honest. Other teams showed a lot more interest prior to the draft, so I was a little surprised. And being from the South, I didn't know much about Boston—all the things that come into play. But the more I learned, the cooler it got. I couldn't be more excited, and I couldn't have been luckier that I ended up here.

DL: *You're a competitor on the field. What are you like off it?*

JP: I do love to work hard, but you can't be serious all the time. I like to have fun.

DL: *Beau Vaughan was a teammate of yours last year. Tell us about him.*

JP: He's a good guy, a bit of a jokester. We became workout partners and pushed each other. Some days I'd push him, and other days he'd push me. He definitely has loads of stuff—tremendous talent. He'll pitch in the big leagues, for sure.

DL: *It sounds like the two of you had some fun together when you weren't working. Are there any good stories you can share without getting in trouble?*

JP: Without getting in trouble? Probably not.

DL: *Any closing thoughts?*

JP: I love being with the Sox, and I just want to play and compete. Put the ball in my hands!

DUSTIN PEDROIA

DUSTIN PEDROIA WAS THE RED SOX' SELECTION IN THE SECOND ROUND OF THE 2004 DRAFT. AN INFIELDER FROM WOODLAND, CALIFORNIA, PEDROIA SPENT THE 2005 SEASON WITH THE PORTLAND SEA DOGS AND PAWTUCKET RED SOX. THIS INTERVIEW TOOK PLACE IN APRIL 2005.

David Laurila: *Let's start with spring training. How did that go for you?*

Dustin Pedroia: It was my first, so I went in not knowing exactly what to expect. I will say that it went faster than a lot of people said it would. I was told it would seem long, but it really wasn't. I got a lot of work in, and having an opportunity to play in a few big league games was an added bonus, a fun experience.

DL: *Was the fan and media attention what you expected?*

DP: I was told there would be a lot of that, and the fans were great. They were there before and after the games, too, not just for them. Red Sox fans are the best in baseball. No doubt about it.

DL: *Where is your comfort level at second base right now?*

DP: I'm getting used to it. I'm putting in the work, so I'm getting there. The biggest differences are having a little more time, with the shorter throw, and turning the double play.

DL: *How is your relationship with Hanley Ramirez so far? Not from a personal standpoint, but on the field as a double play partner?*

DP: It's going pretty well. We've been learning each other for about a month now. In college, I worked with one guy for two years. It's important to be on the same page, and that takes time.

DL: *As an infielder, how important is it to know a hitter's tendencies?*

DP: Being in the right position is the biggest thing with defense. If you can tell the hitter's bat path—if he's inside the ball or not—you'll have a good idea which side he'll hit it to. So yes, it's important.

DL: *Do you like your pitchers to work fast?*

DP: Definitely. Tempo is a big part of defense. Jon [Papelbon] kept the tempo in our favor last night, and it really helps. He threw a great game. Our other pitchers are fun to play behind, too. Gabbard, Lester . . . there are some guys here who can pitch.

DL: *You're probably more than a little tired of being compared to David Eckstein. Who would you compare your game to?*

DP: I'm not much into comparisons, for me or anyone else. But I guess I model my game somewhat after Marcus Giles from an offensive standpoint, and Fernando Vina from a defensive standpoint. Mostly, I believe in playing my own game and not thinking along those lines.

DL: *Have your favorite players tended to be guys similar to yourself or those who do things you can't—say, a Barry Bonds?*

DP: Both. If a guy is good and produces, I'll enjoy watching him, and I'll respect him. And playing the game right is important. I wouldn't model myself after someone who disrespects the game.

DL: *What do you consider the most underrated part of your game?*

DP: I don't pay attention to what people say I can or can't do. I play for the team I'm on and the organization. Winning is what matters, and that's how I try to play—doing what it takes to win.

DL: *Is bunting and moving runners over underrated in today's game?*

DP: For sure. You see that style mostly in the postseason, when the games are more important. The same approach works in the regular season. If you do the little things right, you're going to win more often.

DL: *What are your thoughts on getting hit by pitches—taking one for the team?*

DP: I'm willing to do that—anything, or any way, to get on base. It hurts for what, a minute? You have to be willing to sacrifice yourself. Yeah, I'll take one for the team.

DL: *Do you go up to the plate with a specific plan or just see the ball and hit it?*

DP: I have an idea when I go up there. Everything counts—anything you can use to your advantage. I stay with my approach and hit it where it's pitched. I'll work counts if I can—make the pitcher work harder.

DL: *What's the toughest style of pitcher for you to face?*

DP: One who locates all of his pitches. There are 5,000 guys out there who can hit a 95 mile-per-hour fastball if it's right down the middle. I don't strike out a lot, but getting the fat part on the ball is what you're trying to do. That's harder with well-located pitches.

DL: *Jeremy West, whom you played with at Arizona State, said you're the guy he wants up, or the ball hit to, in the ninth inning. To me, that means you have mental toughness. What are your thoughts on that?*

DP: Obviously, it's a compliment. And respect doesn't come overnight; you have to earn it. I try to do everything I can to help the team win, and I think that's what he's referring to. And if you think you can't do something, you probably won't. If confidence is mental toughness, then I probably have it.

DL: *Are you the kind of guy who comes into the dugout after a great play, high-fiving everyone? Or do you just take everything in stride?*

DP: It's an out, just one of 27. We're here for a reason, and you should act professionally. Will I show a little emotion in a big situation? Sure. But mostly I just go about my business.

DL: *What are some of your early memories of baseball?*

DP: I grew up rooting for the Giants, as did my whole family. I remember that when I was a kid, I'd put on my uniform five hours before the game. Baseball has always been my life and my goal. That's what got me a scholarship, got me drafted, and hopefully will get me further.

DL: *What are you into besides baseball?*

DP: It's mostly baseball, really. I work out a lot, and that takes up much of my time. But I do like movies, especially comedies. *Major League* is one of my all-time favorites.

DL: *Can you give us a good story to close with?*

DP: I traveled to Arizona with the big league club for the final two pre-season games. I wouldn't call it hazing, but a few of the guys gave me the rookie treatment on the plane. If Mirabelli or Wakefield wanted a beer, I'd have to carry it for them. I was their personal stewardess for the flight attendant.

CURT SCHILLING

CURT SCHILLING IS A PITCHER FOR THE RED SOX AND A SIX-TIME MLB ALL-STAR. OBTAINED FROM ARIZONA PRIOR TO THE 2004 SEASON, SCHILLING HELPED LEAD THE RED SOX TO THEIR FIRST WORLD SERIES CHAMPIONSHIP IN 86 YEARS. THIS INTERVIEW TOOK PLACE IN FEBRUARY 2005.

David Laurila: *Before agreeing to come to Boston, you were reportedly concerned about park factors and how they might impact your game. Can you elaborate on why that was important, bearing in mind that you went 22-6 with Arizona in 2001 while giving up 37 home runs?*

Curt Schilling: Obviously, when you look at Fenway, the Monster is right on top of you. Yes, I had some concerns that maybe the park wouldn't work for me. As it turned out, the data gave evidence that I could be successful there, which helped me make the decision. And having seen the data for Arizona, it turns out that maybe the ballpark there wasn't as good as I thought it was. The important thing was that I wanted to go to a place where I'd be comfortable, and I wanted to finish my career there. I have three years left, and after that I'm done. So, having had the luxury of some leverage—Arizona was in a position where they were going to move me—I wanted to make sure it was the right fit.

DL: *You're a believer in scouting reports. But what if a chart says you should throw a hitter a certain pitch in a given situation, and it's not working for you that game? Or what if your gut feeling goes against the reports?*

CS: Reports are preliminary. Overall, feel is important, and ultimately it comes down to incorporating your stuff into the plan. And the plan is going to include more than just one at-bat—you have to plan on getting a guy out three or four times a game. As for having a gut feeling, preparation plays a part in that. You're going to have an idea beforehand, and you're adjusting on the fly knowing what that is. With me, when something isn't working I can always go back to the fastball. I've always had good command, so that's my default pitch.

DL: *Making adjustments is a big part of the game. Can you sense when a hitter is about to adjust to how you've been working him, and if so, do you wait for him to prove that he is, or do you try to beat him to the punch? And is there a difference between "out-thinking a hitter" and "out-guessing a hitter"?*

CS: The thing you want to do is be one pitch ahead of where you have to. The main concern is the game plan. As I was saying, you need to plan three or four at-bats ahead to a hitter—sometimes three or four games. You're going to use a pitch in the first inning to set up the one you use in the seventh with guys on base. And you have to be careful about trying to out-think hitters, too. Some don't think—they just see and hit—so it doesn't make sense to try to figure out what they're looking for. Now, I know a guy like Frank Catalanotto studies, so you have to approach him differently. Michael Young, too. You have to be ahead of them, because they'll have a plan and will adjust. That's part of the beauty of pitching—setting up hitters, pitch by pitch, game by game, season by season.

DL: *It's possible to intimidate a hitter or simply establish the inside half of the plate, without hitting him. That said, it's notable that you've only hit 44 batters in 2,814 career innings. By comparison, Pedro Martinez has hit 115 in 2,296. As you're both known for having outstanding command, how would you explain the difference?*

CS: There are three ways to intimidate a hitter. You can hit him, knock him down, or break his bat. Very few hitters can handle both sides of the plate, and a well-located fastball can help you establish the inside. Pitching inside is part of the game and always has been. There's no doubt that Pedro is intimidating. Going inside has always been one of his weapons, and he's not scared of hitting anybody. But it's his stuff, too. His ball rides in on right-handed batters, and mine doesn't. So he probably hits more guys by accident than I do. Of course, you don't want the hitter to know that it's an accident. That doesn't send the same message.

DL: *When you drill someone, do you respect him more if he stands up for himself and barks at you, or if he just takes his base quietly?*

CS: That's a no-brainer. They should just take the base. But, hey, there's a lot of machismo out on the field. For three-quarters of a century, guys just jogged down to first. But for some reason, the number of guys charging the mound has increased. Getting hit is a part of the game, and I respect the guys who understand that.

DL: *John Smoltz and Dennis Eckersley became great closers after successful careers as starters. Would you be able to make that transition, and is it something you could see yourself doing?*

CS: Could I? Yes. Would I? No. I'm just praying that I can stay healthy and pitch out my career as a starter. But do I respect closers? You bet I do. It's one of the toughest things to do in baseball. There's no worse feeling than blowing a game in the ninth inning, and you have to be mentally tough to handle that.

DL: *Good pitching coaches are an asset to a staff, but just how important are they? Is a Leo Mazzone a difference-maker who can help push a team over the top—or is he simply helpful?*

CS: Both. And it depends on the coach, and it depends on the player. Johnny Podres is the best I've ever had, and he's as responsible as anybody that I'm a big league pitcher. I've always prided myself in being willing to learn, and a pitching coach can help you do that. But you have to be willing to listen and be open to making adjustments, and not everybody is. And more than coaches can help you. R.J. [Randy Johnson] really helped me with my workout regimen—and Pedro with my approach to hitters. He notices a lot of little things, like how a hitter is moving his feet or his hands. I've always been better at preparation, where he notices details during an at-bat.

DL: *You recently said that without the re-signing of Jason Varitek, Boston's chances of winning again in 2005 were nonexistent. With that in mind, what makes a great catcher?*

CS: A lot of it is desire, and yes, I think that about Tek. You have to want to be great, and the desire to call a great game is part of that. Offense is such a big part of the game these days, and some guys just don't work hard enough on calling one. Tek does, as did Darren Daulton, while others I've played with haven't.

DL: *This year, Roger Clemens went 18-4, 2.98, and in 214 innings had 79 BBs and 218 Ks. Ben Sheets went 12-14, 2.70, and in 237 innings had 32 BBs and 264 Ks. Knowing that Clemens won the National League Cy Young, who had the better year, and why?*

CS: Neither. R.J. should have won the Cy Young. He had the best year, but unfortunately a lot of voters had other agendas. As for Sheets, I'd have to look more at the numbers. But there's a lot to be said for winning close games, and 1-0 games. I'm sure Clemens won some one-run games where he had to make the big pitch. And I'm sure Ben would say that he lost a few where he didn't make the pitch at the right time. Pitching well is more than wins and losses, but you still have to know how to win.

DL: *How much should reputation and respect be a factor when assessing a player's career, including Hall of Fame consideration? Is it more than just the numbers?*

CS: Absolutely. When I'm done, my list of top 10 teammates won't be based on numbers. As a matter of fact, people would be surprised at some of the names. The best are the ones who make other guys better. That's how you win. There aren't many Jason Variteks out there.

DL: *Catfish Hunter is in the Hall of Fame, while the comparable Luis Tiant is not. A notable difference in their careers is that Hunter pitched in 22 postseason games, and his team won 10 of the 12 series he played in, while Tiant pitched in only five postseason games. What impact do you think the postseason has—and should have—on who gets in and who doesn't?*

CS: I don't really know the answer to that question. Can you judge a guy by how good the teams were that he played on? Not really, but playing well in the postseason counts for something, too. A lot of guys vote for personal reasons, which isn't right. I remember one guy didn't vote for Nolan Ryan on the first ballot because Don Sutton didn't go in on the first ballot. That's called having an agenda. It probably didn't mean much to Nolan—I don't know—but if you bust your butt for 26 years it's dumb that someone does that. Even in something like the rookie-of-the-year voting. A few years ago, Brandon Webb was the best rookie, in my opinion. But someone didn't respect him and didn't even put him on their ballot. I didn't understand that.

DL: *Warren Spahn once threw 201 pitches in a game at the age of 42— Juan Marichal threw 227 in the same game—and Tiant threw 163 in a World Series outing. Today, a big deal is made if a pitcher is left in for as many as 110. What are your thoughts on this?*

CS: That's how it's evolved, and science seems to have said that's how it is. It's a hard thing to figure out or offer an opinion on. There are a lot more teams now, and the talent is a lot more diluted. And pitching a lot of innings isn't the best way to stay healthy. It's a different game, including the money and the size and strength of the players.

DL: *In comparing today's ballplayers favorably to those of past eras, you once opined that you could blow away Babe Ruth with fastballs, even telling him they were coming. Knowing that he faced Walter Johnson on a regular basis, what do you have that the "Big Train" didn't?*

CS: First, I don't believe that he threw 100 miles an hour. I'd argue that Ruth couldn't get that 42-ounce bat around on a good fastball, and there's zero evidence that guys threw that hard back then. Clocking a fastball with a motorcycle, like they did with Feller, isn't very scientific, but I know what I see with my own eyes and I know the readings. Today's game just moves a lot faster. I'm not saying that they weren't good in his day, but today's players are simply bigger and faster.

DL: *Which type of team would you prefer pitching for—one of the late sixties Orioles squads that featured Brooks Robinson, Mark Belanger, and Paul Blair, or the early eighties Brewers teams with Gorman Thomas, Ben Oglivie, and Cecil Cooper? In other words, do you want a number of Gold Glovers behind you, or run support?*

CS: Obviously, both. And those Brewers teams could catch the ball, too. But if I had to choose, I'd take the decent offense and great defense over the great offense and lesser defense.

DL: *Who are some of your favorite players from a historic perspective, and why do you admire them?*

CS: Roberto Clemente was my first favorite player, when I was just five or six years old. My dad was a Pirates fan, so that's how I grew up. I liked Clemente, Willie Stargell, Dave Parker. As a matter of fact, I only went to one Major League game as a fan. That was Clemente's last, the one where he got his 3,000th hit.

DL: *Whom do the young baseball fans in the Schilling household most enjoy watching?*

CS: My oldest son, who's nine, latches onto guys I've played with. He hangs out in the clubhouse and likes guys who are nice to him. I'd say Scott Rolen is his favorite.

DL: *You obviously grew up with a great love of baseball. But is it possible to truly enjoy the game as a fan when you're a part of it?*

CS: Somewhat. In Boston, more so—there's so much to take in here. And I'm always watching games on TV. You can see a lot of things you can't on the field, and I'm always looking to pick things up. Now, obviously I look at a game differently than you do and appreciate different things. But I still enjoy the game, and recently watched the Pedro/Clemens game—the one where Pedro K'd 17—on *ESPN Classic*. Maybe I'll watch a little differently after I'm done playing. I don't know.

DL: *The media can influence how fans view a player, sometimes unfairly. How much can they influence a player's performance, including making him put too much emphasis on one outing? Your match-ups with R.J. this year would be an example.*

CS: First, I'm definitely going to be looking forward to the match-ups against R.J. That's not on the media, though. They may make it out that R.J. and I don't have a good relationship, but that's because that wouldn't be news. They take whatever they can to make it look adversarial, because that sells better. Misery loves company. But I've been in the game too long to let that affect me. Media attention goes with the territory, but you can't allow it to dictate what you do or think. The onus is on the player to make sure it doesn't. I saw *The Roger Maris Story* not too long ago, and the media played a big part in his stress when he was chasing the record. It's a human element to be affected by what they write and say about you, and some deal with it better than others. I don't let it bother me, because they have no idea who I am as a person.

DL: *You recently commented on how it's impossible for a fan to understand what it means for a player to hold out for an extra million dollars when he's already making as much as 10 to 15.· As someone who is regarded as having a more down-to-earth outlook than many athletes, can you elaborate on that—including how you'd define "respect" from a baseball perspective?*

CS: That's an argument where you can't sound legitimate with your answer. It's about the relationship with players, really. When I signed my last contract, I was acutely aware of it helping set the market. But that's not my most important responsibility. That's to my family, but baseball is a business, too. The owners would pay us a dollar a year if they could, just like we want what they'll pay us. And respect is a part of it, sure, but that's not equated with the size of the contract. I have little respect for the annual value of a player's contract. I have respect for what he puts on the field.

DL: *As people age, they mature and their priorities change. Outside of being a little older and wiser, are you basically the same person you were when you broke into MLB?*

CS: I've changed dramatically, yet not at all. As a player, I'm smarter. As a person, I'm wiser. I've learned. I make mistakes. Of course, because of what I do for a living, I'm often the lead story on ESPN when I do make mistakes. But I want to walk away from this game respected, and I think I'll be able to do that.

DL: *Someday, when you look back at your career, there will be many memories to cherish. Based on the history of the Red Sox and what the team accomplished, I assume 2004 would have to be near the top.*

CS: I'm hoping there are a few more big moments, but right now it's one of them. 1993 is probably a close third, but 2001 and 2004 are the two biggest. They're both special, for different reasons, and I'm certainly proud to have been a part of both. There's nothing like winning a World Series championship.

BEAU VAUGHAN

Beau Vaughan was the Red Sox' selection in the third round of the 2003 draft. A right-handed pitcher, Vaughan spent the 2005 season with the Greenville Bombers. This interview took place in February 2004.

David Laurila: *Your given name is William Lee Vaughan, but you go by Beau. Where does that come from?*

Beau Vaughan: Beau is a nickname my mother gave to me at birth because we have too many Bills in our family. I am actually William Lee Vaughan IV.

DL: *Your name brings to mind two former, and popular, Red Sox players. One is "the Spaceman," Bill Lee. Do you have anything in common with him?*

BV: I am a little young to have witnessed the Spaceman in action. I do remember hearing he wanted to wear 337 because it was his name upside down and reversed. I thought that was pretty clever.

DL: *Explain your personality. What are you like off the field?*

BV: I am a goofball. To me, the greatest thing in the world is to have a good laugh.

DL: *Your name also brings to mind former Sox slugger Mo Vaughn. What kind of hitter are you?*

BV: I love this question. My dad always thought I was going to be a better hitter than pitcher. And I love hitting. I actually batted clean-up through high school and my first year of junior college. If I could, I'd rather be a left-handed-hitting third baseman as opposed to a pitcher.

DL: *More importantly, what type of pitcher are you? What are your best pitches?*

BV: I like to think of myself as a power pitcher. When it comes down to it, I love beating people with my fastball. But at the same time, I love seeing people look stupid on my change-up, my best off-speed pitch.

DL: *Bill Lee once said his idea of a perfectly pitched game is 27 outs on 27 pitches. Would you rather throw a 2-hit shutout with 3 Ks, or allow 3 runs on 6 hits while striking out 18?*

BV: If the team won in both scenarios, I'd want the 18 strikeouts. But I'll take a two-hit shutout win over 18 Ks and a loss.

DL: *Four Vaughans have played in the Major Leagues, including Hall-of-Famer Arky Vaughan. Porter Vaughan is the all-time leader in wins for Vaughans with two. Are you familiar with either, and do you pay attention to baseball history?*

BV: I have heard of Arky Vaughan, but I could not tell you anything about him. Other than that, I have a good knowledge of baseball history. I was actually a history major in college.

DL: *You share a birthday with another Beau who played in the Major Leagues, Beau Allred [Cleveland 1989–91]. He's from the Phoenix/Mesa area, as are you. Have you met him, or even heard of him?*

BV: I do know of him. But again, only by name, and that's because I got one of his baseball cards as a kid. But with that name, birth date, and hometown, he must be a handsome guy. Just kidding!

DL: *Ex-Red Sox [now Toronto Blue Jays] third baseman Shea Hillenbrand is also from the Phoenix/Mesa area. Do you know him?*

BV: Yeah, I know of him, but I don't know him personally.

DL: *You were drafted out of high school in the 39th round in 1999 by the Twins but did not sign. Why?*

BV: When I was drafted by the Twins, it was specifically for a draft-and-follow. They wanted to see me develop for a year. I guess they didn't feel they needed to get me at the time. And they never even offered me a contract, but it worked out for the best.

DL: *The Red Sox drafted you in the third round last year. Explain your development as a pitcher in that four-year period, including who was most responsible for it.*

BV: I went to four colleges in four years. Over the first three, I got more physically mature. I was a late bloomer. I picked up a little bit from each place I went. Finally, when I got to Arizona State, coach Pat Murphy and pitching coach Chris Sinacori basically put the pieces together, and things started clicking.

DL: *Why four different colleges?*

BV: Out of high school, I didn't have colleges banging down my door. I got some mail and a couple of calls from schools. The only two that gave me more than one phone call were Harvard and Dartmouth. I had the grades and SAT scores to go pretty much anywhere. I went to Phoenix College because it was the only school that said I would get an opportunity to hit. But certain promises that were made didn't happen, so I transferred to South Mountain Community College in Phoenix. Things went well, but only two schools offered scholarships when I was there. New Orleans offered a lucrative scholarship, and I went there. However, I barely pitched, and I had a tough time throwing strikes. They said they needed to cut my scholarship in half. I don't blame them. I came back home, thinking I was done with baseball. I was two years away from my degree, and I was going to go to ASU just as a student. While messing around on a team in Phoenix that summer, Jeremy West was on my team and asked me what I had to lose by going to the walk-on tryouts. So I went and made the team.

DL: *What round were you expecting to be taken in, and which teams showed an interest before the draft?*

BV: As the draft got closer last year, people started to tell me to expect higher rounds. First it was the top 10, then the top five, then the third or fourth. I did not really care, to tell you the truth. I was just glad when it was over, because we were going into a super-regional at the time.

DL: *The Red Sox are a storied franchise, with a dedicated fan base, playing in a historic ballpark. What were your thoughts when they drafted you?*

BV: I was glad the team I was going to had such an amazing fan base. Players love playing for fans. If we weren't playing, we'd have the seat next to you.

DL: *Have you ever been to Fenway Park?*

BV: I went to Fenway when I was about seven years old. My parents took me on vacation to the Northeast. We flew into Boston, stayed for a day, went to a game, then drove up to Quebec. It was a great trip. What I remember about the game was that the Sox beat the Blue Jays, and it was a night game. Some of my late nights in college have diminished the details of my memories.

DL: *Which was your favorite baseball team growing up?*

BV: I never really had a favorite team. My dad's family rooted for the Royals because they're from Kansas City. My mom's family roots for the Cardinals because they're from southern Illinois. And Phoenix did not have a team until recently. I definitely never liked the Yanks.

DL: *Comments like that will make you popular here in Red Sox Nation.*

BV: My disapproval of the Yankees isn't because I am with the Red Sox. I just don't like the attitude that the Yankees are all there is to baseball. And I've gotten that impression over the years. Screw them.

DL: *Who were your favorite players?*

BV: I like the hitters more than the pitchers. The art of hitting is a marvel. Guys like Tony Gwynn, Wade Boggs, and Ted Williams are amazing to watch. If I had to pick one, I'd say . . . Gwynn.

DL: *What other sports did you play and follow, and who were your favorite players?*

BV: I love football. I was an all-conference quarterback in high school, and I still go back and help coach in the off-season. I think the best player of all time is Jerry Rice. He's 40 and still performing. Ray Lewis is going to be the best linebacker ever in a couple more years.

DL: *What are your thoughts on this year's Patriots team?*

BV: The Patriots have the greatest concept of team in any sport going right now. Everybody on that team complements everyone else so well, and that extends to the coaching. They've managed to win two Super Bowls in the last three years without a superstar. Everybody does their job, and they're all on the same page. That should be the mold other teams follow, in any sport.

DL: *Someday you may be wearing a Major League uniform, and kids will look at you as their favorite player. What will this mean to you, and will you feel an obligation to be a good role model?*

BV: There would definitely be an obligation there to not do anything embarrassing. But the biggest thing would be personal and relate with the kids. When I was little, players were gods in my eyes. They were unapproachable. Kids should know that players are guys with the same mentality as them, only a few years older.

DL: *What is important to Beau Vaughan, the person?*

BV: The important thing to me is to be happy. Baseball needs to be fun. This isn't a job. I don't know what it is, but it is not a job. It is fun.

DL: *What are your interests outside of baseball?*

BV: I love movies. That is what I do with my free time. As a matter of fact, I would love for someone to challenge me in a game of six degrees of Kevin Bacon. Movies are the greatest.

DL: *Switching back to baseball, what was your biggest surprise when you joined the Lowell Spinners, and became a professional baseball player? Was it any different than you expected?*

BV: There really weren't many surprises. It was what I expected. The fact that the games were sold out every night was surprising. That was great.

DL: *There were a lot of talented young players on the Spinners last year. Which of them impressed you the most?*

BV: Jeremy West has been with me for the last full year. And to see him make the transition from metal to wood has been impressive. But Abe Alvarez has such amazing control. I roomed and played catch with him, and he is amazing.

DL: *Who among your Spinners teammates were the most interesting personalities?*

BV: The best personality on the Spinners last summer was probably Zack Basch. He is so witty and sharp. He is also fun to mess with. We called him Dr. Green, from *ER*, because he looks exactly like him, and he looks 40.

DL: *Going into your second year of pro ball, you'll be hoping to move up the minor league ladder. Do you see yourself as having a better chance to advance through the system as a starter or as a reliever?*

BV: I don't know. I know the Sox want me to be a starter. I love getting as many innings as possible. But I thrive for coming into pressure situations out of the pen.

DL: *Which current or former Major League pitcher would you compare yourself to?*

BV: The management guys asked me the same question last fall, and I told them I have my own style. [David] Murphy told me I reminded him of Kevin Brown a little bit, but I don't know.

DL: *Switching gears again, if you could go back in time and pitch in any era, against any hitters, when would that be?*

BV: Take me back to the late twenties. I want Gehrig. I know I could get the fat kid [Ruth] out with his long swing and heavy bat. But Gehrig is one of the greatest of all time.

DL: *That sounds as confident as Pedro saying he'd like to wake up the Babe and drill him in the ass. Ruth did face guys like Walter Johnson and Lefty Grove. Are you sure you want to stand behind that statement?*

BV: Walter Johnson and Lefty Grove are two of the greatest pitchers to play. And I don't doubt that getting the best of the Babe would be a Goliath-type feat. But wouldn't you want that one shot to see if you could get the best of arguably the greatest player of all time? It's like Matt Damon taking on Johnny Chan in *Rounders*. Maybe I can't do it. But I'd go into that at-bat knowing I can.

DL: *Last question: Someday, hopefully, you'll step onto the mound at Fenway for the first time in a Major League game. When you do, you'll likely sneak a peek over your shoulder at the Green Monster. What will be going through your mind?*

BV: I'll be thinking, "Hurry up and destroy these guys, so we can go get a Guinness." That would be wicked awesome.

COLIN YOUNG

COLIN YOUNG PITCHED FOR THE RED SOX' DOUBLE A AFFILIATE, THE PORTLAND SEA DOGS, IN 2004. A NATIVE OF WEST NEWBURY, MASSACHUSETTS, AND A GRADUATE OF PENTUCKET HIGH SCHOOL, YOUNG ATTENDED FORDHAM UNIVERSITY BEFORE BEGINNING HIS PROFESSIONAL CAREER. THIS INTERVIEW TOOK PLACE IN FEBRUARY 2006.

David Laurila: *You were a ninth-round selection by the Rockies in 1999. What were your expectations going into the draft?*

Colin Young: I thought I was going to end up with the Yankees. There was a lot of draft talk going into my junior year, and because I was at Fordham, the Yankees saw me pitch a lot. They also brought me to the stadium to work out, which was a real experience. They bring you through the tunnel and dugout, and out to the bullpen. Then they bring you to the mound to face live batters. It's a little intimidating, and the first pitch I threw, I tripped and fell on my face! But then I struck a few guys out, so ending up with them was a real possibility.

DL: *As a lifelong Red Sox fan, what would that have been like?*

CY: It's funny, going to school at Fordham, most of my friends were Yankee fans. At that point, I still had all of my loyalties and it would have been kind of a strange deal. Now I wouldn't mind it, because your loyalties have to go out the window once you're involved with the game. But back then, it was, "Oh man, I wish it could be the Sox!"

DL: *Who has helped you the most as a pitcher since you turned pro?*

CY: I'd have to say it was Bob McClure, in my third year. He tweaked my mechanics, including giving me the hesitation I still have in my delivery. Along with slowing me down, it helped me keep my arm-angle up, which helped me get on top of the ball. It also gave me better balance and improved my control. I ended up having a great year in the Carolina League—that was 2001—and they put me on the 40-man roster after the season. Unfortunately, I blew out my groin the following year.

DL: *What happened?*

CY: I was playing in the Arizona Fall League later that year, when I felt something pop a little. My leg was killing me in spring training—this was 2002—but I didn't say anything, because it was my first big league camp and I didn't want be looked at as a complainer. In retrospect, I should have. If nothing else, because they can't option you if you're hurt, I'd have gone on the 60-day DL and gotten some Major League service time. Instead, I ended up pitching maybe 15 games in Double A, but then had surgery and missed the rest of the season.

DL: *You came back and had a good year in 2003 but were released the following spring. Why?*

CY: That's a good question. I was ready to break camp with the Double A team, when on the last day they called me in and said they were planning to send me to A ball. It was either that or they could release me. I didn't understand why, as I had just put up a 2.40 ERA in the Texas League, which is pretty good. The three years before that, my ERA was under 2.00 every time. I guess it came down to more than numbers, which is where the business side comes in. It definitely toughened my skin about the game of baseball, because I felt I had proven myself at the Double A level.

DL: *You were then with the Cubs, but only briefly. Tell us about that.*

CY: I went to extended spring training with them, and they said if there was an opening in Double A, or Triple A, I'd get the call. But for some reason, even though I was throwing okay, they released me a few weeks later. Like with Colorado, I really didn't understand why. To me, it was kind of like, "Thanks for wasting my time."

DL: *That was when you signed with the Red Sox.*

CY: It was, and it was a dream come true. I had other opportunities, but you never know if another chance will come to play for your boyhood team. Unfortunately, after starting well that season, I lost my confidence and started battling myself. My arm-slot was down, and I was slinging the ball. I just couldn't carry any momentum from one outing to the next.

DL: *Results aside, what was the overall experience of playing in the organization like?*

CY: I would say that in the time I was there, the coaches and front office were very likeable and upfront. Ben Cherington is a guy you can talk to, and Ron Johnson was one of the best managers I've ever played for. He's a great baseball person, and he gave me a lot of support. More than once, he came up to me and said, "I know you're struggling, buddy. Hang in there." As an organization, you want baseball guys like that—not guys who think they can coach just because they played, or are too into themselves. Bob McClure and Dave Collins are two other coaches I really respect in the game. If you give them everything you have, they'll support you to the day you die. They're what are called grinders, blue-collar guys.

DL: *Clubhouses typically have blue-collar guys, but they also have prima donnas. Have you encountered many?*

CY: Oh yeah, you see it. When the "prospect" label goes on someone, sometimes he'll try to get away with a little more. I played with a guy who would get in trouble with his teammates—it seemed like an immaturity thing—and the older guys in the clubhouse didn't appreciate it. You want to tell a kid, "You haven't done anything. Try to be a little more humble and do what you're supposed to." You're not too surprised when guys like that end up getting traded.

DL: *Looking at the steroid issue that has plagued baseball, how aware are players as to who has been using them?*

CY: Hopefully, the new testing will take them out of the game, but you knew they were around. There would be some players you'd be pretty sure of, and you always wanted to strike them out more than the next guy. There are certain traits you'll see, and some guys would even tell you they've done it—they didn't hide it. It really became part of the culture. You could look around the room and say, "That guy and that guy." The coaches and managers are there too, so they'd know. But to me, I'd try not to care. It's their body, and even if you don't agree with it, you'd understand why. If you can poke yourself with that needle and hit 10 more home runs and get that big contract . . . some guys are going to do it. You put that question to someone on the street—what would they do?—and it comes down to a moral standard. I'm glad there's testing, and it should help even out the playing field, but there's no doubt a lot of people accepted it as part of the game.

DL: *Switching subjects, while pitching in Portland you were ejected from a game after being called for a balk. Tell us what happened.*

CY: It wasn't one balk, it was four! I had never been tossed, nor had a reason to get that mad, but this young umpire kept calling them on me one game. After the last one, I gave up a double and then completely lost it. Fortunately, Mike O'Keefe came over and stopped me from killing someone, because I was really agitated. It was crazy, because I've been throwing the same way for years and never had a problem. This young umpire was trying to delegate the rules with his own interpretation, which went against how everyone else in the league was calling it. The league must have agreed with me, too, because I never got fined for being thrown out of the game, which was standard procedure. I actually ran into that ump last year in spring training and got into his face about it. I had signed with the Cardinals and was charting the game when I noticed that he was there. He wasn't too happy to see me, either.

DL: *Tell us about last season.*

CY: I had been released by the Red Sox, so I went to spring training with the Cardinals. I pitched three scoreless innings for their Triple A team down there and had been guaranteed at least a bullpen job in Double A, but after 15 days they let me go. Then, during the season, they called my agent to see what I was doing. It's mind-boggling to think about this business sometimes. Anyway, I pitched independent league ball with Nashua last summer and ended up hurting my rotator and labrum. They made me a starter during the year, which was the first time I've done that since 1999. I was bouncing around from role to role, and after throwing 120 pitches in my last outing I was suddenly throwing 75 [mph] instead of 92. I ended up having surgery, and I'm actually feeling great now.

DL: *Going back to your time with the Red Sox, when were you released— how did you find out?*

CY: It was about a week before the World Series. I was with my best friend, Gary, and we were riding in a truck when my cell phone rang. I saw that it was Ben Cherington, so before I answered, I said to Gary, "I just lost my job." Ben thanked me for what I had done for the organization but told me they had decided not to tender me a contract. It was something I didn't want to hear, but the numbers don't lie. I thought to myself, "If I were the organization, would I keep me?" So I was more disappointed in myself than anything. Pitching for the Red Sox was everything I always wanted, and I could still be there had I pitched better. Plain and simple, I picked a lousy time to have the worst season of my career. When I got off the phone, I looked at Gary and said, "Okay, let's go have a few beers."

DL: *What was it like watching the Red Sox win the World Series?*

CY: I was watching with Jack Clark and remember sitting there, wanting to be happy. But I couldn't be. Jack told me, "Don't worry. We all go through these things." So it was bittersweet. I wanted to be a part of that organization. I was there that season—I have the pay stubs to prove it— but there we were, winning the World Series, something I always dreamed about, and I had been released. To be honest, had I never played for the organization, it would have been better.

DL: *Looking at the future, what comes next for Colin Young?*

CY: It's funny, you go back to when you were drafted and think that in two years you'll be in the big leagues. Now, here I am, seven years later, and I just played independent ball. I'm at the point where I'll give myself two more years, because you never know what might happen. I just want one more chance, and if you're a gamer you can always get that opportunity. If you love the game enough, that's what you're going to go after.

CHARLIE ZINK

CHARLIE ZINK WAS SIGNED BY THE RED SOX AS A NON-DRAFTED
FREE AGENT IN 2002. A KNUCKLEBALL PITCHER, ZINK ATTENDED
THE SAVANNAH SCHOOL OF ART AND DESIGN BEFORE TURNING
PRO. THIS INTERVIEW TOOK PLACE IN MAY 2004 WHEN HE WAS
WITH THE PORTLAND SEA DOGS.

David Laurila: *You converted from a traditional pitcher to a knuckleballer last season. Prior to that, you were recommended to the Red Sox
by Luis Tiant, for whom you pitched in college. Tell us what it was like
pitching for Luis.*

Charlie Zink: It was as much fun as I could possibly have had in college. He treated me almost like a son and was a great manager, but it
was his personality that stood out. Sometimes it was hard to know if he
was serious. He'd walk over and start yelling at me in Spanish—knowing perfectly well that I didn't understand a word he was saying. Then
he'd switch over to English and start giving me crap about something
completely off the wall.

DL: *For instance?*

CZ: Things like being from California and wearing an earring. He'd
make fun of me, using every stereotype possible, and then start laughing. It was a riot.

DL: *How about the serious stuff? I'm sure that was there, too.*

CZ: Of course. There's no doubt the man knows a lot about pitching,
and it was great to have him as a teacher. An interesting thing was that
he had me throwing with his old wind-up, turning my back and showing my number to the hitter.

DL: *Seriously?*

CZ: Seriously. I was skeptical at first, but I actually increased my velocity and movement throwing that way. My location suffered a bit, but it
worked out pretty well.

DL: *On his recommendation, the Red Sox subsequently signed you. What did they think of your el Tiante delivery?*

CZ: I actually scrapped it when I turned pro. I wasn't overpowering enough to blow the ball by people, so I figured hitting my spots was more important. I think the organization felt the same way.

DL: *Now that you're a knuckleball pitcher, it's Tim Wakefield tutoring you instead of Tiant. Tell us about that.*

CZ: He worked with me a lot in the spring, and it's invaluable to learn from someone who's mastered the art. He actually talks about how he's still learning, himself, but he's miles ahead of me. I should also add that Wake is a great guy—we hung out a little in Atlanta on the way up north this spring—and it's a pleasure to work with him.

DL: *How often do you speak with him, now that the season is under way?*

CZ: We haven't spoken since Atlanta. I'm a little hesitant to call him with the season under way. He's got his own job to be concerned with, and I can't expect to call every time I need help. I do want to touch base with him, though. It would be helpful.

DL: *Who's helping you right now?*

CZ: Bob Kipper, my pitching coach, doesn't throw a knuckler, but he really understands what I need to do. One of the most important things is consistency, and he recognizes when I'm a little off. He helps me repeat my motion, which is key.

DL: *I believe that Al Nipper tinkered with a knuckleball late in his career. Have you worked with him?*

CZ: He's in Sarasota, so I worked with him a lot last year. He wouldn't show me his knuckler, though, as he doesn't think it's good enough. He thought he'd probably hurt more than help me if he did. Even so, he had a positive impact. He was very supportive, an awesome pitching coach.

DL: *But probably not as much fun as Tiant?*

CZ: He's actually quite a character himself, really funny, and fun to be around. He's really even-keeled, too, and that was a great help to me. I didn't realize what a long grind pro ball could be, and how easy it is to get burned out if you get too high or too low. He helped teach me that it's a long season, and that's one reason I'm not overly concerned about the bumpy outings I've had this year. Once the weather warms up, I hope to be throwing more consistently and for my fortunes to improve.

DL: *How much of a factor is the weather for you?*

CZ: Cold weather is something I'm learning to deal with. I've pitched a few times where I could barely feel my fingers—it's a learning process. There was also a game where it was so windy I almost got blown off the mound a few times, and it really had me wondering how to throw the ball. I think that's what Wake means about still learning on the job—as a knuckleballer, you're always coming across situations that affect how the ball is moving.

DL: *What percentage of knucklers are you throwing right now?*

CZ: I'd say 90 percent or more. That's what they want me throwing— even when I'm behind on the count and need to throw a strike.

DL: *What about early in the count? A lot of guys will take a strike against a knuckleballer.*

CZ: I guess it depends on the game. If a team is clearly not swinging until they have a strike, sure. But other times, I might go into the middle innings before I throw a fastball.

DL: *What about velocity? How hard do you throw your knuckler, and do you change speeds on it?*

CZ: I definitely mix it up. I'm generally around 63 to 66 [mph], but I'll go as slow as 55 and as high as 70.

DL: *What about your fastball? And how hard is it to disguise your delivery when you do throw it?*

CZ: That's one thing I'm doing differently from last year. Right now, I'm between 78 and 82, but with basically the same delivery. Last season I hit 89 at times but tended to tip off hitters when I threw it. The same motion is important, because most guys in pro ball hit an 89-mph fastball when they know it's coming.

DL: *Talk a little about mechanics. How hard is it to stay consistent, and what adjustments can you make when things go awry?*

CZ: I try to do a lot of side sessions when I hit a rough stretch. Like I said earlier, Bob Kipper is good at recognizing when I'm not repeating my motion. Edgar Martinez, my catcher, is, too.

DL: *Catching a knuckleball can be a tall order. Tell me a little about working with Edgar.*

CZ: He caught me in Sarasota last year, too, so he knows how my ball moves. I have great confidence in him. He's a superb defensive catcher. He blocks everything and has the best arm I've ever seen behind the plate.

DL: *That's a big help in stopping the running game. How are you at holding runners?*

CZ: Not too bad, really. I'm fairly quick to the plate, and my move is pretty decent. I do pick guys off on occasion.

DL: *How about umpires? Along with being tough to catch, knucklers can also be hard to call when they're moving a lot. Have you had any issues with not getting strikes you felt you should have?*

CZ: It happens. I've had umpires come to me and apologize, saying they might have missed a few strikes. I suppose it goes both ways, though.

DL: *When you do have a great knuckleball going, I assume it mostly breaks down.*

CZ: For the most part. And I've done a better job of keeping it down in the strike zone this year. As I mentioned earlier, the big issue is consistency. I'd say 7 out of 10 that I throw are good knuckleballs. That's the difference between me and a guy like Wake. My ball probably moves as much as his does—he's just more consistent with it.

DL: *Getting away from the game for a moment, what else are you into besides knuckleballs?*

CZ: I have a big DVD collection. I like tinkering with my car. Depending on my mood, I listen to rock or reggae. Sublime and Jack Johnson are my favorites right now.

DL: *What about your rooting interests in sports?*

CZ: I was a big football fan growing up—Niners all the way. I like the Kings in basketball. As for baseball, I grew up a Giants fan. I have to admit that I love Barry [Bonds]. I liked the A's too, but after they beat the Giants in '89, that changed.

DL: *Who do you hang out with up here?*

CZ: A lot of the pitchers, really. [Chris] Smith. [Abe] Alvarez. [John] Hattig is really the only non-pitcher. Nothing against the rest of those guys, but I guess we pitchers just fit in together.

DL: *You mentioned Alvarez, but he told me he's a Dodgers fan—and you're a Giants fan?*

CZ: Good point. Cross Alvarez off that list.

DL: *One more thing: I've heard that you're a pretty good golfer. Do you have any interesting golf stories to share?*

CZ: I used to golf a bit with Tiant—that was interesting.

DL: *How so?*

CZ: How? Because he cheated.

DL: *Elaborate, please.*

CZ: Maybe "cheating" is too strong a word—let's just say he took liberties. And if I tried to get away with the same things—no way he would let me. Then, if I tried to argue with him, he'd start yelling at me in Spanish! But hey, he's a darn good golfer—shoots around 80, sometimes in the mid-70s; about the same as me. I could never beat him—but mostly for the reasons I just mentioned. Someday though . . .

DL: *And hopefully someday you'll be in the dugout at Fenway, too. Then you can have all the conversations with Wake that you want—and you won't even need his cell phone number.*

CZ: I hope so. That would be cool.

Shorter Views

⚾

JAMES ALBURY

JAMES ALBURY WAS SIGNED BY THE RED SOX AS AN INTERNATION-
AL FREE AGENT OUT OF BRISBANE, AUSTRALIA, IN 2003. A RIGHT-
HANDED PITCHER, THE 20-YEAR-OLD ALBURY SPENT THE 2004 AND
2005 SEASONS IN THE GULF COAST LEAGUE. THIS IS AN EXCERPT
FROM AN INTERVIEW THAT TOOK PLACE IN SEPTEMBER 2005.

David Laurila: *At what age did you first start pitching, and who was
most responsible for you becoming a pitcher?*

James Albury: I started pitching when I was around 11. In Australia,
you can only start to pitch at Under-12 [Under-12 League Baseball]. My
dad was my greatest influence for me wanting to become a pitcher. I
wasn't too bad with the bat, either; I bat left-handed. The chances of me
becoming a pitcher were always high, as I have two uncles who were
very good pitchers, and my dad was a very good left-handed pitcher.
They have all played at "state" level. My two uncles represented
Australia many times and have both been inducted into the Hall of
Fame here in Queensland. Baseball is a very much loved sport in my
family.

DL: *Every year during the Little League World Series, health experts talk
about how kids shouldn't begin throwing curveballs until they reach a
certain age, although that advice is often ignored. Is it any different in
Australia?*

JA: Well, when I watched the Little League World Series this year, I
could not believe how many curveballs these young kids were throwing—probably more curves than fastballs. Now in Australia you can't
throw a curveball until you play Under-16s, and junior rules state that
only 15 percent of curveballs are to be thrown. I think you are like 15 or
16 when you start throwing breaking pitches. Australian baseball is very
big on development, and there are many rules for different age groups
enforced to protect their development.

DL: *How much has interest in baseball increased since Australia won the Olympic silver medal in 2004?*

JA: I don't think the interest has increased that much at all since the Aussies won the silver medal . . . at first, maybe. Winning the silver medal was a great achievement for Australian baseball, though.

DL: *Looking into your future, how would you compare the opportunities to pitch for the Red Sox in the World Series and for Australia in the Olympics? Which would mean more to you?*

JA: I'd say there are plenty of opportunities to pitch for the Red Sox in the World Series. You just have to train hard. Now, to pitch for Australia in the Olympics would be great, too, but the opportunities are not going to be there, since baseball will not be in the Olympics after 2008. Both would mean a lot to me.

ABE ALVAREZ

ABE ALVAREZ WAS THE RED SOX' SELECTION IN THE SECOND ROUND OF THE 2003 DRAFT. A LEFT-HANDED PITCHER OUT OF LONG BEACH STATE, ALVAREZ MADE HIS BIG LEAGUE DEBUT IN JULY 2004. THIS IS AN EXCERPT FROM AN INTERVIEW THAT TOOK PLACE IN MAY 2004 WHILE ALVAREZ WAS WITH THE PORTLAND SEA DOGS.

David Laurila: *You were chosen in the second round last year and are the first from your draft class to reach Double A in the Red Sox organization. You're also the youngest player on the Portland roster at 21. Were you surprised to start the season at this level?*

Abe Alvarez: Very surprised, to be honest. I came into spring training thinking that I'd be in the starting rotation in Sarasota.

DL: *How are things going so far this season, and do you think you can make the jump to Triple A Pawtucket later this summer?*

AA: It was already a big jump to start the season here, so I'm not sure. I came in not quite knowing what to expect. I knew it would be competitive, and it has been. I've been happy with some of my starts, but there are some good hitters at this level and there's a lot to learn. I'm working hard in my bullpen sessions, and that's been a big help. Bob Kipper, the pitching coach here, has been great to work with—showing me what I need to do to improve my game.

DL: *Talk about the transition from Long Beach State to Lowell to Portland.*

AA: From Long Beach State to Lowell wasn't that big of a difference. I faced some guys I had pitched against in college, and I knew how to pitch to them with aluminum bats—now they're using wood. I was confident I could get them out if I made my pitches. It's a little tougher here. There are a lot of guys with more experience, and you can get hit hard if you make mistakes. What I'm trying to do is keep the same approach—pitch my game and do what's made me successful to this point.

DL: *You mentioned growing up a Dodgers fan. You were drafted by the Red Sox, an American League team, but suppose it had been the Giants. What would that have been like? Tell the truth.*

AA: The truth? It would have sucked. I check the Dodgers scores on the Internet every night, so I still follow them. The Giants...that would have been tough, but I suppose you do what you have to do.

EDITOR'S NOTE: A teammate, overhearing this, says, "You still would have cashed the bonus check, Alvarez! Don't try to bull**** anybody!"

DL: *Tell us about how you wear your hat. I've noticed that it's a bit off to the side, similar to how C.C. Sabathia of the Indians wears his.*

EDITOR'S NOTE: Another teammate walks by and says, "The hell with his hat. Tell him to get a haircut!" Alvarez' hair is similar to the style currently sported by Pedro Martinez; Pedro's is a little shorter.

AA: I've been wearing it like that since high school, and believe it or not, it's really comfort more than style at this point. If I straighten it out, it actually feels a little funny—seriously.

DL: *Talk a little about your teammates here. Some of them seem like free spirits—guys who like to have some fun. The long bus rides must be interesting.*

AA: No doubt. We like to mess around a bit. On the bus rides, it's mostly guys arguing over who gets the good seats and yelling at people to turn down their music. But hey, we get along great—we hang out together and eat pizza and do what guys do. And then the next day, we go out and play baseball. That's what we do.

RANDY BEAM

RANDY BEAM WAS THE RED SOX' SELECTION IN THE 18TH ROUND OF THE 2004 DRAFT. A LEFT-HANDED RELIEVER, BEAM SAW ACTION IN BOTH WILMINGTON AND PORTLAND LAST SEASON. THIS IS AN EXCERPT FROM AN INTERVIEW THAT TOOK PLACE IN MAY 2005.

David Laurila: *Your ERA was 0.88 last year, and so far this season it's 1.25. Why do you think you're never mentioned as one of the team's top pitching prospects?*

Randy Beam: I wasn't a high-round guy, for one thing. I've always flown under the radar. Heck, I walked on to my junior college team. But the hardest part is behind me. Getting picked up and given a chance is what's tough. Getting outs is the easy part.

DL: *Tell us about getting drafted and signing with the Red Sox.*

RB: I was following the draft early on, because one of my college teammates, Jeff Fiorentino, was going to go pretty high. He actually got called up to the Orioles a few weeks ago. Anyway, he went in the third round, and I was the first person to call him after he got picked. Then, later on, he was the first to call me when I went in the 18th. I had been thinking that if I got picked, great. If not, I'd hook on somewhere as a free agent. And it was great to come to the Sox, because I've always hated the Yankees. I grew up a Braves fan, and the Yankees are a team you either love or hate. For me, I've never liked them at all.

DL: *You started your pro career in Lowell. What was it like playing there?*

RB: The fan base was great. Last year, in Augusta, 500 fans was a lot. You'd normally get that on "Thirsty Thursday." That was when they'd sell dollar beers. There weren't a lot of fans in college either, but we did get about 1,300 when we played Notre Dame. At the time, it was like, "Wow."

DL: *You pitched in the Alaskan Summer League in 2003. Tell us about that.*

RB: Now, that was a one-of-a-kind experience! It was a fun league with a lot of good competition. I had been interested in the Cape, but Alaska is one of the top five college leagues and a guy from FAU [Florida Atlantic University] said it was a blast to play up there. The sun was always up, so we didn't need any lights at the ballpark. The weather wasn't too bad—usually in the 70s. We were in a town called Kenai, about two hours south of Anchorage. I lived in a nearby town that was so small it only had one gas station. It was a totally different experience, but a good one.

DL: *If you go to a party on a Saturday night, do you feel obligated go home earlier than the starters—guys who know they won't be pitching the next day?*

RB: Definitely. You always have to think ahead, and it's probably not a good idea to stay out until five in the morning, anyway. It's your job—your career—and you have to be ready. I suppose it's a bad analogy, but the president can't stay up all night either, because he has work to do the next day.

JOHN BIRTWELL

JOHN BIRTWELL IS A RIGHT-HANDED PITCHER WHO WAS DRAFTED BY THE DETROIT TIGERS IN 2001. A NATIVE OF WALPOLE, MASSACHUSETTS, BIRTWELL IS A GRADUATE OF HARVARD UNIVERSITY, WHERE HE PITCHED FOR FOUR YEARS. THIS IS AN EXCERPT FROM AN INTERVIEW THAT TOOK PLACE IN JUNE 2004 WHILE BIRTWELL WAS WITH THE TIGERS' DOUBLE A AFFILIATE IN ERIE.

David Laurila: *Talk about that: growing up a fan of one team, but signing a pro contract with another.*

John Birtwell: It's interesting. I think you learn to have a greater respect for the game as a whole. You look at the bigger picture and see teams from a completely different perspective.

DL: *Can you give us an example?*

JB: The Yankees are an obvious one. I grew up hating them but have gained a certain respect that wasn't there before. I still don't like them. I grew up a Sox fan, after all. It's human nature to need a team to root against. It's a yin-versus-yang thing. The Yankees play that role for Red Sox fans. Still, you see how they operate as an organization, and it's impressive. They actually showed the most interest in me before the draft, when I was coming out of Harvard, and they brought me to Yankee Stadium for a workout. Throwing off that mound was a great thrill, a humbling experience. You stand there and think about the guys who have been there before you. It makes you take a deep breath.

DL: *Tell us a little about Bill Monbouquette, who was your pitching coach in Oneonta. He grew up in the Boston area and had a good career with the Red Sox.*

JB: He has some great stories. Monbo claims that he was pitching at Fenway once, and it was "Maine Day." They had things there that Maine is known for, including lobsters and a bear. This was back when the pitchers warmed up near the dugouts, and the bear—it was tame—was tied up nearby. Monbo took a piece of gum out of his pocket after he warmed up, and the bear started sniffing at it. So he reached over to give it to the bear, and it bit down on his entire hand! Now, Monbo is a big guy—forearms like a sailor—and he punches the bear, hard, in the nose! It lets go and backs up, whimpering.

DL: *From your perspective, what is the life of a minor league baseball player like?*

JB: It's a good life, but sometimes it seems like you're going in one direction and the world is going in another. You're not really looking at the days of the week like everyone else—you're looking more at series of games. It's kind of like a family down here. You're all working for the same goals and feeling the same stresses, living the same lifestyles.

DL: *And trying to make the Major Leagues.*

JB: We are, because it's such a great game. Baseball has so much complexity and simplicity, all at the same time. I've had guys—people who've been in the game 40 years—tell me that no matter how long you play, you're always experiencing something new. This is what I want to do. I love playing the game, and in many ways it's all I know.

DL: *That sounds funny, coming from a guy with four years of Harvard among his experiences.*

JB: I think what I mean is that it becomes such a deep part of your life. I look back at where I started and all I've experienced in the game, and it's always been what I loved to do. It's my dream to pitch in the Major Leagues, and when I get there I don't want to forget where I came from, and I don't want to lose my fascination for the game. I hope to be the same person I am now—I just want to be the same person in a big-league uniform.

IAN BLADERGROEN

IAN BLADERGROEN WAS ACQUIRED BY THE RED SOX FROM THE METS IN EXCHANGE FOR DOUG MIENTKIEWICZ IN JANUARY 2005. A LEFT-HANDED-HITTING FIRST BASEMAN, BLADERGROEN WAS HINDERED LAST YEAR BY A WRIST INJURY HE SUFFERED LATE IN THE 2004 SEASON. THIS IS AN EXCERPT FROM AN INTERVIEW THAT TOOK PLACE IN MAY 2005 WHEN BLADERGROEN WAS WITH THE WILMINGTON BLUE ROCKS.

David Laurila: *Tell us about the injury.*

Ian Bladergroen: It was a freak thing. I hit a sac fly last August against the Red Sox—against Augusta—and tore a ligament. It was the TFC tendon in my left wrist, which is essentially the same injury Nomar [Garciaparra] had. It's more or less a case-by-case prognosis as to how long it takes to heal. It was feeling okay until recently, and hopefully will be again soon.

DL: *How has the injury affected your stroke?*

IB: Bob Tewksbury was down here throwing BP yesterday, and he commented on how I was able to drop the head on balls away, but not roll my top-hand over on inside pitches. That's the biggest thing.

DL: *Do you consider yourself a power hitter?*

IB: I have power potential, but I'm more gap-to-gap. If I'm hitting at Fenway someday, I do have power to left center and will be able to hit the wall. I've never been there, but it's obviously a great park. When you think of Fenway, you think about things like the Pesky Pole. You know what that is? It's a great tribute to someone who's a great man.

DL: *You mentioned that you hurt your wrist hitting against Augusta. Which pitchers on their staff do you recall being impressed with?*

IB: You know, it's funny, I mostly remember the hitters. I met Brandon Moss at the All-Star Game, and he and Mickey Hall both impressed me. I don't remember a lot about the guys on the mound, but that's probably my own fault. The Mets organization doesn't stress hitting journals like we do here, so I didn't know them as well as I could have.

DL: *Can you say a little more on that?*

IB: The Red Sox organization places more emphasis on having a good game plan. The Mets had hitters' meetings, but charts weren't mandatory. Here, they are. Pitchers may not throw you what the chart says they will, but if they tend to get hitters out a certain way, there's a decent chance they'll pitch you the same way.

DL: *You were acquired for Doug Mientkiewicz, who made the last putout of the World Series. There's been some controversy over who that ball belongs to. If it were you, do you keep it or give it up?*

IB: Boy, you're putting me on the spot! I think it belongs in Cooperstown or Boston. I don't begrudge Doug if he keeps it, but it means a lot to a lot of people. It's a Hall of Fame ball in my opinion.

JEFF CORSALETTI

JEFF CORSALETTI WAS THE RED SOX' SELECTION IN THE SIXTH ROUND OF THE 2005 DRAFT. A LEFT-HANDED-HITTING OUTFIELD-ER, CORSALETTI HELPED LEAD THE UNIVERSITY OF FLORIDA TO THE FINALS OF LAST YEAR'S COLLEGE WORLD SERIES BEFORE GOING ON TO HIT .357 IN 59 GAMES FOR THE GREENVILLE BOMBERS. THIS IS AN EXCERPT FROM AN INTERVIEW THAT TOOK PLACE IN JULY 2005.

David Laurila: *Compare playing in the College World Series to your first professional game.*

Jeff Corsaletti: It's really different. It's 30,000 fans as opposed to less than a thousand, and pro ball is a lot more laid back. It's not rah-rah like in college. It's a long season, so you're pacing yourself a lot more.

DL: *Still, I have to assume you were a little nervous when you stepped in for your first pro at-bat.*

JC: Totally, I was nervous. It was my first time, and there was definitely a feeling of everyone watching you to see what you've got. Fortunately, I hit a double, which took away a lot of the pressure. Had I gone hitless my first few games, it would have taken longer to feel relaxed and settled in.

DL: *You were drafted in the 22nd round last year by the Indians but didn't sign. Why not?*

JC: To be honest, the money they were offering wasn't worth the year of college. Along with the education, I loved college ball and wanted to come back to win a championship. I also thought I could have a better season and go higher in this year's draft. As it worked out, it couldn't have gone better than it did. I went in the sixth round to my favorite team.

DL: *How did you learn you had been drafted by the Red Sox?*

JC: We were hosting the super regionals at Florida when the draft was going on, and I was in the clubhouse doing interviews. I heard people screaming when I walked out, and then my phone started ringing. My mom, girlfriend, and the Red Sox scout all called at the same time. It was a dream come true to find out it was the Red Sox.

DL: *Being from Florida, how did you end up a Red Sox fan?*

JC: It came from my father, who used to take me to Fenway Park. He grew up in New Britain, Connecticut, and he became a Red Sox fan through my grandfather. And my sister is probably more of a big-time fan than any of us. Like I said, being with the Red Sox is a dream come true—for all of us.

DL: *Along with baseball, you played football in high school.*

JC: Oh, yeah. My dad played football at UMass, and it was my primary sport in many ways. But my choices for college were Division I baseball or Division II football, so it was a clear decision which way to go.

ANDREW DOBIES

ANDREW DOBIES WAS THE RED SOX' SELECTION IN THE THIRD
ROUND OF THE 2004 DRAFT. A LEFT-HANDED PITCHER OUT OF
THE UNIVERSITY OF VIRGINIA, DOBIES SAW ACTION LAST YEAR IN
BOTH GREENVILLE AND WILMINGTON. THIS IS AN EXCERPT FROM
AN INTERVIEW THAT TOOK PLACE IN JULY 2004 WHEN HE WAS
WITH THE LOWELL SPINNERS.

David Laurila: *Introduce yourself to Red Sox Nation. Describe yourself
as a pitcher.*

Andrew Dobies: I'm a lefty with a fastball, curve, slider, and change. I
like to get ahead in the count and move the ball around. I think my fastball and slider work pretty well together. My best control pitch is the
fastball, so I use that to get ahead. My out pitch is the slider.

DL: *Dave Tomlin, your pitching coach, says you command your fastball
to both sides, but that you can elevate it when you want to.*

AD: Yes, I can reach back for something extra at times. I feel confident
that I can throw it by people when the need arises. You don't always
need to throw hard to get hitters out, though. A lot of people think
velocity is big, but you can win with location. I'll hit 91–92 at times, but
88 on the corners gets guys out. Even at this level, 90-plus fastballs that
are located poorly will get hit.

DL: *What were your thoughts on getting drafted by the Red Sox?*

AD: I was certainly thrilled about being taken by such a great organization, but I was a bit surprised. I had talked to the area scout, so I knew
there was an interest. But I also knew they were interested in the college shortstop [Dustin Pedroia]. A few other teams showed more interest, and I thought maybe I'd end up in one of those places.

DL: *Have you been to Fenway Park yet?*

AD: I was there for the first time when I signed my contract. They took
me on a tour that day, and it was awesome. There's so much history.
Then some teammates and I went on an off-day to see Schilling pitch
against Oakland. That was a lot of fun.

DL: *You are from the Pittsburgh area. Were you a Pirates fan growing up?*

AD: Yes. I guess they're my second favorite team now. I liked the way Andy Van Slyke played—all over the field and always hustling. And I really appreciate Roberto Clemente. He played before I was born, but he was my dad's favorite and was one of the greats. I always wore number 21 in his honor.

DL: *Before I let you go, are there are funny baseball stories I can get you to share?*

AD: Sometimes with a guy on base, I'll step up onto the mound like I'm going to go into the full wind-up instead of going into the stretch. It's funny how I'll blank out and do that, and then have to stop and readjust. Fortunately, I always catch myself.

CHRIS DURBIN

CHRIS DURBIN WAS THE RED SOX' SELECTION IN THE 10TH ROUND OF THE 2003 DRAFT. A NATIVE OF WYLIE, TEXAS, DURBIN SPENT LAST SEASON WITH THE PORTLAND SEA DOGS. THIS IS AN EXCERPT FROM AN INTERVIEW THAT TOOK PLACE IN MAY 2005.

David Laurila: *You're rated as the best defensive outfielder in the Red Sox farm system by* Baseball America. *What does that mean to you?*

Chris Durbin: It's an honor, but you're only as good as the day you're out there. You still have to make the plays. It also means you have something to live up to—there are expectations. But that's okay. I don't pay much attention to what people say about me, anyway. I just like to go out there and give it my all.

DL: *What are your strengths and weaknesses defensively?*

CD: I feel like I'm quick . . . when I'm healthy. Right now, I have a hamstring that's not quite 100 percent. I generally get good reads, which is probably the biggest part of playing the outfield. *Baseball America* said my arm was the best in the Big 12 when I was at Baylor, so I'd say it rates as solid. Something I'm working on right now is do-or-die plays on base hits. Lou Frazier is helping me with picking up ground balls and getting rid of them quickly and accurately.

DL: *Luis Soto was recently moved from shortstop to the outfield, and some have speculated that Hanley Ramirez may eventually do the same. What would the hardest adjustment be for someone making that transition?*

CD: Reads can be tough on line drives right at you or directly over your head. In the infield, you're mostly used to ground balls, not balls driven into the air. The throws are different, too. You have to be a little longer with them and over the top, and you need backspin for carry. Any time you're moving to a new position, there are adjustments to make. I know that if I went to shortstop, it wouldn't be easy.

DL: *You put up big numbers in college, and last year in high A hit .279 with 45 extra-base hits in a pitcher-friendly league. Why do you think your reputation is primarily as a good defensive outfielder?*

CD: I don't know, and that's another thing I can't control and don't really care about. In my mind I'm a good hitter. I'm not a power hitter, but I can hold my own up there. Maybe it's because I'm not 6' 4" with a big athletic build. I've always had to prove myself, and all I can do is keep playing hard and let the rest take care of itself.

DL: *Last one: What's it been like following Cla Meredith since he got called up to Boston?*

CD: It's been cool. We were all huddled around the TV in the clubhouse watching him when he made his second appearance. He's had a rough start, but he's a mature enough guy that he'll handle it fine. He really had his stuff going when he was here, and watching him pitch at Fenway shows us just how close we are to the show. We can almost taste it. We just need to play hard and have fun, and hopefully we'll get our chance, too.

KYLE FERNANDES

KYLE FERNANDES WAS THE RED SOX' SELECTION IN THE 12TH ROUND OF THE 2005 DRAFT. A NATIVE OF WESTPORT, MASSACHUSETTS, FERNANDES PITCHED AT MASSASOIT COMMUNITY COLLEGE BEFORE SPENDING MOST OF HIS FIRST PROFESSIONAL SEASON IN THE GULF COAST LEAGUE. THIS IS AN EXCERPT FROM AN INTERVIEW THAT TOOK PLACE IN SEPTEMBER 2005.

David Laurila: *Having grown up in Westport, tell us a little about your history as a baseball fan.*

Kyle Fernandes: I have always been a Red Sox fan. But it wasn't until I was in high school that I became a big fan and really followed them. Baseball was just one of three sports that I loved; soccer and basketball also played a big role in my life, but baseball was my favorite to play and follow.

DL: *I've seen a scouting report that says you throw a fastball, curve, slider, and change-up. Describe the velocity and/or movement of each pitch, and how you typically utilize them in attacking hitters.*

KF: Well, my fastball is usually in the high 80s. I throw 98 percent two-seam fastballs and occasionally will throw a four-seam. I throw my fastball on both sides of the plate. I believe you have to own both sides of the plate, especially with your fastball. My fastball has good movement and it drops out at the end. I will throw my curveball for a backdoor strike or I will throw it right under the hands of a right-hander. When a lefty is up, I try to keep the curveball low and away. The slider I throw occasionally, mainly just to give a different look, and I know I can throw it for a strike and get guys out with it. That mainly is thrown away to lefties, to break off the plate, and to jam right-handers. My change-up I throw to both left- and right-handed hitters, mainly low and away to both. The main thing about all of my pitches is that I have the confidence that I can throw every one for a strike when I want. This way I can't be predictable.

DL: *Tell us a little about your draft experiences.*

KF: I was very happy to be drafted, especially by the Red Sox. I was expecting to go in the 15th to 20th round, but when the 12th round came and they took me I was shocked. Something I worked so hard for finally came true. Before the draft, a lot of people were talking about it to me and asking me a lot of questions. All I said to them was, "Your guess is as good as mine. I don't know what's going to happen. Let's hope for the best."

DL: *What are your favorite memories from your time at Massasoit?*

KF: My whole sophomore year, without a doubt. A lot of those guys I played with for a long time before I even came to Massasoit. That team was by far the closest team I have ever been on in my career. We had a bond like I have never seen. Coach [Tom] Frizzell and coach Zack [Greg Zackrison] were great. They understood what type of kid I was and knew I liked to have fun.

DL: *What about memories from the Gulf Coast League?*

KF: When Goose [Gregson] compared my stuff to Abe Alvarez', who I have not met yet, but am looking forward to it. He is someone I can relate to.

DL: *Tell us something interesting about yourself, perhaps something most people don't know.*

KF: I have a soft side. I mean, I am a nice kid, but a lot of times people don't really see my soft side. There are times when I really feel bad about something, but I don't show it. I wish I could show it better.

KEVIN GUYETTE

KEVIN GUYETTE WAS THE RED SOX' SELECTION IN THE 10TH ROUND OF THE 2005 DRAFT. A RIGHT-HANDED PITCHER OUT OF THE UNIVERSITY OF ARIZONA, GUYETTE SPENT HIS FIRST PROFESSIONAL SEASON WITH THE LOWELL SPINNERS AND GREENVILLE BOMBERS. THIS IS AN EXCERPT FROM AN INTERVIEW THAT TOOK PLACE IN JUNE 2005.

David Laurila: *You just made your first appearance in pro ball. How did it go?*

Kevin Guyette: Not as well as I'd have liked, but it was okay. I worked two innings and gave up two unearned runs and took the loss. Obviously, I was coming in looking for a win or a save. I didn't feel nervous out there, but my ball was all over the place my first inning. My second inning, I threw a lot better.

DL: *How would you describe yourself as a pitcher?*

KG: I'm definitely not a hard thrower. I'm more finesse and have to locate. My fastball tops out around 88–89, and my curve is my out pitch. I guess you could call me a touch-and-feel type of pitcher.

DL: Baseball America *commented on it in your draft bio. They said you've "improved the command of [your] hard, biting curveball this year." What adjustment did you make with it?*

KG: I think the difference was that I started throwing it harder and making it look more like a fastball. Arm speed is the biggest key. Batters are up there hitting against arm speed, so with the same mechanics the break doesn't have to be quite as good. If you have both, you're going to be effective. I didn't have an out pitch before, and it's nice to know you can get a K when you need one.

DL: *What did you study in school?*

KG: I got my degree in business management. Some day, I'll probably go to grad school, maybe even med school or law school. Right now, I have a real estate company with a friend. It's called Student Realty, and we try to sell parents houses that their kids live in while they're away at college. Rather than having them pay rent, they have their roommates paying off the mortgage.

DL: *I assume you played other sports, besides baseball, growing up.*

KG: I was 6' when I was 12 years old, so I actually thought I'd be a professional basketball player someday. But my mom is 5'-nothing, and I quit growing when I reached 6'4". I could play okay and got looked at by a few small D-1 schools, but my future was going to be in baseball, not basketball.

DL: *Your father started on the Kentucky basketball team that lost the 1975 NCAA championship game to John Wooden's UCLA Bruins. Does he talk much about that?*

KG: He really doesn't. He talks more about the mental aspects of competing. He's been there and done that, so he understands how to approach preparing, winning, and losing. He can really help me with what it takes to fight back and deal with a tough loss.

DL: *I understand that he battled cancer a few years ago. How is he doing now?*

KG: He's doing really well. He went through radiation and lost his taste, but otherwise he's doing great. I transferred to Arizona from Georgia Tech when he was diagnosed, because I wanted to be closer to home. It was a blast knowing that he'd be at all of my games. I'm really blessed to have such great parents. There's the old, "My dad can beat up your dad," and mine is the prototype for that. My dad is Superman, and I'm lucky to be his son. And what he went through really helps puts life in perspective for me. I still get mad when I throw a bad pitch and give up a double, but baseball isn't life and death.

DL: *Last one: Who were your favorite teams growing up?*

KG: In baseball, I liked the Red Sox and Cubs. I saw them quite a bit, and they obviously have great histories and ballparks. In basketball, I'm a Phoenix Suns fan. I watched more basketball growing up, because a lot of times when I wanted to watch baseball on TV, my dad wanted to watch a basketball game. So, as you could probably guess, that's what we watched. Dad was in charge!

BARRY HERTZLER

BARRY HERTZLER WAS THE RED SOX' SELECTION IN THE 11TH ROUND OF THE 2003 DRAFT. A NATIVE OF EAST PROVIDENCE, RHODE ISLAND, HERTZLER SAW ACTION IN BOTH WILMINGTON AND PORTLAND LAST SEASON. THIS INTERVIEW TOOK PLACE IN SEPTEMBER 2005.

David Laurila: *How would you assess your 2005 season, and do you feel you achieved your goals?*

Barry Hertzler: In some ways, it's been tough. I've had to work hard at it. A lot of my goals have fallen into place, although most are personal and I don't want to get into the specifics. Some are long-term goals . . . higher-level goals. Others are short-term, more mechanical and fine-tuning. Getting to know myself as a pitcher is an ongoing goal. Last year, I was struggling with the mental part of the game, but I'm over that hump completely. Other things, like getting there . . . getting promoted, are mostly out of my control.

DL: *You made the transition from starter back to being a reliever this year. How did that go?*

BH: The transition wasn't easy, but it's fallen into place. In spring training . . . they weren't really sure where I'd be going into spring training. I went into camp as a starter, but then they pulled me into the office and said I'd go back to the bullpen. They said it was the best way for me to develop as a pitcher. Looking at my pitches and my future, I think I agree with that.

DL: *What is currently in your repertoire, and are you still throwing a splitter?*

BH: Am I still throwing a splitter? Absolutely—that's my change-up. I'm throwing that, along with a curve and a two-seamer. My two-seamer is still my go-to pitch, but I'm confident with all three. The one I most want to work on improving is my curve. I think it's solid, but making it better is a big goal. Overall, mentally and physically, I'm only getting better.

DL: *What was it like pitching in this year's Hall of Fame Game?*

BH: It was a great opportunity and a great time. I had been to Cooperstown before, but this was different. Getting an opportunity to play for Terry Francona . . . being teammates with all of those guys . . . it was a fantastic experience.

DL: What was it like watching the Red Sox win the World Series last year?

BH: I was with friends in Connecticut when we won. I went back there after the season to graduate . . . to finish my degree in criminology. I absolutely expected us . . . the Red Sox, to win it. That's the goal for everyone: to win a championship. That's what I'm thinking now, here in Portland. I'm thinking about more than just being in the playoffs. I'm thinking about winning a championship.

DL: *I understand that you intend to become a police officer after your playing career. Do situations like the post-hurricane lawlessness in New Orleans impact that plan?*

BH: They make me want to do it even more. It's all about helping people. That's what I look at. It's not about writing tickets and making arrests—those are just part of the overall job. It's all about helping people.

KYLE JACKSON

KYLE JACKSON WAS THE RED SOX' SELECTION IN THE 32ND ROUND OF THE 2001 DRAFT. A RIGHT-HANDED PITCHER FROM LITCHFIELD, NEW HAMPSHIRE, JACKSON SPENT THE 2005 SEASON WITH THE GREENVILLE BOMBERS AND PORTLAND SEA DOGS. THIS INTERVIEW TOOK PLACE IN MAY 2005.

David Laurila: *You're from New Hampshire. I assume you grew up a Red Sox fan.*

Kyle Jackson: Oh yeah. I went to my first Sox game when I was about seven or eight. I remember that we played the Brewers. And the World Series this year was obviously great. I was at the two home games with a friend who had tickets. Basically, everyone thought we'd be coming back for a game five, but I knew that wouldn't happen—especially after game three. I could just tell that this was going to be the year. Finally.

DL: *You were taken in the 2001 draft out of high school. As you didn't go until the 32nd round, I assume it was a draft-and-follow situation?*

KJ: It was. The Sox scout, Ray Fagnant, said they wanted me to go to junior college and that they'd monitor my progress. I hadn't played against great competition up north, so I was fine with that. I went to St. Petersburg College, in Florida, and it was a real learning experience. It was definitely a lot of bigger guys with metal bats! It seemed like everybody we played was stacked with a lot of draft-and-follows in the lineup. But I did pretty well, and the Sox decided to sign me.

DL: *Was getting chosen by the team you grew up with a factor in signing rather than staying in school?*

KJ: That was part of it, sure. Everybody dreams of playing for their favorite team. Being on the mound at Fenway is something I've always hoped to do someday. Signing was a thrill, but I only threw two innings after I did, because I had a collateral ligament strain in my pitching elbow. I rehabbed it and came back healthy in 2003 and had a pretty good year.

DL: *Coming into this season, what are you focusing on to improve your game?*

KJ: I came into spring training trying to better control my change. I want a better feel on it, so I know it's a consistent part of my repertoire. You don't want your catcher to put down fingers and wonder, "Uh-oh. Where is this one going to go?"

DL: *You hit 13 batters last year. Was that more a lack of command, or do you like to work inside a lot?*

KJ: A little of both. I definitely like to work inside. My four-seamer moves away from right-handed hitters, rather than tailing in, but if I fly open it tends to come right at them. Most guys that I hit, I hit in the hands. That comes from trying to bust them inside.

DL: *Speaking of hitting, do you enjoy swinging a bat? Do wish you could go up to the plate and hit?*

KJ: Man, I can't remember the last time I hit! Would I want to do it? Not right now. I have enough to worry about out on the mound!

DL: *A few weeks ago, I interviewed Adam Blackley. He told me he rooms with you and Mike Rozier, so I had him give a scouting report on each of you. Give me one on Adam and Mike.*

KJ: They're lefties! So they're different, you know? Adam loves his change-up. I've never seen a guy throw so many, but it's a good one. And he's a fun guy, too—a funny Aussie.

DL: *He actually seemed a little quiet when I talked to him.*

KJ: He was having a bad day. He had just finished a game where nothing was going right out on the mound, and I think his head was spinning. Afterwards, he walked up and said, "Man, you won't believe this. I just did an interview! And I am *not* in a good mood!" But that's not his normal personality. Adam's a fun guy.

DL: *What about Rozier? What does he bring to the mound?*

KJ: He has great movement. If I was a scout and saw him throw, I'd say he has big-time potential. All he needs is more experience—what is he, 19 or 20? And confidence. He needs a good mindset, and to learn from his bad outings, because he has lots of talent.

DL: *You went to the Bucky Dent Baseball School. What was that all about?*

KJ: Boy, I didn't think anyone even knew that.

DL: *They will now, Kyle. What's the story?*

KJ: It's really a good little baseball school. I went three or four times when I was younger. It's down in Florida. My AAU coach had me and a few teammates go down there. You're there for a week, and there's an emphasis on fundamentals. In a lot of ways, it's a week of fun. I never did actually see Bucky down there, though. So I guess it's okay!

DL: *Let's close with a hypothetical question: It's 6 or 10 years down the road, and you're an established MLB pitcher. You're a free agent, and the Yankees offer you a million dollars more than anyone else. What do you do?*

KJ: The Red Sox still want me, right? I guess it depends on who else wanted me, but I'm the kind of guy who'd stay in one place if I was happy. I'd take less money and stay with the Sox.

JON LESTER

JON LESTER WAS THE RED SOX' SELECTION IN THE SECOND ROUND OF THE 2002 DRAFT. A LEFT-HANDED PITCHER AND THE TOP-RATED PROSPECT IN THE BOSTON ORGANIZATION, LESTER SPENT THE 2005 SEASON WITH THE PORTLAND SEA DOGS. THIS IS AN EXCERPT FROM AN INTERVIEW THAT TOOK PLACE IN AUGUST 2004 WHEN LESTER WAS WITH THE SARASOTA RED SOX.

David Laurila: *Outside of being a left-hander, how would you describe yourself?*

Jon Lester: I guess I'd call myself a power pitcher. I throw two- and four-seam fastballs, a curve, and a change. More recently, I've been mixing in a cutter, which is new for me.

DL: *Where is your velocity?*

JL: I sit at 91–92 most of the time, but I'll touch 94 and have been clocked as high as 96. I'll throw my curveball in the low- to mid-70s. Maybe I'll go as low as 70 at times, but not that often.

DL: *Are there any pitchers you model yourself after or try to learn from?*

JL: Mark Mulder is one, and Andy Pettitte's cutter is something I've been paying attention to. He has a good one, and it's something I'm trying to develop.

DL: *As many people know, you almost weren't here this season. You were rumored to be part of the Alex Rodriguez/Manny Ramirez trade that didn't happen. What are your thoughts on that?*

JL: When it first came up, I was shocked. And the more I thought about it, the more unbelievable it seemed. Being part of a deal that included players of that caliber was an honor, I'll tell you that. But hey, I'm glad it worked out the way that it did. A lot of Red Sox fans probably aren't glad, but I love playing for this organization. I'm happy to still be here.

DL: *A deal that did go through was Nomar Garciaparra to the Cubs. One of your teammates in Sarasota also went in that trade: Matt Murton. What was the reaction when he left?*

JL: He was mad that he was leaving, but he understood. Matt is a guy who'll play in the big leagues someday, but he never gets a big head about anything. On the field, he's balls-out all the time, and you have to love teammates like that.

DL: *You signed with the Red Sox out of high school. Given the organization's recent emphasis on drafting college players, do you ever think about how you could have ended up somewhere else—even before the A-Rod rumors?*

JL: Sure, I think most guys do. I know the Mariners, White Sox, and Arizona were all interested, and I hadn't even met the Red Sox area scout yet when I was drafted. He had told my parents that they were considering me, but I was still a little surprised.

DL: *What are your thoughts on the team's current philosophy of taking primarily college players?*

JL: I actually just read *Moneyball*, and that's the way a lot of teams are going these days. They look at college picks as more of a sure thing, and I suppose it's true that the odds aren't as good with high school guys. I'm happy the Sox took a chance with me, though—regardless of where I came here from.

DL: *Scouting reports said you had first-round talent, but you fell to the second round due to signability concerns. Were you intending to play in college rather than sign out of high school?*

JL: You know, I've never really known where that came from. My dream has always been to play pro ball, and I wasn't a big school guy, anyway. I felt I made that clear at the time. I think I was real honest with everyone about my plans and expectations coming into the draft.

DL: *Were you involved with other sports when you were in school?*

JL: I played soccer for about 12 or 13 years. I also played basketball and was first-team all-league my junior year. I didn't play as a senior, though, as I had torn my ACL playing football and my dad didn't want me risking anything with the draft upcoming.

DL: *Have you spent any time in Boston, or at Fenway Park?*

JL: I have, and I love it. The atmosphere at Fenway is awesome. I was first there in '94 or '95 when we had a family reunion in New Hampshire and my uncle got us tickets. Most of my family is back in Washington, but there are a few Northeast connections. My girlfriend, for instance, goes to school at Dartmouth and plays on their soccer team.

JIMMY MANN

JIMMY MANN WAS SIGNED BY THE RED SOX AS A MINOR LEAGUE FREE AGENT IN JULY 2005. A RIGHT-HANDED PITCHER FROM HOLBROOK, MASSACHUSETTS, MANN WAS DRAFTED BY THE TORONTO BLUE JAYS IN 1993 AND HAS APPEARED IN 25 BIG-LEAGUE GAMES. THIS INTERVIEW TOOK PLACE IN SEPTEMBER 2005 WHILE MANN WAS WITH THE PORTLAND SEA DOGS.

David Laurila: *You're from Holbrook. Did you grow up a Red Sox fan?*

Jimmy Mann: Absolutely. I've been a diehard my whole life. I used to love Roger Clemens. My first time at Fenway Park was when I was 12. I won the tickets through my paper route, and my brother took me. I remember being in awe of the whole place.

DL: *What was it like to sign with the Red Sox organization this summer?*

JM: I was obviously extremely excited. Not only was I going from independent ball back to organized ball, I was going to where I've always wanted to be. Ben Cherington called and offered me a spot in Double A, and I was honored to come here.

DL: *Would you have taken a similar offer from another team?*

JM: No, I actually wouldn't have accepted Double A from anyone else, only the Red Sox. It would have to have been a Triple A offer. But with the Sox, I couldn't turn it down.

DL: *You've been with a few different organizations, one of which is the Yankees. What was it like signing with them?*

JM: Really weird. I grew up hating them—not liking anyone affiliated with them. For instance, like most Red Sox fans I didn't like Derek Jeter. But after being around him, he's actually a great guy . . . a great teammate. Signing with the Yankees was just business. I had offers from them and the Rangers, and theirs was better. It goes without saying that I'd rather be here.

DL: *What do you remember about your first Major League game?*

JM: I was with the Mets, and we had a left-hander, Rich Rodriguez, facing the Dodgers' Shawn Green to start the inning. Gary Sheffield was up next, and I knew I'd be coming in to face him. I fell behind on the count 2-0, so I came after Sheffield with a fastball and he got a base hit. Boy does he have fast hands! I have a friend, John Bale, who told me that when he came in for the first time he threw two pitches to the backstop. But I wasn't really all that nervous, and I wasn't going to walk him. I was going to throw strikes and take my chances.

DL: *The first batter you struck out in the big leagues proceeded to get thrown out of the game. Tell us about that.*

JM: That was the next year, with the Astros. We were playing an interleague game with the Indians. I had hit two batters that inning: Juan Gonzalez and Wil Cordero. Bartolo Colon was pitching for them, and I struck him out to end the inning. Colon thought I had hit Gonzo on purpose, so he threw at Scott Service to start the next inning—almost hitting him—and got tossed. I then struck out the next two guys I faced: Kenny Lofton and someone else.

DL: *Along with those games, do you have other favorite moments from your big league experience?*

JM: Oh yeah. One was coming in on back-to-back nights and retiring Sammy Sosa each time. The first night, I got him on a double play, the next on a strikeout on a 3-2 splitter. Another was in Shea Stadium, pitching against the Mets. My mom was there, and it's the first time she saw me play in the big leagues. The first guy I faced was Mo Vaughn, who she obviously knew from his time in Boston. I got him and struck out Jeremy Burnitz to end the inning. Interestingly, my only Major League at-bat came in that game.

DL: *Can I make an educated guess that you struck out?*

JM: Yeah, on a 3-2 pitch against Shawn Estes, but it should have been ball four. No doubt in my mind, but there's no way I'm about to get that call. Anyway, the bottom half of the next inning, Rey Ordoñez comes up and hits a foul ball home run against me. The catcher calls for an inside fastball on the next pitch, and I end up hitting Ordoñez. So the umpire throws me out! The first time my mother comes to see me play . . . and I got tossed!

DL: *What are your plans for the off-season and for next year?*

JM: I'll be playing for Hermosillo in the Mexican League this winter. They called me about playing this past summer, too, but then I got the opportunity to come here. I think Darren Bragg will play down there, too. Next year? I'll be a free agent, and my biggest goal will be to play in the big leagues. Number two would be to stay here and maybe play for the PawSox. Actually . . . let me clarify that. My number one would be to pitch for the Red Sox!

DL: *How long do you plan to stay in the game?*

JM: Until they take my uniform away. When they won't let me play anymore, that's when I'll stop.

BRIAN MARSHALL

BRIAN MARSHALL WAS THE RED SOX' SELECTION IN THE FIFTH ROUND OF THE 2003 DRAFT. A LEFT-HANDED RELIEVER, MARSHALL SAW ACTION IN BOTH LOWELL AND GREENVILLE LAST SEASON. THIS IS AN EXCERPT FROM AN INTERVIEW THAT TOOK PLACE IN SEPTEMBER 2005.

David Laurila: *You were teammates with Cla Meredith at Virginia Commonwealth. Outside of throwing from opposite sides, how similar are the two of you?*

Brian Marshall: In some ways, very. We both loving getting the ball and going after hitters. He definitely has the confidence to bounce back, which you need as a closer, and I like to believe that I do, too. It was a cool thing in college, me and him switching off to close games. He'd come in as the righty with all that movement—that big league sinker— and I'd come in from the left side from different angles.

DL: *In an interview this summer, Cla said you were a smart guy and wouldn't hurt a fly. What are your thoughts on those opinions?*

BM: Yeah, I saw that. Am I a smart guy? I guess. At least I hope I am. The "wouldn't hurt a fly" might be taking it a little far, though. Maybe I'm kind of a softy, but I'm not that soft. I will say that I'm not a mean guy who'll go out and get in bar fights all the time!

DL: *You have a twin brother, Sean, who is in the Cubs system. How is he doing?*

BM: He had a good season. He had a hand injury last year, and it was kind of bothering him this spring. Like me, he stayed down in spring training for awhile. Then he pitched in Daytona and made the Florida State League All-Star team. After the game, he got promoted to Double A. I'm really proud of what he's done. Up until this year, we've pretty much mirrored each other. We were drafted in similar rounds the same year, and last season we both pitched pretty well.

DL: *Why are you a reliever and Sean a starter?*

BM: We were both starters through high school; the one–two punch on the Manchester squad. But when we got to college, he became a freshman all-American while I didn't pitch a lot. He's more of a power guy— over the top with a good curve and fastball—while my approach is more arm-angles and attacking hitters with unique looks. I'm more herky-jerky and will throw anything at any time. Basically, the coaches thought becoming a closer was a better fit for me . . . a good script to success.

DL: *I read bios that said your favorite cartoon character is Yosemite Sam, and Sean's is Homer Simpson. What does that tell us about either of you?*

BM: Not a whole lot, actually. I think we were both probably caught a little off guard by that question and didn't know what to say. To tell you the truth, I like Homer Simpson more than Yosemite Sam, too! Sean's and my personalities are a lot alike, including watching the same TV shows.

DL: *Do you have much in common with Homer?*

BM: Nah, I've got all of my hair still . . . and I'm not fat.

EDITOR'S NOTE: Brian Marshall was released by the Red Sox in spring training of 2006.

BRANDON MOSS

BRANDON MOSS WAS THE RED SOX' SELECTION IN THE EIGHTH
ROUND OF THE 2002 DRAFT. AN OUTFIELDER FROM LOGANVILLE,
GEORGIA, MOSS SPENT THE 2005 SEASON WITH THE PORTLAND
SEA DOGS. THIS IS AN EXCERPT FROM AN INTERVIEW THAT TOOK
PLACE IN APRIL 2005.

David Laurila: *Let's start with this past off-season. What did you do?*

Brandon Moss: Mostly hit. I surrounded myself with baseball.

DL: *Tell us what you worked on in spring training and what your expectations were coming in.*

BM: I didn't know what to expect as far as where I'd play. I met with Ben Cherington early on, and he said circumstances and opportunity would determine where I'd start the season. I definitely got a lot out of spring training. I made a lot of adjustments, and getting deeper into counts was a main focus. I'd say I worked on that more than anything.

DL: *How would you describe your personality? Are you pretty low-key?*

BM: I'm definitely not low-key. Maybe a little bit off the field, but mostly I'm pretty high-energy. I'm out here having a good time, I'll say that. There are a lot of other jobs I could be doing, so I appreciate playing ball almost like a little kid. I want good memories to take with me, because I could break a leg tomorrow and be done.

DL: *You signed out of high school and struggled your first two years in pro ball. Tell us about that.*

BM: I knew there would be struggles, but I was confident that I could handle it. A lot of people don't understand the difficulty of making that jump. They expect you to produce right away. But those are just the uneducated people! It takes time, a lot of effort, and work.

DL: *What type of pitcher gives you the most trouble? For instance, who of your teammates would you least like to face—Jon Lester, Jon Papelbon, or Charlie Zink?*

BM: Don't put me in there against Zink! I like hard stuff. I can handle that. And I don't mind swinging against lefties, even though the ones with good sweeping curves can be trouble. But God help me against a knuckleballer! That can screw you up for days.

DL: *You touched on intensity earlier. Is that how you'd describe Dustin Pedroia?*

BM: In a lot of ways, yes. He's very professional, but he keeps you loose, too. He'll make an out against a guy throwing 98, and when he comes to the dugout we'll ask, "What's he got?" Pedroia will tell us, "He ain't got &*@*!"

DL: *Last one: Along with being a fan, did you collect cards when you were a kid?*

BM: Did I collect cards? Of course, I collected cards! You're not American if you don't collect cards!

DAVID MURPHY

DAVID MURPHY WAS THE RED SOX' SELECTION IN THE FIRST ROUND OF THE 2003 DRAFT. AN OUTFIELDER OUT OF BAYLOR UNIVERSITY, MURPHY SPENT THE 2005 SEASON WITH THE PORTLAND SEA DOGS. THIS IS AN EXCERPT FROM AN INTERVIEW THAT TOOK PLACE IN AUGUST 2004 WHEN HE WAS WITH THE SARASOTA RED SOX.

David Laurila: *As we speak, Hurricane Charley is nearing the Florida coast. How are things going down there right now?*

David Murphy: Pretty quiet, but we're definitely preparing for it. Today's game has already been cancelled, as was yesterday's. We're supposed to be playing Clearwater, but they've evacuated a lot of people from there and didn't want the team traveling. I guess we're expecting it to hit in a few hours.

DL: *Being from the Houston area, I assume you have some experience with hurricane warnings.*

DM: It's kind of funny, because a lot of the guys are getting calls from their families back home. They're all freaked out because they've never gone through anything like this before. Meanwhile, I just talked to my mom and she was perfectly calm. That doesn't mean there's no concern, but I am used to this sort of thing.

DL: *Let's move on to another important subject: your health. You missed some time this summer with a foot injury. Tell us about that.*

DM: We were playing in Lakeland on May 20th, and I rotated my foot awkwardly coming out of the box. It felt like a pinch and got worse as the game went on. A few innings later, I hit a grounder to short and could barely land on my left foot running to first. I had an X-ray, MRI, and CT-scan, all of which were inconclusive. There were concerns that it might be a stress fracture, but they eventually diagnosed it as a deep bone-bruise. It seemed like it took forever for the pain to go away, and it's still not completely healed. It's good enough to play on, but until I can rest it in the off-season it won't be 100 percent.

DL: *Being from Houston, what are your thoughts on living and playing in the Northeast?*

DM: It's kind of funny, because my dad said I was retracing the family's past in some ways. I started my pro career in Lowell and then came down here to Florida. My parents actually lived in Acton, Massachusetts, for a few years and went from there to Miami before moving to Houston.

DL: *Before I let you go, do you have any good stories to share?*

DM: When I was nine years old, I was approached by a couple of scouts. Justin Thompson, who went on to pitch in the Majors, was pitching in a high school game against my future school. There were scouts there to watch him, and a few of them saw me throwing a tennis ball against a wall. They came over and asked me where my dad was and then talked to him for a while. I think one even videotaped me.

DL: *I don't suppose one of them was with the Red Sox?*

DM: Actually, one was.

JEFF NATALE

JEFF NATALE WAS THE RED SOX' SELECTION IN THE 32ND ROUND OF THE 2005 DRAFT. AN INFIELDER OUT OF TRINITY COLLEGE, NATALE SPLIT HIS FIRST PROFESSIONAL SEASON BETWEEN LOWELL AND GREENVILLE. THIS IS AN EXCERPT FROM AN INTERVIEW THAT TOOK PLACE IN AUGUST 2005.

David Laurila: *You hit over .400 in your college career and are over .300 so far in pro ball. What makes you a good hitter?*

Jeff Natale: I don't think there are any big secrets to hitting. A lot of baseball is timing, and I'm seeing the ball well right now. When you're not—if you're not picking up spins and velocity—you'll think pitches are coming harder than they are. I just try to stay back and work the middle. I'm working with Randy Phillips, my hitting coach, a lot. I'm just trying to hit them where they're not.

DL: *You've only struck out five times, in over 80 at-bats, in Greenville. Does that tell us that you put balls into play early in the count or that you simply get your bat on the ball?*

JN: It's probably a combination of both, but I get my share of walks and hit-by-pitches. I've probably been a little lucky in that I've been getting good pitches to hit. I also don't try to do too much with two strikes. It helps that I don't have a long, loopy swing. I try to keep it short and make good contact.

DL: *You're playing second base in Greenville. Is that where you were at Trinity?*

JN: It was actually kind of crazy. I was in left field as a freshman, center field as a sophomore, second base as a junior, and third base as a senior. I also played left field in summer ball. Wherever there's a place for me is where I've been at.

DL: *Randy Newsom, who went to Tufts, is one of your teammates in Greenville. What do you remember about hitting against him, and what do NESCAC [New England Small College Athletic Conference] alums talk to each other about?*

JN: I faced him a bunch of times in college and was also on the same team with him two summers ago. He's a hard thrower and comes from a weird angle. I had trouble with him at times but also a little success. As for what we talk about, we're just normal guys. We talk about baseball a lot. A pitcher from Trinity, Jonah Bayliss, just got called up by the Royals, so we've been talking about him. Bayliss really throws the crap out of the ball.

DL: *What is your history as a baseball fan?*

JN: It's kind of weird. My grandfather was a Yankees fan, but my dad is a Cardinals fan. I think my dad started rooting for the Cardinals when they played the Yankees in the World Series back in the 1960s. Me, I'm more neutral. I always liked the Red Sox because I enjoy rooting for the underdog. It was certainly a huge surprise when they drafted me.

DL: *Are you into other sports?*

JN: I'm a pretty big hockey fan, a Rangers fan like my dad. I grew up loving Brian Leech and also Mark Messier. I played hockey for three years at Trinity, and still enjoy skating and shooting the puck.

DL: *Last one: Despite being a late-round pick from a small school, you're being discussed on the* SonsofSamHorn.com *and* SoxProspects.com *message boards. What does that tell you?*

JN: I didn't know that, but it's great. I'm just trying to find a spot in the organization, and maybe being an underdog is working in my favor. Just because I'm obscure—not a big prospect—doesn't mean I can't play. A lot of people are surprised that a Division III guy can play well against Division I guys. I just hope that I can keep giving people a reason to talk about me.

PAT PERRY

PAT PERRY WAS THE RED SOX' SELECTION IN THE SEVENTH ROUND OF THE 2004 DRAFT. A NATIVE OF NIWOT, COLORADO, PERRY IS A LEFT-HANDED-HITTING CATCHER WHO SAW TIME IN LOWELL AND GREENVILLE LAST SEASON. THIS INTERVIEW TOOK PLACE IN AUGUST 2005.

David Laurila: *You started the season in extended spring training. Tell us about that.*

Pat Perry: I went into spring training thinking that I'd be given a spot, and breaking camp I thought that perhaps I had earned one. But instead, I learned that it takes a lot more . . . that I hadn't done enough. It's kind of tough to explain, but it was a good learning experience for me. I just kept working and earned a promotion to Lowell, and then to Greenville, and it is what it is. You have to look forward, not back.

DL: *You went from Greenville to Lowell late in the season. How did you approach going back down to short-season ball?*

PP: I actually took being asked to come here as a positive. We're trying to make the playoffs, and they think I can help. I know I can make a difference with my defense. I enjoyed my time in Greenville, and I think they felt comfortable with me, but it's exciting to be fighting for a playoff spot. My perspective is that coming here was a good thing.

DL: *You've struggled offensively this year. Why do you think that is?*

PP: My swing has been inconsistent. First it's a toe-tap, then it's a leg-kick . . . I think I've been trying to force things. I just need to return to the old times when I was hitting well. It's funny, I've proven that I can hit . . . but suddenly I can't hit. But I've closed some gaps, and this far into the 2005 season I finally have some offensive direction. From the beginning of last year, people have said, "try this" and "try that," and I'm finally understanding the "why" part of it. Instead of asking for help if I pull off a pitch, or if I do something else wrong, I know it myself. Going into this off-season, I know what kind of swing I need. I'm already looking forward to spring training, because I have it figured out again.

DL: *How would you assess your defensive play?*

PP: If you took snapshots of me last year and now, the difference is night and day. I knew I had to make some adjustments, and feel I've definitely closed some defensive gaps. You need a good blend of quickness and strength, and one thing I've worked on is the follow-through on my release. I think my throwing, blocking, and receiving are all pretty solid now. I've stayed in contact with Rob Leary, our catching coordinator, because I want to make sure I keep improving.

DL: *I understand you have a new prized possession.*

PP: I bought a truck when I got to Greenville, and it's my new baby. When they sent me here to Lowell, I asked if I could take it with me, but they said no—they needed me right away and I had to fly up. So, I left the keys with John Otness. I chose Otness because he has a truck and loves his. It's a truck thing. I'd trust Otness with my life and my truck.

EDITOR'S NOTE: Pat Perry was released by the Red Sox in spring training of 2006.

JUSTIN SHERROD

JUSTIN SHERROD WAS THE RED SOX' SELECTION IN THE 19TH ROUND OF THE 2000 DRAFT. AN OUTFIELDER AND A NATIVE OF BOYNTON BEACH, FLORIDA, SHERROD SPENT THE 2005 SEASON WITH THE PAWTUCKET RED SOX. THIS IS AN EXCERPT FROM AN INTERVIEW THAT TOOK PLACE IN APRIL 2005.

David Laurila: *You were part of the Red Sox contingent that worked out in Japan before spring training. Tell us about that experience.*

Justin Sherrod: It was great. For one thing, I was amazed at the level of respect over there. The team I was with had the league's triple-crown winner, but you'd hardly know it. Everyone treated each other as equals—there weren't a lot of egos like you'll often see over here. We're all just human beings, playing a game, and that's how they seem to approach it.

DL: *What was the level of competition and training regimen like?*

JS: The training focused more on reps than we do here. Maybe a little too much, in my opinion. They give 100 percent in workouts. They go game-speed, which is good preparation. As for the competition, they seem to have a good grasp of the fundamentals and take a lot of pride in that aspect.

DL: *What about the language barrier? Did it make you think about what many Asian and Hispanic players face when they come here to play?*

JS: No doubt. I really felt like I was in a different place, and it gave me a better appreciation of those situations. Most of the guys there didn't speak much English. They seemed to know some baseball jargon, but not a lot more.

DL: *You played third base for a few years before the organization moved you to the outfield. Could you still play in the infield if the need arose?*

JS: I could go back if I had to. I still work out at first and third base, trying to keep my skills, just in case. It's a different game in the infield. Along with fielding ground balls, it's a different throw. When you move to the outfield, you go from a short, quick arm-action to longer throws. With those, you're pulling down with good extension.

DL: *The outfield came into play recently when a fan interfered with Gary Sheffield at Fenway Park. Have you ever had to deal with anything like that?*

JS: No, not really. Sometimes the fans are vulgar, which is something I don't understand. It happens in every park, and you just hope there aren't any kids around. But nothing like that, no.

DL: *Last one: You appeared on* The Bachelorette *last year. Do you have any good stories to share from your experience as a TV celebrity?*

JS: Nah, not really. People were all over that, but outside of getting flown out to California, not much happened. I got my 15 seconds of fame. Maybe 17 seconds. Now I'm just a baseball player again.

EDITOR'S NOTE: Justin Sherrod was released by the Red Sox in spring training of 2006.

MITCH STACHOWSKY

MITCH STACHOWSKY WAS THE RED SOX' SELECTION IN THE 50TH ROUND OF THE 2003 DRAFT. A NATIVE OF POCATELLO, IDAHO, STACHOWSKY SAW TIME IN LOWELL, GREENVILLE, AND PAWTUCKET LAST SEASON. THIS IS AN EXCERPT FROM AN INTERVIEW THAT TOOK PLACE IN JULY 2005.

David Laurila: *You were a 50th-round draft-and-follow two years ago. Tell us about learning you had been drafted and your decision to sign with the Red Sox the following year.*

Mitch Stachowsky: The area scout, John Booher, called to say the Sox had taken me. I had just gotten off work—I laid asphalt for three years—and was getting ready for practice. He told me it was a draft-and-follow situation, so I played my sophomore year at Southern Idaho. I then signed to go to an NAIA school in Idaho—Lewis and Clark State—and it came down to staying home in hopes of putting up better numbers or opting for pro ball. I was on a camping trip when they called to offer me a contract, and the signal on my cell phone barely registered one bar, but the call made it through. The Red Sox wanted me, so I decided to sign and start my career.

DL: *Despite being drafted in 2003, you're only 20 years old and one of the youngest players on the Lowell roster. How much have you matured in the last few years?*

MS: A lot. I graduated from high school and started college at 17, and I've come a long way since then. Most of the guys here have more experience than I do, but I've always played against older guys. That's not an issue. But I am struggling mentally with my hitting right now. I started pressing right at the beginning of the season, in Greenville, and you can't afford to do that. I'm still trying to figure it out.

DL: *Can you say a little more about that?*

MS: I've been trying to do too much. Consistency is a big part of hitting, and I don't have that right now. I've been getting too far out in front and not staying through the ball. I'm fine hitting in the cage, but that's been going out the window once the game starts. I need to start trusting myself more and not press so much. I just saw a video that I think will help, but I'm not close to where I need to be yet.

DL: *You grew up in Idaho. Are you from a city or a smaller town?*

MS: In my freshman year, we moved to a bigger town that had high school baseball, but before that we were in a town with about 1,000 people. We lived down the lane from my grandfather's farm, which had sheep and horses. It was the best thing for me, because my grandfather didn't believe in doing anything half-hearted, and he made me work hard. That was a real key to the success I've had in baseball.

DL: *Before I let you go, let's talk about a few of the guys you've played with this year. Who's the funniest?*

MS: It has to be DK, Dustin Kelly. We're both laid-back guys from the West, and we have a lot of fun together.

DL: *How about the most talkative?*

MS: Austin Easley is always talking. If he's not telling you something, he's asking a question.

DL: *How would you characterize yourself?*

MS: Myself? I'm serious on the field, but less so when I'm not. So I'd say "idiot savant."

DL: *Any final thoughts?*

MS: I had a great time today, a really great experience. A few of us went down to read to a group of kids, including two twin girls who were maybe six or seven and were wearing pink Nomar shirts. It just made me feel good to be doing something for the kids; it was one of those times where you feel like you make a difference.

ADAM STERN

ADAM STERN APPEARED IN 36 GAMES FOR THE RED SOX IN 2005
AFTER BEING TAKEN IN THE RULE 5 DRAFT PRIOR TO THE SEASON.
AN OUTFIELDER, STERN IS A NATIVE OF LONDON, ONTARIO, AND
REPRESENTED CANADA IN THE 2004 OLYMPIC GAMES AND THE
2006 WORLD BASEBALL CLASSIC. THIS IS AN EXCERPT FROM AN
INTERVIEW THAT TOOK PLACE IN JUNE 2005 WHILE STERN WAS
ON A REHAB ASSIGNMENT WITH THE PAWTUCKET RED SOX.

David Laurila: *You were taken in the Rule 5 draft. At what point did you start thinking about the possibility that you could be affected?*

Adam Stern: When the 40-man roster is announced in November, you become aware of it. It's one of those things where you know it's possible, but it's basically a crapshoot. You're told that you're a good candidate, but it's not something you can bank on. All you can do is play, and if it happens, it happens. [Coming to Boston] was a surprise. A team that wins the World Series can hand-select anyone, so it was an honor to have them show an interest in me.

DL: *You were drafted by Toronto in 1998 but elected to go to the University of Nebraska instead. What went into that decision?*

AS: Everybody dreams of playing for the team they rooted for as a kid, but in all reality it didn't seem like the best thing for me. It was more of a draft-and-follow, where they wanted me to go to a junior college for a year. I wasn't sure that I was ready, and it wasn't necessarily a clear path to Toronto if I signed. Going to a top-tier school, getting an education, and going pro later seemed like a better long-term option.

DL: *You majored in sociology. Why was that?*

AS: Originally it was business, but sociology just caught my interest. Learning about people and society was interesting, and there are certainly all walks of life in this profession. Baseball is really its own little sociology class, in many ways.

DL: *Tell us about playing in the College World Series.*

AS: It was awesome. We were playing in front of 25,000 fans in our own back yard, as it's held in Omaha. We were there in my last season, so it felt like I was going out with a bang. It was Nebraska's first trip to the Series, so it was nice to be part of the changing of the guard—part of the group of guys who helped turn the program around.

DL: *What was your Olympic experience like?*

AS: The Olympics are centered around the games, but the opening ceremonies and just being in the village is something else. The energy is something you can't match. It ranks right up there with anything you'll ever do, and there's a lot of pride involved with representing your country. I hope to get the chance to do it again.

DL: *How would you describe your offensive game?*

AS: I'm gap-to-gap and have to use my speed. I'll hit doubles here and there, but I want to put it on the ground. I hate to strike out and will take every measure not to. I don't want to use the word defensive, because you never want to be defensive in baseball, but I'll choke up with two strikes. I'm not trying to drive the ball out of the park, anyway. I want to put it in play and make the defense make a decision.

DL: *How many bunt hits do you get, and do you ever drag bunt?*

AS: For sure, you have to drag one once in a while to keep the defense honest. Overall, I'd say I had about 15 bunt hits last year. Bunting can help in another way, too. Sometimes when you're feeling uncomfortable at the plate or aren't picking up the release point very well, it can help slow you down. You see the ball better, and that can carry over to the next at-bat.

DL: *You haven't drawn a lot of walks in your career. With the Red Sox organization placing a lot of value on working counts and OBP, is that a concern for you?*

AS: Notoriously, I like to swing but a hit counts as getting on base. As a lead-off hitter, you do want to see some pitches and be willing to take a walk, but you can't be afraid to swing, either. Ichiro hits .360, and he doesn't go up there keeping the bat on his shoulder.

DL: *Before I let you go, what are you into off the field?*

AS: I like to be outside a little bit—I like to get away. I used to ski, but can't really do that anymore because of baseball. I enjoy mountain biking. I have a girlfriend. She's from Calgary and played soccer for Nebraska and in the WSA [Women's Soccer Association].

DL: *You're from Canada. No hockey?*

AS: I followed it—the Canadiens because of my uncle, and the Leafs because I was close to Toronto—but I didn't play. I guess I was one of the few who didn't. Baseball is what I've always been into.

CHRIS TURNER

CHRIS TURNER WAS THE RED SOX' SELECTION IN THE 15TH ROUND OF THE 2003 DRAFT. A RIGHT-HANDED-HITTING OUT-FIELDER FROM EL DORADO, ARKANSAS, TURNER SPENT THE 2005 SEASON IN GREENVILLE. THIS INTERVIEW TOOK PLACE IN AUGUST 2005.

David Laurila: *You've improved a lot since last season. What would you attribute that to?*

Chris Turner: It's definitely been a big change from last year. I haven't made any physical adjustments. The adjustments have been mental. I made everything too difficult last year. I'm more relaxed now and have started figuring stuff out, the way baseball is supposed to be played. I'm not sure if I can explain it; it pretty much just clicked. Something clicked in my head.

DL: *You had a poor walks-to-strikeouts ratio last season.*

CT: I agree; it wasn't very good at all. I'd say a good 50 percent of my strikeouts last year came from chasing balls out of the zone, some of them in the dirt. You have to see the ball, and last year I wasn't doing that. This year, I'm being more patient, and if it's not in my zone I'm laying off better. Baseball is situations, and you have to know when to attack pitches and when not to.

DL: *Has improved confidence played a role?*

CT: That's something that comes with time, and you need it to succeed. They have it in the Major Leagues. You have to be confident to hit, and you need it to play good defense. You can't have your doubts. Last year, I did. Now, I'm a lot more trusting in myself. I go up to the plate, thinking, "He's not going to get me out."

DL: *How did you approach starting the season in extended spring training?*

CT: I didn't look at Extended as bad. I looked at it as, "I'm here to get better and to take advantage of the situation." The coaches really helped me down there. They keep you loose and don't put any pressure on you. Being down there helped me a lot.

DL: *You have a lot of power potential. Do you consider yourself a power hitter?*

CT: I consider myself a gap-to-gap hitter, but I have power. I have the strength to drive the ball out to all fields. I've hit balls out to right this year. It's all about squaring up the ball, not swinging hard. You just need to know your strengths and weaknesses as a hitter, and attack the right pitch. I can definitely see myself hitting 25 or 30 home runs a season.

DL: *How would you rate your defensive game?*

CT: I'm definitely not happy with it right now. I'm working a lot on my first step . . . on my reads. That's a big part of playing good defense, and I want to be quicker recognizing out there. I've been playing both right and left field, and I've played five games in center. Not that I'm bad, but there's always room for improvement.

DL: *Which of your Lowell teammates from last year has impressed you the most this season?*

CT: I guess it would have to be John Otness. I already knew he was good, but he's really had a great year. He and Andrew Pinckney. Can I choose more than one? I have to include Andrew, too.

DL: *What are your plans for the off-season?*

CT: Last year, I spent a lot of time working out with friends at my old junior college. I'll do the same thing this year, so I can be in great shape when I report next spring. Maybe I'll go on a cruise, too. I think I'll go to the Bahamas with my girlfriend.

MARK WAGNER

MARK WAGNER WAS THE RED SOX' SELECTION IN THE NINTH ROUND OF THE 2005 DRAFT. A CATCHER OUT OF THE UNIVERSITY OF CALIFORNIA-IRVINE, WAGNER SPENT HIS FIRST PROFESSIONAL SEASON WITH THE LOWELL SPINNERS. THIS IS AN EXCERPT FROM AN INTERVIEW THAT TOOK PLACE IN JUNE 2005.

David Laurila: *You mentioned that mononucleosis contributed to your unspectacular 2004 season. In your draft bio,* Baseball America *attributed your improvement in 2005 to a shorter swing. Was that also a factor?*

Mark Wagner: I feel that I've always had a short swing, but the mono probably made it slower, which might have made it appear longer. At times, it felt like I was swinging a lead pipe. I was pretty sick for a while—I was in the ER twice—and dropped 25 pounds. There were people telling me I shouldn't have come back to play that year, and maybe I shouldn't have, but there's a mentality that if you can be out there, you are—so I played. The results weren't great, and they carried over to the Cape Cod League, but playing at less than full strength was actually a huge learning experience.

DL: *As a catcher, do you think differently than other hitters—going over how you'd be working yourself in an at-bat?*

MW: To be honest, no. If you do that, you start guessing and try to do too much and maybe your swing gets a little too long. I'm more of a see-it-and-hit-it guy. I'll pick a zone on certain counts, but usually not the pitch itself.

DL: *Can catchers learn more from pitchers or from other catchers?*

MW: I'd say other catchers. You watch how they do it—how they move their feet, how they get good balance and position. You learn how they take care of pitchers and why they call certain pitches in certain spots. You can learn from pitchers, but an experienced catcher or catching instructor can help you a lot.

DL: *Catching is a demanding position, and you just played a full college season. How will you approach the fatigue factor that may come into play later this summer?*

MW: I'll try to go back to my Cape experience, where I basically hit rock bottom. That's when I was still fighting back from mono, and I started doubting myself. The game can take its toll on you mentally, too, not just physically. But every day is a new day, and I want to take that experience and use it as a positive.

DL: *If you could catch any one pitcher for one game, who would it be?*

MW: To be honest, I already have. I caught Nolan Ryan. When I was at UC-Irvine, there was an executive day where people could stand in and hit against a special guest. They asked me if I'd come out and catch someone, and I said sure. I had no idea who it was. This guy comes walking down the right-field line, and it's Ryan! He wasn't throwing very hard to most of the guys, but he told me if someone was getting some pretty good cuts off him, he'd give me a wink. That meant he'd wing it a little harder! And let me tell you, the ball still explodes out of his hand! It was really kind of amazing.

J.T. ZINK

J.T. ZINK WAS THE RED SOX' SELECTION IN THE EIGHTH ROUND OF THE 2005 DRAFT. A RIGHT-HANDED PITCHER FROM UNIVERSITY PLACE, WASHINGTON, ZINK BEGAN HIS PROFESSIONAL CAREER LAST SEASON WITH THE LOWELL SPINNERS. THIS IS AN EXCERPT FROM AN INTERVIEW THAT TOOK PLACE IN JULY 2005.

David Laurila: *How long have you been "J.T.," and who first started calling you that?*

J.T. Zink: My given name is James Thomas, but I became "J.T." at a day camp in fourth grade. It came from the TV show *Step by Step*, where the character by that name was a goof-off. My friends started calling me "J.T." at camp, and it just stuck when we moved into fifth grade together.

DL: *How would you describe yourself as a pitcher?*

JZ: I like to work fast and command the game. I'm not a power pitcher, but I do come after hitters. In college, Zach Thomas—who went in the second round—and I were the one–two punch in the rotation. He was the thrower, while I was the pitcher. I'm around 88–90, although I have topped out a little higher. My ball has good sink, and that's what got me drafted. I've always watched how Derek Lowe commands his sinker, and I'm trying to perfect that. He doesn't get a lot of Ks—four or five a game—but he can be efficient with his pitches. That's what I want to do: get ground balls for outs early in the count.

DL: *Lowe tends to wear his emotions on his sleeve. How similar are you to him in that regard?*

JZ: I'm different in that respect. I've talked to a sports psychologist, and I don't think you can ever let yourself be affected by what happens on the field. If someone makes an error behind you, or if you make a bad pitch, you have to stay focused and move on. I'm not saying Lowe doesn't—he's a successful big league pitcher—but I try to be as unemotional as I can.

DL: *Is pitching more like psychology, or is it more like math?*

JZ: I'd say psychology. You can't prepare for a game as though it's a lesser opponent—you have to prepare as if you're facing the Yankees. And you have to be confident in how you go about it. Hitters can smell a tentative pitcher, and you want them to know you're in control.

DL: *What were your expectations going into the draft?*

JZ: I heard a lot of 6 to 10, and a few people said 3 or 4. But I wasn't putting a lot of stock in the 3 or 4 projections. And once those teams got right-handed pitchers early—ones they probably didn't expect to get—I knew it wouldn't be that soon. I knew the Red Sox were interested. Their scout, John Booher, was the first guy to come out to see me . . . in the pouring rain. I had the best relationship with him, and he called me before the draft. He said that he considered me a friend—he was the only scout who said anything like that—and that hopefully they'd have a chance to take me. I was so excited when it happened. Coming to an organization like this meant a lot to me.

DL: *What is it like playing here in Lowell?*

JZ: You hear a lot of talk about the daily grind of the minor leagues, and about how maybe, if you're lucky, there'll be some fans in the park. But here, it's been really great. The first time I stood on the mound, I could actually hear the buzz from the stands. It was a great feeling.

DL: *You recently had a chance to play in Oneonta. What was that like?*

JZ: A lot of people said Oneonta would be bad, but I really liked it. It's definitely an old ballpark—there's actually chicken-wire in the lockers! But it's got that vibe, a real old-time feel. Babe Ruth homered there, Mickey Mantle played there, and I love that kind of baseball history. I'm really excited to get to Fenway for that reason. Some places don't have the tradition, but others obviously do.

DL: *Hypothetical question: If you could face any hitter in Major League history, who would it be?*

JZ: I'll go with Ted Williams. I'd just throw out the book and go with my best against his best. I'm not saying I'd win, but it would be fun!

DL: *What if you could be any pitcher in baseball history, for one day?*

JZ: I'd be Bob Gibson. He was a freaking warrior. He was as old-school as you can get. He came up big when it counted, and if he had to knock somebody down, he did. You have to establish that the plate is yours, and he wasn't shy about doing that. When you're on the mound, you're in charge. It's your game.

Yesterday's Stars

MIKE ANDREWS

MIKE ANDREWS PLAYED SECOND BASE FOR THE RED SOX FROM 1967 TO 1970 AND WAS AN AMERICAN LEAGUE ALL-STAR IN 1969. A MEMBER OF THE 1967 "IMPOSSIBLE DREAM" TEAM, ANDREWS HAS BEEN THE CHAIRMAN OF THE JIMMY FUND FOR MORE THAN 20 YEARS. THIS INTERVIEW TOOK PLACE IN MARCH 2005.

David Laurila: *You grew up in Southern California and were 14 years old when the Dodgers moved to Los Angeles. Did you adopt them as your team when they arrived from Brooklyn?*

Mike Andrews: Absolutely. I grew up in Torrance and really liked Sandy Koufax and Don Drysdale. Before they came, I was actually more of a Pacific Coast League fan. I got to see a lot of the Los Angeles Angels and Hollywood Stars, while the "Major League Game of the Week" was all the big league ball we got on TV. I still followed it, of course. The Yankees and [Brooklyn] Dodgers were in the World Series a lot, so I liked both of those teams. My favorite player was probably Harvey Kuenn. He and Mickey Mantle wore number 7, so I always wanted to wear it when I played as a youngster. I liked Jackie Robinson, Larry Doby, and Stan Musial a lot, too.

DL: *You signed your first contract in 1962, three years before the MLB draft was instituted. Tell us about your decision to sign with the Red Sox.*

MA: I was actually planning to play football at UCLA. I had a scholarship to go there, but my girlfriend and I decided to get married, and we needed the income. So I chose baseball, and to tell you the truth I didn't have a lot of choices. I was all-league in school, but not an, "Oh my God, you have to see this guy play" kind of prospect. The Pirates were the only other team to show interest. Joe Stephenson and the Red Sox liked me more, so I signed with them.

DL: *You made your MLB debut in September of 1966. What do you most remember about your first call-up to the big leagues?*

MA: The Triple A team was in Toronto, and Reggie Smith and I were both getting called up. We made the playoffs, though, which meant we didn't get to Boston until mid-September. I remember driving down with Dick Williams, who was my manager in Toronto. The club had asked him to come to Boston, and he had no idea it was to offer him the job for 1967.

DL: *All Red Sox fans are familiar with the 1967 Impossible Dream story. At what point in that season did you realize something special was happening?*

MA: Probably the second time through. We had so many young guys, and we were just getting comfortable in the big leagues. Once we had played everyone, we started thinking, "These guys aren't any better than we are." And a lot of good things were happening, like winning 10 in a row on a road trip. We really started to believe in ourselves.

DL: *You were in the World Series your first full year, and again in your last, winning it with Oakland. Do the two compare?*

MA: Not at all. In 1967, I felt like I was an important part of the team. In Oakland, I was mostly a good batting practice pitcher. It felt good to win, and it was a really great team that I enjoyed being on, but I was a spare part.

DL: *You committed two errors in the 12th inning of Game 2 of that Series. Afterwards, Charlie Finley, the A's owner, wanted you replaced on the roster. Tell us about that.*

MA: Finley was Finley. He believed in winning at all costs and didn't feel I was helping the team. He wanted Manny Trillo on the roster, but he came up too late in the year and wasn't eligible. Anyway, I didn't make a couple of plays, and he had a doctor examine my shoulder and say I wasn't healthy enough to be out there. He put a lot of pressure on me to sign a paper saying I was hurt, and I finally did—even though I really wasn't. I was off the team for a few days, but the commissioner stepped in and forced them to reinstate me. Of course, once they did, Finley told Dick Williams, now managing in Oakland, not to play me. But Dick was Dick, too. He had me pinch hit, my first game back. The story had gotten a lot of play, so I got a standing ovation when I came up, even though we were playing on the road in New York. Then I grounded weakly to third, so they gave me another ovation!

DL: *At the end of your career, you had throwing problems similar to what Steve Sax and Chuck Knoblauch experienced. How much did that contribute to you leaving the game after only eight seasons, at the age of 30?*

MA: A lot. It was one of those things that can't be explained, and I'm not even sure when it started. And it's strange that it's second basemen that it often to happens to. Of course, it's others, too. When he was with us, Sparky Lyle couldn't throw to first base. In order to keep a runner close, he'd just step off. Or sometimes, he'd just lob the ball over—he couldn't throw it. But yes, that was a big reason I was out of the league after the '73 Series. A broken wrist that didn't heal properly—Harmon Killebrew had run into me at first base—factored into it, too.

DL: *You had a reputation as a good fielder prior to the throwing problems. Were you always a second baseman?*

MA: I was at shortstop in Toronto in '65 but moved to second in '66. It was a pretty easy transition, and I think I fielded the position pretty well. Ken Coleman once told me that I was the tallest second baseman in history when I played—he had looked it up. I'm 6' 3", so I was hard to knock down around the bag. Having no fear is the biggest part of turning a double play. Rico [Petrocelli] and I led the league in double plays once, I'm pretty sure.

DL: *After the 1970 season, the Red Sox traded you to the White Sox in the Luis Aparicio deal. How did you react to that?*

MA: It was crushing, worse than the two errors in the World Series. Baseball was different back then. You had respect for your team and expected to stay there. I felt I was a permanent fixture, but when Dick O'Connell denied the trade rumors and said there's no way I'd be traded . . . well, that's always the kiss of death. The next day, I was at home listening to the radio and heard that I'd been dealt.

DL: *What was it like playing against the Red Sox, and how much fraternization was there at the time?*

MA: On the field, you couldn't talk to your opponent. As a matter of fact, there was usually an umpire watching from the stands before the game, making sure you didn't. As for playing against Boston, I had extra incentive to play well. It was easy to get up for the games. Of course, my years with the Red Sox, especially '67, have always stayed with me.

DL: *You struck out only 390 times in your career, while drawing 458 walks. What type of hitter did you consider yourself, and how would you fit in with today's emphasis on working counts and getting on base?*

MA: I hit 17 home runs one year, but I was by no means a power hitter. My job was to get on base and move guys over. I was a table-setter for guys like Yaz. I always like to tell him that his best years were with me hitting in front of him! As for my approach at the plate, I believed in Ted's theory of seeing pitches and making sure I got a good one to hit.

DL: *You played with some great power hitters. Were any stronger than Dick Allen, and can you imagine what he'd have done with the help of steroids?*

MA: Man, let me tell you, he didn't need them! He was the strongest human being I've ever seen. He was chiseled, and he used to hit bombs to right and left center, well over 400 feet. As for steroids, they disgust me. I agree with Congress stepping in, because baseball isn't going far enough with the testing and penalties. Guys who are caught cheating should get one- or two-year suspensions, or worse. Statistics are a fabric of the game for true fans, and they're being distorted, especially home run records. And the problem goes beyond the records that are being set. There's a trickle-down effect to kids, high school kids who don't think they can compete unless they use them. It's terrible.

DL: *I believe you were there when Don Buford punched out a fan on the field in Chicago. Tell us that story.*

MA: Yes, it was in Comiskey Park and I was at second base. Bart Johnson had thrown one high and tight to Buford. Johnson was known to throw it around a bit. Buford walked out in front of the plate, still holding the bat. He didn't charge the mound or anything, and he wouldn't have needed the bat—he had played football at USC and was a pretty solidly built guy. Anyway, nothing happened, but a few innings later he's in the on-deck circle, and a fan comes out of the stands and runs right at him! He's looking the other way, so we yell to warn him. He turned around just in time, and leveled the fan with one punch! His teammates came racing out of the dugout, and they jumped on the guy, too. It was really something to see.

DL: *You played in Japan for a year after your MLB career ended. Tell us about that experience.*

MA: It was in 1975. I hadn't played in '74 and thought I was done. But I was approached with a big-money offer and decided to take it. It was an interesting experience. I did all right, but not understanding the language or being able to read the newspapers made life a little strange. I was with the Kintetsu Buffaloes, as was Clarence Jones, later the hitting coach for the Atlanta Braves. Clarence had been there a few years, and when we went to the playoffs, he told me, "We're going to get benched now, just watch." I couldn't believe it, but he was right. The manager wanted to win with all Japanese players, just like the Yomiuri Giants had done many times before. After we lost the first few games, he put us back in there, but it wasn't enough and we got eliminated.

DL: *What is the story behind the Red Sox' relationship with the Jimmy Fund?*

MA: The original affiliation was with the Boston Braves, but when they left in 1952, Tom Yawkey established a partnership with the Jimmy Fund. Ted Williams was always a big supporter of the organization, as was Carl Yastrzemski, and others. I can't say enough about what the team has done for us over the years.

DL: *The 1967 team granted a World Series share to the Jimmy Fund. How much was that, and what was your salary at the time?*

MA: Boy, like I said earlier, baseball was a different game when I played. My salary that year was $11,000, which was a real deal for a rookie. And Tom Yawkey actually gave me a $4,000 raise in July. That's the kind of man he was. The World Series shares, if I remember right, were just over $5,000. Yaz made the suggestion that we give a share to the Jimmy Fund, and it was a unanimous vote in favor. One interesting thing about the shares is that, at the time, they were based on the gate. Supposedly, the Cardinals were rooting for a team with a bigger ballpark to win the American League pennant, for that reason. They would have gotten bigger shares if the White Sox, Twins, or Tigers had won.

DL: *Tell us about the Jimmy Fund sign that currently adorns the Green Monster and how much money is donated each year.*

MA: Because of renovations to the park, the Jimmy Fund sign had to be moved from right field, where it had always been. Charles Steinberg had the idea of using the old logo. We're very happy with it, and, again, can't thank the organization enough for all they've done. We raised $47 million last year—that's from everything under the Jimmy Fund umbrella. The Pan-Mass Challenge is our biggest event.

DL: *Any final thoughts, perhaps on the 2004 Red Sox championship?*

MA: It was exciting to see them win. And when the team is doing well, the Jimmy Fund historically does better. People are even more generous. I really enjoyed my days in the game, but what I get out of this job is even more rewarding. As a fan, I was rooting for the Red Sox in October. With the Jimmy Fund, I'm rooting for something even more important.

🔵

DENNIS "OIL CAN" BOYD

DENNIS "OIL CAN" BOYD PITCHED FOR THE RED SOX FROM 1982
TO 1989. ONE OF THE MORE COLORFUL PERSONALITIES IN RED
SOX HISTORY, BOYD SPENT 10 SEASONS IN THE BIG LEAGUES,
COMPILING A RECORD OF 78-77. THIS INTERVIEW TOOK PLACE IN
JULY 2004.

David Laurila: *Your hero growing up was Satchel Paige. Tell us about that.*

Oil Can Boyd: My dad and uncle played with him in the Negro Leagues. They were with the Kansas City Monarchs, and they played some ball together in Mobile, too. My dad was Willie James Boyd, and my uncle was K.T. Boyd. His real name is Mike, but they always called him K.T. We had a lot in common with Satchel, being southern boys and ballplayers and all.

DL: *You had a real style when you pitched, as did Satchel. You also both featured a wide array of pitches. Did you model yourself after him?*

OCB: I inherited the style from my dad and brothers, but I guess it came indirectly from Satchel. He inspired them, and they would have taken a lot from watching him. I used to play a lot of strikeout with my older brothers and had to figure out a way to get them out. That's how I learned to pitch.

DL: *What other players did you admire when you were young?*

OCB: Bob Gibson is one. I liked Dock Ellis.

DL: *Ellis allegedly pitched a game under the influence of LSD. What are your thoughts on that?*

OCB: I don't know, really. Ballplayers are people, so they do some pretty crazy things sometimes. Maybe he did it. Anything's possible.

DL: *Your nickname derives from back home in Mississippi, where oil is a slang term for beer. Tell us a little about that.*

OCB: I'm a country boy from down South and it's a southern thing. Lots of guys have nicknames down there. They follow you around. How you walk, how you talk. Maybe it's a little bit of a black thing, too— an African-American thing. Many of the Negro League guys had nicknames, like Satchel. His real name was Leroy. I give kids nicknames sometimes on the ball field.

DL: *It seems like baseball doesn't have the colorful nicknames it once had.*

OCB: Probably not. I read somewhere that I've got one of the five or six best ever. "Shoeless Joe" Jackson was a great one; Walter "Big Train" Johnson was another.

DL: *If you could have pitched in another era, which would it have been?*

OCB: Oh, man, it would have been the 1940s. That was baseball. I could have seen all the great players. Joe DiMaggio, Ted Williams, Pee Wee Reese! That's the ball I love. And they had great uniforms, too— the best in history.

DL: *You would have had to hit in that era, and you went 6 for 95 in your career. Any thoughts on that?*

OCB: I could hit before they took the bat out of my hands! That all came at the end of my career in Montreal, and I had forgotten how, playing in the American League. By that time, I hardly even wanted to be up there. Major League pitchers are good—I wouldn't have wanted to face myself! But before that, I could hit. I love playing baseball. I like to run the bases and slide—get my uniform dirty. I play a little second base and shortstop these days, and even caught a game last week.

EDITOR'S NOTE: At the time of the interview, Boyd was an owner/ player of an independent league team.

DL: *Back to your nickname for a moment. There's a notable story or two regarding you and drinking. Anything you'd like to offer on that?*

OCB: A lot of guys like a drink after a game. I've always liked to have a beer, maybe a rum-and-coke. Ain't nothing. I always went out there ready to pitch. You have to be ready when you're facing Major Leaguers. I won some games. Probably should have won more.

DL: *What do you remember from your first Major League game?*

OCB: It was at Fenway Park against Cleveland. I mostly remember Toby Harrah hitting me good. He paid me a good compliment after the game, though. He said something like: "From what I saw, he'll be around for awhile." Made me feel good.

DL: *Any favorite memories you'd like to share from your career?*

OCB: There are lots of good memories. One thing I'll never forget is Roger Clemens striking out 20 batters. I was there, and he was bringing it—must have been throwing 100. That young Texas kid was throwing bullets. I've never seen a ball thrown like that.

DL: *You had some bad times, too. Among the widely publicized ones were not getting picked for the All-Star team and not getting the ball for Game 7 in 1986. Which was worse?*

OCB: Both. The All-Star was an individual thing. The Series was different. I would have liked to have won that game. I'm a winner, and we're going to win if I'm out there on the mound for Game 7. I'll always believe that. I wanted that ball in my hand.

DL: *What was it like playing in Boston?*

OCB: This is the world when it comes to baseball. The passion is unbelievable. It's in people's minds, and it passes down from generation to generation. It's the coolest.

DL: *After your career, you signed as a replacement player during the strike. Tell us about that.*

OCB: I wanted to pitch, because that's what "The Can" does. I played with the White Sox, so I got to meet Michael Jordan. My locker was next to his in spring training. If not for that, it would probably never have happened. He's one of the three greatest people I've ever met.

DL: *Who are the other two?*

OCB: Bo Jackson is one. He's a southern boy from Alabama. Walter Payton is the other. I knew him my whole life. A lot of people don't know he was an outstanding baseball player. He could have played in the Majors if he wanted to.

DL: *You've played a lot of Independent League ball since you left the Majors. I understand that you pitched against the Colorado Silver Bullets once—the all-female team.*

OCB: That was cool, man. A girl got a hit off of me! I gave up one hit in two innings, to the first batter of the game. It was Michelle McEneaney; her father pitched for the Reds. She was a little second baseman, and she could really play. So could the blonde center fielder. She went back on a ball over her head and made a wonderful catch. It looked just like Rocco Baldelli, the pride of Rhode Island. It was great to see them play just like us.

DL: *I understand that you have your own Independent League team now. How did that come about?*

OCB: Delino DeShields and I are putting together a team. When I got out of organized ball, I learned about ownership and I still love performing. Now I can do both.

DL: *How long will you keep pitching?*

OCB: As long as I can. I have better stuff now than I ever did. And I know how to pitch. Being smart is the biggest part of pitching, and I've been doing it for a long time.

DL: *How many different pitches do you throw?*

OCB: If you count arm angles, probably 12 to 15. I throw everything.

DL: *Even a knuckleball?*

OCB: I've always had a knuckler. I didn't throw it in the big leagues, but I do now. It's a hard one, too—about 81 mph. I throw it straight over the top and it drops like a forkball. It's a knuckler, though.

DL: *Last question. You spent 10 years in the Majors, but you've also played on teams in places like Sioux City and Bangor. Tell us about those experiences.*

OCB: I loved it. Fans all over got to watch "The Can" pitch. That's why I still love to play. Kids everywhere know me, even though they weren't around when I was in the big leagues. That's me, man. Back home, I'm Dennis Ray, but everywhere else I'm "The Can".

JACK CLARK

JACK CLARK PLAYED FOR THE RED SOX IN 1991 AND 1992. KNOWN AS "JACK THE RIPPER," CLARK WAS A FOUR-TIME ALL-STAR AND HIT 340 HOME RUNS OVER 18 BIG LEAGUE SEASONS. THIS INTERVIEW TOOK PLACE IN FEBRUARY 2006.

David Laurila: *Tell us about your early days as a player, growing up in Covina, California.*

Jack Clark: I didn't start playing baseball until I was 11, when I went out for the Little League team because a friend across the street was playing. We were called the "Firemen," because the coach worked for the fire department. I didn't play my freshman and sophomore years of high school, but another friend said I should try out, so I played as a junior and senior. My senior year we won the championship, and after the game George Genovese of the San Francisco Giants came up and said they were going to draft me. I said "whatever," because I didn't believe him. Even though I grew up in the L.A. area, I liked the Giants a lot more than the Dodgers. The Dodgers were more small-ball, while the Giants had guys like Mays and McCovey.

DL: *Were you a big fan growing up?*

JC: Oh yeah. As a kid, I'd wake up on Saturday mornings and watch cartoons, then in the afternoon I'd watch the Game of the Week. I was born in Pittsburgh, so I mostly liked the Pirates. I was a huge Clemente and Stargell fan. I still love that era of baseball. There were Mays and Mantle, Clemente and Yaz, Koufax and Gibson. Back then, there were real stars.

DL: *You were drafted by the Giants as a pitcher/outfielder. Do you think you could have made the big leagues as a pitcher?*

JC: I had a really good arm, so it's possible. I had kind of a slinky arm . . . kind of a whippy arm. I pitched in rookie ball, but I also hit well when I was playing right field. They asked if I preferred playing every day, or every fifth day, and I decided I'd rather hit. They were actually grooming me to be the next third baseman, to follow guys like Jim Davenport and Jim Ray Hart, but I made a lot of throwing errors in the minor leagues. I never finessed my throws. I liked to throw line drives, and at times I'd sail them past the first baseman.

DL: *Over a two-year period in the early 1980s, you threw out three runners at first base from right field, including Nolan Ryan. Tell us about that.*

JC: I'd read the scouting reports, and against some hitters I'd be playing almost a deep second base. I'd tip off the first baseman that I might try it, and a couple I got, a few I didn't. Of course, word got around and guys realized they couldn't just trot down to first when I was out there. It was fun to challenge runners like that, and the fans loved it.

DL: *You were only 19 when you made your big league debut in 1975. Which veteran players took you under their wing when you got to San Francisco?*

JC: Gary Alexander and I got called up from Double A, and we drove out together from Lafayette, taking short naps in the car on the way. We couldn't wait to get there. Gary Matthews met us at a Holiday Inn when we got to San Francisco, and he was the one who showed us where we needed to go. We hadn't been at spring training, so we didn't know anyone yet, but all of the guys made us feel comfortable. Two years later, in '77, I spent time in the clubhouse with Willie Mays. He taught me a lot about the game.

DL: *What was it like hitting at Candlestick Park?*

JC: It was tough. The summer in San Francisco is like winter time. You go from short sleeves in spring training, in Arizona, to foggy and windy and cutting cold. It was a better place to hit at first, because there was Astroturf and balls would really shoot into the corners. But they got rid of it, because it was like concrete and too many 49ers were getting hurt during football season. The fog would start rolling in late in the day, and by game time the wind was tumbling across from left field to right. It was a jet stream for balls hit to right, but long fly balls to left would get blown back to the shortstop.

DL: *How many home runs do you think Candlestick may have cost you?*

JC: It's hard to say, but it probably took away over a hundred. But it wasn't just me. Look at somebody like Willie Mays. You add another 100 or so to his total, and he has what . . . over 750?

DL: *How was it hitting at Fenway Park?*

JC: For me, it was frustrating. I was more of a line-drive hitter, so the wall actually hurt me. I could hit a line drive as hard, and as far, as anyone in the history of the game, but at Fenway they ran out of room and hit the wall. They would have been gone anywhere else. Not that I didn't like playing in Boston. The fans were great, and I'm a nostalgia and tradition guy, but it wasn't a great park for the way I hit.

DL: *The first time you played at Fenway Park, you were with the Yankees and you homered off Roger Clemens. Do you remember that game?*

JC: I actually don't. There are a lot of things like that I don't remember. For instance, I couldn't tell you who I got my first hit off of. I know my first home run was off Jack Billingham, and I remember the big home run off Tom Niedenfuer in the '85 playoffs. Another is breaking the Giants' record by hitting in 26 consecutive games. That was Willie McCovey's record, and while 26 doesn't seem like that many, 26 in Candlestick is like 46 somewhere else. When you look at who played there, guys like Mays, McCovey and Bobby Bonds, that's something I'm proud of.

DL: *Do you recall your first game in a Red Sox uniform?*

JC: I do, because I hit a grand slam off Dave Stieb, in Toronto, and it was one of the hardest balls I ever hit. It must have broken a seat. But the reason I remember it is that he hit me in the back my next time up. And that's a difference from today's game. Back then, guys didn't charge the mound all the time, so I just jogged down to first base. We took getting hit as a sign of respect.

DL: *You had a three-home-run game at Fenway Park in 1991, the last being a walk-off in the 14th inning. What do you remember about that game?*

JC: I hit a grand slam off Dave Stewart, so it was against Oakland. We came back in that game, and it was one of those salad days for me, one of my best days offensively. I remember that all three balls were legit. They were Jack Clark home runs—they were line drives—not ones that dropped into the basket. They all count, of course, but it's nice when you get into one.

DL: *You're high on the all-time list for extra-inning home runs. Can you comment on that?*

JC: There were a lot of things you did in my era that weren't stats like they are today, like game-winning hits and walk-offs. I was usually good at coming through, and that's another thing I'm proud of. I finally learned that I was out there for a reason and didn't want anyone holding my hand. My father raised me to work hard. I lived that way, and I wanted to be up in a situation where I could win the game.

DL: *In 1989, you set a record by striking out nine times in two games. Do you recall that?*

JC: In '89? I guess I'd have been in San Diego, but no, I don't. My job was to send a message. When I spent that time with Willie Mays, he told me to never let the other team know when I'm not feeling good. There are going to be times when you can't figure it out—maybe you're not seeing the ball well, or you have the flu. Or, like any normal human being, maybe you have something going on in your life that makes it harder to do your job. But you still show up, and you want the opposing team to respect that you can do some damage.

DL: *Having played in both places, how would you compare Boston and St. Louis as baseball towns?*

JC: I guess that because the Cardinals have won more World Series, it was more pride than pressure. In Boston, there was all the frustration and Curse-of-the-Bambino stuff. There was certainly more scrutiny in Boston. Every day, I'd feel it, with people attaching money to production. It seemed like you had to justify the money you were making each at-bat. I know that when I got there, nobody wanted to hit fourth. They didn't want to deal with that pressure. I looked at them and thought, "Are you nuts?" Fourth is the man's spot to be in. You don't want that?

DL: *You played for some notable managers during your career. What was your relationship with them?*

JC: It was all over the board. With Whitey Herzog, it was great. I got along well with Billy Martin, but not Lou Piniella.

DL: *How about Frank Robinson?*

JC: I'd say in-between, and I wish it had been better. That was my fault, because I was young and stupid. When he made me team captain, he said, "I'm naming Jack Clark the captain of this sinking ship." I didn't know if I should take that as a good thing or a bad thing. But all in all, if I could do it again, my relationship with Frank would have been better. He helped me a lot, especially hitting against left-handers. He once had the same problem, which was more mental in approach than mechanical, and he helped make me a more dangerous hitter.

DL: *Going back to your time with the Red Sox, how did you end up in a Boston uniform?*

JC: I became a Red Sox player because of second-look free agency. Back in '87, when the owners colluded against the players, I was a free agent. I had been with the Cardinals, and Dal Maxvill, the St. Louis GM, told me if I didn't take their offer I could go drive a truck in Cleveland, because nobody else would make me one. George Steinbrenner decided to break the collusion, though. He said he knew I loved St. Louis, but if I wanted to play in New York he'd make me a good offer. I took it, and soon Paul Molitor, and everyone else, was getting offers, too. That was a bad time in baseball.

DL: *Because of collusion, that was the only offer you received?*

JC: The Cardinals said they'd match Steinbrenner's offer, once they heard about it. But while I knew I wanted to be in St. Louis, as a man I couldn't do it. Not only had I already shaken hands on the deal, I didn't appreciate what Maxvill had said. For one thing, I have family in Pittsburgh, which is a blue-collar town like Cleveland. It was insulting what he said about going there to drive a truck. $13,000 is the most money my father ever made in a year, but he kept a roof over our heads and taught us trust and to be as honest as the day is long. I had to do what I felt was right.

DL: *How did the collusion settlement eventually land you in Boston?*

JC: After the owners were found guilty, part of the settlement granted second-look free agency to the players originally affected. That was two years later. I had five or six offers that time, and my agent thought the

Green Monster would help me put up the numbers I needed to maybe go into the Hall of Fame someday. It was a nice idea, but it didn't work out the way we had hoped.

DL: *What are you most proud of from your time in baseball?*

JC: I think that what people liked about me was that Jack Clark was real. Maybe that's what some people didn't like about me, too. I stood up for what I thought was right, and I took the blame when I had to. I never caved in. Sometimes, I said things people didn't like, but the truth is the truth even if it hurts. Like the saying goes, if you can't take the heat, stay out of the kitchen. I did the best I could and tried to be a good team-mate. I sleep well at night.

DL: *Last one: How did you get the nickname, "Jack the Ripper," and what is your opinion of it?*

JC: Vida Blue gave it to me when he got to San Francisco. I actually loved it. I think it fit me perfectly.

TED COX

TED COX PLAYED FOR THE RED SOX IN 1977 BEFORE BEING TRAD-ED TO CLEVELAND AS PART OF THE DENNIS ECKERSLEY DEAL. BOSTON'S FIRST-ROUND PICK IN THE 1973 DRAFT, COX SET A MAJOR LEAGUE RECORD BY RECORDING HITS IN HIS FIRST SIX BIG LEAGUE AT-BATS. THIS INTERVIEW TOOK PLACE IN OCTOBER 2005.

David Laurila: *You were one of the top prospects in the game when you debuted with the Red Sox in 1977. Are there any current Major League third basemen who you think are similar, style-wise, to a young Ted Cox?*

Ted Cox: I wish I could say I had the same kind of career, but in a way it would be Alex Rodriguez. I was signed as a shortstop, and at 6' 3½" and 190 pounds was one of the biggest shortstops around at that time. But

Rico Petrocelli was starting to talk about retirement, so they moved me to third. As a hitter, I was more of a high average guy—I hit .330-something my last year in the minors—but I had some power, too. Joe Morgan said I was one of the best clutch hitters he'd had, and Ted Williams gave me a compliment I'll never forget. He told me to never let anyone change my swing. Coming from Ted . . . well, that meant something.

DL: *You were a first-round pick out of high school in Oklahoma in 1973. Tell us about that, including your experience with professional scouts.*

TC: I was pretty athletic. In high school, along with baseball, I played football and basketball. I was recruited by Division I schools at all three. My first experience with scouts came when I was 15. They came to watch one of my teammates and afterwards came over to ask me a few questions. I was kind of shocked when they did. After my sophomore year, my coach arranged for me to go to a tryout. Mike Hargrove was there, too, playing first base. I played well and began drawing a lot of interest from that point on. It was funny; I was going to be the starting quarterback my junior year, but six or seven pro teams were telling me not to play football. I decided not to, which resulted in a lot of people in town barely even talking to me! I did play my senior year, so I guess that worked out okay. The Red Sox then took me with the 17th pick in the first round, although I didn't even know they were interested. The Astros had just worked me out and said they hoped to take me, but they picked a few spots later.

DL: *The Cardinals also drafted an Oklahoma high schooler in the first round: Joe Edelen. Did you know him?*

TC: Joe was from Gracemont, a small town near Binger, where Johnny Bench is from. He played lower-division ball, but we did play against each other. There was a lot of hype for Joe in American Legion and high school ball. He hit a huge number of home runs. Joe did play in the big leagues but as a pitcher rather than a position player. He and I have stayed in touch somewhat over the years.

DL: *You were selected to the Oklahoma all-century high school baseball team. Along with you and Johnny Bench, who else is on the team?*

TC: Joe Edelon is on it, as are Mickey Tettleton and Darrell Porter. Ironically, Bench is only on the second team. There's also an Oklahoma all-professional team—obviously he's on that. Mantle is another one who's not on the high school team. Hard to believe, isn't it? I'm not sure why.

DL: *Tell us about the start of your pro career.*

TC: I started out in Elmira, in rookie ball, and went something like 0 for my first 20. I wondered if I even belonged. But I ended up hitting almost .300. I was hitting .298 going into the last game of the season but didn't have any home runs. A few of my teammates were giving me the business about that, so rather than trying to reach .300 I went out there trying to hit one out. Instead, I struck out three or four times and ended up going down to .293! I moved up the ladder each year, though. In my third year, I led the Carolina League in hitting. My first spring training was the following year, in '76. We were locked out initially, but then finally got going late. I got a hit in my first spring training at-bat, against the Angels. Rod Carew was playing first base, and he said to me, "Nice hit, Ted." I looked at him and said, "You know my name?" He said, "Sure, they announced it when you came up to hit!"

DL: *In 1977, you hit .334-14-81 for Pawtucket and were named the minor league player of the year. In September, you were in the Major Leagues.*

TC: Yes, I had everything going for me. I actually thought I'd made the team out of spring training, but even though I hit .400 I was the last player cut. Don Zimmer had said it would be either me or Butch Hobson at third, and when they decided on Hobson they wanted me playing every day rather than backing him up. We won the league in Pawtucket and went to the playoffs, so it was the middle of September before I got called up to Boston.

DL: *Where you proceeded to set a Major League record by starting your career with six hits.*

TC: I did. I went 4-for-4 in my first game, which was in Baltimore on a day they were honoring Brooks Robinson. Before the game, Ed Yost, one of our coaches, told me I was in the lineup and would be DHing and hitting second. I didn't believe him; I thought he was kidding around with me. After the game, Robinson came up and congratulated me, joking that I had ruined his day. He and Mickey Mantle were my idols growing up, so that was special. The next day, at Fenway Park against the Yankees, I got hits in my first two at-bats.

DL: *What do you remember about your first big league home run, a week later, in Detroit?*

TC: I hit it off of Milt Wilcox, another Oklahoma City guy, a few rows into the stands in left field. Afterwards, there was a rain delay and the guys were kidding me that we'd get rained out and it wouldn't count. Fortunately, that didn't happen. Later that game, Yaz hit one that went onto the roof in right field. I had been calling him "Pops," saying he was old enough to be my dad. After his roof-shot, Yaz came up to me and said, "That's the way to hit them, son."

DL: *You finished that first season with an average of .362 in 58 at-bats. Did you have any idea you might be traded the following spring?*

TC: I didn't. There had been rumors about us trying to get Eckersley, but my name was never mentioned. They signed me to a three-year contract that spring and told me they were looking to trade George Scott. With Hobson at third, the plan was to move me to first base. That's where I was working out; they didn't even have me taking balls at third. But then, eight or nine days before the end of spring training, they started working me out at third again. Apparently, it was to show-case me for the Indians, because the next day I'm in Don Zimmer's office learning that I had been traded. He said they'd had no luck in dealing Scott, so it looked like I'd be a role player if I stayed. In Cleveland, I'd be the everyday third baseman. At least that's how he tried to sell it to me. I was upset. I wanted to be a Red Sox player, and along with all of my friends being in Boston, I didn't want to go to Cleveland. At the time, the big joke about Cleveland was that it was just a stop on the way to the big leagues. Anyway, we were playing a spring training game in Winter Haven when this happened. The people in the stands learned what was going on, so when I walked out of the club-house and left the park, they gave me a standing ovation.

DL: *When you got to Cleveland, you ended up playing more in the out-field than at third base. Why was that?*

TC: When I got to Tucson, where the Indians trained, Jeff Torborg called me into his office. He said they acquired me because they had reached an agreement to trade Buddy Bell to California for Don Baylor, and I'd be replacing Buddy at third. But they had just learned that Baylor said he wouldn't report, so the deal was off. He asked if I had ever played in the outfield. I said no, but that I'd be willing to give it a try. That made for a rough transition for me, learning a new position, for a new team, early in my career. I had hoped to be playing in the infield in Boston. I was told that there were 13 people in Boston who voted on whether to make that trade. Apparently, 11 voted no, but the two who voted yes were Zimmer and Haywood Sullivan, and they had enough power to make it happen. Basically, while the others didn't agree, they wanted Eckersley more than they wanted me.

DL: *Despite high expectations, you were never able to make your mark after leaving Boston. How frustrating was that?*

TC: It was frustrating. I've always wondered, "What if?" Had I stayed, maybe it would have been different. I always hit well at Fenway Park, and when I played with any regularity I hit over .300. There was all the superstar talk when I was traded to Cleveland, but there never seemed to be any stability for me once I left Boston. I ended up playing for seven different managers and four teams in my five seasons. I remember getting a game-winning hit off of Bill Lee in a game in Boston. Afterwards, I had reporters asking me why the Indians traded Eckersley for me and then never really gave me a chance. I know there were other guys involved in the deal too, but I was always told I was the guy Cleveland really wanted. Anyway, one of the reporters was asking about how they always said they were looking for a place for me, and was I tired of putting up with all of the lies. My answer got misunderstood, and the next day the headlines were saying, "Cox calls Torborg a liar." I had to explain to him that it wasn't true. Anyone who knew me understood that I was a team guy, that I'd never say anything like that. That was one part of my career that was frustrating.

DL: *What were some of your other experiences in Cleveland?*

TC: Well, they finally did trade Bell, after the '78 season, for Toby Harrah. When that happened, Torborg went to Gabe Paul, our GM, and said, "Let's put Toby at shortstop and move Cox back to third base." Heck, Buddy even told me he thought I was just as good a third baseman as he was. But even though I did eventually get some time there that season, Paul said, "No, let's leave him in left field." So that's where I was on opening day, which was in Boston. I remember that it was so cold that Bobby Bonds brought pantyhose in for everyone. He said it would keep us warm, so there we were, a lot of guys running around the clubhouse, wearing pantyhose. We lost anyway.

DL: *The Indians traded you to the Mariners after the '79 season. Tell us about 1980 in Seattle.*

TC: Darrell Johnson was the manager there, and he knew me from Boston. That was a good situation, and I was the opening-day third baseman. I got off to a good start, but then I dislocated my shoulder in Chicago later in the season. After that, Darrell was let go and Maury Wills replaced him as manager in August. That was the worst thing that ever happened to me. He was now the guy in control of my career, and we didn't hit it off. I wasn't the only player who had problems with him, either. To me, he was an absolute disaster as a manager. The following spring, in '81, I was released five days before we broke camp. That was bad timing for me, because most teams had their rosters set for the season already. Apparently, Wills didn't want me on the team, which is why I was let go. Soon thereafter, Dan O'Brien, the Mariners' president, asked me if I was willing to sign a minor league contract with them. He said that when they fired Wills, which he expected to happen, they would give me an opportunity to come back up to the big club. They did fire Wills and hired Rene Lachemann in his place, but the deadline was coming up for a possible players' strike so they didn't want to make a move at the time. It turned out that I never did get called up—they released me instead. I ended up in Toronto and had 50 at-bats there, hitting an even .300.

DL: *That was your last season in MLB. As you were only 27 years old at the time, did you hang around in the minor leagues before calling it a career?*

TC: The Mexico City Reds offered me good money, so I played down there in '82. I had thought it might work out in Toronto; they had just hired Bobby Cox, and along with being a Cox he was another Oklahoma boy. I took those as good signs. But they had signed Aurelio Rodriguez to play third, so I was released. Things went well in Mexico, and I figured maybe I'd get another shot the following year. Mexico City controlled my rights though and asked a lot for my contract. Nobody was willing to pay the price, so I sat out the '83 season. I probably should have tried to come back the next year, but never did. That was it for my pro career.

DL: *Do you ever think about what it would have been like to play in today's game, with all of the large contracts?*

TC: It's hard not to, really. I look at the first-round draft picks these days, and they're getting over a million dollars before they even prove they can play pro ball. I look back and think about how I was just an average player. I wasn't anything special, but I played five years and hit around .250. Had the money been the same when I played, I'd have five million in the bank right now. But I don't want to sound like I feel cheated. That's just the way it is.

DL: *To close, tell us a little about your work with the USSSA [United States Specialty Sports Association] Baseball Program.*

TC: I deal with over 2,000 teams, and it's very exciting to be a part of that. You know, when I left pro ball in many ways I was frustrated, and mad and wanted to blame someone for not having a better career. I didn't want to blame myself. But I got over that, and I'm proud to have had the opportunity. That's something I try to pass along to kids now. Every young man has the dream of making it to the Major Leagues, and the odds are long. Not many make it. But I let them know that I did, and hopefully they'll be able to live the dream, too.

CHRIS HOWARD

CHRIS HOWARD PITCHED FOR THE RED SOX IN 1994. A NATIVE OF NAHANT, MASSACHUSETTS, HOWARD APPEARED IN 44 BIG LEAGUE GAMES, 37 IN A BOSTON UNIFORM, FINISHING WITH A RECORD OF 2-0, AN ERA OF 3.13, AND ONE SAVE. THIS INTERVIEW TOOK PLACE IN FEBRUARY 2006.

David Laurila: *You played at the University of Miami before turning pro. Why Miami?*

Chris Howard: When I came out of high school, I was the Massachusetts Division II player of the year, but the only scholarship offer I had was from St. Leo's, in Florida. I had nowhere else to go, so my uncle Pat got letters of recommendation and sent them, along with my baseball résumé, to Miami. They ended up offering me a three-quarters scholarship, but I'd have still needed to come up with another eight grand. Then Miami Dade, which has a great junior college program, contacted me. I talked to their coach, Charlie Greene, who offered me a full scholarship and told me I'd have a chance to play there right away. That's what I decided to do, so I was actually at Miami Dade for two years before I played at Miami. I was the number one starter there, on a pretty good team. I believe we had eight guys drafted.

DL: *You were drafted by the Brewers in 1985 but didn't sign. Why?*

CH: I just felt it was too early for me to turn pro, and I wanted to stay in school. At that point, there were a lot of places I could have gone—a lot of good programs were interested—but Miami seemed like the best place for me. I played one year there and actually led the team in hitting, playing first base when I wasn't pitching. My roomie was Greg Vaughn, who went on to play for the Brewers and a few other teams.

DL: *You signed with the Yankees as a non-drafted free agent in 1986. As a Massachusetts kid, how difficult of a decision was that?*

CH: Being from here, I liked the Sox, but I was actually more of an A's fan. I used to play Strat-o-matic growing up and liked a lot of their players, like Vida Blue, Sal Bando, and Gene Tenace. I suppose that made it a little easier. People were saying I'd be drafted, but when I wasn't, I had an opportunity to sign with the Yankees and took it.

DL: *Where did you start your professional career?*

CH: I was in Oneonta for a month, and then they sent a few of us down to the Gulf Coast League. There were some really talented guys on that team, too, like Bernie Williams and Hensley Muelens. I wasn't pitching, though. I was playing in the outfield.

DL: *When did you start pitching again?*

CH: The next year, this was 1987, I was with the Prince William Cannons in the Carolina League, and I was still an outfielder. Toward the end of the season, I was messing around with some of the pitchers and bet them I could throw harder than they could. I was on the bullpen mound throwing when I noticed that Wally Moon, our manager, had walked over. I started apologizing, but he said it was okay, that I should keep throwing. Two days later, he came up to me and said he had talked to people in the organization, and I could start pitching a little if I was interested. A few days later, he brought me in from right field during a game against the Orioles. That's something you don't see much in pro ball, a guy being brought in from the outfield to pitch in the middle of an inning.

DL: *When did you become a full-time pitcher?*

CH: That off-season I had to decide, but it was really a no-brainer. As a hitter, I was a pretty average guy. I wasn't going to hit forty home runs or steal a lot of bases. It was the right decision, as I made the All-Star team that season as a reliever, pitching in the Carolina League. The following year, in 1989, I went to Double A Albany and pitched for Buck Showalter. Deion Sanders, who was a really good guy, was on that team.

DL: *You were released in May of 1990. What happened?*

CH: This is actually where my career gets kind of cool. I had a little shoulder trouble early in the year—this was in Albany—and they asked me to go down to Florida until I could get my arm healthy again. I was still just 23 years old but didn't want to go back down to A-ball, as I had nothing left to prove at that level. So they gave me a choice, and rather than report, I let them release me. I signed with the Indians a week later, but my arm was killing me, so I decided I was done. I figured I'd just go home and get a job like everyone else. I went back to Nahant and coached a Little League team.

DL: *What happened next?*

CH: Winter came, and some of the guys I used to train with in the off-season—Paul Sorrento, Kenny Hill, Jeff Juden, and Mike Pagliarulo—said I should come and work out with them. One day, they just came and picked me up; they wouldn't let me quit. I went with them, and my arm felt great so I called my agent and asked if he could find me a job somewhere. I wasn't sure what to expect, but the White Sox needed left-handers, so they offered me a Double A contract. When I got to spring training, I met Rick Peterson, who was their Double A pitching coach at the time. He really turned my career around.

DL: *How did he help you?*

CH: He said he had a few things he wanted to change on me, and that they were kind of drastic. He changed my mechanics, including shortening my leg-kick. I struggled at first but then put it together and had the year of my life. I went something like 6-1 with nine saves and an ERA just over 2.00. The changes really helped my curveball and my command. Before that, I tended to be wild in the strike zone, but my control really improved after working with him. He also helped me a lot with the mental part of the game. Baseball-wise, Rick Peterson pretty much changed my life.

DL: *Do you place a lot of importance on the mental aspect of the game?*

CH: Definitely. If you took 10 guys in pro ball and lined them up next to each other on mounds, without numbers, it would be hard to tell the Double A guys from the big leaguers. A lot of guys can throw 92 mph with good breaking stuff. But put them on a big league mound in front of 40,000 people . . . then you can tell the difference.

DL: *You made your big league debut in September of 1993. What do you remember about the game?*

CH: It was in Anaheim, the game was on ESPN, and I was nervous sitting in the bullpen. I knew I'd be coming in, and Greg Hibbard came up to me and said, "I know you're nervous, but even if you're not confident, act like you are." It's a long run in from the bullpen to the mound, and I remember telling myself to make sure I didn't trip over my feet on the way. I know I stepped off the mound a few times that inning, because I was shaking. You try not to be nervous, but you're out there doing something you worked your whole life for. You're at the point where this is it—this is the test you've been studying for. You don't want to fail, because maybe you'll throw five pitches and never get another chance.

DL: *Two weeks later, you got your first big league win.*

CH: That was against the Indians, in the second-to-last game played at the old Cleveland Stadium. What's funny is that before the game, I saw Jack McDowell being stretched out by a trainer and decided to try it myself. I had never been stretched like that before, and when I came into the game in the eighth inning my arm was killing me. The first batter I faced was Jim Thome, and he hit a rocket to deep center that Lance

Johnson ran down. Then, I walked two guys. Junior Ortiz was up next, and he lined a shot to third that Robin Ventura made a fantastic play on, grabbing the ball on a short hop and turning a double play. We scored in the top of the ninth, and I had a win even though I threw lousy.

DL: *Tell us about signing with the Red Sox the following season.*

CH: The White Sox took me off the roster in January. They did offer me a contract, but I turned it down. It was awesome to sign here and put on a Red Sox uniform. I had a great camp, but Tony Fossas beat me out and I got sent to Pawtucket on the last day of camp. In May, we switched places, he went down and I came up. My first day at Fenway, I walked out to the Monster and put my hand on it. I mean, I had been to the park many times, but being on the field is something else.

DL: *You appeared in 37 games that year before the strike ended the season prematurely. What were some of the highlights of your one season in a Red Sox uniform?*

CH: At one point, I retired something like 18 first batters, so that's one. I got a win against the Yankees, striking out Jim Leyritz and then getting another out before we scored in the bottom of the ninth. I got a four-inning save against Cleveland, not giving up a run. I probably made the best play of my career in another game against the Indians. Sandy Alomar was in a big slump, having gone hitless in a bunch of at-bats. He nailed one up the middle, and on my follow-through I was able to throw my glove up behind my back and snag it. I remember him throwing his bat in disgust and starting to swear in Spanish.

DL: *You gave up five home runs in your career. Were any of them notable?*

CH: I know I gave up back-to-back ones to Tino Martinez and Edgar Martinez in Seattle. Roberto Alomar hit one against me at Fenway on the only cut fastball I ever threw. Bo Jackson hit one against me, too. I played with him when I was in Chicago, and I told Bo once, "When you get to heaven, you owe God for that body."

DL: *Your big league career ended the following season. What happened?*

CH: I had been working out in Florida that winter and was driving back to Boston when I heard the news that the strike had ended. When I got home, I went to Wilmington to play catch with Jason Bere and heard something snap in my forearm. My fingers were tingling, and when I got to camp it was still a problem. I had strained a forearm muscle and ended up starting the season in extended spring training. I actually lived with Roger Clemens down there for about a month, while he was rehabbing. From there, I went to Pawtucket, and once my arm was better I got traded to Texas for Jack Voigt. I pitched four games for the Rangers, and the next spring ended up having cervical fusion surgery on my neck and missed the whole season. In '97, I was with the Mets' Double A team, and in '98 I went to camp with the Dodgers. I was throwing a side session with Mike Piazza and blew out my shoulder. That was it.

DL: *Any final thoughts?*

CH: Where I came from—not getting drafted, starting out as an outfielder, getting released, then making it to the big leagues—I did okay. Rick Peterson told us once that whether you have an ERA of 3-something, 4-something, or 5-something, four pitches in the entire season will have cost you that ERA. He said that you can't take those pitches back, so you want to do what you can to stop them from happening. His philosophy is that you throw every pitch like it's your last one. That's good advice, because someday it will be.

BILL LEE

BILL "SPACEMAN" LEE PITCHED FOR THE RED SOX FROM 1969 TO 1978. ONE OF THE MORE COLORFUL PERSONALITIES IN RED SOX HISTORY, LEE SPENT 14 SEASONS IN THE BIG LEAGUES, COMPILING A RECORD OF 119-90. THIS INTERVIEW TOOK PLACE IN JULY 2004.

David Laurila: *The author Tom Robbins was once quoted as saying, "You're never too old to enjoy a happy childhood." Does that describe Bill Lee?*

Bill Lee: I've never grown up and hope I never do. Let's put it this way: You can only be young once, but you can be immature forever!

DL: *Is that a description you'd tag yourself with?*

BL: It is right now. I'm currently serving a suspension for being immature in a Senior League game. One of my outfielders made a mental mistake—I hate mental mistakes—and I threw my glove at the ball when it came back to the infield. Even though it was one of my own teammates I was mad at, the opposition got all up in arms and started complaining. I asked what the big deal was, and one of them said I was being too serious—that it was "only a Sunday game." I answered back: "Did you come up here to look at the trees or to play baseball and try to beat me?"

DL: *I'm guessing they didn't like that response.*

BL: No, and their pitcher had already thrown at me three times, so they weren't being very polite. They had some things to say, but if you talk to me I'm talking back. Vernacular is in my DNA and I majored in "Comebacks 101." Anyway, I'm suspended now.

DL: *Some of the notable things you said and did were as a member of the "Buffalo Heads." Tell us about that infamous group from the mid-1970s Red Sox.*

BL: Fergie Jenkins started it. I was an original member, as were Rick Wise, Jim Willoughby, and Bernie Carbo. Carbo was the only non-pitcher. Alan Ripley joined in at one point—he was actually dating Darrell Johnson's daughter. Rick Krueger wanted to be a part of it, too. Don Zimmer, of course, played a big role in the whole thing.

DL: *I've read somewhere that Dick Pole was involved.*

BL: He wasn't, as he was on his way out by then. I do, however, remember being on the back of the bus with him knowing his days with the team were numbered. I was blasting the Eagles' "Already Gone" on the tape deck, and he was singing along with it—lustily. Zimmer thought it was me, but it was Dick.

DL: *Can you share a good Buffalo Heads story with us?*

BL: We went out the night before the last game of the season, once, and really had a time of it. I believe it was before Brooks Robinson's last game. Anyway, I remember Carbo was sleeping under the trainer's table, and Jenkins was asleep in the bullpen. I had run six miles that morning to get the poison out of my system, but I wasn't doing that great either.

DL: *This was the next day?*

BL: Yes. So the game starts, and Mike Paxton gets roughed up in the first inning. The bullpen phone rings, and they want Jenkins up! Why that was, I'll never know. The guy's a future Hall of Famer and they want him up in a meaningless game on the last day of the season? Hell, we just let him sleep—had the bullpen coach say he wasn't there. I don't think that was a very popular move, but that's what happened.

DL: *Let's talk about pitching and pitchers. We'll start with Oil Can Boyd.*

BL: The Can! Man, he's a great story. As a matter of fact, if they ever do Satchel Paige's life story, Oil Can should play the lead role. He's Satchel, incarnate! I was sort of a left-handed Paige, myself, but The Can was the real deal.

DL: *I brought up Oil Can because he threw such a variety of pitches, and from a lot of different arm angles. Warren Spahn, meanwhile, said you only need two: the one the hitter's looking for, and the one he's not. Where do you fit in?*

BL: I know it's a cliché, but pitching is like real estate: location, location, location. That and changing speeds. It takes guts and confidence to throw slow stuff over the plate, but you have to do it. Greg Maddux pitches like the Spahn quote. He gets hitters looking for one thing and freezes them with another. I think he looks at the plate differently than other pitchers. He looks at it in three dimensions, with a spatial relationship.

DL: *What did you throw and how hard?*

BL: I could get as high as 90, but I was mostly around 86. I could be pin-point at 85–86, so that's where I stayed most of the time. I threw a change and breaking ball, too—sometimes a cutter off my fastball. My change was like a screwball. I threw a 12-to-6 curve, sort of like Barry Zito does now. And I knew enough to stay away from guys who were hot.

DL: *Tell us about that.*

BL: There are times when you have to pitch around guys who are hitting everything. Derek Lowe, for instance, has the problem of not knowing when a hitter is dangerous. Sometimes, you can't attack every hitter—you have to stay away from the guys who are hot. Of course, sometimes the whole team is hot and then you need to get lucky. I once saw Catfish Hunter give up seven consecutive fly-outs to the warning track.

DL: *It sounds like you might be a believer in charts on hitters, more than pitching to your own strengths.*

BL: I believe you should know the hitters, but you should know them— not have to rely on charts. That's one of the problems with baseball. There are too many academics and slide-rule guys, and not enough baseball guys. Why use charts when you can use your mind? That's what your neurons are for.

DL: *If you could have pitched in another era, which would it be?*

BL: For selfish reasons, this one. There's a lot more money, and I could retire on St. Maartens and swim naked every day. I like to scare the fish.

DL: *And if it was a past era?*

BL: I'm reincarnated, so I've actually played in all of them already. I believe I used to be "Iron Man" McGinnity. I was Ed Delahanty, too.

DL: *You grew up in Southern California and were 11 years old when the Dodgers moved to Los Angeles. Tell us about your early days as a fan.*

BL: I followed the Hollywood Stars and Los Angeles Angels before the Dodgers came to town. My grandfather actually played for the Stars. And if you remember *A League of Their Own,* my aunt Annabelle played for them.

DL: *What about once the Dodgers got there?*

BL: I was a big Dodgers fan until I met Al Campanis. I wanted to pitch for them when I left Southern Cal, but he said I didn't have the stuff to make it in the big leagues. That was his opinion—and he was wrong.

DL: *Tell us about your days at USC.*

BL: Everyone on my mother's side of the family graduated from there. I went on a combo scholarship—academic and athletic—and have degrees in geography and physical education. My dad went to UCLA but said I should go to USC to play baseball. He said it's better to be a small fish in a great pond, and he was right.

DL: *You grew up in California but now call Vermont home. Why is that?*

BL: I'm a Vermont kind of guy. I sit here on the planet Earth, but I have to be sheltered somewhere. Up here by the Canadian border I have 300-year-old maples to do that for me. Put it this way: Nobody sees me. Wherever I am, I'm isolated. As a matter of fact, you could call me a compassionate misanthrope.

DL: *And a verbose one at that.*

BL: Like I said, vernacular is in my DNA. I quote Latin all the time. It's pretty neat to know Latin. I'm no expert, but I can read it.

DL: *What else do you read?*

BL: I've read everything. Right now, I'm reading de Maupin, an essayist from France. I like Nathaniel Hawthorne, John Steinbeck, Kurt Vonnegut, Carl Hiaasen. Hemingway's Nick Adams stories—I love those. You mentioned Tom Robbins—I really like his early stuff—what a narrator! Richard Brautigan and I are kindred spirits. *Trout Fishing in America* is on my bookshelf.

DL: *What about music?*

BL: I love good music—all kinds of music—everything from Aaron Copland to Led Zeppelin. I love the blues, jazz, Hank Williams, Jr. I like Hank Williams III, too. I've heard he's always shit-faced like his grandpa, but the songs are good. I like Little Feat, Warren Zevon. I listen to *Carmina Burana* when I need a pick-me-up. Don Henley is one of America's great poets. I listen to everything.

DL: *Have you known many people in the music industry?*

BL: I used to hang out with Zevon. George Thorogood and I are friends. I knew the Eagles—I lived "Hotel California"! Back in the seventies, I lived on the same street as Steve McQueen and Ali McGraw. Neil Young was there, too. Cheech Marin and I played basketball together. Trick-or-treating in that neighborhood was quite interesting!

DL: *Let's jump back to baseball. Who are some of the best teammates you had, and some of the smartest?*

BL: Ben Oglivie did the *New York Times* crossword puzzle faster than anyone I've ever seen. He should have become a GM. Mario Guerrero was a great guy. Jim Willoughby is a computer whiz now—he really turned his life around. I'm still in contact with guys like Carbo and Fergie.

DL: *You gave up your share of home runs. Tell us about the two that you hit.*

BL: The first one cost me the ballgame. I came in with us behind and homered off Cleveland's Ray Lamb to tie it up but then gave up a run and lost. The winning run scored on an inning-ending double-play, believe it or not. The infield fly rule was called on a pop-up to short left, and the ball ended up ricocheting off of Ben Oglivie and all hell broke loose. There was a lot of confusion and the run counted even though the other base runners were out.

EDITOR'S NOTE: Lee remembers this as a non-sequential triple play, but *Retrosheet.org* has it recorded as a double play. The game was played on September 11, 1972.

DL: *Do you remember the other one?*

BL: The other came when I was playing for Montreal. I should have had three, as I hit a triple at Fenway Park that should have been an inside-the-park homer. Eddie Popowski was coaching third, but he was too short to pick up as I was rounding third, so I held up. Third base coaches should be taller.

DL: *Who were the best hitting pitchers you played with?*

BL: Gary Peters could really hit, but Ken Brett was even better. He had a beautiful swing. Someone with an ugly swing that could hit was Luis Tiant. Guys like Oil Can and me swung at everything and tried to hit every ball out of the park—and didn't. I did, however—and this should be duly noted—hit .348 for the Expos in my last year. They thought so highly of that that they released me!

DL: *What are your thoughts on the demise of the Montreal franchise?*

BL: It's a travesty to humanity. Greed and corruption are the reasons behind it, and the only way to save the world is through baseball. Had there been a franchise in Iraq, most of the problems with Saddam could have been avoided. Baseball did the world a great justice by putting a team in Montreal, and now they want to take it away. It's wrong.

DL: *Give us your opinion on Fenway Park.*

BL: It's a jewel of a park. The new ownership is doing just fine fixing it up. They should have the Boston Pops play there every night, though.

DL: *Are there any other ballparks you're fond of?*

BL: I loved Ernie Harwell and Tiger Stadium. I remember climbing the screen behind home plate after a game once to retrieve a ball. The broadcast booth was right there, and I could hear Ernie doing the post-game show—and see him looking at me in amazement. I have another good memory of Tiger Stadium, too—from 1972. We had just lost the pennant on the last weekend of the season, and I got caught up in the crowd leaving. A bunch of Tigers fans recognized me and said not to look so downtrodden, that I should celebrate with them instead. I thought, "What the hell," and the next thing I knew I was 35 miles north of the city partying with a bunch of Detroit fans. I'm not sure how happy Eddie Kasko would have been had he known.

DL: *Who hit the longest home runs off of you?*

BL: Frank Howard hit one off the clock in RFK Stadium against me that I think I jumped for. It kept rising though, and rising . . . and finally stopped when it hit something. Richie Allen hit one into the upper deck at Comiskey Park that is still going. I jumped for that one, too.

DL: *The one you gave up to Tony Perez in 1975 is well documented, but what else is memorable about that game? I assume there were other pitches and other plays that stand out.*

BL: As for the pitch to Perez: I shouldn't have thrown it. But the double play we didn't turn right before that was huge! [Don] Zimmer moved [Denny] Doyle, and that cost us. [Johnny] Bench had been going the other way against me, but you still have to have the second baseman in a position where he can turn two. That's what I remember. Bench played a big role in Game 2 of the Series, also.

DL: *Tell us about that.*

BL: There's no way I should have faced him after the long rain delay. I came back out, and he hit the double down the right-field line, which he said he was going to do! During the delay he was interviewed on national TV and told the reporter that he'd try to go the other way against me. And nobody who heard him say that thought it might be helpful to tell me?

DL: *What kind of manager would you make?*

BL: I'm a Dick Williams when it comes to managing. That's why I'm not doing it in the big leagues—they want touchy-feely guys these days. I'm critical when it comes to bad baseball, and a critic in his own time isn't respected. But I need to get old before I even worry about that stuff, anyway—I'm still a ballplayer. When I do get old, I know one thing: I'm going to wear a suit in the dugout like Connie Mack.

DL: *Last week, there was a bit of a dust-up between the Red Sox and Yankees. Having been involved in a few of those yourself, notably in 1976, do have any comments on Jason Varitek versus Alex Rodriguez?*

BL: Varitek had a golden opportunity to punch him right in the nose! Instead, he sees himself as a Sumo wrestler. Enough said!

DL: *With the Democratic Convention going on right now, perhaps we should introduce politics into the conversation. Is there anything you'd like to say on that subject?*

BL: We get the government we deserve. It's kind of like a rabbit. Someone says, "Here comes a rabbit," and by the time you look, it's gone. Mankind is just a blip on the screen. We're here now, but we're checking out soon. It's all solar energy versus oil, and then we're gone.

DL: *Any closing thoughts?*

BL: I live my life by serendipity and spontaneity, and I'm still playing baseball here on the planet Earth. That's it.

BILL MONBOUQUETTE

BILL MONBOUQUETTE PITCHED FOR THE RED SOX FROM 1958 TO 1965. A NATIVE OF MEDFORD, MASSACHUSETTS, MONBOUQUETTE HAD A NO-HITTER AND A 20-WIN SEASON IN A BOSTON UNIFORM ON HIS WAY TO COMPILING A CAREER RECORD OF 144-112 OVER 11 BIG LEAGUE SEASONS. THIS INTERVIEW TOOK PLACE IN JUNE 2004.

David Laurila: *Let's start with something unique. In 1965, Satchel Paige came out of retirement to pitch one game at the age of 60 [his actual date of birth has long been debated—some feel he may have been older]. You opposed him on this day and struck out in your only at-bat against him. Tell us about that.*

Bill Monbouquette: I'll say this: He had better swings off me than I did against him. He had a lot of motion and surprisingly still threw pretty hard—probably in the mid-eighties. The Athletics had him sitting on a rocking chair in the bullpen, and it was a treat for the fans to see him. I remember Tony Conigliaro saying, "I'll hit one so far against that old so-and-so," but in three innings, Yaz got the only hit off him!

DL: *You weren't known as a good hitting pitcher, but you did have one triple in your career. Do you remember it?*

BM: Of course. It was in Chicago, against John Buzhardt. I blooped the ball over the first baseman's head, and it spun toward the grandstand and rolled into the corner. As I roared into the bag, our third base coach, Billy Herman, actually turned his back on me. I asked him, "What are you doing?" He just shook his head and said, "I can't believe this!"

DL: *You grew up in Medford. Tell us about your early days as a baseball fan.*

BM: The Braves were still here, and it was them that I followed—not the Red Sox. I used to be part of what they called "the knothole gang." We'd pay 10 cents to sit up in the left-field pavilion. The players looked like ants from up there!

DL: *Those would have been the days of Jackie Robinson and the Brooklyn Dodgers.*

BM: Yes. I remember my uncle taking me to see the Dodgers play.

DL: *And then, later, you were with the Red Sox when they finally integrated. What are your memories of Pumpsie Green?*

BM: I grew up in a section of Medford that was pretty "colored." That added to the disappointment I felt with the segregation we faced. I remember being in spring training when Pumpsie couldn't stay in the same hotel with us or always eat in the same restaurant. I didn't like that. I remember talking to him about it. He was such a great guy, and I felt bad about how things were.

DL: *Earl Wilson threw a no-hitter in 1962, becoming the first black pitcher to throw one in the American League. You were his teammate when that happened.*

BM: Yes, and he homered in that game, too. Unlike me, Earl could really hit. He threw hard, too, probably close to 100 mph. His command and location weren't that good when he was here. Later on, after he joined the Tigers, he became more of a pitcher and less of a thrower.

DL: *And, of course, you threw a no-hitter that season, yourself. What are your memories of that?*

BM: I remember that I hadn't won a game for a while, and we were flying to Chicago for the game. I was in the back of the plane, doing a crossword puzzle, and the stewardess asked me, "How are you doing?" I told her that things hadn't been going so great on the field, and she said, "I think you'll pitch a no-hitter tonight." It's kind of funny thinking about her saying that and it actually happening. I guess that game is the highlight of my career.

DL: *You played with Earl Wilson in both Boston and Detroit. You also played with Al Kaline and Denny McLain in Motown. Tell us about them.*

BM: Kaline could do everything, and he never made a mistake. He was a model player, and if a kid ever wanted to copy someone's swing, his would have been a good one. He wasn't flashy, but you sure wanted him on the team. He was a classy individual.

DL: *McLain's reputation was different.*

BM: I actually roomed with him, and while he wasn't always well-liked by everybody, I never had a problem with him, myself. I'll say this, he could pitch. One thing I remember is that he could maintain his stuff for nine innings—he was throwing just as well at the end of the game as he was at the start.

DL: *Tell us about Dick Radatz.*

BM: Dick was probably the best reliever I ever saw. He had great command and velocity, and I remember him once striking out Roger Maris, Yogi Berra, and Johnny Blanchard on nine pitches. I'd love to see some of today's guys hit off of him.

DL: *Why is that?*

BM: Because he was so intimidating. You didn't want to jump out over the plate against him, that's for sure. He was like Bob Gibson or Stan Williams—not afraid to knock you down.

DL: *I assume he saved more than a few games for you?*

BM: Oh, yes. I used to wait on the mound for him when he came in to relieve me. He was nicknamed "the Monster," because he was such a physically imposing man, so I'd hand him the ball and say, "If you don't get them, I'll kick your ass!" He'd snarl at me and say, "Just get upstairs and have a Bud waiting for me; I'll be right up!" I did, of course, and he usually was!

DL: *One of Radatz's claims to fame is that he dominated Mickey Mantle. Were there any guys you always seemed to get the best of, for whatever reason?*

BM: I did pretty well against Mantle, myself. I'm not sure why. Tony Oliva was another. He was a hell of a hitter, but I usually got him out.

DL: *What about guys who had your number?*

BM: Leon Wagner wore me out. It seemed like he knew which pitch was coming every time I faced him. Harvey Kuenn and Bobby Richardson were tough outs for me, too. They were smart hitters who didn't try to do too much with the ball.

DL: *You ended your career in New York, just as Mantle was finishing his. Tell us a little about "the Mick."*

BM: Mickey was a wonderful guy. He would do anything for you, and a lot of people don't realize that he was actually pretty humble—even shy. As for on the field, what a player! He was so strong. I remember him once being so mad after striking out that he bashed his arms against a wall in the dugout, and the whole place shook! He was fast, too, before he hurt his knees. I think he could have stolen 100 bases in a season if he wanted to.

DL: *Mickey had a reputation as a guy who liked the night life.*

BM: I guess so. I never went out with him myself. One thing, though, he was always ready at game time. Someone asked him once: "What do you do with a guy who was out all night and says he's too sick to play?" His response was: "You grab him by the collar and say, 'Don't mess with my money!'" You see, money wasn't so big in those days, and World Series shares meant a lot. Mickey liked to have fun, but he was serious about winning.

DL: *In your opinion, who was better: Mantle or Willie Mays?*

BM: I think I have to go with Mays, but health plays a part in that. He stayed healthy for much of his career, while Mickey didn't. Willie is probably the best all-around player I've seen. Ted Williams may have been a better hitter, but when it came to doing everything well, Mays was the man. He was sure exciting to watch. Pitching against him in the All-Star game was a thrill.

DL: *Ted was still here when you broke in. Talk a little about him.*

BM: When I was just starting out, Ted was watching me warm up and said: "This guy can throw strikes." There's a little extra meaning hearing that from someone like Ted, so I felt pretty good about it. Later on, we got pretty close. We used to joke around in the outfield, shadowboxing and stuff like that. We fished together in New Brunswick. You know how he liked to fish.

DL: *Ted was replaced in left field by Carl Yastrzemski. What can you tell us about Yaz?*

BM: He was obviously a great ballplayer. I had a run-in with him early in his career. I was a veteran by then, and Yaz was going through a rough stretch. He was getting frustrated and people were booing him, especially when he didn't run everything out as hard as he should have. That made it even worse for him, and he said something in the dugout that I didn't appreciate. I followed him into the tunnel and told him: "They run better ballplayers than you out of this town!" It's funny to look back and think that I could say something like that to Yaz, but at the time I thought it needed to be said. It's a veteran's responsibility to make sure young guys play the game the right way, and maybe what I said helped him. There's no doubt, he had a hell of a career.

DL: *Say a little more about that—playing the game the right way.*

BM: When things aren't going well, you have to work even harder. Let's put it this way, it's not how many times you get knocked down, it's how many times you get up.

DL: *Do you think today's players treat the game with the same respect you did?*

BM: That's a good question. I know one thing: In my day, pitchers wouldn't put up with a guy showboating after a home run. No, sir. They'd end up with a ball in their ear the next time they came up to bat—and they knew that. These days, even in the rookie leagues, guys are slapping hands and carrying on after a home run. There's an old saying about acting like you've been there before. Maybe I'm old-fashioned, but that's the way the game should be played.

DL: *Some people claim that you're responsible for Dick Stuart's nickname, "Dr. Strangeglove." Is that true?*

BM: It's not, actually. I did say one funny thing about Dick, though. In 1963, the year I won 20 games, I received the Emil Fuchs award. The plaque itself was very heavy, and when it was handed to me I remarked that it felt like Stuart's glove. That brought a big laugh. I don't want to say anything bad about Dick, though. He was a great guy—one of the real characters in the game. He did take a lot of grief for his defense. I remember once after he struck out, he was getting booed walking back to the dugout and a few fans tossed paper airplanes at him. He reached up and caught one, and the boos turned into a big ovation. That was pretty funny, too.

DL: *Tell us about getting traded from Boston to the Tigers. Did you resent that?*

BM: It was two days after the 1965 season. The Tigers needed pitching, and the Red Sox needed an outfielder and a first baseman. That's just the way it works. I told Dick O'Connell that there were no hard feelings. I enjoyed my years here.

DL: *Is there anything else you'd like to say about your years in Boston?*

BM: This is a great baseball city, and it was an honor to wear a Red Sox uniform. That about sums it up.

JOHNNY PESKY

JOHNNY PESKY WAS AN INFIELDER FOR THE RED SOX FROM 1942 TO 1952 AND THE TEAM'S MANAGER IN 1963 AND 1964. DUBBED "MR. RED SOX," PESKY IS A MEMBER OF THE RED SOX HALL OF FAME AND IS STILL EMPLOYED BY THE FRANCHISE AT THE AGE OF 86. THIS INTERVIEW TOOK PLACE IN MAY 2004.

David Laurila: *Your recent biography, written by Bill Nowlin, is titled* Mr. Red Sox. *Tell us what it means to have such a title bestowed upon you.*

Johnny Pesky: It's flattering, of course. I'm not sure if I warrant it— others deserve it more than I do. I was never very impressed with my own ability, but I have been around for a long time. I'm certainly proud to have been with the Red Sox for so much of my life.

DL: *What does it mean to put on a Red Sox uniform? Have you ever spoken to young players about that?*

JP: I have, many times. The team has always treated me, and my family, with respect. That's important, and it's an honor to be a part of the Red Sox. I tell young players that. Of course, that goes for other uniforms, too—you should be proud to represent your team. Players should have more loyalty than they do these days.

DL: *You've certainly been as loyal as they come.*

JP: And I'm certainly not planning on going anywhere. Nobody else would even take me anymore, so I'm staying right here!

DL: *Tell us about signing with the Red Sox.*

JP: Back then, you could sign with anybody—there was no draft yet. There were a number of teams interested in me, and some offered more money than Boston. My mother and father wanted me to sign with the Red Sox, though, because their scout brought her flowers when he came to the house—and bourbon for my father. They were immigrants, and even though it was the Depression, that was more important than the extra money. I'm glad it worked out the way it did.

DL: *You were born on the day Babe Ruth played his last game in a Red Sox uniform. Is there anything symbolic in that?*

JP: Well, I don't think you want to compare the two of us. It sounds like a memorable date in history, but I was too young at the time to know what it meant.

DL: *Most people have read about your friendships with Ted Williams, Dom DiMaggio, and Bobby Doerr. Who else were you close to in the game?*

JP: There have been many, but the guys you just named are my people. They're the ones I came up with, and we spent a lot of time together, both during and after our careers. Others were close: [Dave] Ferriss, [Tex] Hughson, [Mel] Parnell—but good things happen in your life that you don't forget. My friendships with Ted, Dom, and Bobby are a part of that.

DL: *What about guys you didn't get along with?*

JP: Some people think I didn't like Dick Stuart. That wasn't true. I actually liked Dick—I just didn't like that he couldn't catch the ball. There were other guys, like Allie Reynolds, who were tough and mean. I got along with Billy Martin, for instance. Guys like him and Reynolds were just tough competitors. I got along with [Mickey] Mantle, too.

DL: *Talk about some of the guys on the current Red Sox team.*

JP: I call [David] McCarty "Mr. Harvard," because he's such a smart guy. I know he went to Stanford, but I call him that anyway. [Curt] Schilling likes to get on me about Ted, saying how he'd get the best of him if he played now. I tell Schilling that Ted would hit him—hit him hard. I point to the Williams seat up in right field, and tell him Ted would have taken him even deeper than that! [David] Ortiz and [Manny] Ramirez both like to kid me a lot. They also ask me about my era. Ortiz is a wonderful boy—a pussycat. Manny is very affectionate. He hugs me all the time and kisses me. He calls me "Poppy." Ortiz and [Kevin] Millar have caught on to that, so now they're starting to hug me all the time, too. I might have to start wearing a skirt in the clubhouse!

DL: *What about Pokey Reese?*

JP: What a glove. Defensively, he's one of the elite second basemen of all time, but we need him at shortstop right now—and he's playing great. When Nomar [Garciaparra] gets back, not many balls will get through the middle of the infield with them out there. That's for sure.

DL: *You were close to Shea Hillenbrand when he was here.*

JP: Great kid, great demeanor. He worked as hard as anybody—maybe even tried too hard at times. Jimy [Williams] had me helping him, and after every workout he'd thank me. I'd tell him: "You don't have to thank me—this is my job!" Great work ethic. As you probably know, I hated to see him leave.

DL: *You were in Detroit, late in your career, when Al Kaline broke in. Tell us about Kaline.*

JP: He was a great kid who became a great player. I was a veteran, so the manager, Fred Hutchinson, had me work with him. He was only 18 but very mature for his age. I'd talk to him about what was happening on the field, and he'd take it all in. Some young players aren't good listeners, but he was—he really wanted to learn. Along with Carl Yastrzemski and Jim Rice, he might have had the best work habits of anyone I've seen.

DL: *Tell us about Yaz.*

JP: Wonderful player. Next to Ted, he might be the best I've been around. Not only could he hit, he played different positions and played them well. He worked hard and made himself into one of the best, not only here, but in the game.

DL: *Talk a little about pitchers. You mentioned how Reynolds was tough and mean, and he certainly threw hard. I'm guessing Bob Feller and Dick Radatz are among the hardest throwers you've seen.*

JP: They are. Let me tell you about Radatz. I was managing in Triple A when he was coming up, and in those days guys didn't want to be relief pitchers. But I saw the way he could throw the ball and told him that's what I wanted him to do. He didn't like the idea at first, but I convinced him that it would work out, and it did. For about four years, he was as good as anybody I've seen. He'd just throw the ball by people.

DL: *You were almost impossible to strike out—only 218 times in your 10-year career. Talk about how you learned bat control and how that has changed since your era.*

JP: Heinie Manush had a big part in that. He was my manager when I started out, and he called me over one day and suggested that I choke up on the bat. He didn't try to force anything on me, just explained that big league pitchers can knock the bat right out of your hands. I wasn't that big of a guy, so I wasn't going to hit many home runs, anyway. He had been watching me play pepper and saw that I controlled the bat pretty well that way. Very few guys do it now—there's too much money in hitting home runs—but it's foolish not to listen to advice from guys who have been successful and know the game.

DL: *You also ran very well, but in those years teams didn't run as much. Have you ever thought about how many bases you'd steal if you played today?*

JP: That's a good question. I'm not sure if I know the answer, but it's true we didn't run much when I played. But you have to remember that I hit in front of Ted. We didn't want me getting thrown out, because as often as not he'd knock me in. And if I did steal second, then they'd just walk Ted—we didn't want to take the bat out of his hands.

DL: *Ted was reportedly almost traded for Joe DiMaggio at one time. What was the talk in the clubhouse when that rumor surfaced? Did the players discuss it?*

JP: I've never believed that trade came close to happening. And we didn't really talk about it at the time, no. In those days, you just accepted things and took them for what they were. We didn't pay it much mind.

DL: *You were traded late in your career. What was that like?*

JP: Boston was the only place I played that I really loved, so I couldn't say I liked it. But there were young guys coming up, and I knew how the game worked, so I understood it. Ted didn't understand it, though. He wondered why the hell they would trade me.

DL: *Let's talk a little about Ted. Was "little needle-nosed shortstop" a compliment coming from him?*

JP: Yes, it was a term of endearment. Ted liked me and was a great friend. Back when I was sick—he was still healthy at the time—he called to check on me all the time. He'd shout into the phone: "When the hell are you going to get better?!"

DL: *Tell us about your days as a broadcaster and a little about the greats who have occupied the booth at Fenway, guys like Ken Coleman and Joe Castiglione.*

JP: I was more comfortable on the field than in the booth—I'll say that. I didn't mind the job, but I don't think I was very good at it. Guys like Coleman and Castiglione, they're good at it—they're wonderful. Someone else that's good is [Jerry] Remy. Of all the ex-jocks, he's the best going right now. I like [Dennis] Eckersley and [Jim] Rice, too. They're not as good as Remy, but I like hearing what they have to say.

DL: *There is talk that Tony Conigliaro's number may be retired by the Red Sox next year. There has been similar discussion of retiring yours. What are your thoughts on each?*

JP: Well, I'm not so sure about me. I like the idea for Tony. What happened to him was one of the saddest things I've ever seen. I was managing when he first came up—he was just a kid, like Kaline was. The first time I saw him in the spring, he really opened my eyes. I kept putting him on the field, and he just kept producing. What a great player he could have been.

DL: *Talk about your Navy years and wartime baseball, including base teams.*

JP: There were teams on the bases, yes. Some pretty good ones too, but the top priority was always to do your duty. That's why you were there. That was usually in the morning, and then later in the day you'd play ball. That was secondary, though. Our duties came first.

DL: *Tell us about the war ending and coming back to play.*

JP: Coming back was wonderful. We were all back: Ted, Dom, Bobby— all of us. And we played so well that season [1946]. Ferriss won 25 games, Hughson 20. Ted was hitting like he hadn't missed a beat. The war was over and we were together playing baseball. It was a wonderful time.

DL: *Talk about barnstorming, including the Negro Leagues. I assume you were a part of that?*

JP: Yes. Birdie Tebbetts put together some good groups that I was with. The Negro Leagues and the House of David were a part of barnstorming. You know, some of the guys on those Negro League teams were great ballplayers: Satchel Paige . . . Josh Gibson was wonderful. It was a lot of bull that they couldn't play in the Major Leagues. It was just the way things were, so we didn't really think about it a lot at the time, but it was a lot of bull.

DL: *We spoke to Leigh Montville recently, and he talked about how Ted said the same thing, that he just didn't think about it that much.*

JP: We didn't, and it was a shame. There were so many good players, and they were no less human beings than we were. I remember when Larry Doby broke in with Cleveland. Back in those days, you left your glove on the field and when he came out for his, Ted jogged by and said, "Good luck, kid." A lot of guys weren't like that, and I think that probably meant a lot to Doby. And Doby could play, too—do everything.

DL: *Did you ever hit against Paige?*

JP: Yes, both when we barnstormed and again when he came to the Majors. He was pretty old by then, so he didn't throw as hard—lots of motion, though. I remember finally getting a hit off of him. He was good.

DL: *Talk about some of the men who have managed here, including Grady Little.*

JP: I think Grady did a good job, and I stood behind his decision last year. He had the best pitcher in the game look him in the eye and say he could get it done. You have to go with your best, but in baseball you can't control everything that happens—luck plays a part. [Jorge] Posada tied the game with a bloop hit. There's nothing you can do about that. People always want to find somebody to blame, and that's what happened with Grady.

DL: *Some people blamed you for 1946.*

JP: Yes, and for a short time I was sensitive to that—but I got over it. Fans have a right to their opinions, whether you're talking about 1946 or last year. But it's important to accept responsibility, and I was a part of that play—sure. Could I have thrown him out? I don't know, but I think I would have needed a gun. Something a lot of people don't remember is that Dom got hurt and was out of the game when that happened. With him in center field, I don't think [Enos] Slaughter tries to score.

DL: *Back to managers for a moment: Why, in your opinion, did Joe McCarthy pitch Denny Galehouse in 1948?*

JP: I wish I knew, but you didn't question managers much back then. He pitched him, and things didn't work out. Connie Mack pitched Howard Ehmke in the [1929] World Series instead of Lefty Grove—and ended up looking like a genius. You look good when it works and bad when it doesn't. Baseball is really "the perfect imperfect game." You see new things every day. Sometimes, they go your way, and sometimes they don't.

DL: *There certainly have been some tragic moments in Red Sox history.*

JP: Yes, and if I could explain it, I would. Fate is a God-given thing. Just like He gives you your good looks and a brain, things happen out on the field, too—and you can't always understand why they play out like they do. Joe Morgan's ball fell in front of Fred Lynn in '75; [Ed] Armbrister wasn't called out for interference in that same Series. All you can do is keep playing. This year's team has a chance. We have better pitching than last season. We're good enough to win it.

DL: *Tell us a little about your wife. You've been together for a long time.*

JP: Our 60th anniversary is coming up in January. She's still a pretty little girl. I met her when I was in the Navy during the war, and she accepted that I was a ballplayer. When I went off to spring training for the first time, I didn't think she'd be there when I got back. But there she was, waiting for me.

DL: *Any closing thoughts before I let you go?*

JP: I've had a good life. I've had wonderful friends, a wonderful family. The Red Sox have always treated me fabulously, and that means a lot to me. Yes, it's been a good life—and I'm not done yet.

DL: *We hope you have many more years in the game, Johnny. Thanks for taking the time.*

JP: I hope I gave you enough to work with. Now, I better get back to the clubhouse. There's a game to get ready for.

RICO PETROCELLI

RICO PETROCELLI WAS AN INFIELDER FOR THE RED SOX FROM 1963 TO 1976. A TWO-TIME ALL-STAR AND A MEMBER OF THE RED SOX HALL OF FAME, PETROCELLI SPENT HIS ENTIRE 13-YEAR CAREER IN A BOSTON UNIFORM. THIS INTERVIEW TOOK PLACE IN DECEMBER 2004.

David Laurila: *What are your thoughts on the Red Sox' shortstop situation, including how Hanley Ramirez factors into it?*

Rico Petrocelli: First, we've been dealing with guys who are all good—Nomar, Cabrera, and Renteria. Ramirez looks like he'll be good too, but he's only played as high as Double A and this team is built to win now. You look at the older pitchers we have, like Schilling and Wells, and we're in position to go for it again. Any time you can get a proven veteran who's not too old, it makes sense and it certainly does here. As for the back-and-forth in the negotiations with Renteria, that's the way it works. Agents like to play teams off each other. The idea is to get what the player is worth.

DL: *What was your opinion of the Nomar trade when it happened, and is there any chance that he'd have re-signed had he not been dealt?*

RP: I wasn't surprised, I'll say that. I had been doing a radio show shortly before it happened and said he wasn't coming back. The first few years I think he enjoyed playing in Boston but then began growing tired of the attention and the media. Mo Vaughn had been the leader here, and when he left everyone thought Nomar would take on that role. That's not what he wanted, though. He just wanted to play and then go home.

DL: *Alex Rodriguez moved from shortstop to third base after going to the Yankees. Do you think the Red Sox would have considered playing him and Nomar together had he ended up here?*

RP: No, I don't think we were thinking that way at all. The thought was that we'd be getting the best shortstop in the league—why play him at third base? The plan was to simply move Nomar. It's funny, too, how it played out—not getting Rodriguez. I have to laugh, because in the past things like that would happen and it would turn out for the worst. But not this time.

DL: *It's well known that you moved from short to third during your career, but most people don't know you were originally a third baseman.*

RP: Well, I wasn't really a third baseman to begin with. When I signed, I had pitched and played in the outfield, too. But I was at third in spring training one year—this is when I was still in the minors—and because Frank Malzone only had a year or two left there were six or seven guys working out over there. Johnny Pesky and Eddie Popowski liked the idea of trying me at short, and that's how I ended up there.

DL: *Tell us about the switch from shortstop to third base in 1971.*

RP: The funny thing was that I had gotten stronger and gained weight, so the press had started saying the club should move me to third. Every time I didn't get to a ball, either to my left or to my right, they seemed to bring it up. And then, as it turned out, we had a chance to pick up Luis Aparicio. We had been shopping for a third baseman but apparently couldn't find one. So the club asked me about making the move if we could get Luis, and I said I was okay with it. I knew I'd end up there eventually, and Aparicio was obviously good. Moving was a good experience for me. Frank Malzone was very helpful in teaching the position, too. That made the transition easier.

DL: *You grew up in Brooklyn. Talk about baseball when you were growing up and who you rooted for.*

RP: Sports and baseball were fabulous back then. We had the three great teams in the city—the Dodgers, Yankees, and Giants. I loved the Dodgers and Ebbetts Field. They had a short wall like at Fenway, except theirs was in right field instead of left. There was a lot of hitting. And there were so many wonderful players: Mantle, Mays, and Snider in center field. Maris, Richardson, Campanella, Elston Howard—great baseball.

DL: *Tell us about signing with the Red Sox.*

RP: There wasn't a draft yet, and a lot of teams were interested. All of them scouted me, some as a pitcher. The Yankees and Mets were interested. So were Baltimore and Philadelphia. All of these teams were pretty close to home. But Boston seemed like the best place for me. Right after graduation, I was invited to work out by eight or nine teams, and the Red Sox were the first. Their scout had spent the most time—he was at all of my games. They treated me and my family well and made a good offer. The rest, as they say, is history.

DL: *You made your MLB debut in 1963, playing one game in late September. Tell us about that.*

RP: I came up for the last two or three weeks of the season. They wanted me to see what it was like, which is good for a young player. We were on the road for a while and then came home to play Minnesota. Pesky was the manager, and he came up to me one afternoon and said, "You're in there today." I'll never forget that.

DL: *What did you say when he told you?*

RP: I said, "Oh my God, Johnny!" My knees were knocking the first time I came up to the plate, I know that. Just going out to my position at shortstop—the field looked so big, and everyone in the stands seemed to have their eyes on me. Heck, I was only 19 or 20 years old at the time.

DL: *What do you remember about your first at-bat?*

RP: Guys in the dugout were wishing me luck, saying things like, "Come on, rookie," and "Come on, kid." I was really pumped standing in the on-deck circle, concentrating on getting a good pitch and just letting it go if I did. Lee Stange was pitching, and I hit it good enough—a high fly off the wall in left. I remember running hard, with my head down, and the first base coach yelled to keep going. I never even looked for the ball. I slid into second—a pop-up slide—and then started looking around to see where it was. It would have been pretty embarrassing if the ball had been caught, but the crowd was cheering so I knew it hadn't been. Wow, what a thrill that was.

DL: *What else do you remember about the game?*

RP: I know I made an error! And Harmon Killebrew homered after that, too. It should have been the last out of the inning. I felt pretty bad about it, because Dick Stuart was battling Killebrew for the home run title at the time. Stuart had actually been talking about it before the game, joking that our pitchers would throw it down the middle against Killebrew because they didn't like him. And Killebrew ended up hitting three in that game!

DL: *On opening day in 1967, your second base partner was Reggie Smith. Why was that?*

RP: Mike Andrews got hurt in spring training, and we needed someone to fill in until he came back. Reggie had been a shortstop when he was coming up—boy, he had a powerful arm—so he volunteered to give it a try. He really got taken out at second in that game, too. I shoveled the ball to him, and Tommy McCraw came into him hard—it was a clean slide—and sent him completely head over heels. That was enough second base for Reggie. We didn't want him to get killed.

DL: *Like in '67, we played the Cardinals in the World Series this year. As someone who's been a part of Red Sox Nation for more than 40 years, tell us what this past October meant to you. Did you think you'd live to see us win it all?*

RP: My feeling was almost like we had been released from bondage. There have been so many disappointments, and every time the team lost the fans did, too. And having once been a part of it, I still link to it. The organization has gotten ripped when we've fallen short, and in a way, every time the team is called losers, we as fans are being called losers, too. I know that baseball isn't life and death, but there's a lot of emotion and passion—especially here with the Red Sox. So, in many ways, it was like being set free.

DL: *You hit more than 200 homers in your career. How many would you have hit in today's game?*

RP: That's a question that can't be answered. I strongly believe that you can't compare eras. You can't compare the 1940s to the 1980s, or the 1930s to the 1990s. The number of games has changed, the ballparks have changed—many things have changed. In this era, people like to say things like, "This guy's the greatest ever at this," or "This guy's the greatest ever at that." But how can you say that? You can't.

DL: *The mound was lowered prior to the 1969 season. How much did that change the game?*

RP: That was interesting. I didn't think it would make that much difference at the time, but it definitely increased the hitting. The balls seemed the same coming in—guys like McLain and Palmer certainly got it up there just as quickly—but maybe movement was affected a little. It was hard to say, but the change did what it was meant to do.

DL: *What was your opinion of the designated hitter rule when it was introduced in 1973, and what do you think now?*

RP: I liked it at the time but not so much anymore. It gave older big-name guys a chance to stay in the game, which helped attendance. And as a player, you looked at it as a way to maybe lengthen your own career. But after a while, it began to change, with younger guys DHing more and more. So I guess I'm pretty much against it now. The game was invented for pitchers to hit. It was meant for them to be players, not just pitchers.

DL: *What are your memories of the 1976 deal that would have brought Joe Rudi and Rollie Fingers to the Sox in midseason, only to have it overturned by Commissioner Bowie Kuhn, "in the best interests of the game"?*

RP: Vida Blue was going to go to the Yankees, too, in a separate deal. I remember it well. We were playing in Oakland at the time, and there had been rumors that something might happen. The announcement was made in the middle of the game, and Rudi and Fingers actually came over to our clubhouse. I had come out of the game early, so I was there when they walked in. Somewhere, there are photos of them wearing Red Sox caps and uniform tops, and I'm in the picture with them. But then, the next day, Kuhn vetoed the deal, so they never played with us. It was disappointing.

DL: *Can you say a little more about that?*

RP: Well, Fingers was the best closer in the game, and Rudi was an all-star. We'd have been getting them without giving anyone up, so we were obviously excited and pumped about it. We weren't expecting the commissioner to step in and block the deal, that's for sure.

DL: *Do you think he did the right thing?*

RP: Not really. A deal is a deal, and it didn't seem right for him to block it. Don't get me wrong, teams shouldn't be able to dominate because they can afford to get whatever players they want. But at the time, I didn't agree with it.

DL: *What about in today's game? Should the commissioner invoke "the best interests of the game" in certain situations?*

RP: Quite possibly. Now, we're dealing with things like drugs, which is different. In cases like that, I'd say he probably should.

DL: *Your career ended in 1976 at the age of 33. Tell us about that.*

RP: I got beaned by Jim Slaton, which damaged my inner ear. That's part of the game, and something you accepted back then. It was just one of those things where I never saw the ball, and it caught me flush above the ear. I wasn't quite the same after that and decided to hang it up.

DL: *You were teammates with Tony Conigliaro; what are your memories of him?*

RP: We were good friends. We were in spring training together in 1964, and he had the most unbelievable spring I've ever seen. If he would have stayed healthy, he could have hit at least 400 home runs—maybe even 500. He had amazing power.

DL: *You had good power, yourself. What was the longest home run you ever hit?*

RP: It was in Detroit at Tiger Stadium. The center-field fence there was 440 feet, and I hit one just to the left of center into the upper deck. I just got it all and was kind of amazed that I hit it that far, to tell the truth.

DL: *Who were the hardest throwers you faced?*

RP: Nolan Ryan, easily. Vida Blue was up there, too, and so was Dean Chance. J.R. Richard was over in the National League, but I saw him in the All-Star game. He threw really hard, and the movement on his ball was incredible. Sam McDowell in Cleveland was another one.

DL: *You faced Luis Tiant when he was with the Indians, before he hurt his arm, and then played with him in Boston. Tell us about Luis.*

RP: He threw really hard early in his career, around 96. But he didn't have the good breaking stuff yet, and his slider wasn't as good. When he came here, he didn't throw quite as hard—still a good fastball, though—but he had a lot more stuff. And obviously, he was deceptive, the way he'd twist and turn in his wind-up. Off the field, he was a fun guy to be around. We used to pull a lot of pranks in the clubhouse. Tommy Harper and I would do things like fill a bucket with cold water and douse him while he was in the bathroom. We had to keep on our toes, though, because we knew Luis would get us back eventually.

DL: *Last question: When you're watching the game, do players ever remind you of guys you played with, or against?*

RP: Absolutely. When someone new comes around, your memory will go back and you think of someone with a similar game or style. It's that way with other sports, too. A LeBron James reminds you of Dr. J or Michael Jordan, or maybe Oscar Robertson. That was a guy I loved to watch—Oscar Robertson. When I was in high school, I saw him play in Madison Square Garden when he was at Cincinnati. I played a lot of basketball, myself. I was all-city and had a lot of scholarship offers, but realistically I probably wasn't tall enough to make it. So I chose baseball instead. And the Red Sox.

Shorter Views

JASON BERE

JASON BERE IS A NATIVE OF WILMINGTON, MASSACHUSETTS, WHO
SPENT 11 YEARS AS A BIG LEAGUE PITCHER. CURRENTLY WORK-
ING IN THE FRONT OFFICE FOR THE CLEVELAND INDIANS, BERE
WENT 71-65 FOR THE WHITE SOX, REDS, BREWERS, INDIANS,
AND CUBS FROM 1993 TO 2003. THIS IS AN EXCERPT FROM AN
INTERVIEW THAT TOOK PLACE IN DECEMBER 2005.

David Laurila: *What do you most remember about your first game pitching in Fenway?*

Jason Bere: Probably that I went up against Danny Darwin, and he took a no-hitter into the eighth or ninth. Mike LaValliere caught me that game—he has roots here, too—and he said to make sure not to look up. And he was right. Any direction I looked, there'd be someone I knew or recognized. And that's tough, because pitching is three hours of total concentration. But to pitch here was special. I used to sit in the bleachers as a kid, so it was incredible to be on that field. A lot of times, you'll hear guys say that it's just another game when they're playing in their hometown or against their old team, but those are just words. How can it not be different to pitch in Fenway when you grew up coming here?

DL: *Was that the biggest thrill in your career?*

JB: It was high on the list, but my Major League debut was bigger. To this day, that's the most nervous energy I've had in baseball. I remember getting called up. We were playing in Des Moines, and I had ten Ks in five innings when they told me that was it for the day. Guys were saying that I must be getting called up. Why else would they have pulled me early? After the game, our pitching coach said Skip wanted to see me. When I went in, he asked me how my arm felt. I told him it felt great. Then he asked if I could have gone a few more innings. I said sure, I could have done that. Then he asked if I thought I could go a few innings in Chicago on Thursday. I kind of knew it was coming, but it still floored me.

DL: *How about the game itself—were you pretty nervous?*

JB: Tuesday and Wednesday, I was with the big league team, and I felt fine. No butterflies. Thursday morning, I had breakfast with my family and girlfriend who had flown in for the game. I still felt fine. I was wondering when it was going to hit me. Before the game, I'm warming up and notice that Carlton Fisk is watching me. He tells me to not change anything, to just relax. I thought to myself, man, that's Carlton Fisk telling me that. But I still felt fine. Walking in from the bullpen to the dugout, I couldn't believe how good I felt. But then when I got to the mound and Ron Karkovice squatted behind the plate, suddenly I couldn't feel my legs! It felt like everyone in the stands was looking right at me, and from there the first inning was like a blur. I actually threw my first pitch for a strike . . . somehow. I ended up giving up a three-run homer to Mike MacFarlane with two out, but that probably actually helped me relax. It felt awful when he hit it, but I was able to settle in afterwards.

DL: *I understand that you have a pretty good story about a Porsche?*

JB: Growing up, a lot of guys like cars and I always wanted to get a Porsche someday. After I signed a free agent contract with the Cubs in 2001, I asked my financial advisor, and he said I could afford one. Of course, he also told me it wasn't a good investment. But I bought one anyway, and after waiting a long time for it, it finally got delivered to me in Chicago. The next day, we were playing in Milwaukee, and as it's only about 70 miles, the team let us drive there if we wanted. So I did, and the doorman at the Hyatt let me park it under the awning after the game. I then went to meet Jeff D'Amico for dinner and a few drinks, and told him about my new car. He decided he wanted to see it, so we walked back to the hotel. When we got there, it was gone, so I asked where it was. The doorman said the guy had come to pick it up. I asked, "What guy?" and he said that a guy had come out of the bar and said it was his, so he gave him the keys. At first, I thought it might be one of the guys on the team playing a joke on me, but it was getting pretty late and I realized that wasn't the case.

DL: *So, what happened?*

JB: A little while later, the front desk called and said the guy brought the car back and then left. Apparently, he had just taken it for a joyride. I said, "Wait, we were just down there talking about a stolen Porsche, and you let the guy leave?" So we had the car fingerprinted, and someone did end up confessing to taking it. But as the guy wasn't in possession of it, and there was no damage, there wasn't much we could do. With a brand new Porsche with maybe 100 miles on it, I'll admit that I felt a little violated by the whole thing.

TIM NAEHRING

TIM NAEHRING WAS AN INFIELDER FOR THE RED SOX FROM 1990 TO 1997 BEFORE AN ELBOW INJURY ENDED HIS CAREER AT THE AGE OF 29. CURRENTLY THE MINOR LEAGUE FIELD COORDINATOR FOR THE CINCINNATI REDS, NAEHRING PLAYED HIS ENTIRE CAREER IN A BOSTON UNIFORM, HITTING .282. THIS INTERVIEW TOOK PLACE IN JULY 2004.

David Laurila: *What was it was like playing in Boston?*

Tim Naehring: It was great. I'm very pleased to have been a part of it— the organization treated me very well. I'd have loved to play longer, but unfortunately it didn't work out that way.

DL: *What are some of your favorite memories from your career?*

TN: A few homers versus the Indians stand out, one of them in the playoffs. The 19th-inning game-winner was also memorable. My first Fenway home run was special, too. It was off David West, and getting a curtain-call from 35,000 people is an amazing feeling. Moments like that show you why Boston is such a great place to play.

DL: *Tell us about playing for "Walpole" Joe Morgan.*

TN: Joe was something. He really stuck with me—I owe a lot to him for that. I remember once, there was talk about whether we'd get champagne if we clinched the division. His response was: "I don't like anything sticky on my body. Once, when I was a kid, someone put a peanut butter sandwich down my back, and I didn't like it. So I don't really care one way or the other about the champagne." That pretty much told us where he stood, so we decided against getting any. That was typical Morgan.

DL: *You played in Pawtucket prior to coming to Boston. Tell us about those years.*

TN: My first day at McCoy Stadium was actually quite unique. I drove up from A-ball in Lynchburg, and when I got to the hotel they wouldn't let me check in. I had to come right to the ballpark with my luggage still in the car, and when I arrived we were between games of a doubleheader. They put me right in the lineup, and my first AB was against Ron Guidry, who was down on a rehab stint! He struck me out the first time, but I doubled later, which was quite a thrill.

DL: *I assume you enjoyed your time there?*

TN: I remember my first few nights, meeting Ben [Mondor] and Lou [Schwechheimer]. They knew I wasn't making much money, and really took care of me. That's how they operate. For instance, when I went to Las Vegas to play in the Triple A All-Star game, Ben hooked me up with tickets to a show. Down in Pawtucket, they care about you as a person first and a player second. They're special people.

DL: *And prior to that, you played on the Cape.*

TN: Yes, so I knew what Red Sox baseball meant to New England. Signing with Boston was great, and I was lucky to move pretty quickly through the system. But unfortunately, my career wasn't as long as I'd have liked due to the injury.

DL: *You blew out your arm on a throw from third.*

TN: Yes, and even with two years of rehab, I couldn't make it back. It was frustrating.

DL: *You moved around the infield early in your career. Were you comfortable with that?*

TN: Being versatile helped keep me in the game. Like anything else, there's a learning curve so it was good for my career that I could play different positions. I did enjoy third base when I got established there.

DL: *Kevin Youkilis, like you, is a Cincinnati native. What is your opinion of Youk?*

TN: He's a good player. I saw him play at the University of Cincinnati and in the Instructional League. What he brings to the table is good baseball instincts, which can be hard to find in young players these days. A lot of guys have raw talent, but when the bell rings they struggle with decision-making. That's not the case with Youkilis.

DL: *Several years ago, you built a mini-Fenway Park in the Cincinnati area, with a Green Monster in left. Tell us about that.*

TN: It's the actual field I played on as a kid, and I wanted to give something back to the community. I think that's important. Selling sponsorships has been a big part of raising money to achieve that goal. Right now, we're working toward affording some upgrades.

DL: *Would it be safe to assume you were a Reds fan growing up?*

TN: I was a Reds fan and a [Pete] Rose fan. Everyone who grew up in Cincinnati appreciates what he brought to the game. He's an icon there, and his all-out attitude was a big part of that.

DL: *Would you put him in the Hall of Fame?*

TN: I think the best scenario would be some kind of agreement where it was a win–win situation for both sides. He certainly deserves it, based on his playing career.

DL: *Before I let you go, can you offer an opinion on the rivalry between the Red Sox and Yankees?*

TN: It's the best in all of sports, and it was great to have experienced it firsthand. Right now, the rivalry is as heated as it's ever been, and the new ownership has the team moving in a direction where that will continue. I'll say one thing: in some ways, it's more fun to watch as an outsider. It's sure entertaining.

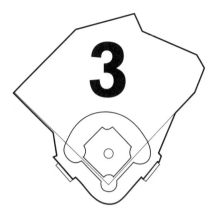

Coaches, Managers, and Scouts

ACE ADAMS

ACE ADAMS IS THE PITCHING COACH FOR THE RED SOX' DOUBLE
A AFFILIATE, THE PORTLAND SEA DOGS. A NATIVE OF
WELLESLEY, MASSACHUSETTS, AND A FORMER RED SOX BATTING
PRACTICE PITCHER, ADAMS HAS BEEN A COACH FOR MORE THAN
20 YEARS. THIS INTERVIEW TOOK PLACE IN NOVEMBER 2005.

David Laurila: *The New York Giants had a pitcher in the 1940s named
Ace Adams. Were you named after him?*

Ace Adams: Maybe indirectly. My dad pitched at Colgate and in the
Yankees organization, so he may have had in mind that it was a good
baseball name. My given name is actually Arthur, but I've been called
"Ace" ever since I came out of the chute. He never told me, but there
could have been some baseball behind it.

DL: *Did you grow up a Red Sox fan?*

AA: Despite growing up miles from Fenway, I have to admit that I was
a Yankees fan. They were unbelievable back then, just rolling. They had

guys like Mantle, Maris, Ford . . . that's who my favorite player was: Whitey Ford. And don't forget, the Red Sox were mostly horrible in the fifties and early sixties. I remember going to Ted Williams' last game, at Fenway Park, and there were maybe 10,000 people there. Imagine that. The greatest hitter ever, playing his last game, and that was it. So, until about 1967, I liked the Yankees more. But don't get me wrong—I liked the Red Sox, too. I went to a lot of games.

DL: *I assume you had a playing career before getting into coaching?*

AA: I did. I was a left-hander and pitched at the University of Michigan. In '73, Dave Winfield and I were all-Big-10 pitchers. Not only that, he's the only Hall of Famer I ever got out!

DL: *Were you drafted by a Major League team?*

AA: I was drafted out of high school by the Cardinals and had to decide between signing or going to Michigan. It wasn't an easy decision. My granddad played at Michigan in 1919—he was a first baseman—and my brother was a catcher there in the early sixties. So that's what I decided to do. After my junior year, I gave up my scholarship and signed as a free agent with the Pirates. They assigned me to the Gulf Coast League, but one day after I struck out seven guys in three innings against the Cubs, they released me! They did re-sign me the following year, but again I didn't make it. That was it for my playing career.

DL: *How did you end up a batting practice pitcher for the Red Sox?*

AA: A good friend, Barry Sullivan, recommended me. He used to coach at Harvard and had been throwing BP for the Red Sox. I did it a little in '82, again late in '84, all of '85, and then part of '86.

DL: *What goes into being a good batting practice pitcher?*

AA: A resilient arm is one thing, and it helps to have a thick skin. Some of the guys are pretty moody and picky about BP. Once, Wade Boggs went five-for-five in a game, and afterwards was quoted as saying that the batting practice pitcher had woken him up by throwing so poorly. He said this to a reporter, and not just "the batting practice pitcher," he said "Ace Adams"!

DL: *Do you have any other good batting practice stories?*

AA: There's another with Boggs that's pretty remarkable. We were in the old ballpark in Cleveland and hitting under the stands because it was raining. Everything was netted down there, and I basically had to throw the ball through a circle between all of the netting. Boggs told me to watch out, that he was going to hit the next 10 pitches back at me through the circle. I figured that was impossible, but I'll be darned if he didn't hit nine of them through it—and the tenth just missed. And it's not like every pitch was in exactly the same spot, either; some were down, others up or away. His bat control was unbelievable. Of course, he had power, too. In games, he'd hit line drives, but in BP he'd hit the ball as far as anyone. And we had some hitters on those teams, too: Rice, Evans, Baylor, Easler. I remember Tony Armas one time in Chicago: he took around 30 swings and hit every one over the wall. That was maybe the most impressive display I've seen. I also threw to Mark McGwire in '97 when I was between jobs and helped out the Cardinals one day—He hit some unbelievable shots, one right after the other.

DL: *Al Nipper was with the Red Sox in the years you were there. Looking back, was it pretty evident that he had a future as a pitching coach?*

AA: Yes, because he was always prepared and always working on his game. He always wanted to learn as much as he could about pitching. In '86, when we got Tom Seaver, Al would talk to him until the cows came home. And Seaver knew his stuff, too. He was also as great a competitor as I've seen. Before Seaver pitched, he'd hang nine uniform tops in his locker. He did that because he'd change after each inning, and every time out he intended to go nine. As to why he changed his shirt after every inning, I think it was probably superstition more than anything.

DL: *I assume Seaver was a real influence on Roger Clemens that year.*

AA: Absolutely. They used to throw together a lot, and it was almost like watching a game. They were so serious and diligent the way they went about everything. They wanted to make everything perfect.

DL: *Have you worked with any young pitchers who you could see becoming coaches someday—guys who already think like one?*

AA: I had Dontrelle Willis when I was with the Marlins, and he was as prepared a person as you'll ever see. The way he goes about getting ready is incredible, so it comes as no surprise to me that he's done as well as he has. I could see him becoming one. As for guys here, a few strike me as potential coaches. Abe Alvarez and Jon Papelbon are both great workers who study the game. Phil Seibel, who's rehabbing his arm right now, is someone else I could see becoming a great coach someday.

DL: *When they were drafted in 2004, Tommy Hottovy was known primarily for his curveball and Andrew Dobies for his slider. This past year in Wilmington, each threw more change-ups and less of his signature pitch. What was behind the change to each of their approaches?*

AA: To me, and I tell everyone this, you won't make it to the big leagues relying on your breaking ball. Commanding your fastball is the number-one priority. At this level—high-A—we want our pitchers to be able to command their fastball 80 percent of the time. That means locating it down in the zone, and in-and-out, not just throwing it for strikes. After that, being able to throw a straight change behind in the count, or on the first pitch, is the most important thing. You get weak contact from a good change, more contact-outs than you'll get with a curve. You still need a breaking pitch, but it's the third priority. But, as I said, locating your fastball is what matters most.

DL: *Despite recognizing that location is more important than a little extra velocity, many pitchers will overthrow anyway. Why do you think that is, and how can you convince them not to?*

AA: It's hard to do at times. A big reason is that the radar gun is there and they want to see high numbers on it. I've had a few guys who have been happy seeing 96s and 97s, even though they haven't been getting guys out. They think that's what will get them to the big leagues. Others will barely hit 87 or 88 but hit their spots and aren't happy without perfection. Which guys do you think have a better chance to succeed? Not that throwing hard doesn't help, but there's more to pitching than that. Perception of a fastball is big, too. I used to have Jorge Julio in the minors, and he'd dial it up there at 98 and still get hit. He didn't hide the ball at all, and hitters could see it coming and adjust to the speed.

Once he improved his delivery and they didn't see it as well, that didn't happen anymore.

DL: *The Red Sox look like they're going to have hard-throwing right-handers in both the rotation and bullpen next year. In many instances, this means we'll see a guy with a 94-mph fastball coming in to replace a guy with a 94-mph fastball. Is this a good thing, or is it more difficult for hitters to adjust to someone coming in and giving them a different look?*

AA: Good hitters will hit anything, so it doesn't really matter. Maybe it makes a difference if it's someone they've never seen, but otherwise they don't really care. Like good pitchers, good hitters make adjustments. Bad ones don't make adjustments.

DL: *Going back to your own career, how did you end up going from coaching at Michigan to working in pro ball with the Expos and now the Red Sox?*

AA: Dave Littlefield was the farm director in Montreal, and I had coached against him on the Cape. Jim Beattie was their GM. They were looking for a coach, and luckily they knew me and felt I could do the job. It worked out well. From there, most of us moved on to the Marlins organization when the Expos' front office changed over. After a year there, Craig Shipley called Theo and recommended me. I interviewed with Theo and Ben Cherington, and it was certainly great to come to the Red Sox. Being a Massachusetts native made it even nicer.

DL: *To close, tell us a little about who Ace Adams is when he's away from baseball.*

AA: He's someone who's home with his family. That would be my wife, Wendy, and our seven-year-old daughter, Abigail. We also have three older kids; two sons who are away at college, Aaron [23] and Kyle [19], and a daughter, Amber [27], who lives in Boston. They come to see me during the season when they can, but for the most part there is no other life while baseball is going on. They don't mind so much, though—they actually love it. Abigail has already seen more games than a lot of people! But not being around them very much for six or seven months out of the year is tough. So when I'm home, I'm perfectly happy just to rake the leaves, do the laundry, and take Abby to go horseback riding. I want to enjoy the time with them while I can, because spring training will be here before we know it.

FERNANDO ARROYO

FERNANDO ARROYO IS A VETERAN OF EIGHT BIG LEAGUE SEASONS AND HAS SPENT THE LAST 16 YEARS COACHING IN THE MINOR LEAGUES. THIS INTERVIEW TOOK PLACE IN JULY 2005 WHILE ARROYO WAS THE PITCHING COACH FOR THE RED SOX' DOUBLE A AFFILIATE, THE PORTLAND SEA DOGS.

David Laurila: *This is your first year in the Red Sox organization. What was your coaching experience prior to coming here?*

Fernando Arroyo: I started out with the Tigers in 1990, at Fayetteville. The next year, I was in Lakeland and then I went to the Marlins organization for three years. After that, I coached in Taiwan for two years, which was a great experience. I got a chance to learn the culture and even learned a little Mandarin Chinese. When I decided to come back, I hooked up with the A's and was with them for six years. I had planned on going back for a seventh, but Boston called and asked for permission to interview me. It was a great opportunity, so I took it.

DL: *What was the deciding factor in coming here?*

FA: It's tough at the rookie level in Arizona because of the schedule and the heat. I also speak Spanish, and there are a lot more Latin Americans in the game today, so I find myself having to repeat myself a lot. And maybe special thoughts I say get lost in the translation, and it wears on me if I didn't get it across to them the same as I did to the English-speaking players. Plus, Boston is a good organization, and they gave me an opportunity to work at the Double A level, which was appealing.

DL: *Did you know people in the organization?*

FA: I knew a few. Bill Lajoie is a longtime friend who I knew from my time in Detroit. Orv Franchuk, who was with me in Oakland, is another. And I had met and liked Ben Cherington. You get to know a lot of people in this game, and there are some quality ones here. Opportunity was part of my decision to come here, but the people were definitely a big factor.

DL: *As a pitching coach, what's the biggest difference between A and Double A?*

FA: At Double A, the talent starts sorting itself out, and the maturity level is different. Once guys reach this level, they start smelling it and are more willing to make the sacrifices. In A ball, a lot of the kids don't get into the programs as well, and they don't understand their bodies as machines yet. They think that everything will come easily, but it doesn't work that way. A lot of times, you have to repeat yourself to them. By Double A, that doesn't happen as often, and they make the adjustments easier. What you're teaching doesn't really differ, but how they react to and understand it does.

DL: *Good command is crucial to a pitcher's success. As a pitching coach, how can you help someone improve it?*

FA: My philosophy is that most pitchers have a similar arm-slot, which is a little over three-quarters. If they drop down or throw a knuckleball, it's a different story, but you don't see that very often. So you want them to know what their arm should do, and you want a consistent arm-track. Everything comes from that. It's like an Iron Mike—a batting machine—that hits the same release point every time it delivers a pitch. That's what you want to try to achieve.

DL: *How should pitchers approach mechanical adjustments?*

FA: They shouldn't think too much on the mound. There are little keys—and you want to make little, quick adjustments—but you don't want to be out there wondering if your arm is a little too long or short. I'm on the bench watching, and it's my job to tell them if there's something wrong mechanically. They should do their thinking in the pen, not while the game is going on.

DL: *How important are radar guns, and how much should a pitcher pay attention to them?*

FA: They're good for detecting within a game. How a pitcher is maintaining his velocity is something you want to know. If he's getting tired, how much is it dropping? It would be nice if everyone on the staff threw 97, but most pitching coaches will tell you that location is more important. A tired pitcher usually won't locate as well. And it can help a pitcher to know he's throwing 87 instead of his usual 90. Not because he should try to force the 90 when his arm doesn't feel strong—he'll likely lose command if he does—but so he can focus more on locating and mixing his pitches.

DL: *Where should a pitcher aim his arm, especially with breaking pitches?*

FA: A good analogy is bowling. You don't bowl to the pins—you bowl to the diamonds in front of you. Like if I extend my arm in front of me, like this, you can see my hand and my face beyond it. You're visualizing the path. You're focusing on the catcher but also on your arm staying down the track.

DL: *Out of 100 pitches, how many should a pitcher throw for strikes?*

FA: It depends on the level and the pitcher. If he's mixing well but not hitting his spots, maybe 60 or 65. If he's locating really well, maybe as high as 75 or 80. What you want to do is be aggressive in the zone and work ahead—adding and subtracting. But everything doesn't have to be over the plate, especially breaking stuff. If you're ahead, you want some of your breaking pitches at the ankles or in the dirt. You want to establish your fastball for strikes, but you can get outs working off the plate.

DL: *I understand that the organization places a lot of emphasis on first-pitch strikes.*

FA: Yes. We want to work inside the box first, and then expand—not work the corners first. You want to hit your spots and mix well, but first you want to establish the strike zone. If you try to be too fine, especially early, you can go to too many long counts and get in trouble. You want to build a tempo in the early innings and not pitch until you have to. For instance, the other day one of our guys got the first two batters in an inning, and then, on a 2-2 count, threw a breaking ball in the dirt. I asked him why, and he said he wanted to use everything early in the game. I asked him, "Why go 3-2 and have to come in with the next pitch? Why not challenge and save the put-aways on the corners for later in the game when the situation dictates it?"

DL: *Did you challenge hitters when you pitched?*

FA: I did the first time I faced Hank Aaron! I had always thought to myself, "When I face Hank, I'm going to go right after him." So beforehand, I'm in the bullpen warming up, and someone tells me, "No off-speed stuff to Aaron, he can hit it." But I'm also hearing, "But be careful, he kills fastballs." So you kind of wonder if there's any way to get him out! I remember walking to the mound and staring right at him. I was living the moment, and it was, "Just you and me, Hank!" I threw him a fastball, and bang—he drives one to deep left. I thought it was gone, but Ben Oglivie goes back and catches it against the wall. Earlier in his career, maybe it's a different story, but I challenged him and got the out. Later in the game, I struck him out with sliders.

DL: *Tell us about the first game of your career.*

FA: I was with the Tigers, and my first game was in Baltimore's Memorial Stadium, in 1975. It was a very exciting moment for me. I remember riding in from the bullpen in the golf cart they used to use, the one with the big Orioles helmet on it. Brooks Robinson was the first batter I faced, and I retired him on a short fly ball. They rolled the ball in for me, and I still have it, signed by Brooks.

DL: *How about your first start?*

FA: It was in Boston, where I actually went 3-0, with three complete games, in my career. Willie Horton hit a two-run homer in the eighth, which won it for us 5-3. Bill Freehan came into the game to catch the last few innings, and I remember him calling for a slider to Rico Petrocelli, and me, a rookie, shaking him off. Freehan comes out to the mound and tells me Rico's a good fastball hitter, which is what I wanted to throw. He asked why I wanted to throw a fastball, and I said that I was just going with my vibes. Remember, this is the 1970s and hippies, and I'm a California kid. Anyway, Freehan walks back behind the plate and calls for a fastball, and we get Rico to ground out. When we get back to the dugout, Freehan starts telling everybody, "This rookie is talking vibes to me!"

DL: *Do you agree that a pitcher has to be comfortable with what he's throwing to be effective?*

FA: I think if you're 100 percent behind what you're throwing, you're going to make a better pitch. And it's your call; the catcher is only suggesting back there. If you throw something you're unsure about and it gets hit, you're going to start second-guessing. That can have a negative effect, because it can cause you to lose focus.

DL: *How much of a psychologist do you and Todd Claus need to be in working with the pitching staff?*

FA: That's a tough part of the job and more complicated than working with mechanics. You try to learn about their backgrounds, but don't always know everything about where they came from and what they need to succeed. We have to be teachers, psychologists, parents, mentors . . . Todd has a great personality for that. Me, I'm more patient than I used to be, but I'm still more old-school. I grew up where respect was expected, but times have changed. Not to say that that most of the guys here don't show it, but it's still very different from when I was in their shoes.

DL: *How does it differ from when you came up in the 1970s?*

FA: When I played, we learned fundamentals and discipline first, and we only knew how to play hard. We played because we loved the game. Today, it's more of a business, with bigger contracts and bonuses. We didn't think about the money. The guys today love the game, too, but you see different ways of going about it with some of them. You get more prima donna attitudes, and if you have one, you better be able to back it up.

DL: *Does a pitcher learn more from adversity or from success?*

FA: It depends on the individual, but there's a lot to gain from negative experiences—but only if you want to learn from them. Jon Papelbon is an example of someone who does that. He's had success dominating hitters and feeds off of that, but he also reacts the right way when things go wrong. He wants to understand why something happened—not make excuses because it did. Earlier this year, when we were having all the rainouts, I was working with Jon on his mechanics. Jon said to me, "I really wish I could get out there and pitch." I said to him, "These rainouts are giving us time to work on what we want to accomplish with your mechanics. We can take some good out of this." Jon looked at me and said, "You know, my dad was just telling me the same thing." Jon understood that the adjustments we were working on were more important than just being out there in a game.

DL: *What did you think when the Red Sox called up Cla Meredith after one appearance in Triple A?*

FA: I thought it was too soon. He made great strides here and merited the promotion to Pawtucket. He was overmatching hitters in Double A and deserved to be rewarded. But he probably needed more time, and a month at Pawtucket would have been good. The game speeds up when you get to the Major Leagues, and the effort level of his mentality came into play. He might have been overthrowing a little. No matter who you are, you need to have the mentality to handle it. He has the right attitude and is going to have success, but he could have used more time.

DL: *To close, tell us about growing up as a baseball fan in California.*

FA: Being from the Bay Area, I grew up with the Giants. My brother had Giants posters pasted all over the walls, but I loved to play more than anything. I'd always be out playing baseball, or any sport that I could. I remember having an Al Kaline bat when I was a kid, and I'd pretend I was Mickey Mantle playing out on the street. When I was pitching, I'd be Juan Marichal with his high leg-kick. He was like an artist with his mechanics. I guess I didn't think of them as mechanics back then, but that's how I think now. I guess that's what happens when you're a pitching coach.

TODD CLAUS

TODD CLAUS IS THE MANAGER OF THE RED SOX' DOUBLE A AFFILIATE, THE PORTLAND SEA DOGS. A ONE-TIME MINOR LEAGUE INFIELDER, CLAUS HAS ALSO WORKED AS A SCOUT AND A HITTING INSTRUCTOR. THIS INTERVIEW TOOK PLACE IN FEBRUARY 2005.

David Laurila: *How would you describe yourself as a manager? Are you more of a Billy Martin or a Walter Alston?*

Todd Claus: I would have to say closer to Billy Martin, although I'm really somewhere in between. I love the fighter in Billy. I love toughness. But I am more of a methodical organizer. I ultimately make decisions based on my gut feel, but strongly value the opinions of my staff, and statistics.

DL: *Have you ever done a good Earl Weaver impersonation, turning your cap backwards and going jaw-to-jaw with an umpire?*

TC: I'd have to say no to the Earl Weaver impersonation. I have been known to get fired up, but I approach umpires with respect until they give me a reason not to. I use a toned-down approach, which I believe has much more impact. Umpires don't hear you when you're verbally abusing them. There comes a time where you have to protect your players and staff, and you "gotta do whatcha gotta do," but for the most part I want the umpires on my side.

DL: *You have three years of managing experience, all in A-ball. Will your job responsibilities or approach be any different in Double A?*

TC: No to both questions. Your responsibility as a manager at any level is to know your players—put them in situations where they can be successful and get the very most out of them. Every player wants to make it to the big leagues and stay there when they do. It's my job to help them achieve those goals in any, and every, way I can. My approach is simple—get better. You do that by diligent work and preparation. The biggest difference between A-ball and Double A is the speed of the game. When you are prepared, everything slows down.

DL: *To a large extent, teaching and development are more important than winning at the minor league level. Have you ever sat in your office after a game and said to yourself, "I'm glad we lost, because I think most of the players learned a valuable lesson by what just happened"?*

TC: I'm never happy to lose—but lessons are often learned the hard way, and that happens at every level. You never stop learning. And teaching and development continue after the minor leagues. Those who stop learning usually weed themselves out.

DL: *You were a minor league hitting instructor for seven years. As a manager, how do you approach working with players in that facet of the game? If you see something, do you go to the player directly or have the batting coach do so? And what if the player comes to you instead?*

TC: Very good question. I strongly believe that personal success comes from surrounding yourself with good people. I also believe that you better have the trust and commitment from your staff. My experience as a hitting coach has been valuable to me as a manager—but they don't mix. Hitting a baseball is the most difficult athletic feat to perform. Multiple voices are bad. If a player comes to me—which they often times do—I solve the problem with the hitting coach and allow him to do his job. I have plenty of ideas and see something every day. I go to the hitting coach and relay my thoughts—almost common sense.

DL: *If you have a tenuous relationship with a player, and he gets promoted to the next level, do you feel a responsibility to inform his new manager of the issues? Or do you let the player move up with a clean, unbiased, slate? Conversely, what do you expect when someone joins your squad?*

TC: Wow! I tell every player they start clean with me. I want to form my own opinion. But there is such a beast known as a "label." There is no way you are going to get along with, or even like, every player who plays for you. I think communication is the key here. I tell players exactly what I think of them, whether they want to hear it or not. They will respect that much more than me telling someone else what I think about them—and hearing it from someone else. As far as passing along information about a player, I reiterate that it's important to know your players . . . and everything helps.

DL: *Many of your players from last year will be moving up the ladder with you to Portland. What advantages and disadvantages do you see in that?*

TC: The only disadvantage I can think of is that players need to learn how to deal with different management styles and personalities—just as coaches need to do with players. It would be helpful to take that quality to the big leagues. However, I feel the advantages far outweigh the disadvantages. I mentioned how important it is to know your players. Obviously, it helps to have had them in the past. You know their strengths and weaknesses, and have a feel for their personalities. It helps with knowing what situations players succeed in. You've heard the saying, "If you can't dance, don't dance." Well, you're not going to ask a guy with two left feet to dance.

DL: *After playing in mostly empty ballparks in the Florida State League, the guys moving up from Sarasota will experience large, supportive crowds in Portland. Do you see this as having any impact on their development?*

TC: Absolutely! Can you imagine having never played in front of a crowd, or even never playing in cold weather, and going to Fenway Park in September? Let's face it—nothing can prepare a player for what he'll experience in Boston. But at least a player can experience what it is like to have people cheer his name and call him a bum. That will most certainly happen. I think the media attention in Portland will also be good for them—if only in a minute comparison.

DL: *David Murphy and Chad Spann went into last year with high expectations but struggled, primarily due to injuries. Talk about the psychological aspect of working with players in their situation, and a little about what we might see from each in 2005.*

TC: Injuries are part of sports, and no one likes to see them. Both kids are solid players and have bright futures, but the unfortunate injury bug bit them both last season. Everyone occasionally likes a pat on the back, but players who are down-and-out and helpless when they are hurt need that extra piece of motivation to let them know you haven't forgotten about them. Look for both of them to come back with a purpose this season and pick up where they left off before they were injured.

DL: *Juan Cedeno pitched in Sarasota last year and despite a lot of talent, had an up-and-down year. Some feel his inconsistency was a result of his ultra-competitiveness, leading him to both overthrow and lose confidence. Is it possible to be too competitive in the game of baseball?*

TC: Nope. Not in my book. But you can be too hard on yourself. No other game has so much failure involved. Three for ten and you're in the Hall of Fame. Give up less than three runs per nine innings—same thing. Dealing with failure is a difficult thing to learn. Some never can overcome it. Those who have figured it out are the consistent performers, year in and year out. There is a fine line between perfection and failure. The good ones understand you have to fail to be perfect. Juan is still very young and learning how to pitch. I would rather tone him down than up. And once he tones down, watch out.

DL: *The players spend an awful lot of time on the field. While doing extra work is often beneficial, do you feel that sometimes a player is better served by taking his mind off the game and going to a movie instead? And does the same go for coaches and managers?*

TC: Without question. Yes to both. This game is mentally, as well as physically, exhausting. If I ask you to give 100 percent effort of what you have in your tank every day for six straight months—it wears you out! I emphasize quality over quantity and firmly believe it. I try to give the players as much R & R as possible, so that when I ask for 100 percent effort, it's available. A fresh mind is better than a tired one. Same for legs, arms, and so on.

DL: *Tell us a little about yourself. What are you like off the field, where did you grow up, and which team and players did you follow as a young baseball fan?*

TC: I'm simple. Friendly. Ridiculously hard-working and motivated to be a good dad. I love working outside in the yard. Hugely interested in real estate. Passionate about fishing and the outdoors. Prefer country over city life and sand over snow. I grew up in South Florida, and we didn't have a professional team to identify with then. I loved Lenny Dykstra. I wanted to be that guy: "Nails." Overachieving tough guy. Football player trapped inside a baseball player's body.

DL: *Last question: You had to deal with a difficult hurricane season in Florida last summer. Tell us about that, along with your thoughts on spending the month of April in Portland with your long underwear and ski cap.*

TC: Man. Talk about scary. We rode the second one out in our home, and it felt like the devil had his hands around our house. Windows and doors were shaking for about 10 straight hours—it felt like it would never end. But it's not like we didn't know any of them were coming. They don't knock on your door unexpectedly and say, "Hi—we're here," like tornadoes and earthquakes. We only experienced minor damage to trees and fences, but our neighborhood looked like a war zone. Screened porches were wrapped around houses. Huge cypress trees were uprooted, and lots of roofs were torn to shreds. It was a mess. As for the cold weather, I'll deal with it. I'm old-school when it comes to that stuff. You won't see all of my layers, but believe me, they will be there.

BRUCE CRABBE

BRUCE CRABBE IS THE MANAGER OF THE RED SOX' SHORT-SEASON
CLASS A AFFILIATE, THE LOWELL SPINNERS. FORMERLY WITH THE
TEXAS RANGERS AND COLORADO SILVER BULLETS, CRABBE WAS
THE HITTING COACH FOR THE WILMINGTON BLUE ROCKS IN 2005.
THIS INTERVIEW TOOK PLACE IN DECEMBER 2005.

David Laurila: *You joined the Red Sox organization in December 2004
and served as the hitting coach in Wilmington in 2005. What brought
you here after spending the previous three seasons with the Rangers'
Triple A team?*

Bruce Crabbe: My time frame had kind of run out with Texas. It was
time for a change, on both sides, and they gave me an opportunity to
pursue other things. Through contacts, I was able to interview here,
and when we sat down the Red Sox liked what I brought to the table.
They liked that I was versatile and had done a lot within the structure
of baseball. The position in Wilmington was a good opportunity, and I
was told there was a chance for future opportunities within the organization.

DL: *When did you learn you would get the Spinners' managerial job?*

BC: At the end of the season, it was mentioned that a dual role might be
available, and it was more than likely that I would get the offer. Along
with taking the managerial position in Lowell, I'm serving as the organization's infield coordinator. First and foremost for me was running the
infield program at our Instructional League. Then I was down at our
Dominican and Venezuelan academies to work with our infielders there.
After spring training, I'll rove until mini-camp and then come up to
Lowell to prepare for the season in June. I'm definitely looking forward
to seeing how the draft unfolds and where the kids will be fitting in.

DL: *How will you handle both positions once the Spinners' season is
under way, and what are your responsibilities as the infield coordinator?*

BC: I'll stay in contact with everyone once I'm in Lowell, and I have the
utmost confidence in the coaches and instructors we have at each level.

Making sure that the Red Sox' infield plan is being implemented throughout the system is the primary role of an infield coordinator. We have a plan for how we want our infielders to go about developing, and there are fundamentals for making every type of play, which we want them to understand.

DL: *The Red Sox organization has a less hands-on approach for first-year players than it does for those in full-season ball. How might that affect your teaching philosophy in Lowell?*

BC: It won't affect it much at all. I managed five years at that level earlier in my career, so I understand the route and parameters that go with it. And while we're less hands-on in some ways—we mostly want to let our first-year players get acclimated to pro ball—we're not hands-off as far as the basics go. There is also a right way approach-wise, which is just as important. So while there are certain things we'll let go—unless they're drastic—there are others we won't. And as a staff, we all have input when making those decisions. That's one thing I like about the Boston organization; input is encouraged from all levels.

DL: *How would you describe your managerial style?*

BC: I guess I consider myself a player's manager. In this day and age, you need to relate to your players. But while I'm pretty low-key, I can raise the bar to get my point across when necessary. I want the players to be comfortable coming to me at all times, but they also have to understand who the boss is. For the most part, I manage based on the ball club and organizational demands. I don't think you can be an extremist, especially at this level.

DL: *This past year, you worked with a Wilmington team that really struggled. How much harder is your job when the team is suffering a lot of adversity?*

BC: I don't look at it as being hard at all. I've been in the game for 21 years now, so I've seen both ends. What's most important is development. I'm not saying that winning isn't important—we teach that it is—but doing things correctly and getting your work in is what matters most. The jump from low- to high-A is harder than a lot of people think, and some of the guys weren't ready to win at that level. But they competed, and they worked hard. And letting players fail can actually be good for them. While a few kids underachieved in Wilmington, with the right attitude they should actually benefit from that.

DL: *Two of the most promising hitters on the Blue Rocks' roster battled injuries last year: Mickey Hall and Ian Bladergroen. What are your thoughts on each?*

BC: Both have Major League potential. Unfortunately, injuries played a big part of their seasons, which is part of the game. Mickey got off to a great start last year, but it's kind of luck of the draw when it comes to injuries. And they can make or break a career. But like I was saying, part of development has to do with adversity. Mickey and Ian both have a lot of talent, and while they had their development hindered by injuries, they can learn from that.

DL: *You played with both Rafael Palmeiro and Mark Grace in the Cubs' minor league system. At the time, each was a young left-handed hitter with a sweet swing but limited power. While it's unclear if the steroid allegations surrounding Palmeiro are true, is this theoretically a classic case of one player gaining an unfair advantage over another?*

BC: I knew Raffy; he and I actually roomed together for a while on the road. He's an extremely talented and gifted guy—one of the best hitters I ever played with. He was great at making adjustments, and in his career learned how to pull the ball effectively. Raffy also played in good hitter's ballparks, with short right-field porches, where he could take advantage of that. Grace never committed to pulling the ball, preferring to hit line drives and use the entire field. Whether or not Raffy ever did anything he's suspected of, I don't know. I just know that he's always been a great hitter.

DL: *Tell us a little about your own playing career.*

BC: I was drafted four times but didn't sign until after my final year at the University of Florida. When I was drafted my freshman year, my dad was ill and made me promise to get my education. This was 1981, and there weren't big bonuses yet. So I finished school and then started my pro career with the Cubs. I made it to Triple A with them and played three seasons in Des Moines. After that, I spent two years in Richmond with the Braves, and then one more in Syracuse with the

Blue Jays. I was a decent player, a career .270 hitter, and versatility kept me around—I played all over the infield. But I was always behind better players. With Chicago, it was Shawon Dunston and Ryne Sandberg, in Atlanta, Mark Lemke and Greg Blauser, and in Toronto, Roberto Alomar and Tony Fernandez. But I don't mean that as an excuse—if I was good enough, it wouldn't have mattered. My last year, I had a hand broken when I was hit by a pitch with a month left in the season. That's when I decided to hang it up.

DL: *Did you go into coaching the following year?*

BC: I took a year off, trying to decide what I wanted to do, and then Phil Niekro called. He had managed me in Triple A and was at the time managing the Colorado Silver Bullets. He was wondering if I was interested in working with their infielders. When a Hall of Famer asks if you want to work with him, it's hard to say no. And I came to find it one of the purest coaching jobs I've ever had, as most of the girls had never played baseball before—they had played softball. We had great people working with the team. Along with Phil, there was his brother Joe, Johnny Grubb, Tommy Jones, and Al Bumbry. While I was there, I also scouted, became the director of player personnel, and in my final season I managed. We played in 15 Major League parks and in Taiwan. It was a wonderful experience.

DL: *Since that time you've coached and managed in pro ball for over ten years. Who are some of the notable people you've worked with?*

BC: When it comes to hitting, I've learned everything I know from Rudy Jaramillo in Texas. Someone else that's been instrumental in my learning process is Alex Rodriguez. Having never played in the big leagues, just watching his work habits in spring training taught me a lot. In over 20 years in the game, I've never seen a kid work harder on his craft than A-Rod. It's eye-opening to watch someone like him in the cage and in the weight room. Work ethic is number one in my book, and he has it. Not everyone is going to make it just because they work hard, but it will help your chances a lot.

DL: *Tell us a little about what you enjoy doing off the field.*

BC: I'm big into golf and fishing, being outdoors. My wife and I like to travel when we can. We don't have kids, but I consider myself a family guy. And I enjoy giving private lessons in the off-season, both hitting and infield. I love to teach kids—of all ages.

DL: *To close, do you have a favorite story from your time with the Silver Bullets?*

BC: One of the highlights—or maybe you can say lowlights—was when one of the girls charged the mound in a game. It was in Albany, Georgia, although I forget just who the team was that we were playing. But they were really cocky and weren't showing us any respect. We were giving them a good battle, which they didn't like, and their pitcher drilled one of the girls in the back with a pitch. It was definitely on purpose, and it really threw everyone under the bridge when she charged the mound. It was a sight to see. The pitcher didn't know what to do, because she came right after him—she wasn't backing down. The benches emptied, and there were some bruises that came out of the fracas, too. It just goes to show that baseball is a game of pride. At any level.

RAY FAGNANT

RAY FAGNANT IS THE NORTHEAST REGIONAL SCOUTING SUPERVI-
SOR FOR THE BOSTON RED SOX. A NATIVE OF CHICOPEE,
MASSACHUSETTS, FAGNANT RECEIVED THE GEORGE DIGBY AWARD
AS THE RED SOX' SCOUT OF THE YEAR FOR 2005. THIS INTERVIEW
TOOK PLACE IN FEBRUARY 2006.

David Laurila: *Let's start with your background as a baseball fan.*

Ray Fagnant: I grew up a dyed-in-the-wool Red Sox fan in Western Mass. I have no recollection of 1967, because I was only two years old, but I know that I was in the Yaz Club. I always wanted to be a professional player. My father never pushed me into it, though, not like what I see in scouting a lot of the time. But he was always there for me, throwing me batting practice and coming to my Little League games. I was big into Carlton Fisk. I remember 1975 vividly and was heartbroken when he left. After that, my favorite player was Gary Allenson, probably because I was a catcher. Interestingly, I ended up playing for Gary in 1991, when I was at New Britain.

DL: *Tell us a little about your playing career.*

RF: I played four years at Assumption College and then signed as a non-drafted free agent with the Pirates in 1987. I was signed by Bob Whalen, whose son is now the coach at Dartmouth. I spent '87 and '88 in Bradenton but got released and started playing semi-pro ball while working as an actuary in Connecticut. Then, on June 21, 1989, I got a phone call from Ed Kenney, Jr., asking if I was interested in playing in the Red Sox system. I told him, of course, I was. He asked if I could report to the Double A team in New Britain, and I almost fell over. I told him I could be there in 20 minutes!

DL: *What happened next?*

RF: They needed a catcher because Todd Pratt was injured, so I reported that night. Butch Hobson was the manager, and I was there for two weeks until Pratt came back. They sent me down to Florida, and I played a game in the Gulf Coast League the next morning. Then, because John Flaherty had broken his hand, they sent me to Winter Haven the same night. That meant I actually played at three levels in just over 24 hours! In one of the games, I faced Jack Morris, who was down making a rehab start, and went 2-for-3 with a home run off an 85 mph rehab fastball. I should have quit right then!

DL: *How did you go from the playing field to scouting?*

RF: I knew I wanted to stay in baseball, and in 1991, my last year as a player, Lee Stange asked me if I could throw good batting practice. That told me they were interested in possibly keeping me around after I was done playing. In the spring of '92, I was close to signing with the White Sox, who would have sent me to their co-op team in California. That's when Bill Enos, who was about to retire, called and asked if I'd like to stay in the organization. At the end of the summer, I interviewed with Wayne Britton and Eddie Kasko, and in '93 I was at the MLB Scouting Bureau School.

DL: *What are some of the first things you learned there?*

RF: Because I had played, I thought I knew a lot about baseball, but as it is with everything, you don't know what you don't know. That said, while it isn't a necessity, having played pro ball does provide a great background and perspective you can't get anywhere else. It's a big plus, especially when explaining to a young player, or his family, what they'll experience themselves. Overall, the program was very good, and I learned new things every day. The first days were spent in the classroom, where there's a lot of procedural stuff you need to go through, from filling out reports to regulations. Then, they sent us out to watch an Instructional League game, assigning us a player we had to watch and write up. After that, it was a high school game, where you don't have names, numbers, or hardly any information on the players. That teaches you how to get what you need from different sources. You also learn what can be corrected, and what can't. You learn how to project, because what a player will look like five years down the road is important. That goes for both physical projection and as a baseball player. Make-up is big. A player can get better, but he has to be willing to work hard to reach his ceiling.

DL: *Is there any one quality that all good scouts share?*

RF: There's an assumed notion that you need instincts and a feel for the game. You're taught to trust your instincts, and you have to be aggressive. The organization you're with is going to have a say in that, and for 14 years I've been blessed to have had the Red Sox allow me to do that. I've also been fortunate in having learned from legends like Buzz Bowers, George Digby, Bill Lajoie, and Bill Enos.

DL: *What are your current responsibilities?*

RF: Geographically, I cover New England, New York, New Jersey, and Eastern Canada. Most of my focus is on the draft, but once that's over I have the New England Collegiate Baseball League, half of the Cape Cod League, and part of the Eastern League. I also do a lot of tryout camps.

DL: *Give us a brief overview of the amateur scouting process.*

RF: Everything is geared to the draft, and we have around 100 days to see thousands of players. We start with a list of players, a follow list, and go from there. My final draft list will typically change, in part because New England players are often late bloomers due to the shorter season. I look at all players optimistically, but a scout is still going to fail 19 out of 20 times—but that's still a success if that one guy makes the big leagues. We have 12 scouts who cover the country. We also have three cross-checkers, one each for the East, West, and Central regions. Then, there are two national cross-checkers who see all of the top players.

DL: *Who are a few of the top prospects in the Northeast region going into the 2006 season?*

RF: Billy Rowell, from New Jersey, has a great bat. He's a high school third baseman and a good example of someone we've done a lot of prep work on. We already have a good read and foundation on how we'll scout him. Dellin Bettances, a high school pitcher from Brooklyn, is another player we've seen a lot. Both are examples of guys we have a history on. I've been in their homes and have been getting a feel for what kind of kids they are.

DL: *In covering part of the Eastern League, would you have had a role in the Red Sox signing David Bacani as a minor league free agent this off-season?*

RF: I've handed in reports on Bacani that would have gone into making that decision. Jamie Vermilyea would be another player I've seen and turned in reports on. That includes what he did two years ago too, as history is important. You'll even look back at amateur reports, because information is power. You want to know as much about a player as possible. In the Eastern League, I'll make sure I see my teams at least seven or eight times, because the information can be critical in trades, Rule 5 selections, and signing released players. We have at least two scouts for each team at every level. The scouts in our professional department are assigned four or five organizations. In my department, amateur scouting, our priority is the draft. Once that's over, we're divided into geographic areas.

DL: *Which is more important in assessing a player, workouts or game action?*

RF: Ideally, you want both. I'd say the most important is games, but you can see 80 swings in practice. In a game, you might see someone get pitched around and barely get any at all. At a workout, you can also talk to a guy and see what he's thinking. And, to some extent, you can create game situations to evaluate with. Overall, each can show you things the other may not on a given day, so you want to mix if you can.

DL: *We're watching a college team scrimmage right now. From a scout's perspective, run down what we're seeing from the right-hander on the mound.*

RF: Well-proportioned with a strong build on a sturdy frame. Well-developed thighs. Loose upper body with long arms. High three-quarter delivery. Slight head-jerk at release. That's not a plus; a quiet head is better. Throws across his body, but good fluid arm action. That's important. A delivery you can fine-tune a little, but you can't fix arm action. I'm seeing an inconsistent delivery. On three pitches, he's landed a little differently each time. Velocity is okay.

DL: *Can you usually tell within a few miles an hour how hard someone is throwing?*

RF: I couldn't give you an accurate reading, but you can see hard without out a radar gun. And you can tell a lot by how the hitters are reacting. One game last year, I saw a guy in Trenton throwing 96, and he couldn't miss a bat. Later that night, I saw Shawn Chacon throwing 87 and dominating big league hitters. There are some guys you just don't get good swings off of, and velocity is only a part of that. Of course, especially at an amateur level, you have to be able to project what a guy is going to do against better competition.

DL: *As this is a spring scrimmage, are you as concerned as you'd be if it were a real game? Do you think the pitcher we just saw may not have been bearing down as much?*

RF: No, I think he was bearing down. Look at him walking off the field. He looks like he's pretty unhappy with how he was throwing. You watch for things like that. You watch how a guy acts when he leaves the field. You want all the information you can get about someone, including what's in his head and how he carries himself.

DL: *What about the guy coming up to the plate right now—how would you describe him?*

RF: Compact build on a strong muscular frame. Well-developed wrists and forearms, which is good. Square, parallel stance. A bit of a bat-wrap. Bat speed not great, but that was only one swing. I'd want to see him for at least a few more at-bats.

DL: *When you're watching a hitter, what are you hoping to see?*

RF: Confidence, good command of the barrel of the bat, and command of the strike zone. And that doesn't mean a guy who walks a lot. You can get a good pitch to hit without walking. The reason players get on base is because they can hit. If they can't, they're not going to walk, either. Some people don't want to believe it, but hitting is a tool.

DL: *How do you balance a player's tools with his numbers?*

RF: You pay attention to the numbers, but stats don't tell you why. In scouting, to project "why" is important. Numbers don't just happen. You need skills to put them up, and you have to be able to project those skills to the next level.

DL: *Some hitters are said to have a hitch in their swing, while with others, that movement is called a trigger. What's the difference?*

RF: A hitch is someone who drops his hands before he swings. A trigger is a movement to get your hands ready to hit. It's almost semantics, but there's a difference. It's kind of a half-full or half-empty thing, and it depends on the hitter. You want good mechanics, and maybe you can shorten a trigger at times, too, improving someone's swing.

DL: *How can you tell a correctable flaw from a problem—not just with hitters, but also with pitchers and in the field?*

RF: One thing you can identify is guys who have a fear of the ball, which is more obvious in high school than in college. Muscle-memory, subconscious things are hard to change. Maybe a guy flinches a little on an inside pitch or before he catches the ball. It's often subtle, but the game speeds up at each level, so you're not going to be able to get away with as much. Of course, you're going to find an exception to every rule. Mechanical deficiencies can sometimes be overcome by great talent and athleticism. That's the exception rather than the rule though, and consistency and clean mechanics are going to help your chances.

DL: *One of the players you've signed is Manny Delcarmen. When did you first see him pitch?*

RF: He was recommended to me when he was a sophomore at West Roxbury High School, but I didn't see him until I had him come to a tryout camp in Pawtucket after his junior year. Not that many people knew about him at the time, although there aren't that many secrets in scouting, either. Scouting might be the fastest network in the country. We then saw him at a workout at Milford High School, and he really stood out. A lot of kids were throwing 75–80, and he was at 91–92. The first game he pitched at West Roxbury as a senior, on a dreadfully cold day, he had something like 21 Ks in nine innings. I had a radar gun, and he was hitting 90 in the ninth inning, even though he had thrown about 180 pitches.

DL: *What is it like watching someone you signed make his big league debut?*

RF: It's not unlike being a proud father. You're happy for the player, and it helps validate the hard work you did. You scout for the organization, not for yourself, so it's a good feeling to see him contributing. I remember Manny's debut vividly. I hadn't even known he had been called up until hearing it on the radio at about 5:30, and I was driving on Route 84 from somewhere when Joe Castiglione said he was warming up in the bullpen. I was about 10 miles from home and started flying to get there in time to see him pitch. I called Buzz Bowers, too, because we had been together a lot watching him. We had both been in Delcarmen's home and had talked to his high school principal together. I couldn't have been more nervous had Manny been my own son.

DL: *Is it like that for most of the guys you've signed?*

RF: Not that many make it, so it's always exciting. I remember Carl Pavano's first game, Brian Rose's, Lou Merloni's. He was my first big leaguer. When Craig Hansen made his debut last year, I was on my knees on the floor, by the coffee table, as close to the TV as I could get. I was nervous, but I was proud, too. That's why you do the job. You want to see your guys play in a Red Sox uniform.

◉

ORV FRANCHUK

ORV FRANCHUK IS THE RED SOX' MINOR LEAGUE HITTING COOR-
DINATOR. A NATIVE OF WANDERING RIVER, ALBERTA, CANADA,
FRANCHUK HAS BEEN A COACH FOR MORE THAN 20 YEARS. THIS
INTERVIEW TOOK PLACE IN AUGUST 2005.

David Laurila: *Before we get to hitting, let's start with a little of your background. What was your baseball experience prior to joining the Red Sox organization?*

Orv Franchuk: I went to Pepperdine on a baseball scholarship and was having a good senior year. The Mets were going to sign me, but I tore my Achilles before the season ended, and they decided I was too big of a health risk. So, I went into coaching instead. For 20 years, I scouted and coached at different levels—but mostly short-season ball in the summer, and taught PE and biology in the off-season. That was in Edmonton during the glory years of Wayne Gretzky and the Oilers, which was great because I love hockey. I actually could have gone to Denver on a hockey/baseball scholarship. I was probably better at hockey than I was at baseball. Anyway, I scouted for Cincinnati, and coached and scouted for the Angels and Oakland before coming here. I also managed for a season and was the hitting coordinator in Oakland.

DL: *As the organization's minor league hitting coordinator, what is your primary responsibility?*

OF: My primary responsibility is to get everyone in the farm system to the big leagues . . . just kidding. My job is to ensure that our organizational hitting philosophy is followed. In three words, that philosophy is: selectively aggressive hitters. Results come from good mechanical fundamentals, but we want our hitters to swing at strikes. We want them to be aggressive to a pitch when they get one in their zone.

DL: *What is your relationship with the hitting coaches in Lowell, Greenville, Wilmington, Portland, and Pawtucket?*

OF: I oversee them to make sure that the program is being followed. I make sure they understand the needs of each individual. They call after every game, and we go over all of the players. That includes everyone who played, plus guys who did extra work before the game. Communication is important. That goes for every facet of life, from talking to your wife to the game of baseball.

DL: *True-or-false question: The Red Sox organization expects hitters to take a lot of pitches and draw walks.*

OF: False. We expect them to think swing on every pitch. Location and spin will dictate whether you take or swing. We want our hitters to be selective within a zone and not go after borderline strikes, especially early in the count. The end result of that might be a walk. There will also be Ks because of that process, because it may result in deep counts. But if a pitcher starts you with fastballs over the heart of the plate or a pitch in your happy zone, we want our hitters to be aggressive.

DL: *How does the approach change with two strikes?*

OF: You expand your zone a little. A good hitter can't be afraid to hit with two strikes. Some guys will swing at borderline pitches early in the count, because they're afraid of getting two strikes. They're afraid of striking out, so they don't wait for a pitch in their zone. In a nutshell, you need to be patient and trust your ability, which is part of having a good plan.

DL: *Some players—Nomar Garciaparra is an example—are much more comfortable being aggressive than they are at being selective. How do you approach situations in which a player is having success while not adhering to the organizational philosophy?*

OF: On-base percentage and walks-to-strikeouts ratio are two things we look at. If a guy hits .380 but doesn't walk a lot, okay. He's being successful. And let's say a guy hits .450 for a month with no walks. That doesn't mean he wasn't being selective, because you're not going to hit .450 swinging at bad pitches. It more likely means that he was being aggressive to his strengths.

DL: *Nomar—a former MLB batting champ—is one example, but how about if we're talking about a guy having a good month in A-ball?*

OF: We'd probably just remind him of what we feel is the best approach, and that at the next level he may not be as successful. But it's hard to teach aggressiveness, and we wouldn't want to take that away from him, either.

DL: *Most people will tell you that good pitching will beat good hitting. How true is that, and do you want your hitters to believe it?*

OF: I don't talk to hitters about that, because it's a negative. What's important is that they're prepared. If they know the pitcher and have a good approach, they can have a quality at-bat. And you can have a quality at-bat and strike out.

DL: *What constitutes a quality at-bat?*

OF: That's something we stress. We're focusing on good at-bats—quality plate appearances—not hits. If you do that—if you're selectively aggressive—the results will follow.

DL: *What qualities do all good hitters share?*

OF: Selectivity is one. A good hitter is confident, because he knows he'll be successful if he swings at strikes. He trusts himself. Work ethic is another.

DL: *Pitch recognition is important. How do you develop that?*

OF: By getting ready early and being on time. You want to get your body in a strong position to hit so you can identify the pitch. If you're late, your mechanics will suffer and be out of sync. Guys struggle because their timing is bad. Being on time lets you get to a power position, and allows you to be quiet and see the ball better. Sometimes a hitter will walk back to the bench and say, "What's wrong with my swing?" But it won't be his swing so much as a bad read, which means something happened before the swing.

DL: *Two-word question: Charley Lau.*

OF: He has his philosophy, and some guys can hit like that. George Brett was a Lau guy. As far as cloning a guy to hit a certain way . . . I think you have to be your own man. Maybe I'll suggest to a particular hitter that he emulate someone, but he still has to be himself. I don't like to create robots or teach hitters to hit a certain way. Everyone is different, and you have to take into consideration their athletic ability, their intelligence, and their ability to make adjustments.

DL: *If a guy you've never seen before steps into the cage and takes 10 or 15 swings, what can tell you tell about him?*

OF: Athleticism. Hand–eye coordination. Actually, I prefer to call it eye–hand coordination. You have to see the ball before your hands and body work, not the other way around. Aptitude and work ethic are important, too, but I think I can tell a lot from 10 swings. It's kind of hard to explain, but you can get a feel for someone if you've seen enough guys hit.

DL: *You often hear people talking about a hitter having good hands. What does that mean?*

OF: All good hitters use their hands. I can shake a guy's hand and generally tell what kind of hitter he is. From the elbow down is where you hit. The rest of the body takes care of itself.

DL: *Is it the hands, or is it really more the wrists?*

OF: It's the hands. The hands control the barrel in the zone, and you want the barrel in the hitting zone for as long as possible. The wrists should roll after contact, not before. If they roll before, you'll roll over contact. You'll also come out of the zone faster.

DL: *Should a hitter pay attention to how the defense is playing him?*

OF: Only if he's a guy who'll bunt for hits. Unless there's a violent, notable shift, you don't want to let it dictate what you do. You need to stay with your approach and hit the ball hard somewhere. After you've made contact, the baseball gods will determine if you get a hit or not.

DL: *Good catchers can recognize things a batter is doing—perhaps with his hands or feet—which the pitcher can use to his advantage. What can a hitter see from a pitcher that may give him an edge?*

OF: Savvy hitters will notice things, and we want our hitters to watch for them. Maybe the pitcher will turn his wrist in the glove when he's about to throw a breaking pitch. Maybe he'll fan his glove for a certain pitch, or he'll dig the ball into it when he's going to throw a change. Of course, sometimes these things are easier to see from the dugout than from the batter's box. We want to watch the pitcher at all times, not just when we're hitting. We're watching both mental and physical things.

Does he throw harder from the wind-up than from the stretch? Does he change his pitch sequence with runners on? In the pen, does he have good command or is he all over the place?

DL: *In a recent game at Fenway Park, a Kansas City pitcher came in and proceeded to throw nine consecutive balls. On his 10th pitch, David Ortiz grounded out—with the bases loaded—to end the inning. What is your opinion of Ortiz not taking a strike in that situation?*

OF: My philosophy is, other than for maybe a guy in the big leagues . . . I'm not a happy camper. Guys in the Major Leagues are different. They know themselves and they know the pitcher. The information they're taking into the at-bat is like an educated prediction. But would I want most guys to do that? No. You have to make a pitcher prove that he can throw strikes. If you do swing, you better do some damage.

DL: *In a similar situation, Johnny Damon led off a recent game and was retired after a 12-pitch at-bat. Rather than taking the next offering to help build up the pitch-count early, Edgar Renteria swung at it. Your opinion?*

OF: I have no trouble with a hitter doing that, but he better do damage if he does. You're giving up an at-bat if you go after a first pitch and it's not in your zone. Renteria would have been on deck watching the 12 pitches to Damon, so he should be confident on what he'd see, himself. But he has to go after a good pitch.

DL: *Manny Ramirez is said to be hard to fool with the same pitch twice in the same game. Why do you think that is?*

OF: You could make an argument that Manny can be hard to understand from a social perspective, but from a mental and physical hitting process . . . he's incredible. Listen to him talk about hitting and the preparation that goes into hitting, and he's in his own category. He's very good about being prepared for who he's facing. He sets pitchers up as well as anyone.

DL: *And he knows how to make adjustments.*

OF: You have to be able to make adjustments. You also have to be able to fix yourself and deal with failure. That's the first thing I teach. Big leaguers understand that, and they know how to prepare.

DL: *We're into the month of August, and Kevin Millar has only four home runs. Why might a hitter who has shown consistent power over the years suddenly see his power numbers drop that much?*

OF: There are a few different possibilities. Sometimes, a guy gets labeled as a power threat and gets pitched to more carefully. They'd rather go after the guy behind him or in front of him. Not playing every day can be another thing. Maybe you're not as selective or relaxed, because you're trying to do more to make sure you're in the lineup the next day.

DL: *David Murphy has received some criticism for not producing a lot of power yet. How different is the situation for a young player who is still looking for his home run stroke?*

OF: I don't like to talk about power that much, asking, "Why aren't you hitting home runs?" Players have to go through a time period and at-bats. They have to go through the process and get experience. They need confidence. All the tools and ability are there for David, and hopefully it will start clicking for him. He's a good young hitter.

DL: *Last year, Chris Turner had a terrible walks-to-strikeouts ratio at Lowell. He then started this season in extended spring training but has since rebounded to put up good numbers in Greenville. What happened?*

OF: Like I was saying, it takes experience and at-bats, and for some guys it just takes a little longer. He simply needed to figure it out. Chris hadn't played a lot growing up, and I don't think his confidence was very high. He worried about things he couldn't control. You have to be patient with guys like that, because they have the tools. You can't always just fix something.

DL: *What advice do you give when a knuckleballer is on the mound?*

OF: Look for balls up in the zone. If it doesn't start on top of the zone, or slightly above, you want to lay off. If it starts as a quality strike, it's probably going to end up at the ankles or in the dirt.

DL: *Last one: As a fan, who are some of your all-time favorite players?*

OF: Growing up, I was a big Mickey Mantle guy. He was a power-hitting switch-hitter and a lot of fun to watch. Maybe he had some less-than-desirable qualities off the field, but as a kid you only see the on-the-field stuff. I was a big Yaz fan, too. He was a real blue-collar player, a guy who really knew hitting. And it was funny, the first year I got here, I arrived in camp and he's sitting right next to me. He's a great guy to talk hitting with. The players may change, but the hitting process doesn't.

BUTCH HOBSON

BUTCH HOBSON WAS THE RED SOX' THIRD BASEMAN FROM 1975 TO 1980 AND MANAGED THE TEAM FROM 1992 TO 1994. HE NOW RUNS THE BUTCH HOBSON BASEBALL ACADEMY IN NASHUA, NEW HAMPSHIRE, AND COACHES THE INDEPENDENT LEAGUE NASHUA PRIDE. THIS INTERVIEW TOOK PLACE IN FEBRUARY 2006.

David Laurila: *You have sons playing Little League baseball. Tell us about them.*

Butch Hobson: I have three boys, and yes, all of them are playing. K.C. is 15 and a freshman at Nashua North. He plays football, too, and was the first freshman starter at quarterback there in 60 years. Baseball is his game, though. He's a big 6' 3" first baseman and a lefty. Hank is 13. He's my third baseman and a real team player. Noah is eight and a lefty–lefty. He's still a little boy compared to his brothers, but he's starting to come around.

DL: *Tell us about your own life growing up with sports.*

BH: My dad was a football coach, and in Alabama if you didn't play football you didn't eat. We were an athletic family: football, baseball, hunting, fishing . . . and school if we could find time for it. But seriously, school should always come first. We stress to our kids that they should do what they enjoy, be it sports or guitar lessons or reading, but school is what's most important.

DL: *How would you describe your teaching philosophy, primarily when working with younger players, but also at the professional level?*

BH: At my camp, on the back of our shirts is, "No excuses." There's no excuse for not running hard, for not playing hard. I tell the kids that they're going to make mistakes, but they can learn from them. I want them to take responsibility for their actions, and I want them to leave it on the field.

DL: *You played football at the University of Alabama for the legendary Bear Bryant. How did he influence your life?*

BH: Coach Bryant was a people person. Getting to know the players and their parents was at the top of his to-do list, and he taught more than just football. He taught us about life after football. That's one thing I try to do now, whether it's to youngsters or in independent ball. He was also a motivator. His preparation process was second to none. Another thing I learned from him is to be tough but fair.

DL: *You played in the 1973 Orange Bowl against Nebraska. In which ways did that help prepare you for the Major Leagues?*

BH: It helped me, although I didn't play until the fourth quarter when our starting quarterback got hurt. I ended up leading us in rushing that day, but it's because I spent most of my time running for my life—Rich Glover was chasing me all over the field. But even though we lost, that game was meaningful for a lot of people. Afterwards, my mailbox was filled with letters telling me how I exemplified Bear Bryant's 110-percent attitude because I never gave up. And while I knew I wasn't going to the NFL, in order to make it in baseball I was going to have to stay humble and work hard to prepare myself. I think playing for Coach Bryant and getting an opportunity to play in the Orange Bowl helped me do that.

DL: *How would you compare the Alabama/Auburn rivalry to Red Sox/ Yankees?*

BH: Wow. They're different sports and different levels of competition, but when you go to see Alabama/Auburn it's almost like a pro game. The intensity is there, even between the fans. You hope a game like that will bring out the best in everybody, but sometimes it's the worst instead. You know what it's like with New York and Boston. When I was managing the Red Sox, it wasn't quite as intense as it is now, but when I played it was a war. It was Thurman versus Pudge, and everything that went with it. It was important to beat them. And in Alabama, you could be 0-9 going into the last game, but if you beat Auburn the season would still be a success.

DL: *As the Red Sox' manager, you were similar to your predecessor, Joe Morgan, in often going with your instincts rather than strictly by the book. How do you view today's increased emphasis on statistical analysis in the dugout?*

BH: The technology is different today. We didn't have that. We could get information from Howe Sports Data and find out what Don Mattingly hits against Tony Fossas, but these days you have access to a lot more and don't have to go out of your way to get it. We were a lot more fundamental in our approach then, because that's how the game was played. Had the information been available, I'm sure we'd have made use of it. Of course, Sparky Anderson once gave me some good advice, too. He said you're only as good as the horses you have in your stable.

DL: *While managing in Boston, you were often referred to as "Daddy Butch." What was your opinion of that?*

BH: I liked it. Bear Bryant used to walk out of the meeting room on Sundays and say, "I love you guys. Now go home and call your mothers." Whether it wins a game for you or not, you want your players to know you care about them. When the game is over, win or lose, you want them to be able to go home and relax—not take the game with them. And playing and managing here is tough, so don't sign here if you can't handle it. Terry [Francona] was hammered all year in '04. But as for what the media said about me, I didn't have a problem with that. I think I gave them what they needed, and I got along with them well. To be honest, I kind of liked being called "Daddy Butch."

DL: *What value do you put on clubhouse chemistry, and how accurate was the "25 players, 25 cabs" reputation of the Red Sox teams of the 1970s and 1980s?*

BH: I think more is written about team chemistry now than it was before. The A's won in the seventies without it. As for the "25 cabs," I didn't see it. We all rode the team bus together and got along fine. We didn't have trouble in our clubhouse—we had leaders. We fought the other teams, not ourselves.

DL: *Who were the team leaders?*

BH: A lot of times, you go into the season looking for 25 and end up with 1. But we had a lot of guys. Andre Dawson took a strong leadership role when he was here. Danny Darwin was a leader. Mike Greenwell was one. Roger was a leader—in Roger's own way. Different guys lead in different ways. When I was a player, it was Yaz, and he led more by example.

DL: *Who were some of the more notable "personalities" on the teams you've been with?*

BH: Bill Lee, without a doubt. I saw him not too long ago, and he's still a beauty. George Scott is another, and Luis Tiant definitely kept everyone loose. And I should include Luis as one of the leaders, too. He was important to our clubhouse.

DL: *What are you most proud of from your time managing both the Red Sox and Pawtucket Red Sox?*

BH: In Pawtucket, we won the division and I got the manager of the year award. I'm proud of that. I guess in Boston I'm most proud of getting to manage Hall of Famers like Boggs and Clemens, and Andre Dawson is close. I got to manage Mo Vaughn early in his career and see him become a great player. But I guess what's more meaningful than anything is that I was given the chance to manage the team I played for.

DL: *What do you remember about your first big league games, as a player?*

BH: I played the last game of the year in '75, the day after we clinched, but opening day in '76 was special. It was my first game at Fenway, and I hit a double off the wall against Jim Palmer in the early innings. Then, later on, I hit one off the wall near the flagpole in left-center. The ball hit a seam and rolled away from the outfielders, and I ended up with an inside-the-park home run.

DL: *Of the home runs you hit in your career, which were the longest?*

BH: One of them wasn't even a home run. I hit a speaker in the Kingdome—I think I was the first to do that—and I absolutely crushed it. Fortunately, I never pimped it around the bases, so even though it caromed back onto the field, I ended up sliding head-first into third with a triple. But probably the longest one I hit was in Cleveland, off Jim Kern. It was in '77, and I remember my mom, dad, and grandparents were there. I was sick as a dog that day, but played anyway and hit the ball into the upper deck in left field to win the game. It was a bomb.

DL: *In retrospect, should you have played third base for most of the 1978 season when your elbow injury severely hindered your ability to throw?*

BH: No, I shouldn't have. As a matter of fact, I went to Zim [Don Zimmer] late in the year and told him I was killing us. After that, I just DHed, because I could still hit. But there was no need to [go to Zimmer] until around the All-Star break—I was okay until then. I had torn a hamstring, but I was going to play. I'd have played with a broken leg. That was the mentality back then—nobody wanted to miss games.

DL: *You were traded to California in 1980. How surprised were you when it happened, and would you have liked to spend your entire career with one team?*

BH: I was very surprised. And I was very, very disappointed. Would I have liked to spend my whole career with one team? Of course—if it was Boston. Not if it was Milwaukee or a lot of other places. This is a special place to play.

DL: *Do you have any good stories you can share—maybe of oddball things you've seen on the diamond?*

BH: Back in the seventies, you'd see some goofy things. Streakers ran across the field a few times, and back then the security guards could hit people if they wanted. One interesting thing happened in, I think, '79. Somebody in right field let a bird dog loose on the field; it was a high-strung setter, and nobody could catch it. I had raised them back in Alabama, so I was wondering if it had been trained. When you train them, you always teach them "whoa"—it's called whoa-breaking a dog—so when it ran by third base, I yelled, "Whoa!" and it stopped like it was frozen. I got a standing ovation—probably the biggest one of my career!

DL: *You've been quoted as saying that drugs were a part of the game when you played, and they may have taken a few years off of your career. How would you describe the baseball culture you were a part of as a player, and how much do feel it has changed?*

BH: When I think back, drugs were readily available, and it seemed like everybody was doing them. I didn't have the knowledge to know it was wrong—I just thought it was what you did as a celebrity . . . as a ballplayer. As athletes, we're blessed, but there is also an arrogance factor and a tendency to think you can't do wrong. It was a social aspect that wasn't good, and maybe I'd have spent 15 years in the game had I been smarter. The problem will always be around, but today there are programs to enlighten and educate players. I know that I try to help guys, but that's all you can do. You can't change people.

DL: *Who do you owe the most to, both in baseball and from a personal standpoint?*

BH: From the personal side, it would have to be my wife, Krys. She's stuck with me for a long time, through all the ups and downs. Even when I was arrested in '96, she was there for me. She's helped maintain a good Christian household and raised four beautiful children with me. If it wasn't for her, I probably wouldn't even be around.

DL: *What about in baseball?*

BH: You know, it's probably not any individual persons. It's the game of baseball itself. I've never gotten tired of it, and I'm fortunate that it's given me an opportunity to make a lot of friends. I've been lucky to have been a part of the greatest game there is.

DL: *Last one: When all is said and done, how does Butch Hobson want to be remembered?*

BH: I believe that the fans in New England liked the way I played, my mentality of always giving 110 percent. I hope I'm remembered as a guy who did that. I also hope I'm remembered as someone who tried to give as much back to the game as he got. And do you know what? I got a lot from baseball.

ROB LEARY

ROB LEARY IS THE RED SOX' MINOR LEAGUE FIELD COORDINATOR. A ONE-TIME CATCHER IN THE MONTREAL ORGANIZATION, LEARY JOINED THE COACHING RANKS IN 1990. THIS INTERVIEW TOOK PLACE IN JULY 2005.

David Laurila: *Your title is minor league field coordinator. What does the job entail?*

Rob Leary: I'm in charge of coordinating spring training, the mini-camps, and Instructional League. I assist our director of player development, Ben Cherington, in the development of organizational teaching philosophy and standards, including communication with staff, daily oversight at spring training, in-season, and Instructional League, and enforcement of disciplinary measures when necessary. I'm responsible for the enforcement of organizational fundamentals and act as the liaison to the Major League staff on development of organizational fundamentals. I assist Ben in minor league staffing decisions and the development of individual minor league staff members. I assist Ben in the development and implementation of the individual player plans. I also seek out and research new and progressive means to improve the operation of the department.

DL: *Do you look at your responsibilities more as instruction or as evaluation?*

RL: Both, actually. As the field coordinator, I oversee all field operations. Like all of our managers, coaches, and instructors, I am constantly evaluating each player. Part of my responsibility is to also evaluate the staff. I'm also the roving catching instructor, so I'm directly involved with the catchers' instruction.

DL: *What approach is behind the evaluation process?*

RL: Evaluating our players correctly is critical to the success of our department and the organization. We cannot afford to make mistakes with our players. Obviously, we're working with our guys on a daily basis and should get to know them well enough to make an accurate evaluation. Because baseball is not an exact science, it's unfair to expect perfection with our evaluations, but we are doing a very good job in this area. There's so much more to an evaluation than just saying whether a guy will make it to the Major Leagues or not; what type of player will he be when he gets there, is he going to be an impact player right away or ever, will he be a productive postseason player, etc . . . As you can imagine, we are constantly discussing the players, their abilities, and how we can help further their development.

DL: *Is there any formal evaluation during the course of the season?*

RL: There is. Our staff turns in a progress report on each player in June. We then write up a player plan for each player. The staff of each team then meets with each player on their team, and they discuss the plan with the player. It's important to know the meeting is a dialogue and not a monologue. We want to know what players think about their development and their season. We want to talk baseball with them. We get a thorough understanding of the players through these plans, and their comments and conversation.

DL: *What about for the new draftees—guys just joining the organization in June?*

RL: They'll have one in Instructional League or in spring training if they don't go to the Instructional League. We have scouting reports which give us an idea of their skills, personality, and work ethic. Personally, I like to observe each player before I look over the scouting report. We want them to show us why they're here—what was it that made our scouts interested in them. We teach them the system, but we're hands-off with trying to change very much their first year. This is a major transition for them, and we want them to get comfortable with the system, programs, and people.

DL: *How are the organizational philosophies modeled, and how are they implemented?*

RL: We have an organizational manual with all of the programs spelled out. It covers pitching, catching, hitting, infield, outfield, and base running. We take a systematic approach to developing players. We're trying to develop the most complete, winning baseball player.

DL: *What are the organization's expectations regarding discipline and behavior?*

RL: Discipline means a lot of things. We want our guys to be disciplined both on and off the field. Our expectations are that a player will be professional and respect the game. There's a correlation: the more disciplined a person is, the better chance he has to be a productive player. Behavior includes respecting the Red Sox organization and your teammates. Acting professional on and off the field, always keeping in mind you are representing the Red Sox. We have an orientation in spring training and right after the draft, and we let everyone know the rules and regulations—what we consider professional behavior to be.

DL: *Dustin Pedroia, who is small of stature and not noted for his tools, was just promoted to Triple A, a mere 12 months after he was drafted. What does that tell us?*

RL: He's a winning player, and that's the best compliment I can give him. It all starts with his work ethic. There's no time off with Dustin. Everything he does has purpose. He's never off the clock. He's all baseball, and along with physical work, he takes the mental part of the game seriously. Whether it's talking baseball with his teammates, the staff, or studying the opponents, he puts 100 percent into each facet of the game. He's a guy who came to us disciplined and professional.

DL: *What can you tell us about Luis Soto's transition from shortstop to the outfield?*

RL: Coming into spring training, the plan was to keep him at shortstop. He was continuing his development there, but after a lot of discussion with a lot of people, we decided to make the change. It wasn't something that was decided overnight. It was a decision based on seeing him play over the course of a year, including the winter in the Dominican. Ben Cherington, Craig Shipley, and Victor Rodriguez all met with him, and he had no problem with it. We feel Luis has a better chance to make it to the Major Leagues as an outfielder, and he understands the importance of that.

DL: *What was your experience prior to coming to Boston?*

RL: I managed in the Montreal organization at the Single A level from 1991 through 1994. I went to the Florida Marlins as their catching instructor in '95. Midway through '96, I became the field coordinator and held that position through '98. In 1999, I was promoted to director of field operations and held that position through 2000. In 2001, I was the Marlins' Major League advance scout.

DL: *What about playing experience?*

RL: I was drafted in the 12th round and spent five years in the Montreal organization as a catcher. I got as high as Triple A. Before that, I played junior college ball at the College of San Mateo and then at LSU in '85 and '86. I was truly blessed and lucky to be coached my whole life by quality coaches. They taught me a lot about the game, and good coaching and instruction is essential if you're going to succeed. That's what we're trying to accomplish in the Red Sox organization. As I said before, we're trying to develop the most complete, winning baseball players.

Shorter Views

JOE MORGAN

"WALPOLE" JOE MORGAN MANAGED THE RED SOX FROM 1988 TO 1991, LEADING THE TEAM TO TWO DIVISION TITLES. A MANAGER IN THE MINOR LEAGUES FOR 16 YEARS BEFORE TAKING THE HELM IN BOSTON, MORGAN PLAYED FOUR SEASONS AS A BIG LEAGUE INFIELDER FOR THE BRAVES, ATHLETICS, PHILLIES, AND INDIANS. THIS INTERVIEW TOOK PLACE IN JULY 2004.

David Laurila: *You managed for several years in Pawtucket. Tell us about that.*

Joe Morgan: Like anywhere in the minors, you'll have good teams and bad ones. I had both. My first team was bad, even though I had the two best players in the league: Jim Rice and Fred Lynn. We finished $33\frac{1}{2}$ back. That was in 1974.

DL: *What about the good ones?*

JM: We won the pennant the first year Ben Mondor owned the team. I think we only drew 76,000 people all year, though. Attendance wasn't good back then. I remember that after we won, I told Ben: "It's not that easy."

DL: *What are some of your favorite memories of managing in Boston?*

JM: Nothing beats the "Morgan Magic" days. It rained the first day I had the job, and then [Roger] Clemens was on the mound when we finally played. We won 12 in a row, which was something.

DL: *Which no manager had ever done to start his career.*

JM: No, and it was kind of ironic. The old record was held by Fred Haney, my old manager, who took over the Braves and won 11 straight. A few years later, in 1959, he sent me down to Louisville. All those years later, I eclipsed his record.

DL: *Did you follow the Red Sox growing up in Walpole?*

JM: I followed them and also the Braves. I actually came full circle with those teams. I signed with the Braves in 1952 and got fired by the Red Sox in 1991.

DL: *Did you have a favorite player when you were a kid?*

JM: The closest to a favorite would be Jimmie Foxx. He was a great hitter and played many different positions, even pitcher and catcher.

DL: *I'm familiar with him as a first baseman.*

JM: Yes, he played a lot of first, over 1,900 games. But he also played a little third, some outfield, a game at shortstop, caught 109 games, and pitched 23 innings.

DL: *What have you been doing since your managerial days?*

JM: Mostly spending money. I've done some gardening, played some golf, gone to the Kentucky Derby.

DL: *How often have you gone to the Derby?*

JM: Every year since. It's my favorite event.

DL: *What is your opinion on clubhouse chemistry?*

JM: It doesn't matter. If you're good, you'll win, and if you're not you won't. Simple as that.

DL: *You don't buy into it at all?*

JM: No. It's overblown, mostly by the media. When the players get on the field, they don't want to shame themselves. It's what they do out there that counts.

DL: *What are your thoughts on last year's Red Sox team, and this year's?*

JM: This year is the same as last year in many ways. We're trying to catch the Yankees. What is it, seven games now? And at present, we're battling for a wild card. That's one of the toughest parts of today's game, having to go through the playoffs to win. In my day, you went right to the World Series.

DL: *Back in your day, there weren't so many teams. If you played today, you probably wouldn't be sent down to Louisville.*

JM: No, I'd be a star. But it was tough to make it when there were only eight teams in each league, that's for sure.

DL: *One more question: How does Joe Morgan want to be remembered?*

JM: I'd like to be thought of as a guy who knew most aspects of the game. I studied them. There's no thinking, hoping, or praying. You have to know it, or you don't. Pretty simple.

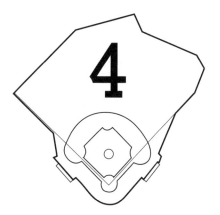

The Front Office

BEN CHERINGTON

BEN CHERINGTON IS THE RED SOX' VICE PRESIDENT OF PLAYER PERSONNEL. A NATIVE OF MERIDEN, NEW HAMPSHIRE, CHERINGTON IS A GRADUATE OF AMHERST COLLEGE AND HAS BEEN WITH THE ORGANIZATION SINCE 1998. THIS INTERVIEW TOOK PLACE IN NOVEMBER 2004 WHILE HE WAS THE TEAM'S DIRECTOR OF PLAYER DEVELOPMENT.

David Laurila: *Let's start with the World Series championship. Who were the first people you thought of when it was over?*

Ben Cherington: Since most of the front office was in the clubhouse after we won, I thought mostly of people who weren't there—namely, our minor league staff who work so hard each year to help put the team in a position to do something like this, and also my family who puts up with me throughout the year.

DL: *Tell us about your background and how you came to work for the Red Sox.*

BC: I coached for a year at Amherst College and got a master's degree in sports management. After that program, I was fortunate enough to be hired as an intern by the Cleveland Indians where I was able to work and learn from some great baseball people like John Hart, Dan O'Dowd, Mark Shapiro, Josh Byrnes, Paul DePodesta, and Neal Huntington. I took my first full-time position with the Red Sox as a mid-Atlantic area scout in November of 1998. I spent a year in that job and then moved into the office in Boston. Since then, I've been a baseball ops assistant, advance scout, coordinator of Latin American scouting, assistant director of player development, and now I'm finishing my second year as director of player development.

DL: *You're responsible for helping build future championship teams. What are some of the most important things you've learned since you first took the job of director of player development?*

BC: Building a good minor league system requires hard work from a lot of people and also a lot of patience. Our scouting department, both amateur and international, has done a very good job of identifying and signing players with talent and the makeup to succeed. Once they sign, we try to create an environment that is conducive to their development in all facets of the game. The most important part of my job is to hire the right people. If you hire the right people, they end up making us all look good.

DL: *How many games did you see at each level this past season, and what drives the decisions regarding when and where you go?*

BC: I saw each of our affiliates play between 20 and 25 games each. We are fortunate to have three teams in New England, which are all very easy to get to. I also visit our academies in the Dominican Republic and Venezuela once each. The schedule is pretty much dependent on where teams are playing and convenience. I tend not to make decisions on where to go based on how players are doing, unless there are extreme situations. Our staff, at each level, is more than capable of handling any development issues regarding players, so my job is really just to support them and offer some perspective.

DL: *Managers and coaches play an important role in the development of prospects. What goes into the process of selecting them for each level of the minors, specifically the managers?*

BC: We look for people who have a passion for the game and for teaching. It is also important that they believe in, or are willing to adjust to, our philosophy. We believe that each of our staff members is a member of the "player development staff" more so than they are the "Portland manager" or "Lowell pitching coach." A staff member might be really valuable at a certain level one year and then more valuable at a different level the next year, depending on the mix of players we have on a particular team, and so on.

DL: *How important is it to keep everyone on the same page between all levels, and which are the key organizational philosophies stressed throughout the system?*

BC: Very important. Without getting into the specifics of our philosophy, we have some standards in our teaching program as well as standards for behavior and discipline that must be met, and it is the job of the staff to enforce those standards. We believe the staff should have freedom in how they teach, but not what they teach.

DL: *How much latitude do coaches have in changing a prospect's mechanics? For instance, if a pitching coach wants to alter someone's arm-slot, at any level, does he need to "go upstairs" to do so?*

BC: We promote and maintain open lines of communication between managers, coaches, rovers, and front office. Any major mechanical changes are done after pretty thorough conversations between all of those parties.

DL: *Although the organization will always take what it considers the best player available, there has been a clear trend toward those with college experience. What are your thoughts on the following assessment of this year's draft by* Baseball America: *"[beyond Mike Rozier] ... an otherwise conservative draft class of advanced players who should move quickly but don't have huge ceilings."*

BC: In the end, it's all about where they end up. If a college pitcher who is deemed to have a "limited ceiling" helps our Major League club as a solid member of the pitching staff for a few years, does it really matter what his "ceiling" was considered? There is no empirical evidence that suggests that the average high school player has a higher ceiling than the average college player, based on the history of the draft. That said, we have and will continue to take the best player available based on the scouting factors that are most important to us, no matter where he is from.

DL: *How does being a large-market team impact decisions regarding the draft, player development, and the trading of prospects?*

BC: Theo and the rest of the front office have a responsibility to put a contending team on the field every year. There are a lot of different ways to do that. Being a large-market team doesn't effect our decision-making as much as wanting to put together a winning team does. In the end, our decision-making process when it comes to drafting, trades, etc., is really not that different from other teams. We have to evaluate what we are getting back on our investment [opportunity cost] and make a value-based decision on what is best for the Red Sox.

DL: *How much does character factor into the draft process and retaining/trading players?*

BC: It's important. Baseball is a tough game, and it is especially challenging to play in Boston. There are certain character traits that may give a player a better chance for success here.

DL: *What about when it comes to filling the Triple A roster? Does leadership play much of a role when you sign minor league veterans?*

BC: It's a factor, although not an overwhelming one. Ultimately, our Triple A roster needs to be filled with players at each position who could play the corresponding position in the Major Leagues if the need arose. That is what drives our decisions on filling the Triple A roster, more than anything else.

DL: *Many people feel the failed A-Rod negotiations adversely affected Nomar last year. Are there similar concerns regarding younger players like Jon Lester [who almost went in the A-Rod deal] and Beau Vaughan [reportedly almost dealt to the Mets for Eric Valent]?*

BC: I won't comment on who may have been involved in trade talks in the past, but if any of our players were I don't think it really affects them. They care most about playing, and besides, if you are being asked for in exchange for a good Major League player, it is a compliment.

DL: *Abe Alvarez got a spot-start this year and then went back to Double A. How much thought went into him moving to Triple A after his outing versus Baltimore, and what goes into that type of decision?*

BC: We felt this was Abe's year to develop in Double A. We needed someone to start a game in the Major Leagues, and it was Abe's turn. He was able to stay on schedule and then go back into the rotation in Portland right away.

DL: *Alvarez didn't make the Eastern League's top-20 prospect list, in large part because he lacks velocity. How does the organization compare tools versus results when drafting and developing players?*

BC: It's a balance. The higher the player gets, the more results matter.

DL: *Shortstop looks to be a strength within the organization, while the depth at catcher beyond Kelly Shoppach is arguably lacking. Which positions do you feel may need an upgrade, and are any typically more or less important than others?*

BC: We're pleased with the shortstop depth we've begun to create with Kenny Perez, Hanley Ramirez, Dustin Pedroia, Christian Lara, Luis Soto, et al. Catching is a hard position to find in general, but we do like some of our younger catchers. As an organization, we are never satisfied with our depth at any position, even those that are relatively stronger than another.

DL: *Can you comment on the recent franchise shifts involving Sarasota/Wilmington and Capital City/Augusta? What were the biggest factors in these moves?*

BC: We believe the Carolina League is the best high-A league in baseball and that Wilmington is the best franchise in that league, so when it became available it was a no-brainer. We have a good relationship with the Burke family through Dan's ownership of Portland. His son, Frank, is part of the ownership group in Capital City, and we wanted to be in a situation where we had a good relationship with the ownership/management group.

DL: *Last question: Will a World Series championship have any impact on the player development system, or will you and your staff go about things in basically the same way—albeit with a bigger smile on your face[s]?*

BC: It won't make any difference in the mission of the department. It should allow us a little more freedom and time to continue pushing our program forward.

DAN DUQUETTE

DAN DUQUETTE WAS THE GENERAL MANAGER OF THE BOSTON RED SOX FROM 1994 TO 2002. A NATIVE OF DALTON, MASSACHUSETTS, DUQUETTE NOW RUNS THE DUQUETTE SPORTS ACADEMY IN HINSDALE, MASSACHUSETTS, AND THE PITTSFIELD DUKES OF THE NEW ENGLAND COLLEGIATE BASEBALL LEAGUE. THIS INTERVIEW TOOK PLACE IN FEBRUARY 2006.

David Laurila: *You were replaced as Red Sox GM when the current ownership group took over. Do you ever wonder what might have happened had you moved in, rather than out, in 2002?*

Dan Duquette: I can't really answer that, but I can say they inherited a good ball club and a productive farm system. They traded a number of players we had acquired or developed to help build a championship team. We had aggressively signed free agent pitchers from places like Venezuela and the Dominican Republic, and tried to develop them so we had guys to trade. It's no secret that teams with pitching can be players in the trade market. Overall, I think the current group fulfilled our vision for the farm system. The idea some people tried to perpetuate, that the organization wasn't healthy when they took over, was a myth in my opinion.

DL: *Do you feel your philosophy of building a team was any different than that of the current Red Sox management?*

DD: The philosophy for winning in baseball is the same everywhere. You try to be as powerful offensively as you can, you need good pitching, and you need good defense. The overall philosophy doesn't really change when management changes. Maybe you weigh some of the tools differently, but you're basically trying to do the same thing.

DL: *Your utilization of statistical analysis and interest in acquiring undervalued players was similar to today's* Moneyball *approach, yet you were often criticized for your methods. Do you think the fans simply weren't ready to embrace what has proven to be an effective approach?*

DD: I believe that the public accepted our ball club and our philosophy of building a winning team. We did use saber-tools and computer analysis to evaluate players, but so have a lot of clubs, to varying degrees. Of course, the current regime brought in Bill James, who improved a lot of the models.

DL: *Why do you think Mike Gimbel, whom you utilized as a statistical consultant, wasn't better accepted?*

DD: I think some of his freak interests away from the game detracted from his work and from the image of the organization. But we had other men doing sabermetric work, too. The work saber-guys do is to focus on the on-the-field results and quantify them. That makes cost–benefit analysis easier, so you can know within reasonable certainty what you'll get for your investment. Gimbel made relative comparisons of offensive and defensive production of players at the Major League level. We also had people working on minor league projections and economic evaluations.

DL: *How similar was your decision not to re-sign Roger Clemens and Mo Vaughn to Theo Epstein and company not re-signing Pedro Martinez and Johnny Damon?*

DD: I wasn't intimately involved in the Pedro and Damon decisions, so I don't know that I can speak to the concerns of the current administration. I do know that they have a consistent philosophy when it comes to contracts, and they stuck to it. Individual decisions need to be secondary to the overall philosophy of putting the best team on the field, not only for that season but in the future. Having a budget and a farm system are paramount in doing that successfully.

DL: *Can you address Vaughn's departure and the subsequent signing of Jose Offerman in 1998?*

DD: Offerman had been a good player for Kansas City—a good offensive player—and he had been dependable. We needed a second baseman, and he did a good job for us for two years. As for not re-signing Mo, that was actually one of the better decisions we made, because it freed up millions of dollars. We took the money his contract would have absorbed and put it to use for several years by investing it in salaries of other players. If you look at the commitment involved, and his production over the life of the contract that he signed in California, it was extremely one-sided in favor of not signing him.

DL: *When you acquired Pedro from the Expos in 1997, how long did it take to put the deal together, and were Carl Pavano and Tony Armas, Jr., the players Montreal initially asked for in return?*

DD: We talked to the Expos for about two and a half months. Eddie Haas did a lot of the groundwork with Jim Beattie and their scouts, and he also found out which other teams were involved in talks about trading for him. We had a few pitchers they were interested in. Pavano and Armas were just two, but they were definitely players they wanted. Of course, we knew Pedro well, because we had acquired him from the Dodgers when we were in Montreal. I also had talks with Claude Brochu, the Expos' president, during the negotiations.

DL: *In dealing Jamie Moyer for Darren Bragg in 1996, you were trading a 33-year-old pitcher for a 26-year-old outfielder with good speed. What other factors went into that deal?*

DD: That one was pretty straightforward. In trading Moyer, the manager wasn't using him, and he had come up to me and said he wasn't going to re-sign with us. He said he wasn't comfortable here, and his family wasn't happy here, so we could trade him if we'd like—otherwise, he'd leave after the season. We had signed him to a one-year deal, so rather than get nothing for him we made the deal for Bragg. Bragg was a good fourth outfielder, which was something we needed at the time.

DL: *Looking back at the Carl Everett/Jimy Williams situation, should it have been handled any differently?*

DD: As I was saying earlier, the best interest of the team is more important than that of the individual. In the case of Carl Everett, we had a multi-year financial commitment to a player that was guaranteed. Jimy wanted him off the team, and Carl didn't want to play here anymore. One of the tenets of the Yawkey ownership was that the team was not going to release players with multi-year financial commitments; either we were going to keep a player on our roster and play him, or we were going to trade him. There were teams waiting for us to release him so they could pick him up, but that wasn't going to happen, and our trade options were limited at the time. Jimy may not have agreed with the team's position, but economically it was the right thing to do for the franchise, particularly because the team was for sale. If we released Everett from the contract but still maintained the financial burden, it probably would have been considered an economic liability by the new owners. Fortunately, at the end of the season and before the team was actually sold, we were then able to trade Carl to Texas, and most of the Everett salary obligation became the responsibility of the Texas club.

DL: *How would you describe the relationship you had with Jimy Williams?*

DD: Jimy did a good job for us, especially in 1999. We had some issues where I thought the interests of the organization were more important than his perspectives as the manager, but those things are going to happen. But it was never a situation where I dictated what he did. As manager, he was in charge of the team, the clubhouse, and the lineup. Jimy had as much autonomy as any manager in the business during his tenure in Boston.

DL: *What about your relationship with John Harrington?*

DD: He was essentially the managing partner, and I will always appreciate that John gave me the opportunity to lead the Red Sox baseball organization, which I have told him several times. John was very supportive of me both personally and professionally. I understood his philosophy and did my very best every day to fulfill his vision for the team as the senior baseball executive on the staff. I knew that John had a fiduciary responsibility to the Yawkey Trust but also that he took very seriously his responsibility to the fans. I also understood with the team for sale, we would have to give more weight to the present. You have to understand that the team's operational philosophy can change when the team is for sale. Unfortunately, in 2001 we had so many injuries with Pedro and Nomar and Manny, and then Carl Everett, and one that is often overlooked but very important was that Varitek missed the entire second half of the year. That really hurt our chances to be a top-flight team that final season of the Yawkey ownership.

DL: *Can you elaborate on the "win now" philosophy in that later part of your tenure?*

DD: It's always "win now" in a major market. That only changes if you have a lot of injuries or fall out of contention for some other reason. Of course, you have to balance that with the team's long-term goals, but when the team is for sale the owner has a right to put all of the resources into the current team. It's his last chance to win. What's the value of the farm system to the former owner after the team transfers to a new owner? When I was with the Expos, we had built a great farm system, but when it came time to sell, Charles Bronfman got all of the executives together one day and he said he wanted to make it clear that we were going to do everything we could to win now. When it came time for Dave Dombrowski to evaluate Randy Johnson and Mark Langston, Johnson was traded for Langston, a solid third-starter type, because Langston would help us more that season. The future wasn't a part of the consideration of the trade, because the only future the owner had with the team was that season.

DL: *What went into the decision to hire Joe Kerrigan to replace Jimy Williams in 2001?*

DD: He was one of the most capable pitching coaches in the industry, and I gave him an opportunity to manage and see if he could get us over the hump. Joe is a diligent worker and a good baseball man. It remains to be seen if he's a Major League manager, because he didn't get much of a chance after we hired him.

DL: *One of your goals when you were hired in 1994 was to improve the farm system. How do you feel you did in that regard, and what is the story behind the team's inability to sign Mark Teixeira after drafting him in 1998?*

DD: We made an aggressive offer to Teixeira, but Scott Boras wanted him to go to college. There wasn't much we could do about that. We also tried hard to sign Pat Burrell a few years earlier but weren't able to for the same reason. But we still improved from one of the least-productive farm systems to one of the most productive over a 10-year period. Wayne Britton and I rebuilt the scouting staff, as a lot of our scouts had gotten old at the same time. Ed Haas, Lee Thomas, Kent Qualls, and I worked very hard to redefine the farm system. By any account, it takes around seven to eight years to rebuild a farm system, and looking at the results I feel we did a very good job with the farm system. Considering that the current ownership group traded over 35 contracts from the farm system that our scouts signed, to staff the recent Major League teams, and the core of the club they inherited has averaged almost 95 wins a year, speaks very favorably for the work of the baseball operation during my tenure as general manager.

DL: *Along with acquiring Pedro, what would you consider your best player moves?*

DD: The Johnny Damon signing was terrific. By signing him, we got a center fielder to help the pitching staff, one of the best leadoff men in the game, a dependable player who played every day and became a matinée idol in Boston. Drafting and signing Nomar Garciaparra, and bringing him up through the system was important, too. As the best cleanup hitter in the league, Manny Ramirez certainly stabilized the team offensively for a long time, and needless to say, acquiring Jason Varitek and Derek Lowe was a trade that helped us enormously.

DL: *Heathcliff Slocumb for Varitek and Lowe was one of the best trades in club history. Take us through that deal.*

DD: In 1997, it was clear that we were out of the race going into the trading deadline. Philosophically, I always believed that you owe it to your fans to get what you can for certain veteran players if you're out of contention in a given year to restock for the future . . . to give your club a better chance, in other words, so you can win later. Fortunately, we were able to make a terrific deal and acquire two players who became mainstays on our championship-caliber teams. We were looking for someone to replace Mike Stanley at catcher. Everyone in baseball knew about Jason Varitek. But a lot of people were frustrated with Varitek, because he hadn't started his pro career as soon as he could have. The perception of his value wasn't equal to his ability because he was drafted several times by Major League clubs before he decided to sign and start his professional career. I had seen him play a lot, because I had scouted Nomar when they were both at Georgia Tech and seen him play every year in spring training against the Atlanta Braves when Georgia Tech came south to start their spring trip. I had also seen him on the Cape, and I always liked his power, his hands, his leadership, and his work ethic.

DL: *How about Derek Lowe?*

DD: Gary Rajisch had seen him in the Pacific Coast League, and told me he felt Lowe had a chance to pitch in the big leagues. One of the best parts of the deal is that a week before the deadline, Lou Piniella saw Slocumb throw 95-96-97 in a game with a great breaking ball and good command. It was probably his most dominant game while he was here. Seattle was looking for bullpen help, but then they signed Paul Spoljaric and I thought maybe they were done. So I called Woody [Woodward] back and asked, and he said no, they were still interested in Slocumb. You always need starting pitching, so we were focusing on having a guy named Ken Cloud, who was in Double A at the time, included in the deal. Woody said, "Along with Varitek, why don't you look at this other young pitcher from Michigan, Derek Lowe? A few other teams are interested in him." Our scouts had Cloud rated over Lowe, so we kicked it around the office and decided to hold out for an additional arm. I talked to Woody several times the night of the trading deadline, and he said he didn't know if they'd give up another pitcher, so I said I'd have to think about it. In the interim, Slocumb blew a save for us. When Woody called back, he said, "Don't tell me he blew that save." I said, "Okay, I won't tell you." He said, "Did he?" I said, "Woody, I said I wouldn't tell you!"

DL: *What happened next?*

DD: It got down to 11:20, so I thought I'd take one more crack at it. We needed another catcher, so I decided I'd make the deal straight-up for Tek, if necessary. I called Woody and reminded him that we had to have it in by midnight, and I'd need to talk to Mr. Harrington first, so what could we do to get it done? He said, "If you take Lowe, we'll do it." As it's turned out, not only has Varitek become maybe the best catcher in team history, even with the great career Carlton Fisk had, but Lowe went on to win all three clinching games in the 2004 postseason. That is the definition of a clutch pitcher. Derek Lowe pitched well when he had the opportunity to win the pennant and the World Series. He really came up big when it counted.

DL: *Can you give us snapshots of the Brian Daubach, Tim Wakefield, and Troy O'Leary acquisitions?*

DD: Dave Jauss recommended Daubach, so he deserves most of the credit there. He had seen him in the Dominican Republic when Mo was a free agent, and Daubach ended up having some very productive seasons for us, hitting over 20 home runs four years in a row. Eddie Haas and Eddie Robinson recommended Wakefield. We then hired Phil Niekro to help him, and Wake has turned into a good long-term signing and an asset to the team. He's the senior member of the team now, not to mention a good guy. O'Leary I originally signed out of high school, in Compton, California, in 1987. Ruben Rodriguez was the scout. We went to see another kid play but ended up drafting O'Leary instead, I believe, in the 13th round. He had that quick bat, and the huge grand slam against Cleveland in the playoffs.

DL: *The Red Sox were the last Major League team to sign an African-American player and remained poorly integrated until your tenure as general manager. Do you consider that one of your greatest accomplishments?*

DD: I'm very proud of having helped diversify the organization. We integrated from all over the world, from Korea and Japan to Mexico and the Dominican, and we evaluated strictly on ability. We did the same thing when we built our farm system in Montreal. Our scouting didn't see color—race and ethnicity meant nothing. That changed the culture both on the field and in our office, and it extended to throughout the community. At the end of the day, we were more diverse, and it made us a more interesting brand all over the world.

DL: *Besides the integration of the team and player acquisitions, what are you most proud of from your time in Boston?*

DD: A great moment was the 1999 All-Star game at Fenway Park. Having the all-time team there, the last on-the-field public appearance of Ted Williams, the greatest hitter of all time, and then Pedro blowing away the National League hitters—it was a great moment for Boston. Having all of that tradition together on the field that day was truly a memorable and proud moment for the team and city and the fans.

DL: *If you could get one mulligan for your time here, what would you do differently?*

DD: In retrospect, having an opportunity to reflect back, a number of things. I gave my best to the Red Sox organization and the fans for many years. And I tried to fulfill the ultimate goal for the fans each and every season, and leave a foundation for hope for the next season. While it was satisfying to see the club win with the group of core players that we assembled, naturally it would have been more satisfying to have been part of the organization at the time the team won the World Series. Prior to him leaving, I also wish that we could have convinced Roger Clemens to make the adjustment required . . . to convince him of the need for additional conditioning at that stage of his career. To his credit, Roger made those adjustments after moving to another city, but Roger was one of the greatest pitchers in the history of the club, and it would have been nice if he had played his entire career in Boston. One trade that I regret was not acquiring equal value in return for trading Aaron Sele for Jim Leyritz. Aaron was an effective pitcher for us, and we should have at least gotten another pitcher back in the deal. Ted Williams would always scold me about that one. He'd say, "For crying out loud, how in the hell could you trade a guy who throws a curveball like that?"

DL: *Last one: What did 2004 mean to you and your family?*

DD: I grew up a Red Sox fan, as did my dad and mom and my grandparents, so it was fun to be in St. Louis to see it happen. It was meaningful to us as a family; we're four generations of Red Sox fans. Personally, I dedicated my professional life to bringing a World Series championship to the city of Boston and the fans of New England from the time I was 18 years old, so it was satisfying to see the key members that I assembled play vital roles for the Red Sox team that finally won it all. I was thankful to have had the opportunity to see Lowe, Varitek, Damon, Martinez, and Ramirez, the series MVP, bring home the Holy Grail! Everyone who ever waited up for a game on the West Coast, or who suffered through any, or all, of the missed opportunities, was delivered by one final moment, and as far as I was concerned, everyone who was ever a Sox fan could die happy now . . . finally, we beat the Yankees and won the World Series. And the ones who didn't get to see it live, I bet they were also relieved from a heavy, heavy burden, too!

CHARLIE ESHBACH

CHARLIE ESHBACH IS THE PRESIDENT/GENERAL MANAGER OF THE RED SOX' DOUBLE A AFFILIATE, THE PORTLAND SEA DOGS. ESHBACH HAS BEEN IN PROFESSIONAL BASEBALL FOR MORE THAN 30 YEARS AND FORMERLY SERVED AS PRESIDENT OF THE EASTERN LEAGUE. THIS INTERVIEW TOOK PLACE IN APRIL 2004.

David Laurila: *Minor league baseball returned to Portland in 1994. How did that come to be, and what role did you play?*

Charlie Eshbach: When MLB granted franchises to Florida and Colorado, minor league baseball needed to expand in order to accommodate them. At the time, I was president of the Eastern League, and a committee was formed—comprised of representatives from the three Double A leagues—to decide which two cities would get franchises. There were 13 applicants, and Portland became one of four finalists, along with New Haven, Atlantic City, and Long Island. Dan Burke [the current owner] had previously expressed interest in bringing a team to Portland, and he asked for my help in accomplishing that goal. He was able to work with the city and put together a good proposal, and here we are.

DL: *Was there a stadium in place at the time?*

CE: That was a big part of what Dan was able to accomplish with the city. Hadlock Field, at the time, was a high school facility—inadequate for baseball at this level. They were able to come up with a plan to enhance Hadlock and bring it up to Double A standards, with a capacity of 6,975.

DL: *Why did you choose to step down from your position as president of the Eastern League and move into your role with the Sea Dogs?*

CE: There were a few reasons. First, Dan Burke is a quality individual. Second, it was an opportunity that appealed to me. And third, Portland is a wonderful place to raise a family.

DL: *Portland had been without a professional baseball franchise for 45 years, and the Maine Guides folded in 1988 after only 5 years. Why was it felt that the Portland area was now ready to support minor league baseball?*

CE: Baseball has a long history in Maine, going all the way back to Louis Sockalexis [the man for whom the Cleveland Indians were named, in 1915]. The Red Sox have always had a huge fan base up here, and with it being the major business center in the state, Portland was well-positioned to succeed. Old Orchard Beach is much smaller, and it was hard for them to adequately support a team for that and other reasons.

DL: *The Sea Dogs were affiliated with the Florida Marlins from 1994 to 2002. In 2003, they became the Red Sox' Double A affiliate. Tell us what that meant to the franchise, the fans, and the city of Portland.*

CE: The city supported the team very well while the Marlins were here, but obviously getting the Red Sox was a boon. There's always been a "hometown team" relationship with the fans, and as I alluded to earlier, nearly everyone up here follows the Red Sox. Having them here is ideal. It feels almost like a birthright.

DL: *Prior to the Red Sox moving from Trenton, there were accusations that the organization was not always providing the team with a competitive roster. Did you have any concerns regarding support, or with building a working relationship with the Boston organization?*

CE: None whatsoever. You have to remember that John Henry was with the Marlins before he came to Boston, so we were used to working with him and his staff. It was, and is, a great relationship. As for any problems with providing a competitive roster, it's something that happens periodically at this level. In most cases, it's something you have to deal with for a day or two at most—no big deal. There haven't been any problems, and I couldn't be happier with how we've been treated.

DL: *General managers in MLB are responsible for acquiring players and building rosters. How much of a role, if any, do they play at the minor league level?*

CE: That responsibility falls outside our purview. We're essentially in charge of running the business but only what happens off the field. We certainly interact with them [the Red Sox], but they call the shots when it comes to player personnel.

DL: *So when a player at the MLB level needs a rehab assignment, you can't lobby to have him in Portland for a few days?*

CE: No, I'd never do that. A lot of times, the schedule is a determining factor. If Pawtucket is on a road trip and we're at home, it's often easier to send someone here—or vice-versa. We did have a few guys here on rehab last season, and it's always a treat for the fans. I don't ask for them, though.

DL: *You've seen a lot of talented players come and go. Who are some that had "star" written all over them?*

CE: Off the top of my head, I'd say Edgar Renteria, Charles Johnson, and Josh Beckett, all in the Marlins system. Nomar [Garciaparra] and Derek Jeter played here as visitors, and it was easy to see how good they were going to be. These are guys who fit into the category of "when, not if."

DL: *Who impressed you on the 2003 Sea Dogs team?*

CE: Kelly Shoppach is an obvious one. Kevin Youkilis, too, although he had a pretty rough start defensively. To his credit, he worked his tail off and became a very good third baseman by the end of the year. That impressed me. Jorge de la Rosa [now with Milwaukee after going to Arizona in the deal that brought Curt Schilling to Boston] was another, as was Anastacio Martinez. Jeremy Owens is a guy I should mention. He was a pleasant surprise. And something I should add is what quality people they are—it was a pleasure to have them here as individuals, not just as players.

DL: *Kevin Millar played in Portland. Tell us a little about him.*

CE: Kevin is a great guy. Two notable things about him: one is that he wasn't looked at as a big-time prospect when he came here, but he worked hard and really stepped up his game. The other is that he was good in the clubhouse. Each of those is a testament to his character. He's a class act.

DL: *Are today's players any different from when you started out in the game?*

CE: I think the main difference is education. I'd say 70 percent of today's players come here out of college, while years ago it was 70 percent out of high school. There's a big difference. There's more of a mix now, too, with players coming from a variety of places and backgrounds.

DL: *Have salary structures changed much in minor league baseball?*

CE: Compared to MLB, not very much at all. It's still basically an apprenticeship. You're working your way up to where the big money is. Guys on the 40-man roster get paid a little more, and signing bonuses are much greater than they used to be, but the base-salaries haven't changed appreciably.

DL: *Entertaining the fans is an important part of running a minor league team. Talk about some of the things the Sea Dogs have done to attract and retain fans.*

CE: Experience tells me that people come to baseball games for a wide variety of reasons. No two fans are necessarily the same. We try to make people feel comfortable, and we try to keep them entertained. One notable enhancement to Hadlock Field this summer is a new video board. It's state-of-the-art and will provide fans with a lot of information and replays. We're excited about that.

DL: *What about the young fans?*

CE: Our mascot, "Slugger" the Sea Dog, has always been popular. So, too, has the "Trash Monster."

DL: *Tell us a little about him.*

CE: The "Trash Monster" is a creature who helps keep the ballpark clean. He walks around the stands and people can "feed" their garbage into him. Kids get a big kick out of that, and it helps keep the place tidy—sort of a dual-purpose value!

DL: *Tell us about Hadlock's other "Monster," the one in left field.*

CE: This is something Dan Burke first mentioned several years ago. With a relatively short distance to the fence in left, much like at Fenway, he proposed putting up a similar wall. Once the Red Sox came here, it was only natural to have our own Green Monster—37 feet high—so up it went.

DL: *Let's go back in time, prior to your involvement in organized baseball. Where did you grow up, and what led you to make the game your life's work?*

CE: I grew up in both Weymouth and Amherst, and always loved baseball and the Red Sox. When I was at the University of Connecticut, I worked in their sports information department, so I got paid to go to games. That idea appealed to me. After graduating, I got a job with the Elmira club. That was in 1974, and I've been in the game ever since.

DL: *So, you were a Red Sox fan growing up. Tell us about that.*

CE: I went to my first game in 1959 at the age of seven, so I got to see Ted Williams play. I'd say that Bill Monbouquette was my favorite, though.

DL: *What do you remember about 1967?*

CE: It was a great year to be a Red Sox fan—obviously. What I remember most is going to Games 2 and 6 of the World Series. I was a sophomore in high school, and I sent in for tickets. Much to my surprise, I was lucky enough to get them. Game 2 was when [Jim] Lonborg threw the one-hitter.

DL: *Last question: You've been in the game for a long time. What are your favorite memories, and what are you most proud of?*

CE: I think I'm most proud of having started out as a kid who wanted a job in baseball, didn't know anybody in the game, and here I am, 30 years later. That said, I also feel quite fortunate.

DL: *How about the memories?*

CE: Well, I hope to add more, but to this point there have been several. I was the GM at Bristol before becoming president of the Eastern League, and we won championships in '75, '78, and '81. Those were special. The first game at Hadlock Field was memorable—ditto the first one here as a Red Sox affiliate. There was also Game 6 of a playoff series in 1996. We were down 3 games to 2 and were trailing 6 to 1 in the bottom of the ninth. Their pitcher was dominating us, and we were about to be eliminated. Despite this, the entire crowd stood up—it was a full house—and they gave us a rousing and heartfelt ovation for a full half-inning. That was something special. That's baseball in Portland.

LOU GORMAN

LOU GORMAN WAS THE GENERAL MANAGER OF THE BOSTON RED SOX FROM 1984 TO 1993. A MEMBER OF THE RED SOX HALL OF FAME, GORMAN HAS BEEN IN PROFESSIONAL BASEBALL FOR MORE THAN 40 YEARS. THIS INTERVIEW TOOK PLACE IN MARCH 2005.

David Laurila: *You're currently an executive consultant for the Red Sox. What do you do in that capacity?*

Lou Gorman: I do a lot of PR-related work, a lot of entertaining. I haven't been in the baseball operations end for some time now. John Harrington asked me to stay involved when Dan Duquette replaced me as GM, so I was senior VP for a few years—but I moved on. I miss baseball ops—I did that for 36 or 37 years—but I'm happy where I am now and delighted to still be a member of the Red Sox organization after 42 years in baseball.

DL: *You grew up a Red Sox fan in South Providence, Rhode Island. Tell us about that.*

LG: My dad was a fire chief and took me to Fenway Park for the first time when I was 9 or 10. Just walking down the ramp and seeing all that green—the green field, the Green Monster . . . it became a part of my life. I was enamored with the game. My dad wasn't a big fan, but I was and wouldn't stand for us leaving before the game was over. I admired Ted Williams greatly, so I talked my dad into waiting by the players' parking lot to get a glimpse of Ted afterwards, which I did.

DL: *You went on to sign a pro contract yourself.*

LG: I played baseball, football, and basketball in high school, at LaSalle Academy in Providence, and am actually in the Rhode Island Gridiron Hall of Fame. In baseball, I played in the New England All-Star game at Fenway Park. I played first base for the New England All-Stars, and Harry Agganis was the first baseman for the Boston All-Stars. I ended up signing with Philadelphia; I was only 17 years old. I remember going to camp and being around guys like Richie Ashburn, Del Ennis, and Robin Roberts. That was a real thrill. I then started my career in Appleton, Wisconsin, but really struggled. The whole team did. They released six of us, myself included. It took me two weeks to build up the courage to go home and tell my dad what had happened—that I had failed in my dream to become a Major League player.

DL: *So, you enrolled at Stonehill College.*

LG: Yes, my dad said that if baseball wasn't going to work out, I should either get a job or go to college. After Stonehill, I joined the Navy and had eight and a half years of active duty, with two tours in Korea. I'm proud of that. I remained in the active reserves for 34 years and retired as a Navy captain. But I still wanted to be in baseball, so in 1961 I went to the baseball convention in Tampa and talked myself into a job with the Giants. I've been in the game ever since.

DL: *Is it fair to assume that being a New Englander played a key role in your decision to leave the Mets and join the Red Sox organization in 1984?*

LG: Very much so. It was hard to leave the Mets, but I was coming home to my roots. I knew the Mets had a chance to be very good. Their nucleus was outstanding. Guys like Gooden and Strawberry could have been Hall of Famers, but for personal problems, and we had developed some great young players like Lenny Dykstra, Kevin Mitchell, Mookie Wilson, Randy Myers, Billy Beane, and others. Coming home was simply an opportunity I couldn't pass up.

DL: *How different, and difficult, was it running the team you grew up cheering for? Theo Epstein is now dealing with the same situation.*

LG: Theo has done an outstanding job. He is very calm, despite the media pressure he faces, and he helped put together a championship team. In fairness to Dan Duquette, he deserves credit also. He acquired a number of players who were very important to the team's success.

When I took the job, I knew that Red Sox baseball in New England was part of the culture and passion. But I still didn't know until I got here that every day there would be 20 or 30 reporters, and it was something you had to learn to live with. And it wasn't like coming to a place like Kansas City, where you can start from scratch and be patient. There was constant pressure to win now. The fans had waited nearly 70 years for another world championship.

DL: *When you became the Red Sox GM, how did you approach reshaping the roster?*

LG: It was a good ball club when I took over. The nucleus was there, and I knew there were only a few things I needed to do to make the club a contender. I started by sitting down with my baseball operations staff to get their input. I wanted to evaluate the club before I made any moves. I decided that we could use another bat or two, with some pop, and a steadier shortstop. I went out and acquired Dave Henderson and Spike Owen. Henderson had some big hits for us, and Owen was very steady and competitive. I also acquired Don Baylor, who hit 30 home runs, and Hall of Famer Tom Seaver, late in the season. He would win big games for us before becoming disabled.

DL: *Overshadowed by the 1986 World Series is one of the greatest games in Red Sox history, Game 5 of that year's ALCS. What do you remember feeling as that unfolded?*

LG: There's no question that it was an incredible game. I thought we were done. I was sitting there in Anaheim Stadium with Mrs. Yawkey and Haywood Sullivan—I'm pretty sure Ted was there, too. The din of noise was incredible, and the Angels fans were getting on the Red Sox pretty bad. I started thinking that we needed to get out of there, and I had turned up the aisle to look for an escape route when Henderson hit the ball out. I didn't actually see it. All of a sudden, there was complete silence. I knew something had happened. I turned around, and there was Henderson, circling the bases. It was a truly dramatic win for us.

DL: *Let's move on to Game 6 of the '86 World Series. In the book you wrote about your life in baseball,* One Pitch from Glory, *you recall that with one out to go in the infamous 10th inning, you said to yourself, "No God could ever be so cruel as to allow this victory to slip away." Prior to last October, did you ever allow yourself to think that maybe there really was a curse?*

LG: The curse was a media-type thing—a legend. It never meant much to me or most of the players. Some players probably didn't even know who Babe Ruth was. It wasn't something I believed in. I knew it would happen one day—we would win. Of course, I hoped it would be when I was the GM. It almost didn't happen in 2004. For instance, if Tony Clark's ball doesn't one-hop into the stands in Game 5 of the ALCS, and it just barely skipped over the short right-field fence, Gary Sheffield might very well have scored all the way from first base and we lose to the Yankees four games to one.

DL: *You also wrote that you had never seen Mrs. Yawkey as intense and nervous as she was in Game 6 in 1986. Did you think of her last October?*

LG: No question. She was the first person I thought of when Foulke underhanded the ball to Mientkiewicz and we were finally world champs. I had decided to stay back in Boston, rather than travel to St. Louis. My wife and I watched together. We had a bottle of Chardonnay. And I never thought we'd sweep the Cardinals. Maybe win, but in seven. And I felt badly that Mrs. Yawkey wasn't around to see it. I know what it would have meant to her. But I did think that, somehow, she and her husband, Tom, knew it happened—and smiled.

DL: *Mrs. Yawkey looked you in the eye after Game 6 in '86 and said, "Do you understand what I'm telling you? Your manager cost us the world championship."*

LG: I could see the tragedy on her face after that game. I was almost afraid to look at her. She was referring to John McNamara not bringing in Stapleton. I knew then that he'd get fired the following year if we struggled—whether it was fair or not. Of course, that's what happened. And I think McNamara was a better manager than most of the media gave him credit for. As for not bringing in Stapleton, I think Buckner talked him out of it. He wanted to be on field when we won it all.

DL: *You've been asked countless times about Clemens coming out of that game. Did you think back to that when Grady left Pedro in too long in 2003?*

LG: Definitely. And Clemens in '86—I've been asked a million times about that. Like Pedro, he was a tremendous competitor, and I doubt that he'd have ever asked out of such an important game. But I had tremendous respect for McNamara, too. He was very honest and upfront with me. I think it was really a misunderstanding about whether Roger could continue. His finger was bleeding, and when he indicated that he was having trouble throwing his breaking ball, McNamara may have taken that as an indication that he wanted out of the game.

DL: *Last summer, Oil Can Boyd told a reporter that he went out drinking after being told he wouldn't start Game 7. Tell us about the decision to pitch Bruce Hurst instead.*

LG: I haven't heard that, but I can believe he reacted emotionally. Dennis was a tremendous competitor and really wanted the ball. I knew when we made the decision to pitch Hurst that he'd be upset. I told John McNamara that I'd be with him when he told Dennis. McNamara said it was his responsibility, and he'd do it himself. I loved Dennis, but we thought the Mets were vulnerable against left-handed pitching, and Hurst had obviously pitched brilliantly so far in the Series. He probably would have been MVP had we won.

DL: *Have you ever pondered what might have happened if Tom Seaver was healthy at the time?*

LG: Many times. He could have made a huge difference. He was used to pressure, and we acquired him knowing that he could win big games for us. Unfortunately, he was injured and never got that opportunity in the postseason.

DL: *The following spring, Boyd was involved in an episode where he neglected to return X-rated videotapes. What are your memories of that?*

LG: It's a funny story. We were down in Florida, and a police chief came in to tell me that a warrant would be served on one of our players. It was Dennis, who had rented a few videos a year earlier but never returned them. The owner of the video store had decided to report them as stolen. I arranged to pay for them and apologized to the store owner for the situation. That should have been the end. A local reporter, however, found out and decided to look into the titles of the videos. It turns out they were X-rated. I think one was *Dixie Does Dallas*, or something like that. Reporters approached Dennis in the clubhouse about the videos, and when I arrived I found him ranting and raving at them, extremely upset. I pulled Dennis into the trainer's room and calmed him down as best I could.

DL: *Back to Game 7 in '86; Clemens was going to close if the opportunity arose. Did you ever ask John McNamara if he considering bringing him into the game instead of Schiraldi in the seventh inning?*

LG: I never did. But you're right—the plan was to use Roger as the closer if we had the lead. Schiraldi had pitched pretty well for us, and Mac thought he could get it done. We had a chance to win that game, but it just wasn't meant to be.

DL: *A few years later, you traded Schiraldi and Al Nipper for Lee Smith. Why were you able to make that deal, and do you consider it your best as Red Sox GM?*

LG: I think picking up Nick Esasky and Rob Murphy really helped the ball club, too. Esasky hit 30 home runs for us, and Murphy really solidified our bullpen, pitching in over 70 games one year. Of course, once Esasky left, he had the trouble with vertigo and his career was over. As for the Smith deal, I think the Cubs—Jim Frey was their GM—were simply down on him. Lee never really liked to work hard off the field. Of course, once he got on the mound he gave 110 percent and was a helluva pitcher. He might go in the Hall of Fame some day. Anyway, Frey and I were talking, and he let me know Smith was available. I tried to act like I was mildly interested and gave him the names of some guys we'd be willing to trade. I tried to make it look like I was doing him a favor by making the deal. Once it was done, the media was shocked. They thought something must be wrong with Smith. There wasn't, and it was a good deal for us.

DL: *Can you address Bagwell-for-Andersen, and whether Scott Cooper was ever discussed in that deal?*

LG: Bagwell was the guy they asked for from the start. I've never understood where the Cooper story came from. Their scout simply did an outstanding job. We were badly in need of a pitcher. We had guys hurt. Jeff Gray, a twice-released player, was holding our pen together. I asked Eddie Kasko and Wayne Britton to find someone who could help, and they said Larry Andersen was the best set-up guy in the National League. None of our talent evaluators plussed Bagwell's power. I double-checked before making the deal, and the report was that he couldn't play third base. We'd have to move him across the diamond. It also said that he'd hit for average only—not for power. We all know how it worked out, but it was a deal we had to make at the time to stay in contention, but Bagwell went on to prove us wrong about his power and became an All-Star National League player. He was an outstanding competitor.

DL: *And, of course, you lost Andersen after the season.*

LG: Yes, and Larry Andersen had pitched well for us, too. That was the year of the collusion settlement, and we knew he could potentially be impacted by that. I went to the league office before making the deal, and they assured me he wouldn't. But then, after the season, he was made a free agent anyway, by the ruling of an arbitrator.

DL: *What about the Mike Boddicker deal?*

LG: We needed a pitcher, and Boddicker did an outstanding job for us. When we traded Schilling in that deal, we knew he had a great arm. And we knew he was a great competitor. We wouldn't have won the World Series [in 2004] without him. But at the time, we figured he was five years away. He ended up going to Houston, and then Philadelphia, after Baltimore. That's when he started to win, and obviously he's had a great career and has become an All-Star. His competing spirit was brilliantly displayed in the 2004 World Series when he pitched in pain.

DL: *You mention in your book how difficult it is to release players. Tell us about the decision to let Dwight Evans finish his career in Baltimore.*

LG: Dwight had back problems. In August, he had played the first game of a double-header but came up to see me, in street clothes, afterwards. He told me, "My back is too bad to play anymore. I'm going to retire." I had to talk him out of it. I asked him to come back the next day to discuss it, and Art Pappas and I got him to agree to go into traction at UMass Hospital. We didn't disable him, though, as we didn't want him out for 15 days if we could help it. That actually led to some criticism, as we were shorthanded and ended up with Rick Cerone in right field at one point. But the traction helped, and Dwight went out to see if he could hit. I remember he had us bring in Yaz, who he really valued as a mentor, to help him. The team was on the road, so we brought in a college pitcher from BC to throw to him. He came back, but when it came time to sign him after the season we still had concerns. He was always one of my favorites. Dwight was very dedicated. But we felt he'd want more than a one-year deal, and we weren't sure he could stay healthy enough to honor that. Letting him go was a business decision but a hard one for me to make. I had great admiration for him.

DL: *You were involved in many difficult contract negotiations and often looked like the bad guy because the player wanted more than your bosses—ownership—were willing to pay. How have agents and salaries impacted the game?*

LG: It's a different world today than it was when I started out. It used to be that when you made a proposal to a player, you met him once, no agents, and finally we would shake hands after we both agreed on the terms. Maybe some players were taken advantage of in the past, but for the most part, the agreements were fair. Now you have as many as 10 meetings with his agent, and you never know what he's reporting back to the player. And the Union—the Players' Association—has tremendous power in the game. Arbitration is another thing. It's possible to win the battle but lose the war. You have to remember that when the hearing is over, the player still wears your uniform. You have to do everything in your power to make sure he knows you were being fair in the arbitration process, but you also have to work within the financial parameters of your ball club.

DL: *Your negotiations with Roger Clemens in 1987 led to the now-infamous line, "The sun will set . . . and I'll have lunch tomorrow," which was repeated over and over by a certain scribe. What are your thoughts on the Boston media?*

LG: Sometimes they get too personal or mean-spirited. Some guys are looking for anything negative they can find and try to make major issues out of nothing. Of course, others aren't like that; they're fair and professional. My problem was that I'm a people person and upfront. I'd tell someone what I thought, and they'd try to make a story out of it. If you make a mistake, nothing will change that. You accept that and go on, but the media will remember it and repeat it, over and over.

DL: *You opine in your book that Haywood Sullivan was "old-school." Do you consider yourself "old-school," or more in tune with today's way of looking at the game?*

LG: Haywood, in a sense, was old-fashioned, yes. He grew up in a game that never included agents, unions, and astronomical salaries. He didn't really like the game changing as it did. And I can see where people would look at my era and think that I was that way, too. But I've always tried to think outside the box. I talk about *Moneyball* somewhat in my book. I think that stats are important, but they serve as adjuncts rather than as the primary evaluation. Computers can give you certain facts, but eyeball-to-eyeball scouting, for me, is essential. Guys like Joe Torre, and even Earl Weaver before him, would use stats. But they wouldn't overburden or inundate themselves with them. You need to look at both sides of everything, but primarily the scout's advance scouting-reports, and the computer reports secondarily. In the *Moneyball* theory, they would seldom draft high school players, primarily college players. I believe you never pass up an outstanding prospect because he's a high school prospect.

DL: *You once refused to allow the ambidextrous Greg Harris to pitch left-handed, "for the integrity of the game." Tell us about that.*

LG: I'd seen him throw left-handed in BP, and he while he believed he could get hitters out left-handed, I was very skeptical. Could he throw left-handed? Sure. But in my opinion, it wasn't good enough to get Major League hitters out. I liked Greg a great deal. He was a bit of a character, but in a good way. I had him earlier in his career, with the Mets, before acquiring him to pitch for the Red Sox. He was an excellent competitor.

DL: *You mentioned Torre a moment ago. I understand that you almost hired him once.*

LG: That was when we initially hired "Walpole Joe" Morgan as our interim manager. I knew Torre well when he managed the Mets when I was there. At the time, Torre was doing the color commentary on the Angels' broadcasts. I had recommended Morgan highly, and Mrs. Yawkey liked him also, so he became our manager. Joe didn't even care about the money—he just wanted to prove he could manage. Once we hired him, the team went on that great winning streak and "Morgan

Magic" became a rallying cry. If things hadn't worked out with Morgan, Torre was the guy I had in mind to hire as our manager.

DL: *Last one: In your book, you talk about how in Game 6 of the '86 Series, your mind kept going back to all the minor league parks you'd been in—all the years and all the games. Baseball really is more than just the Major Leagues, isn't it?*

LG: You know, with all the controversies and scandals—the money, the steroid scandals, etc.—between the white lines it's still a game, a great game. All over the country, the minors bring families out to see base-ball. In 42 years, I've been to a lot of great minor league parks in New England. Up here, Pawtucket is great, Portland is great, Lowell is also great. Minor league baseball is fun, and baseball, to put it simply, is America. I have been blessed to have spent so much of my life in a game I also love a great deal.

Jason McLeod

Jason McLeod is the Red Sox' director of amateur scout-ing. A former pitcher in the Houston organization, McLeod is a native of San Diego. This interview took place in June 2005, shortly after the amateur draft.

David Laurila: *Did the draft go pretty much as expected, or were there surprises in the first few rounds that impacted our strategy?*

Jason McLeod: I'd say we were pleasantly surprised at how our first six picks shook out. We did mock drafts beforehand—with different sce-narios—and they seemed to indicate we wouldn't get everyone we wanted. We knew Hansen could fall because of the Boras factor, but we didn't think it would be far enough for us to take him. We focused a lot on Jacoby Ellsbury, Trevor Crowe, and Cliff Pennington at the top. When we heard that Cincinnati and Pittsburgh were taking high school outfielders, we knew we had a pretty good shot at getting one of them.

DL: *Did we go into the draft with a checklist of specific goals?*

JM: Not really. In the draft, you have to pretty much roll with the punches and select the best talent that's available. I know this is a pretty vanilla answer, but you want to get guys that you like in every round. We're happy with how things worked out.

DL: *We obviously took more high school players than in recent drafts. Can you comment on that?*

JM: Because of what we've done the last few years, some people were surprised. And all things being equal, maybe we'd have gone with more college guys again this year. But with so many teams using the so-called *Moneyball* approach this year—the stat-ball approach—by the time we got to our sandwich picks and the fourth and fifth rounds, the ability of the high school guys we took was just too good. We projected them higher than the college players available, and we weren't going to pass them up just to be taking college guys.

DL: *Last year, 8 of our top 26 picks didn't sign, and 7 of them were either high school or junior college guys. As we took 9 such players in the first 15 rounds this year, what signability issues might we be facing?*

JM: We selected with a pretty good feeling that we'd be signing the players we drafted. We still have a few to go, but we're getting guys signed. Egan and Blue are down in camp. Engel and Bowden are still in school, and we can't sign them until they've graduated. There are always questions, but we should be okay.

DL: *How many pre-draft agreements did we make, and is there a timetable as to how quickly we hope to sign our picks?*

JM: Most of our college guys are signed already, and a few others are still playing. We didn't have any agreements during the draft, but you have a pretty good idea from the pre-draft workouts and other conversations you have.

DL: *Among the guys we drafted, whom did we bring to Fenway Park for workouts?*

JM: We had about 25 guys in on June 2, and we drafted a handful of them. Egan was here, Alvarez, Engel, Criaris. We worked out Buchholz and Fernandes prior to that. I think that's it.

DL: *When will the decisions be made as to who is assigned where, and are most of our high school picks going to the GCL or Lowell?*

JM: We have a pretty good idea when we draft them. Ben Cherington is there, and when a guy is taken we'll tell him where the guy should probably start off. The high school guys will all be in the GCL. With the college guys, part of it is when they sign. Hansen could take longer, and there's a decent chance he'll start higher than Lowell. Ellsbury will likely start at Lowell. Other guys we plan to have there are Buchholz, Lowrie, Zink, Yema, Corsaletti, Wagner, and Guyette.

DL: Baseball America *said our fifth round pick, Reid Engel, "May not be physically ready yet for pro ball." Do you agree, and is he the fastest player we drafted?*

JM: He's fast, but I'd say Ellsbury is faster. Engel isn't physically mature yet—he looks like a high school player is supposed to look rather than a weight-room guy. He's lean, a Steve Finley body-type, and a good athlete who can swing. It will be a good test for him to play in the GCL, but we expect him to be fine.

DL: *We didn't take a shortstop until the 14th round. How much was depth in the system a factor in that?*

JM: We do feel good about the position, but if a guy deserved to be picked, we'd have taken him. We took Jed Lowrie, even though we have Dustin Pedroia playing second base right now. We have guys like Hanley and Christian Lara in the infield, too, but we thought Lowrie was too good to pass up.

DL: *Prior to the draft, there was speculation that we had a lot of interest in Cuban shortstop Yuniel Escobar, who went 75th overall. How much truth was there to that?*

JM: We had an interest and worked him out. He's very athletically gifted, but there was more of an unknown factor that played into the evaluation process. It was going to cost a lot to sign him, and we were maybe a little uncomfortable, not knowing as much about him as we'd have liked.

DL: *In the first 10 rounds, we selected 2 catchers, followed by several more in later rounds. How need-based were those picks, and how much consideration was given to Taylor Teagarden and Nick Hundley?*

JM: If you talked to people in the organization, they'd say it's an area of need. We did look at Teagarden and Hundley, but their signing demands didn't seem like they'd match our assessments and evaluation of them. Teagarden was the best defensive catcher in the draft. Hundley had his good days and bad days when we saw him. Overall, we thought we were better served with the guys we drafted.

DL: *We took Jon Egan in the second round. Are we projecting him as a catcher or at another position?*

JM: Right now, his offense is ahead of his defense. He's a big kid—about 6' 4", 215—but he sits low and is nimble. We'll have to see. He hasn't had a lot of instruction, but we feel Rob Leary and his staff will really be able to help him. He'll get every opportunity, and he has the bat to project at another position if necessary. The other catcher we took in the earlier rounds, Mark Wagner, is very strong defensively. He threw out over 40 percent of runners this year, and he calls a good game. Unlike Egan, he needs his bat to catch up with his defensive skills.

DL: *With the system in need of power, and character highly valued by the organization, how hard would it have been to pass on John Mayberry, Jr., had he been available when we made our first pick?*

JM: He's one of those guys where when you walk in, your eyes go right to him. He's really an imposing presence, and he has a lot of talent, but Jed Lowrie out-homered him the past two years, which you wouldn't think could be the case. As I said earlier, along with Crowe and Pennington, Jacoby Ellsbury was the guy we liked at the top of our draft.

DL: *Tell us what made Ellsbury our first pick.*

JM: Coming in, we wanted an athletic college guy who was also a baseball player. We liked what Ellsbury brought to the table, which was performance at a high level to go with good tools and great makeup. He's a good hitter, a plus-plus runner, and a plus defender.

DL: *Craig Hansen is a big right hander with overpowering stuff and was a closer in college. As that sounds like a description of Jon Papelbon, how does Hansen compare to our top pitching prospect, and how is he being projected?*

JM: Hansen has had a lot more press and notoriety than Papelbon did. He definitely has the repertoire to start, and people have been asking about that possibility. If he signs quickly, we'll likely leave him in the closer's role for the rest of the summer. He certainly could move more quickly through the system in that role. As for projecting his future, that's a question we haven't answered yet. First, we need to get him signed, and then we'll sit down and make that decision.

DL: *What were the deciding factors in drafting Hansen over Luke Hochevar and Matt Torra?*

JM: It really just came down to having him rated higher. There's no complicated explanation beyond that.

DL: *A lot of people are intrigued by our selection of William Blue. What can you tell us about him, and why did we take him as high as the fourth round?*

JM: It was a case of getting a guy we wanted, and if you do that you're probably not taking him too high. We kept pretty quiet on him but really liked that he has a big, strong, durable body, and he can touch 92 with a good curve and good command. A lot of scouts don't see guys in his area of northern California, but we knew a few other teams were interested. When a few high school guys fell off the board, we thought that if we wanted him we'd have to take him when we could. Scouting instincts were a big part of it.

DL: *Clay Buchholz and Michael Bowden are both said to be great athletes. How much importance do you place on athleticism with pitchers, and with his limited experience on the mound, is Buchholz much more advanced than the high schooler Bowden?*

JM: We do value that a lot. Craig Shipley and I talk about it. Being able to repeat your delivery and make physical adjustments are important. If you're a good athlete, you're going to be able to do those more easily. Buchholz has a streamlined, athletic body and was getting looks as a shortstop in high school. Bowden is a bigger, bulkier kid—more physically mature. Besides being two years older, Buchholz has faced much better competition than Bowden. He pitched in a very good junior college conference.

DL: *The report on J.T. Zink, our eighth-round selection, says he has a sidearm delivery and throws a good sinking fastball. How similar is he to Cla Meredith?*

JM: They're not really the same types. Zink is low three-quarters, while Meredith is more from the side. And Meredith's sinker is hard and heavy—a strikeout sinker. Zink's is a lighter sink—a truer, shorter sink.

DL: *Last one:* Baseball America *rates the tools of its top 200 prospects, and Jacoby Ellsbury and Craig Hansen are each listed in more than one category. Of our other picks, who would you rate as having the best power, best fastball, best breaking ball, and as being the best pure hitter?*

JM: I'd say Jon Egan has the most power potential. Next to Hansen, the best fastball would be either Buchholz or Bowden. Next to Hansen's slider, Bowden's curve might be the best breaking pitch. Buchholz has a good slider, though, and Guyette's curve is very good. As for best pure hitter, Lowrie, who's a switch-hitter, has a very good stroke from the left side. From the right side, Egan has a very good swing. Someone else with a good swing is Engel. He has a short, quick stroke and centers the ball really well. He hits pitches where they're supposed to be hit, which is impressive.

⚾

MIKE TAMBURRO

MIKE TAMBURRO IS THE PRESIDENT OF THE RED SOX' TRIPLE A AFFILIATE, THE PAWTUCKET RED SOX. ALSO CONTRIBUTING TO THIS INTERVIEW WERE THE TEAM'S LONG-TIME OWNER, BEN MONDOR, AND ITS GENERAL MANAGER, LOU SCHWECHHEIMER. THIS INTERVIEW, WHICH FEATURES MEMORABLE STORIES FROM THEIR TIME IN PAWTUCKET, TOOK PLACE IN JUNE 2005.

David Laurila: *You've been with the team for almost 30 years. Who gets your vote as the most colorful PawSox player ever?*

Mike Tamburro: Win Remmerswaal is the premier character in the history of the franchise, and it's not even close. Win played here in the early 1980s and was Dutch. Dick O'Connell signed him out of a tryout camp in Europe, and in my opinion, Win came here as a tourist first and a ballplayer second. He threw in the nineties and pitched in the big leagues for a while, and he was as colorful as they come.

DL: *What's your favorite Win Remmerswaal story?*

MT: One of the best is the time the team was flying back from either Norfolk or Richmond and had to change planes in Washington D.C. Win was famous for missing team buses, and he never made it onto the plane in Washington. We got back to Pawtucket, and no Win. The next day, no Win. We had no idea where he was. Finally, on the fourth day, he comes strolling into the office. He has a box of cigars for Ben—he knew Ben liked cigars—and we asked, "Win, where have you been?" He said, "I realized that I was in the nation's capital, and that I may never see it again. So I decided to stay for a few days and look around."

DL: *And there are more?*

MT: There are a lot more. Once, when he was up with the Red Sox, the team was playing in New York in September. He missed the team bus from the hotel, so he hopped into a cab and told the driver to bring him to the stadium. When he got there, he went to the visiting locker room only to have the attendant tell him, "Son, there are no Red Sox here. This is Shea Stadium. The Jets are playing a football game here today."

DL: *It sounds like he should have rented a car.*

Ben Mondor: Not necessarily. His roommate was Julio Valdez, and they did occasionally rent cars. Now, that was an interesting duo to begin with. One spoke Dutch, the other Spanish—neither had perfect English. They got pulled over because Win was driving on the wrong side of the road. And I think they had rented the car with wrong identification, because neither had a credit card. Somehow, they talked themselves out of it—maybe because the cop knew they were ballplayers. Win apparently told the cop, "That's how we drive in Holland. I didn't know."

MT: Another time, Win was driving a rental car down the Mass Turnpike and ran out of gas. He walked to the nearest town, but instead of going to a gas station he rented another car. He just left the first one sitting by the side of the road. It sat there for a week until they tracked it and found out it been rented by someone with the ball club. They brought it to the ballpark—this was at the end of the season—and left it there. Butch Hobson knew what had happened, so he decided to drive it home to Alabama. When he got there, he just left it in a parking lot near his house.

DL: *Did Remmerswaal get along well with his teammates?*

MT: He did. He was a likeable guy and very bright. He spoke several languages. Win used to come into Ben's office to call his father, and Ben would tell him he could use the phone in the back room if he wanted privacy. He'd say to Ben, "Ben, we'll be speaking Dutch. It doesn't matter!"

The guys on the team nicknamed him "Poundcake," and a local announcer once asked Win what his biggest dream was. He told the guy that he wanted to be in Fenway Park; it's Game 7 of the World Series, and he's the closer. It's the ninth inning of a close game, and as he comes jogging in from the bullpen, 35,000 fans are chanting, "Poundcake, Poundcake!"

DL: *Who was the manager while he was in Pawtucket?*

BM: It was "Walpole Joe" Morgan, who was the greatest umpire-baiter I ever saw. He'd agitate umpires just for fun. There weren't a lot of fans back then, and Joe liked to give them a show. His favorite trick was to run out after a close call went against us and start gesturing in an animated fashion to the umpires. The fans would cheer him on, thinking he was giving them hell. What Joe was really doing was yelling, "That was the right call . . . you got it right . . . you're a hell of an umpire!"

DL: *And he got away with that?*

MT: A lot of the time, sure. They couldn't toss him for agreeing with them. One year, he was having an ongoing rhubarb with an umpire named Fields. It had been going on from city to city. Fields had run Joe recently and was umpiring first base when the first batter of a game hit a routine grounder to the second baseman. He was out by a good four steps—an easy call. Joe came charging out of the dugout and right up to Fields. He said, "You're right," and then turned around and walked back to the dugout.

DL: *I'm sure there were times he was truly mad, though.*

MT: Absolutely. For some reason, we always seemed to get bad calls in Columbus, which is where the league office was. One game, Joe went absolutely berserk over a call and sat down on second base and refused to move. He was there for 10 minutes and demanded that Harold Cooper, the league president, talk to him before he'd leave. He knew Cooper was upstairs, and finally Cooper gestured for him to go to the dugout to take his call. Joe went over, picked up the phone and said, "Harold, how the hell are you?"

Another good story is the time a center fielder named Dick Sharon made two great plays for us in a row. First, he made a diving catch going to his right. Then, he made a diving catch going to his left. Joe goes running out to center field to shake his hand . . . and it's still the middle of the inning. There were only two outs. Joe didn't care—he liked to entertain the fans.

DL: *Oil Can Boyd played in Pawtucket. Do you have a favorite Oil Can story?*

MT: Dennis used to come into the office every day to talk. We'd pump him up and give him confidence, which he seemed to need. Anyway, there was a fan who used to bake for us once a week, and one day she brought in a big chocolate cream pie. She put it on the desk—Dennis was there—and a few minutes later the phone rang. It was Lou Gorman, so I told Dennis to sit tight for a few minutes while Ben and I took the call in the back room. When we got back, Dennis—all 160 pounds of him—had eaten the whole thing. He was just sitting there with a big smile on his face. That was Dennis.

DL: *Any from Wade Boggs?*

Lou Schwechheimer: Wade was superstitious, as most people know. And he obviously loved to hit. One Sunday afternoon, he had gone two for four and afterwards talked us into throwing him BP in the empty stadium. Then, when it started to get dark, he begged us to turn on the lights so we could keep going. We wouldn't, so he challenged us to a game of wiffle ball in the parking lot. The whole team is packing up to go, so finally he gives up and gets his own stuff together. He has a red PawSox bag with his name on it, and he's got his bats in there. He didn't want them with everyone else's. He said the other bats would give his bats bad habits.

DL: *Any from Mark Fidrych, who made a comeback bid with the PawSox in the early eighties?*

MT: When Mark was here, there were Marlboro Man billboards in all the ballparks. We had a pitcher named Dennis Burtt, who convinced Mark that there was a spring behind the billboard, and if the Marlboro Man got hit below the belt he'd bend over. A little later, Mark was out there with a bucket of balls, trying to hit the sweet spot.

DL: *Who else has a good story?*

MT: Luis Aponte was involved in "the longest game," which went on until 4:09 in the morning. Afterwards, he showered and went home like everyone else, but his wife had locked him out of their apartment. He didn't have a key for some reason, and she didn't believe that he was coming from the game and wouldn't let him in. He had to come back to the ballpark and sleep on the trainer's table.

DL: *Can we have a few more?*

MT: Buddy Hunter was here in the seventies; he was a cerebral guy who later managed in the organization. He was playing second base one game and knew the hitter on the other team was coming off knee surgery. There was a guy on first, so he let a pop fly drop and took the force-out instead. That put the guy with the bad knee—his name was Braziele—on base instead of the faster runner. They jawed with each other a little, but I think it was in good humor rather than anger. The next day, Braziele gets to the ballpark early and steals Hunter's glove out of the clubhouse. When Hunter got there, it was hanging from the top of the flagpole in center field.

DL: *Can we close with another Remmerswaal story or two?*

LS: The first time Win got called up, the big club was in Milwaukee and we went to his place to let him know. It was eight o'clock in the morning, and we had booked him a ten o'clock flight. We knocked on the door, but there was no response. So we changed his flight to noon and kept knocking. Still no response. Some time later, Julio Valdez pulls up in their rental car. It's missing the front bumper, and the windshield is broken. We ask Julio if he knows where Win is, and he says let's go in and check. We walk into his bedroom, and we see two black socks sticking out from under the blanket—that's all we can see. We said, "Win, is that you?" He said, "Yeah, it's me." We said, "We've been knocking for a couple of hours—why didn't you answer?" He said, "I figured it was probably you, and that maybe I was getting called up, but if they really want me, they'd be willing to wait."

DL: *One last one?*

BM: Win's brother came from Holland to visit once. After he had been here a few weeks, one of us asked him when he'd be going back. Win said he wasn't sure, but that his brother's visa was going to be running out in the not-too-distant future. We told him he should check into it, and he asked what would happen when it ran out. We told him they'd send his brother back, so they just let it happen—his brother got a free flight back to Holland. Win just shrugged and said, "He wanted to go home, anyway."

DREW AND JOANN WEBER

DREW AND JOANN WEBER HAVE OWNED THE RED SOX' SHORT-
SEASON CLASS A AFFILIATE, THE LOWELL SPINNERS, SINCE
1997. ONE OF MINOR LEAGUE BASEBALL'S MOST SUCCESSFUL
FRANCHISES, THE SPINNERS HAVE SOLD OUT EVERY GAME AT
LELACHEUR PARK SINCE THE MID-POINT OF THE 1999 SEASON.
THIS INTERVIEW TOOK PLACE IN JUNE 2005.

David Laurila: *Prior to purchasing the Spinners, what did each of you do for a living?*

Drew Weber: I was in the men's clothing business. I was a partner with my brother, and we were based in New York City.

Joann Weber: I raised our two children, Michael and Kate, and was a sculptor for 20 years. I also taught English to Russian immigrants at our temple.

DL: *Why did you decide to buy a minor league baseball team?*

DW: I used to know a lot of Major League players through my business. Dave Bergman was one, and he and a few others used to tell me I should buy a team someday. He'd come in with some of his teammates on the Tigers, and I got to know him and Sparky Anderson pretty well. When I decided to sell my business, I thought back to what was essentially a semi-serious suggestion and liked the idea.

JW: Timing is everything, and our youngest had just left for college. That lent itself to doing something like this, because we didn't have the same obligations as before. We decided to look for a team, and the one thing we wanted was to not have partners. We wanted to run things ourselves rather than be part of a larger group.

DL: *What went into purchasing a team? I assume it wasn't a simple endeavor.*

DW: Not at all. We knew some people and were able to arrange having dinner with the president of Minor League Baseball. He was very congenial, but in reality, that and fifty cents will get you on the subway.

JW: We learned that it's a "good old boys" network, and you really need to know somebody. We really only knew people who knew somebody, which wasn't enough.

DW: We put a lot of homework into it, too, and probably knew as much as anybody who wasn't in the game. We went to the El Paso seminar to learn as much as we could, and we talked to a lot of baseball people in a lot of places. I even worked as an intern for a week with the team in Jamestown, just to learn more about the business—I was probably the oldest intern in history! But it was hard to get our foot in the door, and it got pretty frustrating.

DL: *How did you finally get an opportunity to purchase the Spinners?*

DW: In 1995, we went to the winter meetings in L.A. We did a lot of networking, which consisted mostly of 20-second conversations, letting people know we were interested in purchasing a minor league team. Most of the people there were wearing sport jackets or knit shirts with team logos on them. Then we spotted a guy wearing a University of Cincinnati shirt, which immediately struck me as a positive sign. We started talking to him, and instead of 20 seconds we spent most of the evening together. The fellow's name was Clyde Smoll, who was in the process of moving his Elmira team, which was a Marlins affiliate, to Lowell to be associated with the Red Sox. We kept in touch with Clyde, in large part because we were so interested in the process. I had really become obsessed with the idea of getting a team . . . but I certainly had no idea it would be his.

JW: Obsessed is a good word for it.

DW: Right about the time I was getting ready to throw in the towel—this was August of '96—Clyde called. He was having health issues and had decided to sell the team, and was wondering if we were still interested. The next day, we were in Lowell watching a game.

DL: *Why was Lowell such an appealing opportunity?*

DW: To be honest, it was our first opportunity. We had looked into teams all over the country and didn't know anything about the Lowell area. But they were talking about a new stadium here, which was state-financed and factored into the purchase price, and it looked like a good situation. We were just looking to break even, anyway. There were a lot of other business ventures that would have been more profitable. We wanted to be in baseball.

JW: To put it simply, we came in saying that it was a labor of love. That's what it was, and still is.

DL: *How much of a time investment has it been?*

DW: The truth of the matter is, we used to be a lot more involved in the day-to-day than we are now. We won't ever take anything for granted when it comes to the sell-outs or the fan experience here, but we're fortunate to have a great staff. That enables us to be a part of the community without the pressure of worrying too much about how things are being run.

DL: *How do you view your relationship with the Lowell community?*

JW: It's part of our responsibility. To give back to the community is very important, and giving time or helping with charities is a part of that. I was sick last year and got a lot of cards from people who are season ticket holders or simply knew us from the community. That was very important to me.

DW: To a certain extent, the community becomes a part of your extended family. They've been very supportive of us, and we don't want to lose sight of that.

DL: *The Spinners have received accolades for off-the-field entertainment, both between innings and with promotions. How important is what you provide to the fans beyond the game itself?*

DW: We think it's a good combination. I remember when we came here, people said Boston-area fans were too conservative and it wouldn't work. We love the baseball, but want fans to have as much fun as possible. The team has matured into the community, and the entertainment we provide is a part of that.

JW: One hundred percent, we love entertainment.

DL: *Which teams and players did you follow growing up?*

DW: I grew up with the Brooklyn Dodgers, who left town when I was 14. Duke Snider was my favorite player. I went to the same school as Doris Kearns Goodwin, who also grew up following them. After the Dodgers left, I started following the Mets.

JW: I followed players like Maris and Mantle, like my friends did. I didn't know as much about baseball then. My father was a huge Jets fan. He was all football.

DL: *What are your some of your biggest baseball memories, either from those earlier days or from your time here in Lowell?*

DW: Believe it or not, I get a big kick out of being in New York among Yankee fans now. I always rooted against them, and in a way I wonder where they all came from. When I was a kid, I hardly knew any. There were three teams in New York back then, and who rooted for who isn't like it is now. A lot of it was based on the social and cultural dynamics of the time, along with what part of the city you lived in. Today, Yankee fans are different, and right now they're not quite as smug as they were before last year.

JW: A memory that stands out for me is from the first year we owned the team. We had this big guy on the team who wore a lot of chains and was very popular with the fans. One day, I was told that we'd be sending him home after the game. When he came out of the office, he had his head down and he was crying. It was very traumatic, seeing a young, confident guy—a very big guy—having his dreams ruined. That's by far the worst part of baseball.

DL: *What is your relationship with the players?*

JW: The ones we get to know better are the ones with interesting personalities. It's like with any group of people, anywhere—some are quiet and others are more outgoing. These are college kids, and most of them are friendly and unassuming. Most of them are very nice, as are their families.

DW: The way it's set up here—where the clubhouse and offices are—we have a lot of contact with them. I remember when Hanley Ramirez was with us. He walked by the office one day, and I asked him if he was happy here. He smiled at me and said, "No" and kept walking. He didn't know much English yet, and I don't think he had any idea what I had just asked him! We don't go out of our way to talk to the players, but we see them a lot.

DL: *One last question: Do you have a lot of contact with other owners in minor league baseball?*

DW: We know the people down in Pawtucket pretty well. And, of course, having been here eight years, we know everyone in the New York–Penn League. What's actually kind of fun is taking calls from people who want advice about purchasing a minor league team. I remember when it was us making those calls, and who was helpful to us, and who wasn't. It's hard to believe that it was so long ago

SHORTER VIEWS

CHRIS KEMPLE

CHRIS KEMPLE IS THE GENERAL MANAGER OF THE WILMINGTON BLUE ROCKS. THE BLUE ROCKS BECAME A BOSTON FARM CLUB PRIOR TO THE 2005 SEASON. THIS IS AN EXCERPT FROM AN INTERVIEW THAT TOOK PLACE IN JANUARY 2005.

David Laurila: *Start by telling us about the affiliation change. Why did the Royals leave Wilmington, and why are the Red Sox coming in?*

Chris Kemple: We had been an affiliate of the Kansas City Royals for 12 years, and they were terrific to work with. Thus, it was a difficult decision to leave them. However, we as an organization felt the Red Sox had more to offer. First, it is a much better fit geographically. There are many more Red Sox fans in Delaware than Royals fans. Second, the Red Sox are one of the top teams in baseball, not to mention one of the premier sports organizations in the country. We felt it would be an honor to associate with such an organization. Also, since the Red Sox train in Florida and not Arizona like the Royals, it gives our fans the opportunity to go to spring training to follow the team.

DL: *How long was the move in the works?*

CK: The affiliation change was rather quick. Matt Minker, the team president, and I met with Ben Cherington and Peter Woodfork in early September and the contract was signed shortly thereafter. After our initial meeting, we knew the Red Sox were the right fit. It was sort of like the Jerry McGuire "you had me at hello" scene.

DL: *Cherington was quoted as saying, "The Blue Rocks are the top franchise in the most respected high-A league in baseball." What are your thoughts on that?*

CK: Ben paid us a tremendous compliment. While we would like to consider our organization the tops in Class A baseball, it's always nice when a Major League executive takes notice.

DL: *The working agreement you signed with the Red Sox is for two years. Why two, and what is typical in the industry?*

CK: The typical player development contract is for either two or four years in duration, thus the two-year agreement is quite standard. For those not familiar with a player development contract [PDC], it is a standard contract between a Major League team and the minor league team. It follows the basic agreement, which is the agreement between Major League Baseball and Minor League Baseball, outlining who is responsible for what. For example, the Major League team pays for 75 percent of all bats and balls used, while the minor league team pays the remaining 25 percent; the minor league team is responsible for the first 17 hotel rooms used, and the Major League team pays for all meal money on the road.

DL: *Let's close by touching on ballpark atmosphere. When fans come to Frawley Stadium, what can they expect?*

CK: I believe the stadium atmosphere is terrific. The fans really get into the game, and we keep everything active with all the in-game promotions. In addition, our mascot, "Rocky Bluewinkle," puts on a great show and then there is the popular "Mr. Celery," who runs on the field and dances every time the Blue Rocks score a run.

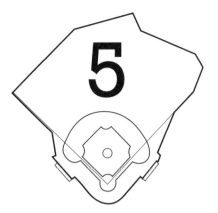

Voices of the Game

CARL BEANE

CARL BEANE IS THE RED SOX' PUBLIC ADDRESS ANNOUNCER. A
NATIVE OF AGAWAM, MASSACHUSETTS, AND A LIFELONG RED SOX
FAN, BEANE HAS BEEN THE VOICE OF FENWAY PARK SINCE THE
BEGINNING OF THE 2003 SEASON. THIS INTERVIEW TOOK PLACE
IN AUGUST 2005.

David Laurila: *What did you do before you became the Red Sox' public
address announcer?*

Carl Beane: I began as a musician, a drummer. I was, and still am,
devoted to Buddy Rich. I played with some local bands but was good at
playing with people who didn't make it. I did play with Chuck Berry
once, though, when I was about 16 years old. He was having one of his
annual duels with the IRS and didn't have a traveling band. Musicians
hung out at record stores back in the sixties, so he'd call one in the town
he was coming to and line up local musicians. I was in a store in
Holyoke, and the manager asked if I wanted to play with Chuck Berry.
The night of the show, we're standing around waiting for him when this

big Cadillac pulls up. We asked if he wanted to do a sound check, but all he wanted was to know that we had played his songs. He said that we'd start a song when he waved his guitar, and we'd end it when he waved his guitar. That was it.

DL: *What did you do besides music?*

CB: Radio. I knew in fourth grade that I wanted to do radio. I went to broadcast school and graduated in 1972. When I got out, I started working at WMAS in Springfield. I was a disc jockey and also did some sports, which included high school basketball. After that, I went to WBRK in Pittsfield, where I was a nighttime DJ and produced a sports show. From there, I went to WARE, in the town of Ware, and I've been associated with them ever since. One of the interesting things I've done is host a Sunday morning polka show. I called myself Beane-ski. There's a big Polish population in the Ware area, and I took a lot of requests. I had a three-page list of people I had to say hello to every show.

DL: *Do you currently do any radio work outside of WARE?*

CB: I do. I work as an independent contractor, and my voice is on around 400 stations. In the offseason, I'm with WBZ and ESPN radio. I do updates on WFAN. I do sound-bites for Westwood One. I figured out a long time ago that if I worked for a lot of people, there'd always be work. I've been in radio now for 33 years.

DL: *Have you done any play-by-play or color outside of high school sports on WARE?*

CB: Oh, yes. One thing I did was work with Dick Irvin on the Montreal Canadiens' broadcasts. I did color for him, on English radio, for three years when the Canadiens came to Boston or Hartford. That was in the 1980s when he worked alone and would use local guys when he was on the road. A little bit like Chuck Berry, in a way.

DL: *When you decided to audition for the Red Sox' PA job, what did you put on your demo tape?*

CB: I didn't do a demo tape. I've been going to almost every Red Sox game for 28 years because of my radio work. I was a known commodity as a reporter. It had been suggested to me that I look into the job, and one day at the dinner table I got a bee in my head to call and ask about it. This was in March, and they asked me if I wanted to come down to Ft. Myers to try it out. I was the only one to get a live audition. By the third inning, I knew that I really wanted to do this. They kept me there to do a second game, and afterwards said that I was the frontrunner. They still had to check out their other candidates, but I understood that. One hundred and sixty-five people applied for the job, and they gave it to me after I had decided, almost on a whim, to call and ask about it. My theory is that God was talking to me that day, because I can't think of a better explanation.

DL: *Are you a celebrity now? Do people recognize you, or your voice, when you're in the supermarket or a restaurant?*

CB: They do. It took a little getting used to, but I like it just fine. I had a taste of it from radio, but being associated with the Red Sox brings it to another level. When I took the job, the Celtics and Bruins had changed PA announcers, and the Red Sox had done so twice since Sherm Feller. In each case, it was without much notoriety, so I didn't expect it. But I enjoy people, so I don't mind. If someone wants to walk up and say hi, and see my World Series ring, that's okay. The most amusing thing is when I hear people doing impressions of me. As the saying goes, imitation is the sincerest form of flattery.

DL: *There's a funny NESN promo with Tim Wakefield and Don Orsillo, where Orsillo pretends to do voice exercises to get ready for a broadcast. Do you do anything to keep your voice in shape?*

CB: The "announcer boy" promo? Yes, that's a good one. Do I do anything for my voice? No, I was simply blessed with a good set of vocal cords. My voice changed at the age of 11, so it was God-given—simply the sound of the noise coming out of the hole below my nose. I try not to do anything to abuse it—I don't drink or smoke—but that's all. I've always liked to read aloud. Maybe I have what I have from that.

DL: *In a recent broadcast, Jerry Remy was mispronouncing the last name of Kansas City outfielder Chip Ambres. Interestingly, his broadcast partner, Orsillo, was pronouncing it correctly. How do you ensure that you get the names right?*

CB: When a team comes in, I talk to their media relations person or their announcer. If I have an opportunity, I'll ask the player himself. I'll walk up to him and say, "Say your name." Kansas City also has a player named Gotay. But it's not pronounced "go-tay," it's "go-tie." It's my job to have it right, so I always check.

DL: *At one point in his career, Tim Raines preferred to be called "Rock" Raines. What do you do regarding nicknames versus given names?*

CB: If they are a visiting player, it's their given name. Ivan Rodriguez is "Pudge" in Detroit, but here it's Ivan. Nicknames are for hometowns. Home is different. If he played here, it would be "Pudge," if that was his preference.

DL: *Do you announce all players the same, or does anyone get special treatment?*

CB: It's always the same, with one exception: Derek Jeter. I pause just a little longer between the Derek and the Jeter. He knows it, too. After one game, he came up to me in the clubhouse and said, "I know why you do that. You do it so they can boo me twice." I admitted that it was true, and the next night when I did it, he looked up at me and nodded. But it's funny, there are players who get more boos than he does. A-Rod and Sheffield get it worse. Jeter's boos aren't vicious; they're more like Mantle-boos. He's booed out of respect.

DL: *What is the daily routine that goes with your job?*

CB: I get here three hours before the game. The first thing I do is let everybody know I'm here. I don't want them walking around and saying, "Is Beane here yet?" Then I set up my computer and check the rosters, looking for injuries and additions. I start checking the pronunciations, to make sure I get Joachim Benoit right. I get myself something to eat, then wait for the daily script that covers the pregame festivities. Depending on the game, it's anywhere from 6 to 15 pages, and I always read it aloud. It starts with the greeting, and then there are things like the honorary ball boy, the kid who says "Play ball," the person throwing out the first pitch, the person singing the national anthem, and more. Those are all names I have to get right. Of course, sometimes there are last-minute changes and I have to wing it. Everything is timed out perfectly. It's very structured.

DL: *How do you know exactly when an inning is about to start, and how are you kept apprised of lineup changes?*

CB: The normal break between innings is 2:05, and it's 2:20 when it's an ESPN or FOX game. The second base umpire keeps time on the field, and I keep track myself on my watch. I take my cue from the throw down to second base to announce the first batter of an inning. When they start throwing the ball around the infield, I know the batter will be walking toward the plate. As for lineup changes, the home plate umpire is supposed to wave and point if there's an official change, so I have to watch him. Of course, some umpires are better at that than others.

DL: *Play-by-play guys have told me there's a kind of brotherhood that exists within their industry. What is your relationship with other PA announcers?*

CB: Before I had the job, I'd stick my head in once in a while when I was in a new ballpark. I was interested in the set-up and wanted to check it out. They'd ask me what I wanted, and then let me take a quick look. But once I got the job, I instantly joined the fraternity. Everyone became friendlier and invited me to stay and talk for awhile. They all wanted to know about Fenway. Everyone wants to know about Fenway.

DL: *In some venues, PA announcers look at themselves as entertainers—think "Let's get ready to ruuummmble"—rather than simply suppliers of information. You don't do that. Why not?*

CB: If I did, people would boo. The fans here wouldn't want me to do that. The only schtick—I suppose that's what you'd call it—is in the seventh-inning stretch, when I say, "streeetch." But beyond that, the fans' expectations are that I just do my job. Some places expect something different, but this is Fenway Park. It's all about tradition. You don't need to tell people how to or when to cheer. Places like Fenway Park, Wrigley Field, and Yankee Stadium don't need cheerleaders. There's been a precedent set, a way it should sound.

DL: *What was your relationship with Sherm Feller?*

CB: I introduced myself to him in 1977 when I started working here as a reporter. That was 10 years after he took the job. He was a very approachable and friendly man. He enjoyed interacting with people, and within five minutes it's like you've always known him. His style and philosophy were perfect for the job. He believed—and I agree—that anybody can do this job. He was humble. I enjoyed talking with him.

DL: *What did you talk with him about?*

CB: We'd talk baseball. But we'd talk about other things, too. He had a million stories. Like me, he did radio first. As a matter of fact, I believe that he was the first radio talk-show host in Boston. He had a long-time career in radio. And he really knew music, including a lot of Tin Pan Alley. He was an accomplished songwriter. Along with writing "Summertime, Summertime," he also wrote a symphony.

DL: *A lot of people don't realize that it wasn't you who replaced Sherm when he stepped down. Who did?*

CB: His last year was 1993, and he passed away in January of '94. Leslie Sterling replaced him and had the job for two years. It was a difficult job to move into, for two reasons. One, she wasn't Sherm Feller. Two, she was a woman. There aren't many women in the job, although San Francisco has had one in the position for roughly the last 10 years. Leslie did a fine job and left to become the pastor of a church. She was replaced by Ed Brickley, who did it for four years and also did a good job. Ed actually still works here at Fenway. One of the things he does is the tours. When he left, I took over.

DL: *Along with Sherm Feller, are there other people you've admired or learned from?*

CB: I listen to a lot of guys, but not really to educate myself. It's more just to compare and hear what they do. However, Bob Sheppard is someone I do go to for education. He's been doing it for a long time— 55 years—and I know him through visits to New York. Over the years, we've struck up a friendship—he's affable, like Sherm. He's different than Sherm in that Sherm was more blue-collar. Bob is a retired speech teacher, from St. John's, and is more educated and elegant. I've learned a lot from each of them.

DL: *While you obviously had a great appreciation for Sherm, do you think it would be fair to say that you also sound like him?*

CB: I think we share a similar cadence. We each have a deep baritone that fills the place—it kind of rumbles—and it carries well. He definitely had it. I'm told I have it.

DL: *Final thoughts?*

CB: I'm often one of the last people to leave the ballpark after a game, and I've sat in the parking lot, overwhelmed by where I am and what I'm doing. I've been coming here for 50 years, and I can imagine this place talking to me. Actually, it does talk to me. I hear it talking to me in my own voice. At least, I hope it sounds like me.

TOM CARON

TOM CARON IS THE STUDIO HOST FOR THE NEW ENGLAND SPORTS NETWORK'S COVERAGE OF RED SOX BASEBALL. A NATIVE OF LEWISTON, MAINE, CARON HAS BEEN WITH NESN SINCE 1996. THIS INTERVIEW TOOK PLACE IN DECEMBER 2005.

David Laurila: *As a native of Lewiston, Maine, I assume you grew up a Red Sox fan.*

Tom Caron: Absolutely. The earliest picture of me is sitting with a Red Sox pennant in front of the house. Once a year, we'd drive down to Fenway, and it was always a magical moment to walk up the ramp and see all that green. If I was lucky, there'd be a second trip. My parents let me stay up late in '75 to see Fisk's home run. By '86, I was a TV sports anchor in Plattsburgh [NY] and had to go on the air right after Game 6. I had been planning to call my dad the second the game ended and had dialed all but the last number prior to the wild pitch and the ball going through Buckner. I never did dial it, and a few minutes later it was, "Here's Tom with the big Mets win." That was pretty painful.

DL: *Where were you in 2004 when we won it?*

TC: I was there with Jerry Remy and Bob Tewksbury, and we were scrambling to get to the studio for the postgame show. But ever since '86, I had promised my dad I'd call him right away if we won, so I did— I finally got to dial that last number. And right as I was hanging up, my wife called with our eight-year-old son. That was great: an 84-year-old, a 40-year-old, and an eight-year-old all celebrating the moment. It's something I'll never forget.

DL: *How did you come to cover the Red Sox and the rest of the New England sports scene, for NESN?*

TC: I studied journalism in school, so my goal was to be Oscar Madison—a fat slob sportswriter. Instead, here I am—a fat slob television host. I worked for a small newspaper—the *Barre Montpelier Times*—as a stringer while I was at St. Michael's College and took a job with them when I graduated. I was already interested in TV, but there were no jobs and I wanted to eat, so I took the news job. That lasted for less than a month, though, as I landed a job at WPTZ-TV in Plattsburgh as their full-time weekend sports anchor. I put in about 70 hours a week there, and it was almost a paid internship as I was making all of $100 a week. I did that for a year and a half while working 9 to 5 at Radio Shack to make ends meet. But I got to cover the Vermont Reds and the Montreal Expos, and that's where I really caught the love for doing this.

DL: *What was it like covering those teams?*

TC: It was great. The Vermont Reds had some great players at the time: Paul O'Neill, Chris Sabo, Rob Murphy, Jeff Gray. And it was interesting going up to cover the Expos. For one thing, we had a viewing audience in Montreal because there was no NBC in Canada—they'd tune in to stations like ours from across the border. I grew up reading about the adversarial relationship between players and the knights of the keyboard, but it wasn't like that in Montreal at all. There really wasn't even much coverage to speak of. I remember being a 22-year-old kid and going up to Tim Raines. He had just got back from playing in the All-Star game and I asked if I could talk to him. He said, "Sure, I'd love to." He was just standing there by himself—there was no crowd of reporters surrounding him like there'd be here.

DL: *I believe you worked in Portland after that.*

TC: I was actually in White River Junction [Vermont] first, then Portland. I did the play-by-play for the Portland Pirates of the American Hockey League and also served as their director of communications. I had begun to think I was tired of broadcasting, but being close to a team again got me back into it. From there, I came to NESN, in August of '95.

DL: *What were your first NESN assignments?*

TC: I came in hosting *Front Row*, which was kind of a magazine show— sort of a chronicle of sports. In '98, I began working on Bruins games, which I'm no longer involved with. I'm pretty much year-round with the Red Sox now. In 2002, I started with the Sox as a roving reporter, doing "Not Your Typical Fan" [an in-game segment on NESN], which inevitably resulted in me being on camera, having an inane conversation with someone while big home runs were being hit. In the spring of 2004, I started hosting the pre- and postgame shows.

DL: *How do you approach your role on the* Red Sox Postgame Show?

TC: I'm a TV host. I try to keep it fun and entertaining, but it's not about me. I'm like a traffic cop, getting us from point A to point B. If I'm next to Eck, they don't need me to opine on how Foulke was throwing. Or if it's Jim Rice—a former MVP—he's the one to explain what happened in an at-bat, not me. It's all about keeping things flowing, and I try to tee it up for those guys.

DL: *Do you always use the same approach?*

TC: I try to tailor it to the analyst I'm working with. One will have more stats and facts—others will react more with analysis. It's not brain surgery, but I want to adapt to their own approach if I can. We don't have scripts or teleprompters, so things are constantly changing on the show. No one has ever told us what we can and can't say, and I take pride in that you'll never see us stage a point–counterpoint. Somehow, arguing seems to have become viewed as good TV, but you don't need that for a good show.

DL: *How do you prepare for the* Postgame Show?

TC: I sit with the producer and that night's analyst during the game, and take notes. And if the analyst makes a good point, I make sure he uses it in the *Postgame Show*. I don't want it to be wasted. One thing we strive to do is have good story-lines, not just highlights. For instance, if Matt Clement is pitching we might chart first-pitch strikes as a story-line. We want to break down the game. While our pregame show is a little *Baseball Tonight* mixed with a little *Letterman,* our postgame is more serious baseball. I also want to know what the fans are thinking, because here they're as educated as anywhere, and you don't want to insult them by not being as informed as they are. So I have a laptop in front of me, and I surf the Net, checking the message boards to see what the pulse of Red Sox Nation is.

DL: *Tell us a little about NESN's new show:* Red Sox Now.

TC: It airs on Wednesday nights at 7 o'clock, and it is part of our effort to have more Red Sox coverage, even in the off-season. We used to do *Inside Out,* which ran from January to spring training, but we decided we needed to do more. The producer, Mike Barry, and I came up with it. We started the first week of November, and the idea is to have up-to-date news about the team. We've had Bill Lajoie on the show and Dave Wallace; we had a good interview with Terry Francona. We also have different co-hosts, people like Gordon Edes and Nick Cafardo. We tape the show a few hours before it runs, but we'll be doing it live from Ft. Myers the first week of spring training. What it boils down to is that fans have wanted more Red Sox programming, and we're trying to give it to them.

DL: *You mentioned earlier that you did play-by-play for the Portland Pirates of the AHL. Have you done any baseball play-by-play?*

TC: A little, but not much. The first time was actually the Division III College World Series, in Battle Creek Michigan, when Southern Maine beat Wisconsin-Oshkosh. I've mostly done hockey, but I consider myself a reporter—not a play-by-play guy. I enjoy it, but it's not my primary interest or something I aspire to do on a regular basis.

DL: *You did once serve as the play-by-play announcer for Roller Hockey International's New England Stingers. What can you tell us about that?*

TC: The owners of the Portland Pirates bought the roller hockey team, and the league was trying to make it a big-time sport. We played in the Spectrum in Philadelphia, the Montreal Forum, the Aud in Buffalo. The venues were big, but there were no more than a few hundred fans at each game. The actual paid attendance was probably even smaller—I was told it was 50 for one game. Finally, I was in the Omni in Atlanta getting ready to do the game on radio one night, and when I called in to get the line set up, they told me not to bother. They had just bought out the contract, so they didn't have to cover the games anymore.

DL: *I assume there are a few more good stories.*

TC: I can't even begin to tell you. It could almost be a Farrelly Brothers movie. I remember one time we were playing the Minnesota Arctic Blast, and one of our players came up to me and said he was going to score that night—the goalie for the other team was a buddy of his. The games would usually end up about 14-12, but he was one of the few guys in the league without a goal. But just like he said, early in the game he let one go and it went right by the goalie, who hardly moved. Another time, we were playing in Atlanta and the game went to a shootout—and the team let me decide who would go out for it. Because there were hardly any fans at the games, instead of putting me in the broadcast booth I was set up in the stands and called the game from there. The coach and players just looked up at me, I'd announce a guy, and he'd take it. We ended up winning, which was our first one all year. So, in a sense, I coached our first win. Let me tell you, it was a goofy, strange, summer.

DL: *In your NESN bio, you list your favorite players growing up as Bill Lee and Bobby Orr. That's a somewhat odd pairing, so let's close with that one.*

TC: When I was a young kid, growing up in Maine, Orr was everything. My first skates were Bobby Orr models; I had an Orr sweatshirt. Then, when I reached my rebellious years, Lee and the Buffalo Heads are who I grew up with. Those Red Sox teams were fun to watch. I remember in 1978, I was on the freshman football team when we played the Yankees in the one-game playoff. We were listening to the game on a transistor radio during practice. I also remember someone smashing it when we lost. But Lee and Orr . . . I guess maybe those are the traits for me: wackiness and hard work.

JOE CASTIGLIONE

JOE CASTIGLIONE IS THE RADIO PLAY-BY-PLAY VOICE OF RED SOX BASEBALL. CASTIGLIONE BEGAN HIS MAJOR LEAGUE BROADCASTING CAREER IN 1979, IN CLEVELAND, AND HAS BEEN WITH THE RED SOX SINCE 1983. THIS INTERVIEW TOOK PLACE IN MAY 2004.

David Laurila: *Let's start with something you use as an ending. After the final game of each season, you sign off by reading from Bart Giamatti's "The Green Fields of the Mind". Tell us about that.*

Joe Castiglione: This was actually started by the late Ken Coleman—I can't take credit for it. I simply continued the tradition after he left the booth, in 1990, and have done it ever since. The Giamattis and my family actually grew up together in the same neighborhood in New Haven, so I had the pleasure of knowing Bart. He was a great man, and it's a pleasure to share with everyone his homage to the game he loved.

DL: *Tell us a little about your beginnings in baseball—both as a fan and as a broadcaster.*

JC: I grew up, as I said, in New Haven [Connecticut]. My father, along with the rest of the family, was a Yankee fan. They loved DiMaggio. He was, after all, Italian like we are. So that's who I followed as a youth—Mantle was my favorite. From the broadcasting angle, I loved listening to Mel Allen. My childhood dream was to grow up and do Yankee games, just like he did.

DL: *Instead, you're up here doing the Red Sox.*

JC: Yes, and there's nowhere else I'd rather be. My days of following the Yankees are long gone. The Horace Clarke era played a part in that, as did the arrival of George Steinbrenner. You also have to remember that the Red Sox weren't very good when I was a kid—it was easy to root for the Yankees at the time. But, as I said, that's ancient history for me.

DL: *So you plan to stay in Boston? You've been here a long time now.*

JC: Definitely. I've moved before—I used to broadcast in Cleveland—but I hope my moving days are over. I'm very happy here. For one thing, I have the pleasure of working with Trupe [Jerry Trupiano], who's a great partner in the booth.

DL: *Tell us a little about that—your relationship with Jerry and other broadcast partners you've had.*

JC: I've been blessed to have worked with some great ones. I've gotten along with all of them, which helps a lot, and formed wonderful friendships. Trupe and I, for instance, have a lot of common interests.

DL: *Such as?*

JC: Music is one, specifically rock-and-roll. He's not nearly as progressive as I am though—Trupe is kind of stuck in the past.

DL: *And you?*

JC: I enjoy some of the older stuff he likes, but also a lot of things he hasn't even heard of: Coldplay, Dido—people like that. I've always loved music.

DL: *It sounds like you'd make a good DJ. Did you ever do that?*

JC: In college, sure. As a matter of fact, had I not become a sportscaster that's probably what I would have done—been a disc jockey.

DL: *Ernie Harwell—one of the best ever in your business—penned over 60 songs. Did you know that?*

JC: I did. Ernie and I are actually good friends, and he was somewhat of a mentor to me early in my career.

DL: *Tell us about that.*

JC: I've always marveled at his work. I heard him doing Tiger games a lot while I was in Cleveland—it's easy to pick up WJR from there. One of my memories of listening to him was when [Luis] Aparicio fell down rounding third in 1972.

DL: *In what ways did he impact your career?*

JC: I first met Ernie in '79 when I was doing television in Cleveland, and he was very supportive of me and complimentary of my work. He was also instrumental in piquing my interest in Baseball Chapel and I often went to him for advice. He remains a dear friend.

DL: *What type of advice did you seek from him?*

JC: An example would be the Wade Boggs/Margo Adams controversy. His advice was, "If it affects the game on the field, it's something that needs to be addressed. If it doesn't, leave it be."

DL: *Can you elaborate?*

JC: The Wil Cordero incident is an example of something that affected the play on the field. He ended up missing games because of it, so that directly impacted the team. The Boggs issue, meanwhile, really only affected him and his family—not the team.

DL: *Sticking with Ernie, there's a great story of his mistakenly believing that a game had been called because of rain, and getting in his car and driving off. While on the freeway—and it was fortunate that he had the radio on—he heard his broadcast partner say, "Ernie, if you can hear me, come back! We're playing baseball today!" Do you have any similar stories?*

JC: No, nothing quite like that. I do remember having the wrong pitcher in the game once in the mid-eighties. Curt Young came in to pitch for the A's, and we thought it was Tim Birstas. We ran down all of Birstas' statistics, and had him going the entire inning. That made for a little confusion when he [Birstas] came in to replace Young.

DL: *What about odd plays that you've called? Things you don't see every day?*

JC: A favorite was in Tiger Stadium in '83, with Tony Armas playing center field and Lou Whitaker on second base. Kirk Gibson hit a shot to deep center that banged off Armas' glove, and Whitaker should have scored easily. However, he somehow misread the play, and by the time he came barreling into the plate, Gibson—who could really run—was right on his heels. There was a collision, and [Rich] Gedman first tagged out Whitaker, then Gibson. But the home plate umpire had been bowled over, so the first base ump had to come hustling in to make the call. He should have ruled each of them out, but he saw a ball lying on the ground, and assuming it had been knocked free he called the second runner, Gibson, safe. What actually happened was that when the home plate umpire was knocked down, a ball rolled out of his pouch—that's what he saw. Gedman was still holding onto the game ball, but somehow wasn't able to convince the umpires of that fact.

DL: *What about oddities you weren't involved in? For instance, how would you have called Eddie Gaedel's pinch-hitting appearance?*

JC: That's a good question. I'm not sure what I'd have said, but Dennis Eckersley would probably have referred to him as a "sandblower."

DL: *A sandblower?*

JC: A few years back, we were doing a game in spring training, this guy comes up to the plate—couldn't have been more than 5' 6". Eck, who was in the booth with me, referred to him as a sandblower. When I asked what that meant, he said, "You know; one of those guys who's built so low to the ground that when they pass gas, sand blows across the field." And then, after the inning, he grins at me and says, "I bet you're really glad I didn't say 'fart.'"

DL: *I'm not sure if I have a good question to follow that with. . . .*

JC: Eck's a good guy, but sometimes he'll say things that kind of make you wonder.

DL: *Here's one that seems appropriate. Are good broadcasters born, or are they are made?*

JC: Both. It's something that can be developed, but there's also an innate quality to it. I think I was born with an ability to describe a play, but it's not as simple as that. I had to learn to be a reporter, and to be more descriptive as a play unfolded. For instance, not every ground ball to second is the same. Was it a grass cutter, did it take two hops, was it right at the second baseman or off to one side or another? You can teach someone "approach." You can teach preparation.

DL: *The subtitle of your upcoming book,* Broadcast Rites and Sites, *is* I Saw it on the Radio, *which is also the subtitle of Terry Cashman's fine song, "Play by Play." Is a good play-by-play man like a good writer—he evokes true images in the mind's eye?*

JC: That's the goal. I've always loved that expression and appreciate Terry giving me permission to use it for my book. You're trying to capture the moment, so you hope your words can do exactly that.

DL: *You mentioned getting advice from Ernie Harwell. Who else did you learn from?*

JC: Ken Coleman, certainly. One thing he taught me was to wait on fly balls hit to left at Fenway. It's too easy to misjudge balls hit toward the wall, and you want to be accurate with your call. Another person who stressed accuracy was Gabe Paul, the former GM in Cleveland. He said to make sure I was never wrong when it came to rules—that's a sure-fire way to lose credibility.

DL: *Let's talk a little about each. We'll start with the rules.*

JC: We keep a rulebook in the booth, but I also have an index card I rely on. I have it organized in such a way that I can usually find things pretty quickly. And if I can't, that's where patience comes in handy.

DL: *Like in calling fly balls to left. You do seem to read balls pretty well off the bat—much better than other announcers I've listened to. Is that a knack or something you've developed over time?*

JC: A little of both. I think I've always had a knack for it—more so than for playing the game itself.

DL: *I assume you dreamed of playing in the Majors when you were a kid growing up in New Haven.*

JC: Of course. Dreaming of being the next Mel Allen was secondary to playing, but as Ernie Harwell so eloquently describes it, "I wanted to play in the worst way—and that's exactly how I played." So, here I am, in the broadcast booth instead.

DL: *While we're on Ernie again, what was it like broadcasting from Tiger Stadium? I understand it was interesting.*

JC: Scary is a better word. I think the broadcast booth was closer to the plate than the pitcher's mound. I remember one time a ball was fouled straight back, and it hit Trupe on the carom. It was a great vantage point, but you always had to be on high alert. Ernie and his partner always kept a net in front of their booth, but we didn't have one for ours. Believe it or not, I actually did a few games from there wearing a glove!

DL: *Let's talk a little more about some of your favorite calls. What are some that stand out?*

JC: Trot Nixon's game-winning homer in the playoffs last year was big; Mo Vaughn's walk-off grand slam in the home opener a few years back; the last outs of the no-hitters; Lou Merloni's home run in his first at-bat at Fenway—you know, him being a local kid and Italian to boot. Brian Daubach's game-winning double in the really long at-bat a few years ago was memorable. He and I have actually become good friends.

DL: *Tell us a little about your relationships with the players. You just mentioned Dauber.*

JC: Brian's a great guy. He's down to earth, unassuming—just a genuinely nice person. He got married this past year, to a wonderful girl named Chrissie, and I actually played a role in them being together.

DL: *Tell us about that.*

JC: I've been getting my hair cut for years at a salon Chrissie owned in the Little Italy section of Baltimore. I told Brian he should get his cut there, and I told her that there's this guy that she should meet. I didn't actually introduce them, but they both give me credit for helping them get hooked up. When they got married, they asked me to do a reading at their wedding, which was an honor.

DL: *Who are some of your other favorite people in the game?*

JC: There are a lot. You see many of these guys every day, so you build up a lot of friendships. Mo Vaughn is a good friend—we've done Jimmy Fund work together. Roger [Clemens] and I got along well. Darren Lewis, Tony Peña, Lynn Jones . . . there are really too many to name. Andre Thornton, in Cleveland, is a wonderful person. I used to enjoy talking to Oil Can Boyd. No, let me rephrase that: I liked "listening" to Oil Can Boyd—he loved to tell stories. Lou Gorman is a good friend—my kids used to call him "Uncle Lou." Al Nipper taught my daughter how to roller blade. I can't say enough good things about Johnny Pesky. I should have mentioned him earlier when I talked about people who helped me with my career. He really did a lot to help me get established, which I'll always appreciate. He also hit countless ground balls to my kids, which says a lot about what type of person he is. He's a wonderful man.

DL: *What about your relationships with the managers? You obviously interact with them a lot—pregame and postgame shows, etc.*

JC: There have been 12 of them, 9 here in Boston. I've gotten along with the majority. I obviously looked up to Ralph Houk. Jimy Williams is a good friend, a wonderful man. Grady [Little] is another. Joe Morgan might be my closest friend in the game; we speak often. There haven't been many bad apples in the dugout during my time here.

DL: *You mentioned Mo Vaughn and the Jimmy Fund. Tell us a little about the Jason Leader story.*

JC: Mike Andrews told me about Jason, who was a Jimmy Fund patient, and how he wasn't doing very well. Mo was his favorite player, so I asked him if he could call Jason to wish him a happy 10th birthday. He did and went on to tell him that he would try to hit a home run for him that night [the Red Sox were playing in Anaheim]. I was aware of the conversation, so when Mo homered I related the story—on the air—about how Mo promised to hit one for him. It was a wonderful moment, and even though Jason has since passed on, it is a memory to be cherished.

DL: *Players get a lot of fan mail. What about broadcasters? Who writes to you, and what do they say?*

JC: The most interesting and moving ones come from shut-ins. This includes the disabled, the elderly, even prisoners. Their letters really strike a chord, because it shows how something as simple as broadcasting a baseball game can touch people's lives. To many of these people, baseball—Red Sox baseball—is their only source of joy. Knowing that helps me take my job seriously, and I hope people enjoy my work—I know I do.

ANDY FREED

ANDY FREED IS THE RADIO PLAY-BY-PLAY VOICE OF THE TAMPA BAY DEVIL RAYS. A NATIVE OF MARYLAND, FREED DID RADIO PLAY-BY-PLAY FOR THE PAWTUCKET RED SOX FROM 2001 TO 2004. THIS INTERVIEW TOOK PLACE IN JANUARY 2005, SHORTLY BEFORE FREED WAS HIRED FOR HIS FIRST BIG LEAGUE JOB.

David Laurila: *Prior to Pawtucket, you did play-by-play for the Single A St. Lucie Mets and then the Double A Trenton Thunder. Are most broadcasters like young ballplayers, looking to move up the ladder and reach the Major Leagues?*

Andy Freed: Most minor league broadcasters are looking for a way to break into the Major Leagues. When I mapped out a plan for my career many years ago, I felt that the best way to achieve that goal would be to come through the minor leagues. All things considered, it may not be the quickest way to get there, but I do believe that it is the best way to learn the craft. There is no better way to improve in this field than by doing it every day, and by living the life of a team's play-by-play voice. There is no way to simulate any of the unique aspects to this job. You just have to live it. In the end, hopefully when that rare Major League chance happens, the person who has put in the time and "paid his dues" will be prepared to handle the job.

DL: *You got your start as an intern in Baltimore working with Jon Miller. What did that mean for your career?*

AF: Jon Miller came to Baltimore when I was 11 and had a huge impact on me. I was already obsessed with becoming a Major League announcer, and listening to him every night on the radio was akin to taking a course in how to broadcast baseball. His descriptive abilities, the emotions he expresses in his vocal inflection, his friendliness, his knowledge of even the most obscure rules of baseball, and a million other things endeared me to him. In fact, when I spoke with him for the first time when I was in college, I felt like I knew him. Having the opportunity to intern with him, and having him take an interest in me and my career dreams has meant the world to me. When I interned with him, I would broadcast Orioles games into a tape recorder and he would sit with me after the game and go over my tapes. Having that kind of instruction was invaluable, and so is his friendship and support to this day.

DL: *Your partner in the booth is Steve Hyder, who was chosen from among 144 applicants. Talk about that process, including your own experiences in getting the jobs in St. Lucie, Trenton, and Pawtucket.*

AF: Every baseball broadcaster knows what it is like to go through the process of competing for a job, especially one as sought-after as with the Pawtucket Red Sox. It is always humbling to realize just how many people apply for one job. When Steve applied, we were in the market for someone to work with me, and while I wasn't part of the hiring process, I saw just how competitive it was. As for my experiences in St. Lucie, Trenton, and Pawtucket, each time I was selected out of hundreds of candidates. Because each was a job I really wanted, it was a nerve-wracking couple of weeks waiting for the decisions. It always feels good to get the job interview. If you can get to the interview, then you've done something to make an impression on the decision-maker. Fortunately, I have been able to secure these jobs, but there were certainly lots of sleepless nights thinking about if my tape would even be listened to among the sea of applicants.

DL: *You also do games on TV. How does that compare with radio, and what is it like working with Bob Montgomery?*

AF: Working with Monty on the PawSox television games is one of the highlights of my job. Of course he brings tons of credibility with his experience as a Red Sox catcher and broadcaster for so many years. One of his greatest qualities is that he communicates his points so well. I routinely learn things about baseball from him and appreciate the time I get to spend with him. Television itself is quite a different medium than radio. One doesn't have to "paint the word picture" on TV, so the idea is provide the best caption possible to the picture while holding interesting conversation with your partner. Fortunately, working with Monty and the entire crew at Cox Sports Television makes things comfortable. Steve McDonald is also a big part of our telecasts and is someone I admire and enjoy working with. Broadcasting the games on radio is what I have always loved, and I have grown to love doing the TV as well.

DL: *Who are your heroes and role models in the business?*

AF: Fortunately, over the years I've gotten a chance to meet and become friends with many of the people whom I would consider role models. It is such a great feeling to meet someone that you have respected greatly—and they turn out to be great people. Of course, Jon Miller is such a talent and has been so nice to know over the years. Gary Cohen [Mets play-by-play and former PawSox broadcaster] is one of the best in the business today and has become a great friend and incredible support. Joe Angel [Orioles play-by-play] is someone I've known since my internship days in Baltimore and has also been a valued confidant and friend. Don Orsillo is also someone I respect immensely. Not only is he one of the most talented young broadcasters in baseball today, but he is the person I followed here at the PawSox so there is a kinship I feel we share. I would also be remiss without mentioning the person who first inspired me to enter this field. Legendary Hall of Famer Chuck Thompson was the voice of the Orioles for decades, and it was his abilities and style that introduced me to the art of baseball play-by-play.

DL: *Are minor league broadcasters employed by the team itself or the organization? For instance, had you still been in Trenton when the Red Sox moved their Double A team to Portland, would you have gone with them or stayed with the Thunder and their new parent club, the Yankees?*

AF: It varies from situation to situation in the minor leagues [and the Majors, for that matter]. In St. Lucie with the Mets, I was employed by the station. In fact, during my time there, I was fortunate to switch stations and move with the broadcast when they changed to a new radio home. In Trenton and Pawtucket, I have been employed by the teams. Ultimately, if they were to switch affiliations, you switch with them. So if I had still been with the Thunder when they joined the Yankees, it might have felt strange, but I would have joined with them!

DL: *Every broadcaster has experienced slips of the tongue, misidentified players, and not known he was on the air during a break. What are your own horror stories?*

AF: I don't know if it is a horror story, but certainly the strangest moment I've ever experienced on the air was in 2001 when PawSox slugger Izzy Alcantara infamously kicked the catcher after he was nearly hit by a pitch. I've never had a moment like that when my jaw actually dropped, and wasn't sure what the heck was going on. I can recall trying to describe the moment as best as I could, but it happened so fast, and frankly, that had never happened before! The pitch came in, and he instantly "karate-kicked" the poor backstop [Jeremy Salazar of Scranton]. It seemed like the players on both teams, the fans, even the umpires were stunned. What made it especially strange was that to know Izzy was to like him. He's funny, laid back, and very friendly. That is one of the best things about baseball—you never know when you are about to see something for the first time . . . even something that has never happened before!

DL: *Do you have any favorite stories regarding other broadcasters—ones that make you either laugh or cringe?*

AF: A few years back, I saw something that made me cringe and laugh a little bit, too. These days, having a laptop computer is incredibly handy to a broadcaster because you can read lots of newspapers and keep up to date on the happenings of the game around the country. There was a play-by-play man who kept his laptop in front of him during the games so he could refer to it whenever he wanted. So there comes a really exciting moment in the game and he must have bumped it with his hand, and the computer, almost in slow motion, tumbled out of his booth and end-over-end all the way down the backstop. The poor guy watched in horror as his priceless link to the world slowly bounced and skipped and twirled across the netting for seemingly an eternity, until it finally reached the bottom and exploded into a million pieces when it hit the ground. It was so sad, and a fear those of us who rely on their laptops have had, that all you could do was laugh. He even laughed himself . . . and cringed!

DL: *Tell us about growing up and deciding that you wanted to do this for a living. What did your family and friends think, and what do they think now?*

AF: Contrary to what you might expect, my family was not into sports at all when I was growing up. I probably would have never gotten into it had it not been for my uncle who took me to an Orioles–Brewers game when I was eight years old in 1979. I've often said that that night, whatever path my life was heading, it forked into something new. There was a long rain delay that night, and I will never forget listening to the Orioles broadcast piped inside the stadium as we waited out the delay. Something about it was just captivating to me. To say that I fell in love with baseball that night would be an understatement. Overnight, I was obsessed with baseball and especially the broadcasters who described the game. Corny as it may sound, I knew right then what I wanted to do with my life. I spent much of my childhood lugging my tape recorder out to Memorial Stadium and holed up in my room broadcasting my favorite game, Statis Pro Baseball [a tabletop baseball game] into my tape recorder. Truthfully, I don't think my parents knew what to make of it until I got a job in St. Lucie with the Mets after college. Even then, I don't think they thought it was a "real job" until years later. Now, of course, my Mom, Dad, and brother are three of my biggest fans. My wife and daughter are my two biggest supporters—there is no way I would be anywhere without them as my base in life. The overall goal in this, or any career, is to balance professional life and family. I've been blessed to have the best in both categories.

DON ORSILLO

DON ORSILLO IS THE TELEVISION PLAY-BY-PLAY VOICE OF RED SOX BASEBALL ON THE NEW ENGLAND SPORTS NETWORK. PRIOR TO JOINING NESN IN 2001, ORSILLO WAS THE RADIO VOICE OF THE PAWTUCKET RED SOX FROM 1996 TO 2000. THIS INTERVIEW TOOK PLACE IN OCTOBER 2005.

David Laurila: *I understand that you and Carl Beane, the Red Sox' PA announcer, have a thing where you meet in the hall and acknowledge each other by saying: "Cool job." What makes what you do a cool job, and would you even refer to it as that: a "job?"*

Don Orsillo: I think what you are referring to is something Carl said last year. He said, "We have cool jobs." I think he was joking, but really they are fun jobs and as you point out, calling them "jobs" might be a stretch. For Carl and me, both positions are our dream jobs. After growing up a life-long Red Sox fan, I am extremely grateful to be able to drive to Fenway Park every night during the summer and call Red Sox games.

DL: *You were in radio prior to joining NESN. How hard was it making the transition to TV, and what is the best advice you received when you did?*

DO: It was a long trip through the minor leagues: 10 minor league seasons in baseball at Single A, Double A, and Triple A locations, and 5 seasons in the American Hockey League—all of it primarily on radio. My last season in Pawtucket [2000] was really my first season of doing games on TV. I started to make the transition that season, and then when I got the September call-up at the end of that season to Boston, I did some more. The transition my first year in Boston [2001] was a challenge. I no longer had to paint the picture. Everybody could see the picture. My best advice came from a former professor of mine at Northeastern University, Joe Castiglione: "Put a caption under the picture, don't paint it."

DL: *Talk about the process of growing into your current job and handling the inevitable criticism of your work.*

DO: It has been a great deal of fun and a dream come true. I was born in Melrose, Massachusetts, and until high school lived in the North Conway/Madison, New Hampshire area of the White Mountains. I grew up listening to Ken Coleman and Ned Martin, and hoping to have the chance to do this someday. I was fortunate to achieve my goal at 31 years of age. I am happy to say the excitement has never worn off. Five years have gone by very quickly. I think it takes a long time for people to get used to your voice and style over a number of years. All you can do is the best you can; there will always be people who are critical of your work. Not everyone will like you. It is sort of a fact of life.

DL: *Image is important in television, and your broadcast partner's "RemDawg" persona has proven both popular and marketable. Do you see your "Announcer Boy" promos branding your own image, and is that a good thing?*

DO: Ah, no. . . . They have been a fun thing that actually started last year with Tim Wakefield. We were doing an NESN promo and he was ad-libbing some and threw out there the term, "Announcer Boy." It was the part where he was working me out and standing over me as I was about to pass out. Tim has been a great friend and someone I respect a great deal. But to answer your question, the promos have been fun, and the players have had fun being part of the NESN monthly promos, but I think as far as branding an image, that comes from years and years of doing the same job.

DL: *While familiarity is said to breed contempt, the opposite appears to be true when it comes to baseball announcers. Do you think most fans would favor having the same good play-by-play voice for two decades over three or four very good ones over the same period of time?*

DO: I think looking to the past in New England and around MLB, the guys who last the longest period of time seem to be the most loved and appreciated. I think over time, there is a comfort level that people develop with announcers. Generations grow older and you remain in the same capacity. My partner, who has just concluded his 18th season, certainly falls into that category. Part of that longevity is being successful over time, as well. Jerry is one of the best in the country.

DL: *While you grew up listening to Red Sox games in New Hampshire, you spent your high school years in Los Angeles. Talk about the broadcasters you heard in each part of the country and the influence they've had on your career.*

DO: Having grown up a Red Sox and Ned & Ken fan, the American League was all I knew when my parents transplanted me to Los Angeles. I have learned over the years what a great announcer Vin Scully of the Dodgers is, but when I moved out there I watched the Angels. Bob Starr was the TV voice, and I liked his delivery and his style. In a weird twist of fate, the two main voices of my youth on each coast I would end up working for, in 1989 and 1990. While at Northeastern, I was the statistician/intern for Red Sox Radio and sat next to Ken Coleman for his last season [1989] and with Bob Starr for his first season [1990] in Boston. That was an experience I will never forget, and reaffirmed what I wanted to do after college.

DL: *When the Red Sox regular season comes to an end, so does your own. How hard is it to step aside just when the games begin to mean the most, and what is your opinion of the jobs ESPN and FOX do with their postseason coverage?*

DO: It is very hard. It starts in February when you arrive in Ft. Myers, and just when the entire season comes to its most exciting point, your season is over. I wish we could at least do the ALDS. In the NHL, the local TV outlets are allowed to do the first two rounds. I think the guys who do the postseason are very good, and it is hard to please each fan base while trying to please the rest of the country, all at once. It is not easy, but I think they balance it fairly well.

DL: *The Red Sox won the World Series last year. When it happened, where were you, and what did you do—besides envy Joe Castiglione?*

DO: I was part of the postseason and postgame show on NESN. I was on the field in St. Louis conducting interviews with all the players and staff. It was an incredible experience that I will never forget. In some ways, I still cannot believe it happened. I was extremely happy for Joe, as well. To think he is the only Red Sox announcer to have the opportunity to say "The Red Sox are World Champions" in the history of the franchise is amazing, and he deserves it.

DL: *Broadcasting history is filled with colorful characters, some of whom have pushed homer-ism, eccentricity, and/or excitability to the extremes. While you might not want to emulate them, who do you enjoy that fits any of those descriptions?*

DO: I like them all. Curt Smith has written several books on voices of the game. He writes about all of them, and they are all different in their own way. All of them were themselves. Harry Caray was very different from Harry Kalas, and so on. They are all unique and great announcers. I think as a local broadcaster, you are able to let your emotions run a little more than a national announcer.

DL: *As baseball is a game where anything can happen at any time, and often does, are concentration and discipline the most underrated qualities a play-by-play announcer possesses?*

DO: Without a doubt. You can be flawless for 3 hours and 10 minutes of a game, but if something happens and you are not ready, or locked in, you can blow it and it ruins the entire game completely for you. You can never let down, no matter how long the game is, because something major will always happen unexpectedly.

DL: *How often do you get information through the headset while broadcasting a game, and what does it typically consist of? Also, how important is your working relationship with your producer?*

DO: From time to time, our producers will come in our ears with some statistical information, which is very helpful, because no matter how much you prepare it helps to have someone else thinking along with you so that you do not miss anything. Mostly, they are telling us what graphical information they are putting up next to coincide with what we are discussing. The relationship is huge, and it's a good one with our very talented producer Russ Kenn.

DL: *For members of the print media, especially columnists, a good story line is arguably more important than the result of the game itself. As a broadcaster, how do you look at what happens from the first inning to the last out?*

DO: That's just it. The writers look at the game as a whole. We are pitch-to-pitch, and when it's over, so are we. Our contributions are all in-game. We react and explain what is going on as it happens, rather than after. It changes moment-to-moment; a good play, a bad play. The key is to be consistent all the time, good or bad, and to be ready.

DL: *I've read that your favorite player growing up was Dwight Evans. Why Dewey, and who else would be on your short list?*

DO: When I was a kid, Dwight to me was just cool. He had power and had a great arm, and seemed to hit well in the clutch. Many of the games I attended at Fenway, I was seated down the right-field line, and I watched him a great deal. Sadly, my Little League stance was similar, pigeon-toed and all—with very little success, I might add. It was great getting to know him, as he was on the coaching staff in my second season. Butch Hobson, Yaz, and Eck were other favorites.

DL: *Like most kids who grow up in New England, you once idolized those who wore a Red Sox uniform. Now you interact with them on a daily basis. To phrase what is best described as a silly question as simply as possible: What is that like?*

DO: It is pretty cool. I think it without question wears off, though. When I arrived, the fact that I knew 65 percent of the clubhouse helped. In my five years in Pawtucket, I got to know players and coaches alike who made their way through the system. So when I arrived, I already knew Nomar, Trot, Hatteberg, Varitek, Lowe, Merloni, Daubach, et al.

DL: *You mentioned earlier that Tim Wakefield had a lot of fun shooting a NESN promo with you. Who are some of the great guys on the team—ones we're maybe not aware of from their public personas?*

DO: I think people have a pretty good grasp on most of the players. The teams the last few years have had some very good people on them. One thing the current ownership group has done, very successfully, is bring in good character people/players. While not all of these players enjoyed successful seasons on the field, none were really unpleasant to be around.

DL: *Every announcer has a few funny, if not embarrassing, stories from his time behind the microphone. Do you have any you're willing to share?*

DO: I would have to say my most embarrassing moment was when I attempted to explain what a lunar eclipse was during a game. It was supposed to take place late one evening and we came back from break and there was a shot of the moon. So I started to explain it, realizing that I was not really entirely sure what it was. Jerry, realizing this, decided to let me explain it completely. Sadly, under my scenario, we would all be fried and not be here today. Many times, I have had trouble stopping laughing, and this was the worst case. I received a great deal of mail from college professors and fans explaining what it is. I think Northeastern University cringes every time I speak.

SHORTER VIEWS

DAVE JAGELER

DAVE JAGELER IS THE RADIO PLAY-BY-PLAY VOICE OF THE WASHINGTON NATIONALS. A NATIVE OF WINDSOR, CONNECTICUT, JAGELER PREVIOUSLY WORKED IN THE BOSTON SPORTS RADIO MARKET AND WAS THE PLAY-BY-PLAY VOICE OF THE PAWTUCKET RED SOX IN 2005. THIS IS AN EXCERPT FROM AN INTERVIEW THAT TOOK PLACE IN JULY 2005.

David Laurila: *Who have been your role models in the radio business, and why?*

Dave Jageler: I followed those that I listened to when I was growing up. My basketball role model was Johnny Most, since I was a Celtics fan. Sometimes I would sound like Johnny when I would get on a referee while doing college hoops. For baseball, it has to be Sean McDonough, who I had the pleasure of working with at AM 1510. When I made the decision to go into the business, he was someone I paid a lot of attention to and listened to carefully. His versatility and ability to do several sports well is outstanding.

DL: *Tell us about your decision to work in sports radio. Was it made in college, or much earlier?*

DJ: Much earlier. I knew I wanted to be a sportscaster back before high school. I was smart enough to know I wasn't going to be a Major Leaguer so it seemed like a good way to get into sports. When I played baseball in high school, I was an outfielder and I used to practice my announcing in left field. That was great until the broadcast was interrupted by a double down the line. I also worked at a local-access cable television station in Windsor while in high school. I used to broadcast the school's high school hoops games, so I got some great experience doing that.

DL: *Prior to Pawtucket, what was your experience doing play-by-play at the professional level, and why did you decide to get back into it?*

DJ: In terms of baseball, I was the number-two announcer for the Charlotte Knights [the Marlins' Triple A affiliate back then] in 1995 and '96. I also filled in on some games in 2001. Most of my experience was in basketball. I was the radio voice of the Charlotte 49ers of Conference USA and now the Atlantic-10 for seven years. When I moved to Boston, I also got to fill in as the play-by-play man for the Boston Celtics on about 10 games, which was a dream come true: to call NBA games.

I really wanted to get back into play-by-play full time because it is what I truly love to do. It is so much fun to be in the atmosphere of the game with the crowd noise and the sounds of the game. Talk radio is so sterile, going into a studio every day. I love going onto the field and hanging out at the batting cage and then doing the pregame show as the crowd is filing in. Then the high point is when the crowd builds after the crack of the bat and the ball leaves the yard, and you are describing it as it happens. It is quite a rush.

STEVE LENOX

STEVE LENOX IS THE RADIO PLAY-BY-PLAY VOICE OF THE WIL-
MINGTON BLUE ROCKS. WITH THE BLUE ROCKS SINCE 2001,
LENOX IS ALSO THE TEAM'S DIRECTOR OF BROADCASTING AND
MEDIA RELATIONS. THIS IS AN EXCERPT FROM AN INTERVIEW THAT
TOOK PLACE IN JULY 2005.

David Laurila: *Do minor league announcers typically have a broadcast partner?*

Steve Lenox: It depends on the team and their needs, but I think most do. My partner is Kyle Berger, who does all of the home games with me. He only travels to a few of our road games, so when we're not at home I am doing it solo.

DL: *How does that compare to having a partner in the booth?*

SL: It's a lot different. A conversation is different from a monologue, and you can do point–counterpoint with a partner. Sometimes when I'm playing two arguments off each other—by myself—I worry that I'm beating them into the ground. All in all, if you have a good broadcast partner, your job is a lot easier.

DL: *What does it feel like to be alone in the booth?*

SL: At times, it can be lonely. If you're on the road alone and there are maybe 75 fans in the stands, you can wonder who it is that you're talk-ing to. For that reason, I carry a card with me that has a picture of Fenway Park with the World Series banner. That helps remind me of my ultimate goal and keeps me motivated to do the best job I can. Probably the best advice I've ever received is to bring my A-game every time, because you never know who might be listening. A great experi-ence I've had is getting a call from Don Wardlow after doing a Staten Island game in Niles, Ohio. Wardlow, who is blind, is a long-time radio color guy and is very well respected in the industry. He called to say he really enjoyed my broadcast, and hearing something like that—from someone like Don—meant a lot.

DL: *Who listens to Wilmington Blue Rocks games on the radio?*

SL: There are certainly some diehards, including fans who come to the ballpark, and I'm sure there are many who just check in once in a while. I wish we had some better numbers to know just how many are listening. But like what I was just saying about Don Wardlow: you never know who might be tuning in. Earlier this year, I was in a Blockbuster video store, and a guy asked me if I was the Blue Rocks broadcaster. He had recognized my voice, and you kind of put your chest out a little when that happens. It feels good to know that people are listening.

EDITOR'S NOTE: Lenox left the Blue Rocks in April 2006.

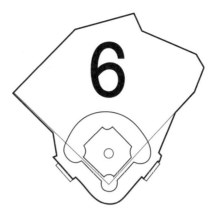

Stat-heads and Historians

DICK BRESCIANI

DICK BRESCIANI IS THE VICE PRESIDENT OF PUBLICATIONS AND
ARCHIVES FOR THE BOSTON RED SOX. A GRADUATE OF HOPEDALE
[MASS.] HIGH SCHOOL AND THE UNIVERSITY OF MASSACHUSETTS,
BRESCIANI HAS WORKED FOR THE ORGANIZATION SINCE 1972 AND
IS A MEMBER OF THE RED SOX HALL OF FAME. THIS INTERVIEW
TOOK PLACE IN DECEMBER 2005.

David Laurila: *Let's start with a little background. When did you first become interested in baseball?*

Dick Bresciani: I came from an athletically oriented family—a large family—and baseball was the big sport when I was growing up. Like most kids, I dreamed of playing in the Major Leagues someday, but you come to learn that good-fielding, no-hitting second basemen are a dime a dozen. Still, I've always had a tremendous interest in baseball, and I had a knack for statistics and an enjoyment of scoring games. I was lucky enough to turn that into a career with the Red Sox.

DL: *Can you elaborate on what you mean by "a knack for statistics"?*

DB: I'm referring to things like the recognition and understanding of what's important, and the derivation and accuracy of putting them together. Some of what I did—we're talking a number of years ago—included things like hitting with runners in scoring position, allowing inherited runners to score, and driving in runners from third with less than two out. I was in charge of the team's statistics from 1972 to 1996, and a lot of that data wasn't available like it is now—especially earlier on. And dealing with it in those days, there was no basis for what was good. If someone drove in 72 percent of runners from third with less than two out, was that good, poor, or average? You need to build up data to deduce that. In those days, you couldn't just go on the Internet to find out.

DL: *Once compiled, how was that data utilized?*

DB: Some of it went into our media notes, but it was mostly used by the ball club. We'd put out an in-house report after every season: statistical analysis—strictly hard numbers—with no human element. We did situational hitting charts, how many bases runners were advancing in which situations, where balls were hit against certain pitchers. For instance, if Luis Tiant or Rick Wise were pitching against the Yankees, we'd know where their guys typically hit the ball against them. And with four-man rotations and fewer teams in those days, we'd have a pretty good sample size to work with. We were also one of the first teams to keep pitch charts, in the 1970s. We tried to supply any and all information that we could use to our advantage. Trends were important. Of course, it all served as a gauge, not as an end-all.

DL: *Were you the first person to compile most of those numbers for the Red Sox?*

DB: Everything grows from what other people started, and I took what my predecessor, Arthur Keefe, did, and expanded on it. Like most teams, we weren't that good about keeping statistical records until the 1970s. Even then, there was typically just a PR director who did a lot of everything, and he did it on a typewriter. Baseball has never had a great method of scoring. The AP used to do play-by-play for years, but mistakes were made and seldom corrected. In 1964, my eventual boss, PR director Bill Crowley, started keeping a day-to-day book on the players here, but it wasn't comprehensive. In 1968, Art Keefe was hired to be the first Red Sox full-time assistant PR director, and he traveled with the team, and kept notes and official stats. He bettered what Bill Crowley started. When I came on in '72, I took Art's good work and expanded on that.

DL: *Let's go back to my initial question about when you first became interested in baseball. Did you grow up a Red Sox fan?*

DB: As a very young boy, I was actually a Joe DiMaggio fan and liked the Yankees. A lot of that had to do with my Italian heritage and the Yankees having players like DiMaggio, Berra, and Rizzuto, and before that Crosetti and Lazzeri. But I changed that tune growing up. My father and uncles used to take me to Sunday doubleheaders at both Fenway and Braves Field. We'd pack a lunch and go spend the afternoon at the ball-park. We'd normally sit in the bleachers, but once in a while we'd splurge and pay the $2.25 to sit in the grandstand. I was crushed when the Braves moved to Milwaukee in 1953. I was a knothole gang member at Braves Field when I was a boy. Boston was very fortunate to have two teams, and I followed both, but those days are long gone.

DL: *How did you come to work for the Red Sox?*

DB: I was the assistant sports information director at UMass for 11 years, and I wrote a letter to the Red Sox telling them of my interest and asking them to keep me in mind. They responded by saying there was nothing available, but that I was welcome to write back in six months. In the meantime, I got rejection letters from many other teams I had also contacted. Nothing happened right away when I got back to the Red Sox, but then, in May, I got a call. They said Art Keefe was going to be interviewing in Milwaukee, and if he went they might have something for me. Art did go to Milwaukee—that was Memorial Day weekend in 1972—and the next thing I knew, I was telling the chancellor at UMass, "I'm going to the Major Leagues!"

DL: *Along with UMass and the Red Sox, you've also been involved in the Cape Cod League. Tell us about that.*

DB: I knew I wanted to work in sports when I graduated from UMass, and luckily for me, they created a position that I was able to move into.

It was a nine-months-out-of-the-year job, which gave me an opportunity to get involved in the Cape Cod League. At the time, they were making changes in order to be fully accredited by the NCAA and eligible for grant money from MLB. This was in 1967. To do that, they had to make the league college players only—no pros, high school, or noncollege players—and make jobs available to them. Back then, the Basin League in the Dakotas was probably the top summer league, with guys like Jim Lonborg and Jim Palmer having played there. The Alaskan League had begun by then, and others like the Central Illinois and Shenandoah Valley leagues were also strong. The Cape Cod League was in the mix, but it wasn't what it is now. I'm proud of the work I've done for them. And it helped my own career, as I've met a lot a people, from all over baseball, on the Cape.

DL: *You've been elected to the Cape Cod League Hall of Fame, but I want to ask you about another hall. What can you tell us about the Red Sox Hall of Fame?*

DB: Long-time broadcaster Ken Coleman used to tell me we should start it, so in the early nineties I contacted teams that had one. I learned what their criteria was, what type of ceremonies they held—things like that. Our owners, Haywood Sullivan and John Harrington, agreed that we should establish our own, and we decided that making it a first-class event was a priority. They also wanted the net proceeds from the induction dinner to go to charity. Every two years a maximum of six players and/or managers can go in, along with one non-uniformed inductee and one memorable moment. We have a 15-person selection committee, and the players have to meet two requirements: They have to have spent at least three years in a Red Sox uniform and been out of baseball for at least three years. Anyone inducted into Cooperstown is an automatic selection. Our former GM, Lou Gorman, has done tremendous work coordinating the induction dinner.

DL: *Are there plans to establish an actual physical Red Sox Hall of Fame, similar to the one in Cooperstown?*

DB: Larry Lucchino and the owners talk about it a lot, and definitely want it to happen. Location is the problem. We need it to be part of the fan experience of coming to Fenway, so we shouldn't have it any distance from the ball park. We need to figure out the logistics of where we can put it, but eventually we'll get one.

DL: *Retired numbers are somewhat controversial, as many people feel there are deserving players who have not been recognized. Johnny Pesky is perhaps the most widely cited. What are your thoughts on that?*

DB: For years, numbers like 9 and 4 weren't given out by the ball club, and in the winter of 1983 we decided to make it formal. Yes, it's controversial, but it's a matter of exclusivity and we don't want to get into a situation where we're making exceptions. For instance, if we retire Johnny Pesky's number, what is the argument against also retiring Dominic DiMaggio's? And if we retire Dominic DiMaggio's, why don't we retire so-and-so's, and right on down the line. We had a huge hue and cry when Tony Conigliaro passed away, but if we retire his number, what about Harry Agannis'? A lot of people have agendas as to who should be honored—and some of those agendas are quite meaningful—but you don't want to get trapped into a situation of "If player A, why not player B?" So we made it objective rather than subjective. There are three key rules—three requirements—which Haywood Sullivan, John Harrington, and I came up with: you have to be in the National Baseball Hall of Fame, you need to have longevity—at least 10 years—with the team, and you need to have been loyal, which means finishing your career with the team. In the case of Carlton Fisk, it's a situation where the requirement doesn't read "playing career." Yes, that's a bit of a loophole, and in this case we're fortunate that it exists, as Fisk deserves the honor.

DL: *You mentioned Tony Conigliaro. The organization does present an award in his honor.*

DB: Every January since 1990, someone in the game is honored for courage and perseverance in facing adversity in his baseball career. We started a national award, endorsed by former commissioner Fay Vincent after Tony C passed away, and feel it's an honor befitting his life. It's not awarded just to Red Sox players; every club in MLB can nominate someone. An 11-person independent committee decides on the award each year.

DL: *To close, the Baseball Hall of Fame will be announcing its 2006 inductees next week. Tell us your thoughts on that.*

DB: This is a big voting year for Jim Rice, and we compiled and sent out information on his career that is tremendously revealing. His dominance over a 12-year period was phenomenal, and I think we did a good job of showing that. If you compare his numbers to those of his peers, it's eye-opening how he stacks up in many of the important offensive categories. He was one of the greatest players I've had the pleasure of watching, and I think he deserves to be inducted into the Hall of Fame.

BILL JAMES

BILL JAMES IS A RENOWNED SABERMETRICIAN AND THE AUTHOR OF SEVERAL INFLUENTIAL BOOKS ON BASEBALL, INCLUDING *THE BILL JAMES HISTORICAL ABSTRACT*. A NATIVE OF MAYETTA, KANSAS, JAMES IS CURRENTLY A SENIOR BASEBALL OPERATIONS ADVISER FOR THE RED SOX. THIS INTERVIEW TOOK PLACE IN OCTOBER 2004.

David Laurila: *How did your association with the Red Sox come to be, and did you pass up similar opportunities prior to coming here?*

Bill James: John Henry got my e-mail address and asked me if I had ever thought of being a part of a Major League front office. I had worked with other teams in a limited form, and I had also passed up opportunities to do so.

Whether these were "similar" opportunities or not depends upon what you consider to be similar. The Red Sox are different in that the people who run the Red Sox—John Henry and Theo and many others— already had a good understanding of how I think, and thus were very easy for me to communicate with. When I had worked with other teams, I was always fighting rear-guard actions against mistakes, based on ways of analyzing the move that people didn't understand, which is sort of like trying to persuade a Chinese policeman to stop beating you if you don't speak any Chinese. When I came here, I could use a term like "defensive spectrum" without dragging the conversation back 18 steps to explain what I was saying.

DL: *How does your approach differ now that you're no longer independent—is your perspective notably different?*

BJ: Well, I'm not a full-time employee here, and I'm still somewhat independent. But my perspective on the game is very, very different from inside than it was from outside.

DL: *Although you visit Boston on occasion, you still live in Kansas. How often do you communicate with the front office, and do you feel it's an advantage to keep a distance from the day-to-day activity and media coverage of the team?*

BJ: I communicate with somebody here nearly every day, usually many times during the day. But what I do—what I do for the Red Sox, and what I have always done—is, in essence, to walk away from the problem and look at it from a great distance, to try to see the size and proportion of each element of the problem. That's much easier to do from a distance than it is from close up. What I worry about is getting too close to the team—getting so close to the team that I can't see the library for the books.

DL: *Can you give us a scenario regarding your work with the front office? For instance, what type of assignment might you be given, and what is your process in carrying it through?*

BJ: I'm not sure I can answer. I'm given all kinds of assignments, little ones requiring immediate feedback, big ones requiring months. I don't know that I can generalize accurately based on this question.

DL: *Let's address a few questions involving player personnel decisions: When constructing a roster, how much weight should the dimensions, and other relevant factors, of your home ballpark come into play?*

BJ: Well, if you can't play Major League baseball, the park won't help you. If you're Honus Wagner, you can play anywhere. Stated in analytical terms, if you're an .800 player—a superstar—it makes very little difference what park you play in. If you're a .300 player—a Triple A player—it makes no difference whatsoever what park you play in. But there are players who are .480 players in some situations, .520 players in others. The park makes a big difference in the decision if the player is near the margin, and the margin is about .380.

DL: *It has been argued that the Red Sox are hindered by Fenway Park, and that replacing it with a more conventional home field would be beneficial. What is your opinion on that?*

BJ: Horse Hockey.

DL: *This year's team was reportedly "built to win in the playoffs," rather than the regular season. Do you buy into that theory, and if so, what are the differences?*

BJ: I'm answering these questions during the playoffs. You'd have to ask me another time.

DL: *You argued, in your* Historical Baseball Abstract, *that Roy White was better than Jim Rice. While you have statistical formulas to back that up, would you still, hypothetically, take White over Rice if you were a Major League GM? Also, thinking back to the previous questions, would your home ballpark play into the decision?*

BJ: Well, Jim Rice was an MVP. Obviously, he was a very good player. He and I are now teammates, in a sense. I see him in the aisles of the offices. It wouldn't be appropriate for me to criticize him, or to say anything that might be interpreted as criticism. He was a tremendous hitter.

DL: *Given the same hypothetical option, how many of today's GMs do you think would take White over Rice, and what should their priorities be in making the decision?*

BJ: Ibid. But to answer as much as I can, certainly many would, and sometimes they're right, and sometimes they're dead wrong. But different people see things differently. If the Minnesota Twins could choose between them, they'd choose Roy White. That's why we had the opportunity to sign David Ortiz.

DL: *While arguably overrated, Rice was probably the most "feared" slugger in the AL for a number of years. Conversely, players like Darrell Evans were underrated and more typically described as "respected." What are your thoughts on the relative merits of these reputations when it comes to HOF consideration?*

BJ: I wrote a book about the Hall of Fame, and I said there what I have to say about it. The Hall of Fame is not a serious evaluator of players' skills. Never has been. It has always been arbitrary, superficial, and prone to pick irrational favorites. So if you ask what their standards "should" be, they should be serious, thoughtful, systematic, and fair-handed. But, unfortunately, they're not, and it is impossible to guess what their standards would be if they were.

DL: *How would you compare Ryne Sandberg and Roberto Alomar? Who was the better player, and should either be in the HOF?*

BJ: They're very comparable in terms of the "gross weight" of their on-field contributions. Thus, choosing between them rests on the other issues, the things perhaps beyond what we can measure. I guess what I am saying is that Roberto Alomar may well have been a greater player than Ryno, but I have a failure of enthusiasm in endorsing him. Also, I don't have any idea what the Hall of Fame standard is, and frankly, neither does anybody else.

DL: *In your opinion, who's the best player not in the HOF?*

BJ: Ron Santo.

DL: *Can you comment on Rogers Hornsby, who some feel is the best right-handed hitter of all time? You rated him as the third-best second baseman of all-time, behind Joe Morgan and Eddie Collins.*

BJ: He was a great hitter. Greatest right-handed hitter ever? Was he a greater hitter than Hank Aaron, Willie Mays, Honus Wagner, or Jimmie Foxx? I doubt it. He was a below-average second baseman and a perpetual pain in the butt. To me, Joe Morgan or Rogers Hornsby is not a hard choice.

DL: *In ranking Arky Vaughan the second-best shortstop in history, you note that he was not an outstanding defender. Taking the pitching staff into consideration, are many teams not better off with an Ozzie Smith at this position?*

BJ: No, they're not. And Arky Vaughan was a better defensive shortstop than Rogers Hornsby was a second baseman.

DL: *Looking at a team as a whole, rather than a group of individuals, how much importance do you place on defense up the middle?*

BJ: I always look at the team as a whole, rather than as a group of individuals. But relative to what? It's like asking "How important do you think water is?" or "How important do you think silverware is?" Looking at the meal as a whole, how important do you think silverware is? Relative to what?

DL: *In center field, you have Dom DiMaggio rated below Cesar Cedeno and Amos Otis. Similar to the Rice/White comparison, which of the three would you rather have on your team, and why?*

BJ: Below Otis and Cedeno, but ahead of at least three Hall of Fame center fielders. Dominic played 1,400 games in his Major League career; Cedeno and Otis played more, even if you give DiMaggio credit for time missed in World War II. They had power; he didn't. But it's a marginal call. Who you would take would depend on the needs of your team.

DL: *It has been argued that stolen bases are overrated, but what about the impact of having a running threat on first base? How much added value is there to getting a hitter more fastballs—not uncommon in that situation—not to mention the disruption of a pitcher's rhythm?*

BJ: The impact of having a running threat at first base, on many teams, is negative, not positive. It is very clear that this is true if you start with the facts, rather than the theory. What happens on a lot of teams is that the hitter takes pitches in order to allow the runner to steal, and finds himself hitting behind in the count. It's a bad trade. It's another way the running game will bite you in the ass if you give it a chance.

DL: *Thinking about this year's NL Cy Young award, who of the following do you feel had the best year: Roger Clemens, Randy Johnson, or Ben Sheets?*

BJ: Randy was very, very good, even though his teammates didn't give him much opportunity to shine. I haven't run the numbers, but intuitively, I would guess Randy was the best of the three.

DL: *It's fairly clear that Barry Bonds is the NL's best player, but is he also the MVP? As he wasn't given as many opportunities, especially in key situations, is it fair to argue that he was too respected to earn the honor? Isn't an Albert Pujols a better choice, because his extra-base hits and RBIs are more valuable than Bonds' free passes?*

BJ: I thought Pujols was the MVP a year ago, and so argued. This year, I think it's back to Bonds. Pujols drove in 22 more runs, but made 160 more outs. It's hard to see how that's an advantage for him.

DL: *Hideki Matsui has historically fared poorly against Pedro Martinez, while Enrique Wilson, a comparatively inferior hitter, has excelled. If you were Joe Torre, which of the two would you rather have up against him in a key situation?*

BJ: Matsui, obviously.

DL: *Can you please elaborate? Some would argue that Wilson's 11 for 25 versus Matsui's 3 for 22 would indicate otherwise.*

BJ: A great many people would. Statistics derived from 20 or 25 trials don't really mean much, and there are few situations in which I would make a decision based on them. If Wilson was 22 for 50 against a given pitcher and Matsui was 6 for 44, that still would be much more likely to be a fluke outcome than actual evidence that Wilson would hit this pitcher better than Matsui. If it was Matsui against Bernie Williams or Soriano or Giambi, somebody comparable to Matsui as a hitter, that would be different.

DL: *When assessing predictive statistics, how many at-bats do you feel are necessary to accurately project future production? Also, how do age and level of competition factor into the equation?*

BJ: As to the at-bats, there is no magic cutoff at which the numbers become meaningless. It's the wrong question.

DL: *Let me rephrase my question: If you're looking at a statistic that is generally considered more predictive [OPS] than descriptive [RBIs], I am presuming that you can more accurately project future performance based on a sample size of 2,000 at-bats than 2. Somewhere in the middle is, theoretically, a number-range where you can say, "I think there's enough here to try to assess future performance." Is there such a number?*

BJ: No, there is no magic number at which the data becomes reliable. It is a mistake to think that there is such a number. If there was, then you wouldn't need to look at other factors . . . scouting reports, health, etc. But there isn't. It is always a matter of balancing stats against other information—whether the player has 2 at bats or 2,000.

DL: *When assessing the risk of trading a prospect, what is the relative importance of tools versus production?*

BJ: I apologize, but I just can't answer a question that general. It's exactly like asking, "What is the relative importance of education versus intelligence?" Education without intelligence is wasted. Intelligence without education is limited.

DL: *While most people agree that it's harder to project pitchers than hitters, what is your opinion on the importance of velocity? R.J. Swindle in the Sox organization, and Jon Connolly with the Cubs, have questionable stuff but are proving they know how to get hitters out. Are they marginal prospects because they don't throw hard, or miss enough bats, or does that really matter?*

BJ: There are good pitchers who don't throw hard. The editor of the 1892 *Reach Guide* argued—paraphrasing it from memory—that fans were always impressed by fastballs, but that it was control and knowledge of what to do with the pitches which won the game at the end of the day. This has always been true to some extent, and the development of the radar gun has made it more true. There are people who will never believe that Bronson Arroyo is really a good pitcher, because he doesn't throw all that hard. But there are some pitchers who are very, very effective without throwing 95 or, for that matter, 91. John Burkett won 25 games in his last two seasons for the Red Sox throwing 84–85 miles an hour.

DL: *Last question: In your book,* The Politics of Glory, *you quote an unnamed coach as saying, "We use statistics the way a drunk uses a lamppost—for support, not illumination." What does that quote mean to you and the work that you do?*

BJ: Almost everybody "uses" statistics to prove their point, rather than using them to understand the question. Almost all sports writing "analysis" begins with the answer, or begins with a position on the question, and then defends that answer or that position. This has never been what I do. I begin with the issue itself, rather than with a position on the issue. In other words, I never begin by saying that "Manny Ramirez is the MVP, and here's why." I always begin by saying "Who is the MVP, and why?" To many people, this is irritating. Most people just want to know what your position is; they could care less how you got there. Do you think Manny Ramirez is the MVP or don't you, damn it? This is what most of your questions here are about . . . Ryne Sandberg or Roberto Alomar, damn it? Stop stalling. But . . . that's me. I am always more interested in the question than I am in the answer.

PETE PALMER

PETE PALMER IS THE AUTHOR AND CO-AUTHOR OF SEVERAL BOOKS, INCLUDING *THE HIDDEN GAME OF BASEBALL* AND *TOTAL BASEBALL*. A RESIDENT OF HOLLIS, NEW HAMPSHIRE, PALMER IS ALSO THE CO-EDITOR OF *THE BASEBALL ENCYCLOPEDIA*. THIS INTERVIEW TOOK PLACE IN FEBRUARY 2006.

David Laurila: *There was much debate as to whether Alex Rodriguez or David Ortiz was the AL MVP in 2005, with Ortiz's frequent late-inning heroics among the arguments in his favor. Who do you feel was deserving of the award, and why?*

Pete Palmer: I have an objective program which computes the probability of winning the game [based on a table generated by simulation], before and after each at-bat. Ortiz led the league, with about nine wins over the average player, while Rodriguez was second with about six.

However, I would still give the nod to A-Rod because of the fact that he held down a reasonably important field position. His fielding stats are not exceptional, but just the fact that he contributed on defense is important. Ortiz did have one great season at the plate, though.

DL: *Superstars make a lot of money, but how many more games do they actually help their teams win than players who are simply "good" [and not such a drain on the payroll]?*

PP: Our encyclopedia [the *ESPN Baseball Encyclopedia* published by Barnes & Noble, due out this spring for its third edition] explains our rating methods. Since we don't have play-by-play for all games in history, I use season-statistics, and rate players in number of wins above or below average. This involves batting, pitching, fielding, and base running. There is also a positional adjustment. Since it takes less skill to play some positions [like left field, right field, first base] compared to others [like catcher and shortstop], each batter is compared against others at his position rather than the league as a whole. Thus in the Ortiz/Rodriguez case above, Ortiz is compared against DHs and Rodriguez against third basemen. DHs are expected to hit better and therefore must do so in order to be equal to less-demanding positions. If you take a good hitter who is a shortstop, he is more valuable to the team than an equally good hitter who plays left field on another team. That is because the first team can add a left fielder to the lineup who on average will be a better hitter than the shortstop added on the second team. The actual difference in this case could be a couple of wins a year. So allowing for the fact that some positions are expected to have better hitters than others, it is rare for any player to be worth more than 3 or 4 wins a year to his team over a period of years. There can be season-to-season variations which cause this number to be higher or lower for a particular year. For example, Manny Ramirez has been consistently rated at 2 to 4 wins a year every year for the past decade. Once in a while, you get a player in the 5–6 wins a year range, like Rodriguez or Albert Pujols. Even Bonds was only 7–8 wins until his late resurgence, which was around 10, since 2001, until his injury last year. This puts him in the class with Ruth and Williams. Aaron was 4–5, but he did it for a very long time, Mays 5–6 for a shorter time, Mantle 5–8 for even a shorter period. Ty Cobb was 4–6 wins a year. For pitchers, Maddux was 4–6, Clemens was less consistent [at 3–7], but his lifetime total was about the same. Walter Johnson was about the only pitcher to be rated higher. Thus, any player who can contribute more than 3–4 wins a year is one of the all-time greats.

DL: *How would you compare the careers of Dwight Evans, Andre Dawson, and Jack Clark, and do the three compare favorably to Tony Perez?*

PP: Perez was probably not a good choice for the Hall. I have him rated at 10 wins, well below the limit. Dawson is 18, closer, but still not a good choice. These two were better at quantity than quality, good solid players, but not at the Hall-of-Fame level. Evans, on the other hand, is rated at 25, right in the middle of the marginal level. Dwight dropped off the ballot after three years, falling below the 5 percent level. Evans has a much higher on-base average than Dawson and only a slightly lower slugging average, and Dwight also shows up as a better fielder. Dawson has gotten strong support [61 percent in the last elections] and might even get in eventually. I can't give you a good reason for it. Perhaps Dawson was often considered the best player on his team, where Evans had Yaz, then Lynn, Rice, and Clemens to take away the spotlight. Clark is another player who I rate highly but got very little support from the Hall of Fame voters. I have him at 30 wins above average, making him a good candidate. His skills were fairly obvious, slugging and on-base.

DL: *Some people feel Bobby Grich is deserving of the Hall of Fame. Do you agree?*

PP: Bill James had Grich rated fairly highly, although he picked Ron Santo for the most deserving of the Hall of Fame who has not been elected. I have Grich at 52 wins above average, while Santo is 45. Along with old-timer Bill Dahlen, these are the top three. Grich is overlooked because his skills were more diversified. When Gene Autry was trying to win a pennant with the Angels, he acquired Rod Carew, Reggie Jackson, and Grich. The other two were first-ballot Hall of Famers, while Grich struck out in his first chance with less than 5 percent of the vote and never will be considered again. I have him rated ahead of the other two, but Carew had batting average and Jackson home runs. Grich had relatively good on-base and slugging, and played a difficult defensive position well. Without his bad back, he might have made the Hall of Fame, anyway.

DL: *Why are there so few third basemen [9] enshrined, and how much should a player's position be a factor?*

PP: Third base is a difficult position because it is not a hitting position or a fielding position, but a combination. Outfielders and first baseman can contribute a lot with their bat, while catchers, second baseman, and shortstops can do it defensively. Third basemen handle only about three chances a game in the field, so they have less opportunity to make a difference there, but the defensive skill needed is still more than the hitting positions, so they tend to be not as good at the bat. That is because hitting and fielding are different and it is the rare player [like Rodriguez, Wagner, Ripken, and Hornsby] who can do both well. Of 110 batters over 30 wins, I have only 9 third basemen, whereas 13 would be expected. This is about the same as catchers, who are lower because the rigors of their position prevent them from playing as many games. Another factor is that some third base slots are held by former shortstops who moved to the right of the defensive spectrum [like Ripken, Rodriguez, and Joe Sewell] and others are lost by those who move further to the right [like Killebrew, Richie Allen, and Jim Thome]. Position is important. Since positions require different amounts of fielding skill, normally the average batter in a more difficult position will not bat as well. I take this into account as positional adjustment. If a left fielder produces 20 more runs on the average than a shortstop, that does not mean that if you put the left fielder in at shortstop that the team would allow 20 more runs a year. It would be a lot more than that. But it does mean that a shortstop who hits as well as the average left fielder will help his team more than if he played left field, because the team will expect to get 20 more runs from the average left fielder they now need, rather than the average shortstop. So for Hall of Fame purposes, a player's batting stats should be compared to others at his position. In the 1920s, the average regular outfielder batted about .325. Half of them are in the Hall of Fame, which is a mistake, because the position and the era were not taken into account. Beyond this, if a player is a good fielding shortstop, that should be worth more than a good fielding outfielder because a shortstop gets more chances each game to show his skill. Thus, you get credit for being an average fielder at a more difficult position, and even more credit for being a better than average fielder.

DL: *Where do we currently stand in regard to defensive metrics? Will it ever be possible to accurately gauge the difference between an Ozzie Smith and an Omar Vizquel, and how many games they helped win with their gloves?*

PP: My defensive stats are based on putouts, assists, errors, and double plays per defensive inning compared to the league average. I also take into account pitcher strikeouts, which affect the number of chances for other fielders, and the left–right composition of the staff, which also has an effect. In addition, I consider double-play opportunities for the team derived from the number of runners who reach first. Since we don't have detailed hit location data much before 1988, I can't use that for all players, so I don't use it for moderns. There are many other factors which influence fielding opportunities, like ground-ball/fly-ball pitching staff tendencies and park configuration. The trouble with ground-ball/fly-ball is that you can't separate a lot of chances for the infield based on good fielders from that based on ground ball pitchers. If you take the pitchers into account, you end up comparing infielders only against the other players on the team, rather than on the league. I thought our fielding numbers were pretty reasonable, except for catchers and first baseman. For catchers, see the next question. First baseman can pile up a lot of assists by throwing to the pitcher on almost every grounder. I would like to analyze current data and try to filter that out. I did a study for 1969 to 2003, measuring the percentage of time a first baseman threw to the pitcher on a grounder, and it varied from 20 percent to 50 percent. There is no clear pattern on poor fielders doing it more often, so perhaps some just didn't get to many balls away from the bag. Bill Buckner was famous for throwing to the pitcher, and he is one of the 50 percent guys. Supposedly, he did it to train the pitcher to always come over so he would be there when Bill needed him, but it also could have been because he couldn't run. I think fielding ratings can be improved for current players. I believe MLBAM [Major League Baseball Advanced Media] is trying to do something with videotape. You need to track the position of the fielders and the trajectories of the balls. It would be interesting to see what they come up with.

DL: *Are defensive metrics for catchers realistic, with players like Jason Varitek bringing intangibles to the position that are difficult to quantify?*

PP: I worked hard on improving the catcher rating by tabulating stolen bases and caught-stealing allowed. We have it from Gary Gillette's project scoresheet/baseball workshop data from 1984 and Dave Smith's retrosheet for 1960 to 1983. Before then, I used team data and allocated that among the catchers. There is no caught-stealing data for 1926 to 1950 National League, so I used a combination of factors, including catcher assists, out on base, and American League success rate to come up with estimates for teams and then divided them among the catchers as before. Johnny Bench had a negative rating in the old system, because he had very few assists. This was because players did not run on him. I had Bench rated at −11 fielding wins, while a study by Bill Deane showed that he was +11 based on stealing alone. When I took that into account, Bench got credit for few stolen bases allowed, a high caught-stealing rate and also more assists on non-stealing plays, so his fielding went to +8, a swing of 19 wins. This put him up among the lifetime leaders for catchers, where he belonged. Iván Rodriguez also got a big boost out of the improved system, although Gabby Hartnett is number one among catchers. Bill McNeil has a new book out on catchers, and he also selects Hartnett, but Bill does not rate Bench as highly as I do. I give the catcher credit for 10 percent of the pitching success of the team, which is just a token. I admit that there are other aspects of a catcher's job that are hard to measure, like calling pitches, rapport with the pitchers, general field leadership, and others. Still, I think our top-rated catchers make a pretty good list.

DL: *While quality pitchers are very desirable, good defensive players are generally not valued as highly. Just how much more important are pitchers than the defenders behind them when it comes to preventing runs?*

PP: Dick Cramer did a study years ago where he determined that 85 percent of fielding plays are routine, which I suppose means they could be handled by any professional player at any level. My studies show that the range of fielders in total chances varies about plus or minus 15 percent, which agrees with Dick's findings. Thus, I believe that the pitcher is the main contributor to team defense. Walks, strikeouts, and homers are beyond the reach of the fielders, and these are the main components of good pitching. Voros McCracken got a lot of publicity for stating that there is absolutely no difference in outs made on balls in play for any pitcher. He later backed off from that a bit. I found that there is a small difference. There is a good reason for this, though, and that is as stated above, the method strips away a lot of what makes a good pitcher. A good pitcher will turn a homer into a double, but since the double is not turned into an out, his number of hits allowed goes up. If he turns a double into a single, it is unaffected. If he turns an out into a strikeout, his outs on balls in play goes down. If he turns a walk into a ball in play, it is unaffected. The only time he gets a boost is if he turns a single into an out. Thus, outs over balls in play has a very strong leveling factor which undermines the difference in pitching skill. A good defensive player can save some number of runs a year, but in most cases it would be less than that of a good pitcher.

DL: *Bill James once disparaged your Linear Weight System, saying that "runs-scoring is not a linear activity." What are your thoughts on that, and how would you describe your relationship with James?*

PP: Bill is technically correct. The nominal values of linear weights are for average Major League play. On a good hitting team, a hit is worth more and an out costs more because of the good hitters around you. These differences are small, however, and the nominal values work pretty well for the actual levels of play encountered. Besides, I think it is fairer to rate players on what they would contribute to an average team and not give them credit for having good teammates. The values are normalized to the league average by picking an out value, which makes the average player come out zero [with pitcher batting excluded].

Bill and I are good friends, and I see him once in a while, usually at SABR [Society of American Baseball Research] conventions. He is always cordial in person but manages quite a few jibes in his writing. I remember he told me after his first historical abstract came out, which seemed very much concerned with touting his stuff over mine, that he was going to tone down the revisions a bit, but he never did. This does not bother me, however. Bill is a much better writer than I am, and he is very good at turning a phrase. I credit him with popularizing statistical analysis, which made it easier for me to have my work get exposure. I remember how he disparaged my rating of Gene Tenace as a hitting catcher. I used his exact formulas to show that he would have had Tenace ranked ahead of Cochrane, Dickey, and all the rest as a hitter, and did not get a response. Of course, Tenace was not a great fielding catcher, did not play for a long time, and saw a lot of action at first base. Tenace batted .241, but had a normalized OPS of 137 [37 percent above average]. He has since been passed by Mike Piazza [149] but is still ranked 2nd.

I find it amusing that it took Bill 20 years to figure out how to convert runs created in wins [via Win Shares]. Actually, it is quite simple; 10 more runs means one more win. The actual number varies somewhat year to year, based on the average level of league scoring [the actual formula is 10 times the square root of runs per inning by both teams, which is usually around one. It is almost always between 9 and 11 and with the large variation due to chance between runs and wins, 10 works as well as anything [including Bill's vaunted Pythagorean theorem]. Take a team that scores 800 runs and allows 700. Using the 10 runs per win method, you take [800–700]/10 which is 10. This indicates the team should win 81+10 or 91 games, for a percentage of .562. Pythagoras says .566 [800 squared over the sum of 800 squared plus 700 squared]. My method is much easier, with no calculator needed, and just as accurate. Bill's method does work a bit better in extreme cases, where I would invoke the more complicated formula mentioned above. In his *Win Shares* book, Bill states that 95 percent of a player's value is being average. I would disagree with that. I rate an average player at zero, which is very different from saying he is worthless, or that you and I are also at zero and therefore just as good. What zero means is that the player contributes nothing toward making the team win more than half its games. It takes a great deal of skill to be an average player. Heck, it takes quite a bit of skill to even be drafted or play in the low minors. But at the Major League level, it is all about winning and in order to win you need better-than-average players. At three or four wins a year from superstars, you need four or five of them plus a fair amount of luck just to make the playoffs. And you need average or near-average players at the other positions so you don't fall behind. Using Win Shares, a 20-year average player can pile up over 200 shares [at 13 or so per year] and rank ahead of a very good player who only played 15 years. If I tell you a player is plus 10 wins for his career, you know he was pretty good, independent of how long he played, whereas 30 wins shares [three shares per win] is pretty much meaningless without a take on how much play was involved.

DL: *Let's say two batters have an identical OBP of .350. Player A hit .25 points higher, while player B made up the difference by drawing more walks. Many would argue that player B is more desirable, because he displayed better plate discipline. Others might argue that player A helped his team more because his base hits advanced runners further than player B's walks. Your opinion would be . . . ?*

PP: The player with more hits would also have a higher slugging average. I developed on-base plus slugging because it is easy to calculate and very closely matches the more complicated linear weight method, where each item is multiplied by a value which reflects its worth in runs. A single is worth about half a run, and each extra base or walk is worth about 3/10 of a run. An out is around −.25 runs. So if you look at the overall spectrum, normalizing roughly to a quarter of a run, a walk is worth 1, a single 2, a double 3, a triple 4, and a home run 5. This is about the same as in on-base plus slugging because with on-base, each is worth 1, while in slugging, a walk doesn't count and the others are 1-2-3-4. So if you add them up, you get the 1-2-3-4-5 pattern I mentioned. Adding up OBP and SLG is quite easy these days, as many stat forms show them side by side. This does not take into account park factors and positional adjustments, however. Recent studies have shown that on-base is actually worth more than slugging; however, the difference in correlation of team runs is small.

DL: *You were on the cutting edge of statistical analysis in the 1970s and have been credited with introducing OPS as a stat. When you look at how the teams of today utilize such information, what do you think?*

PP: Well, Michael Lewis's book on the A's was enlightening. I was honored to be mentioned in that book, as well as Alan Schwarz's book on numbers. I would have thought Billy Beane would have liked to keep whatever he was doing secret for competitive advantage, but evidently not. I think they have done a lot in looking for high-OPS players who might not look that impressive otherwise and also in trying to teach plate discipline. They still had trouble impressing Miguel Tejada, however. I wrote a piece in the mid-seventies which stated that a player with a 1-0 count produces twice as many runs in that appearance as one at 0-1, and that an eighth-place hitter with the same 1-0 count is a better hitter than a cleanup guy with 0-1. But I still think a lot of people don't believe it. I know the Red Sox talked about not using the traditional closer strategy when the 2004 season started, but after a couple of weeks I didn't see a lot of difference there. I think definitely some teams like the A's, Red Sox, and Blue Jays are cutting down on the use of strategies that most of us outsiders [beginning with George Lindsey in the sixties] have criticized, like stolen bases, sacrifices, and intentional walks. But the actual difference in number of runs saved over the course of a season is small. The owners still are paying very high salaries over a long period of time to moderately good players. I have not done the research, but it appears to me that there has not been a really big contract [like $100 million or so], where the team was happy with it after a couple of years. Surely, the Red Sox could not have expected Manny Ramirez to play any better than he has, and yet they tried to unload him for no return, and no team took him. In most of these cases, the original signing team has to pay someone to take the player off their hands, and yet they keep doing it. It's hard to explain.

DL: *Long-time SABR member Cliff Otto offered an interesting opinion about statistical analysis recently, saying, "You also have people doing analysis who really do not understand the underlying mathematics, and people who accept it as gospel because it fits with their notions." What are your thoughts on that?*

PP: Cliff is a good buddy of mine, and we have shared data over the years. I believe in some cases that an analyst comes up with a conclusion and then tries to find supporting data, which is probably part of human nature. I know I was surprised when I did a detailed analysis of sending the runner in on a fly ball. It turns out that if the fly ball is the second out, then the runner has to be safe only about 35 percent of the time to make it a good decision to send him, where the actual success rate is around 98 percent. I stand by that conclusion, but when I figured out how many runs might be gained in a season, even at a 50 percent success rate, it was only a few runs a year. Certainly, one thing that a lot of analysts don't understand is the large variation due to chance. There are probably 10 players every year with batting average changing 60 points or more from the previous year, just by chance. A team's wins from season to season with no changes, just from luck, has a standard deviation of 9 wins, meaning 5 percent of the teams [one or two a year] will be 18 wins off just by luck, good or bad. Thus in a short series, like the playoffs, it is basically a crap shoot, with chance easily dwarfing any real difference between the teams. I guess I would like to get more detail from Cliff on what he meant, to fully answer the question.

DL: *Tell us a little of the history behind Pete Palmer, including your rooting interests in baseball.*

PP: Well, I have certainly been a Red Sox fan since the days of DiMaggio, Pesky, Williams, and Doerr. I have helped out Dick Bresciani and Rod Oreste in the publications office from time to time with various research projects. I started out collecting baseball cards like most of us diehard fans and got interested in the stats, compiling quite a few various lists of one type or another. I got into the analysis part in the sixties, working on correlating batting statistics to runs and runs to wins, using linear weights to rate players. I collected a lot of individual player home-and-away data. Then I got into strategy in the seventies. I kept writing to A.S. Barnes, who was publishing the current baseball encyclopedia, pointing out all the mistakes, and they finally gave me the job of editing, which I did for several years in the seventies. This also gave me the opportunity to start my historical database. Then I met up with John Thorn through SABR, and we collaborated on *The Hidden Game of Baseball,* which was basically an outgrowth of a paper I did for *The Sporting News.* They were going to publish it in 1969 but backed out at the last minute because they thought it was too technical. John and Mike Gershman got *Total Baseball* going, of which I did seven editions, and then Gary Gillette and I made the contact with Barnes & Noble to do their encyclopedia, now in its third edition. In the meantime, I had hooked up with *Who's Who in Baseball* for 15 years and worked with Steve Gietschier at *The Sporting News* to help with their record books, both projects still active. SABR is currently in the process of putting my data on its site for research use by members. I have also done a fair amount of football work, including being a member of the Patriots' stat crew for more than 30 years, doing *The Hidden Game of Football* with Bob Carroll, and am now working on a football encyclopedia for Barnes & Noble. I retired from work as a software engineer at Raytheon in 1998 and have been devoting more time to sports work, with my new family, wife Beth, and kids Emily [4], Daniel [2], and Stephen [2 months]. We spend about half the year in New Hampshire and the other half in Florida.

@

ALAN SCHWARZ

ALAN SCHWARZ IS A SENIOR WRITER AT *BASEBALL AMERICA* AND THE AUTHOR OF *THE NUMBERS GAME: BASEBALL'S LIFELONG FASCINATION WITH STATISTICS*. HE ALSO WRITES THE "KEEPING SCORE" COLUMN FOR THE *NEW YORK TIMES*. THIS INTERVIEW TOOK PLACE IN JULY 2004.

David Laurila: *Who does MLB rely on for their stats?*

Alan Schwarz: This gets very, very complicated. I believe that after several years of sorting things out, MLB now keeps its own stats through its *MLB.com* scoring network. These statistics are then sent to the Elias Sports Bureau for proofing and blessing. Other services such as STATS Inc. have their own networks that supply numbers to *ESPN.com*, etc., which have—either occasionally or often—proofed their stats with MLB's to make sure there aren't any differences, though of course there will be from time to time. For example, several years ago, Benny Agbayani of the Mets hit what one outfit called a double, and another called a single advance on a throw, and they never ended up agreeing. But this is very rare.

DL: *What is your opinion of the "*Moneyball*" approach to statistical utilization?*

AS: *Moneyball* was a book, not an approach, and not a philosophy. That's my first and most important point, one that I pray people recognize as we move forward. To the extent that I obviously know what you mean—what is my opinion of organizations using statistical evaluation?—they have been doing that for more than 100 years. The question is which statistics do they follow, and to what extent. Now, the A's are more "draconian" [Billy Beane's own word] than others, but several teams have been doing similar, in-depth stuff for a long time, well back into the 1980s, a very rich history. Just because a famous author wrote a [good] book about the modern A's doesn't change that.

DL: *What is your opinion of Win Shares?*

AS: I like it very much to examine certain questions, such as the aging of players and the amateur draft, where you really want to have one base-lined system to compare all types of players. Given that, while I'm not a huge expert on WS derivations, it does feel to me as if starting pitchers are undervalued a bit, but I think we have to give Bill [James] the benefit of the doubt. He spent a ton of time on the system and had well-thought-out reasons for what he did at every turn.

DL: *Are individual hitter-versus-pitcher stats valuable, or is the sample size usually too small to be meaningful?*

AS: I would only look at them for at least 20 at-bats. Not that that is very significant in a statistical sense, but if a hitter is 1-for-20 off a certain pitcher, today he's gonna know about it, and it might affect him mentally.

DL: *Thinking about regression to the mean, who has a better chance to get a hit off of Pedro Martinez in a given situation: Hideki Matsui [a good hitter with poor numbers against Martinez] or Enrique Wilson [a poor hitter with good numbers against Martinez]? Which way does a "numbers-savvy" manager go?*

AS: Great question. [For those who don't know, Enrique Wilson has a crazily high lifetime batting average against Pedro.] The numbers-aware manager goes with Wilson. The numbers-savvy manager, probably Matsui.

DL: *From a fan's point of view, statistics that reflect the past are usually more important. From a baseball executive's, it would be stats that predict future performance. What do you consider the best examples of each?*

AS: The distinction between descriptive and predictive statistics is probably the most misunderstood aspect of baseball statistics today. As for the ones that describe the past, the ones that reasonably knowledgeable fans rely on to see who had the best year, I'd have to say RBIs [depending on the spot in the batting order, Coors Field, etc.], ERA, and OPS for the more stat-savvy. Generally, you need to be pretty stat-savvy to care about future performance, and there we find things such as adjusted OPS, DIPS ERA, maybe WHIP. But no one statistic tells you everything you want to know. They all have to be taken in context.

DL: *A quote in your book states that the naked eye can't tell the difference between a .275 hitter and a .300 hitter . . . without the numbers. Taking chance into consideration—a key component of the game—is this true without a very large sample size? Comparing two hitters, could a talented scout not tell you more than the raw numbers in a season's worth of games?*

AS: I think a very talented scout might be able to. Then again, the talented scout is going to remember line drives, not necessarily hits, and who knows how many times those line drives and good swings wound up as outs? Batting average is such a horrible statistic, so dependent on luck both in the short term [whether a certain ball falls in for a hit] and the long term [an intrinsically .300 hitter can still hit .200 over two weeks, easily] that it corrupts almost every conversation about statistics from the start.

DL: *Why do Cy Young Award voters seemingly put so much emphasis on won–lost records when they should know better?*

AS: You've answered your own question. They don't know better. They should, but they don't. It's the "just win, baby" syndrome. The problem is, a win for a pitcher only means that the pitcher's team outscored his opponent while he was on the mound. It doesn't really say if he pitched that well.

DL: *What is the most underrated number in baseball history [example: Bob Gibson's 1968 ERA]?*

AS: Great question. I think we're about to see it. Barry Bonds this year is going to hit an absurd percentage of strikes for home runs. As for old numbers, Gibson's ERA was great, of course. It might actually be Tip O'Neill's .492 batting average [in 1887] believe it or not. People dismiss it because it came during the one year that walks were counted as hits. But he still would have hit something like .438 under conventional rules. So tip your hat to Tip!

DL: *What rule changes over history most affect the comparing of eras from a statistical point of view?*

AS: I think nothing changes the game more than the strike zone—everything depends on the strike zone. After that, the size of ballparks has been a big one, both with the weird parks [Baker Bowl, Polo Grounds] that existed in the first half of the 20th century and the smaller ones we see built today.

DL: *What can you tell us about Babe Ruth's 715th HR and similar debates over "official" statistics?*

AS: The hit you're referring to was unearthed when Information Concepts Incorporated was putting together the first *Baseball Encyclopedia* in 1969. This is the discussion of it from my book: "On July 8, 1918, at Fenway Park, Ruth came to the plate for the Red Sox in the bottom of the 10th with the score tied 0-0, with one out and Amos Strunk on first. Ruth belted Stan Coveleski's pitch deep into the right-field bleachers. But this was not a home run, according to a rule in effect before 1920; it was only a triple, because Strunk's run effectively ended the game with Ruth at third. [Had Strunk originally been at second, Ruth would have gotten credit for a double.] Only after 1920 did "walk-off home runs," as they are now called ad absurdum, go down as actual home runs. ICI discovered 37 of these phantom shots from before 1920—belonging to such legends as Sam Thompson, Jimmy Collins, and one George Herman Ruth. "Computer Finds Ruth's 715th Homer," the *Times'* headline declared, sharing the era's wonder and distrust for the intimidating machines. ICI briefly gave Ruth credit for 715 home runs—but because of the resulting controversy, that number was changed before the book went to press. It has remained 714 ever since.

DL: *In generations past, before television and detailed statistical analysis were present, baseball had more of a mystique. The Negro Leagues are a good example of ignorance being bliss—at least from the standpoint of building myths. Are too many numbers detracting from the romance of the game?*

AS: Absolutely not. For every person who's turned off by the numbers, there's another who derives his or her romance for the game *from* the statistics, perhaps more. As for the mythological nature of the game, that dissipated a long time ago, principally due to television.

DL: *Statistical interest is high, yet keeping score at the ballpark [or at home with the radio] is seemingly a dying art. What is your explanation for this?*

AS: I'm not convinced it's a dying art. I haven't seen any polls or anything. If it has declined at all, it's probably because so much statistical information is now available on the scoreboards. But what's wrong with that? It doesn't keep you from scoring the game; it makes it easier to enjoy for those who don't want to. Complaining that the technology keeps people from scoring games like they used to is akin to lamenting the microwave because iron stoves are more quaint.

DL: *What role have baseball cards played in our fascination with statistics?*

AS: I think that kids, mostly boys, entered a little fantasy world when looking at the backs. All the numbers were a separate little universe. You could see a player's home run totals go up and down, his average ebb and flow. You could use them to argue which player was better than another. Remember, there was no true *Baseball Encyclopedia* until 1969. Most kids got their stats fix through newspapers and Topps baseball cards, which were, of course, very portable.

DL: *Your book notes that Jack Kerouac had a great interest in baseball statistics. What can you tell us about that?*

AS: Like many boys throughout the 20th century—particularly before the widespread popularity of dice games such as Strat-o-Matic or APBA—Kerouac invented his own game, complete with players, teams named after cars, and what-not. He wasn't alone. Hundreds of boys did the same thing. He just grew up to be famous.

DL: *You're a senior writer at* Baseball America. *What is BA's approach to statistics with the publication, and do you think it should be handled any differently?*

AS: We print [conventional] minor league statistics in every in-season issue, but what you probably mean is the magazine's approach to statistical analysis, particularly compared to traditional scouting. I would say that, of course, the magazine is rooted in traditional scouting—talking with talent evaluators and executives about the top minor leaguers, who has real talent and who doesn't. But, of course, we look at the statistics, too. And not just batting averages, but BB-SO ratios for hitters, H-IP ratios for pitchers, and things that have predictive value. [Just because Jose Martinez goes 20-3 in the Sally League doesn't make him a prospect; everyone knows that—you have to look at more, both in the statistical realm and the scouting realm.] Lots of new-age stat folks give *BA* a hard time because of its scouting bent, but it's far more even-keel than people want to realize. Jim Callis, for instance, is as knowledgeable about statistics as you could ask for. He just knows how to balance the two sides, which is, of course, the healthiest approach.

DL: *In your book, you opine that "Women are almost certainly the next untapped talent pool for baseball front offices." Can you elaborate on that?*

AS: Right now, off the top of my head, only about 5 of maybe 300 front-office personnel are women. Given that the game is moving away from its old requirement that executives played the sport in the Majors or even professionally—what you need is not strong thighs or a quick bat but intelligence and a strong work ethic—it stands to reason that this huge untapped pool of talent, women, will be incorporated, and fairly soon.

DL: *"Statman" Mike Gimbel was reviled during his days as a consultant to Dan Duquette. Why are most Red Sox fans embracing Bill James, and the team's current phiolosophy, considering that Gimbel was treated as little more than a bad joke?*

AS: Gimbel was an unknown weirdo for many reasons, including keeping all sorts of exotic animals in his house. Bill James is a legend and a [generally] respected baseball mind. That being said, I'm not sure how universally accepted he has been. Most Red Sox fans seem to be griping that the team doesn't bunt or steal enough and blame it on Bill—when he has very, very little to do with that kind of thing.

DL: *Along with Henry Chadwick and Bill James, who else is a first-ballot electee in a* Baseball Statistics *HOF?*

AS: F.C. Lane, who wrote dozens and dozens of fascinating sabermetric-type articles for *Baseball Magazine* from 1908 into the thirties. The guy was generations ahead of his time, trying to figure out linear weights formulas 30–40 years before Pete Palmer was even born. I have hundreds of pages of the guy's work, and it's just incredible.

DL: *What is the basic difference between the Elias and Bill James' publications?*

AS: As I say in the book, Elias gave people fish. Bill James taught people how to catch them.

CHAZ SCOGGINS

CHAZ SCOGGINS HAS BEEN THE PRIMARY OFFICIAL SCORER AT FENWAY PARK SINCE 1978. A LONG-TIME SPORTSWRITER FOR THE *LOWELL SUN*, SCOGGINS IS THE AUTHOR OF GAME OF *MY LIFE: BOSTON RED SOX*. THIS INTERVIEW TOOK PLACE IN DECEMBER 2004.

David Laurila: *You've been the team's official scorer since 1978. How did you get started?*

Chaz Scoggins: When the Baseball Writers Association of America was formed early in the 20th century, the organization offered to provide official scorers as a courtesy to Major League Baseball, and for the next three quarters of a century, members of the BBWAA did all the scoring. If you had an interest in official scoring and were a member of the BBWAA, after you had been in the organization for five years and were judged by your chapter to be qualified, you could become an official scorer. That's how I became one.

DL: *Tell us a little more of the history—both yours and the profession's.*

CS: At the time I started there were three other members who were scoring, so we divided up the 81 home games, getting about 20 each. Back then, scorers were paid $25 a game. Now the fee is $125, but when figuring in the cost of living since then, I think we're earning less than we were 30 years ago. Most fans [and even players] presume we're hired and paid by the clubs, which is why they expect close decisions to go their way. We're actually paid by the league. Shortly after I began scoring, there were some controversies over scoring decisions in no-hitters and near-no-hitters. The first one, I recall, was in San Francisco, and the scorer, Joe Sargis, who worked for the old wire service United Press International, was forbidden to score by UPI after that. UPI's argument was that their reporters were there not to make the news but to cover it. Not long after that, there was another controversy in Pittsburgh, and the newspapers there forbade their reporters to score for the same reason. That prompted a national reassessment of the scoring duties by newspapers. One after another, citing a conflict of interest over being paid by the sport they were there to objectively cover, the papers began ordering their reporters not to score anymore, and by the mid-1980s the BBWAA told MLB it could no longer provide scorers. Naturally, almost overnight, there was a critical shortage of qualified official scorers.

DL: *So what happened?*

CS: In some cities, retired writers continued to score, but in many cities there was no one. While scorers continued to be paid by the league, the onus was on the clubs to find them. Some were amateur umpires or college coaches, but a lot of scorers came from unusual backgrounds. A couple of times, my newspaper, the *Lowell Sun,* considered ordering me to give up scoring. The argument being used was pretty much the same at the other newspapers: If you tick off the players with a scoring decision and they won't talk to you because of it, then you can't do your job. Fortunately for me, the Red Sox in those days were a difficult club to deal with for all writers, and my argument was that sometimes the only time the players *would* talk to you was when they were ticked off. Anyway, I always managed to convince them that by scoring I was devoting my full attention to the game, rather than walking around the press box chatting with other writers or hanging around the snack bar, and that guaranteed I was paying attention to my job. Also, I pointed out that many of the newspapers that stopped their writers from scoring had given them raises to compensate for the lost income. The *Lowell Sun* decided that ethics weren't nearly as important as money. So the paper has continued to let me score, making me one of the few active members of the BBWAA still doing it.

DL: *With fewer sportswriters doing the job, who is?*

CS: In some cities these days, I think they just crawl out of the woodwork. Maybe they're termites. But if you want to see really bad scoring, take a trip through the minor leagues. I really think MLB needs to start training scorers the way they train umpires. But I doubt that will ever happen because of the expense.

DL: *Talk a little more about conflict-of-interest issues with being both an official scorer and covering the team for the* Sun. *Do they exist?*

CS: The editors think they do. I don't. While I've had my differences of opinions with players, there has never been one who refused to talk to me because he was mad at me about a scoring decision. If anything, the opposite might be true. A player might think that if he's nicer to me, he'll get a scoring break next time. [He won't.] I have always been able to separate the two duties and not let worrying about one affect the other. Whether or not they're nice or not so nice to me about a decision will never affect my next decision involving them. But I'll let you in on a little secret: If they want to think that way, it makes both my jobs easier, so I'm not going to tell them any different. Unless they read this, of course. Then the cat is out of the bag.

DL: *How many games do you score each season, and how many do you think you've done in your career?*

CS: I can tell you exactly how many I've done. I have scored 1,375 regular-season games, 8 ALDS games, 16 ALCS games, 13 World Series games, and 3 All-Star games. Since the BBWAA got out of the scoring business about 20 years ago and I became the chief OS at Fenway Park, I have never scored fewer than half the Red Sox home games and have scored as many as 65 in a season. Generally, the number is in the 50–55 range. We have a minor league team in Lowell, affiliated with the Red Sox, and I enjoy covering their games, too. [I do not score them. I believe the minors should be the training ground for future Major League scorers, and I don't want to deny scorers in Lowell the valuable experience they need.]

DL: *You mentioned that you work for the American League rather than for the Red Sox. Do official scorers have a boss they report to, and do they get performance reviews? And do they ever get reprimanded or fired?*

CS: Actually, since the offices of the two leagues combined a few years ago, I work for Major League Baseball now. My nominal boss is one of the VPs, Phyllis Mehrige. She handles the administrative chores, making sure we get paid and have scoring forms and get new rulebooks every year, but she doesn't look over our shoulders or evaluate us herself. There is no fixed system for reviewing the performance of official scorers. But if she starts hearing too many complaints about someone, she'll look into the matter. If the feedback is that the scorer is incompetent . . . well, I've never heard of a scorer being overtly fired. But there are ways to keep an incompetent one from being rehired. Sometimes even a competent one.

DL: *Any examples?*

CS: One of the scorers I trained in Lowell, an outstanding scorer in my opinion, with six years of minor league experience, finally got a chance to score a couple of Boston Red Sox games back in 2001. Wouldn't you know it: In his very first game as a Major League OS, Hideo Nomo, who had thrown a no-hitter earlier in the season, takes a no-hitter into the seventh inning. Then right fielder Darren Lewis breaks the wrong way on a fly ball, rushes back in, and has the ball hit off the end of his glove as he tries to make a diving catch. The OS correctly rules it a base hit because Lewis committed a mental error by breaking the wrong way, not a physical error. Naturally, because he's a rookie OS, the play is even more controversial than it should have been. Red Sox GM Dan Duquette even puts pressure on him to change it to an error, but to his credit he sticks to his guns. But after finishing his two-game assignment the next night, he never works at Fenway again. A couple of years later, after he had been fired, I learned that Duquette had ordered his PR department, which is technically in charge of assigning official scorers, to never let him score another game. For all intents and purposes, he was fired for making the right call.

DL: *Do official scorers ever get overruled?*

CS: Until a few years ago, officials scorers were rarely overruled, and then only in their interpretation of the rules. A fellow named Seymour Siwoff is MLB's scoring guru, and has been ever since I've been around, and he overruled me a couple of times, illegally in my opinion. For example, I once credited Lee Smith with a save after he entered the game with a 2-0 count on a batter and walked him, a walk that was charged to the previous pitcher under the rules. It hadn't been a save situation until that batter walked, but because the walk was charged to the previous pitcher, and there was nothing in the rulebook that addressed this situation, I ruled that Smith had not created his own save situation and was entitled to the save. Seymour overruled me, even though the rule in question states that "The scorer shall have the authority to rule on any point not specifically covered in these rules." I was not happy. There are some other quirky scoring rules that Seymour and I have disagreed on.

DL: *Is there a process for questioning rulings?*

CS: Now that almost every game is on TV and videotape of almost every play can be obtained for review, clubs and players can protest a scoring decision and ask for a review from MLB. A committee of four or five people will look at the videotape and either uphold the decision or recommend it be overturned. The OS, however, can refuse to go along with the recommendation. Until 2004, I had never had a play submitted to MLB for review. There are at least three that I know of from last season, one of which was recommended by a 4-0 vote that it be changed. I was adamant, however, believing I still had the play right, and refused to let it be overturned. MLB has to protect the integrity of its scorers, just as it has to protect the integrity of its umpires, and while the panel disagreed with me, MLB backed up my original decision. On the other plays, I assume MLB agreed that I got it right.

DL: *With hindsight being 20/20, how many times have you been wrong?*

CS: I can only remember one decision that I regret as being absolutely wrong. A couple of years ago, a runner should have been doubled off second base on a line drive, but the second baseman dropped the ball. He should have been charged with an error, but since there had been one out on the play, I applied the grounded-into-double-play rule, and let the error slide. It was wrong.

DL: *Do you have a reputation, either for your judgment [hits versus errors, etc] or approachability? If so, do you think it's accurate?*

CS: MLB asks that its scorers be willing to review plays when their decisions are challenged. As long as the request is made in a civilized manner, I'm always willing to do so. But if I receive uncivilized treatment, that person forfeits any future appeals with me unless I get an apology.

MLB wants scorers to report such incidents of incivility, and transgressors can be reprimanded or fined. But I have never reported such an incident to the league, preferring to handle it in my own fashion.

I think I have a reputation for being a fair scorer. Frequently, I have had players complain to me that they don't get favorable scoring decisions on the road, so they have to get them at home the way other home team players do. I tell them I can't be concerned with the scoring practices in other cities, that it's my job to be fair to both teams. Several times I've had visiting players express their surprise to me that I've approached them to talk about a play, that they've never had scorers in road cities solicit their input.

While I know a lot of Red Sox players would disagree, I think I'm perceived as a generous OS when it comes to giving players hits. But it's not generosity. In Rule X, the Rules of Official Scoring, the words "ordinary effort" appear nine times, and I'm big on interpreting ordinary effort. Nothing in Rule X says to hold Major Leaguers to a higher standard of fielding than minor leaguers or amateurs. So even though a Major League player might be capable of making a tough play nine times out of 10, I'm not going to stick him with an error the one time he doesn't make that play. Sure they can—and often do—make those plays look routine. That's why they're in the Major Leagues. But that doesn't mean they should be expected to make them every time. So the rule of thumb I use for determining hits and errors is this: When a play isn't made, I ask myself, "If he had made that play, would I have silently said to myself 'Nice play'"? If the answer is yes, then it would have taken more than ordinary effort to make it, and I'll rule it a hit.

DL: *How often do players complain about your decisions, and has that changed much over your 27 years on the job?*

CS: On average, I would guess my decisions are challenged about four times a year. I probably change half of them. Usually, the challenges come early in the season, and from new players who don't know where I've drawn my line in the sand. Once they learn, the complaints dwindle. I have found that when the Red Sox are contending, players pay less attention to their personal stats. Some of the worst years I had were when the Red Sox were losing, and players became more selfish. The 1992 and 1993 seasons were particularly difficult. The 2004 Red Sox were the exception to the rule. Almost every ruling I made was challenged, not just by players but by the manager and even the GM. That was baffling.

DL: *Can you elaborate on that a little?*

CS: Sure. Here was a team that was a contender all year long, even during a mystifying three months of mediocrity, yet some of the personnel were consumed by personal stats that are usually all but ignored when a team is in a pennant race. I think that might have been a reflection on the manager, Terry Francona, who seemed to be at the forefront of every question. If a player doesn't approach me directly, I assume I got the call right. When the manager contacts me instead of the player, I have to wonder if he's getting involved on his own, perhaps because he feels a happy player will play better for him. I don't know what Francona's reasoning was. I know when Butch Hobson was managing the Red Sox a decade ago, he wanted all the players who disputed a scoring decision to go through him first. I tried [unsuccessfully] to talk him out of it, explaining there was no reason for him to get involved. I preferred to deal with the players involved directly. That way, nothing could be lost in translation. Theo Epstein even lobbied for a change on at least one occasion. He's a young GM, though, and maybe he doesn't yet realize that getting involved in scoring decisions is not within his purview.

DL: *Over the years, which players have been the most notorious questioners of rulings?*

CS: Mike Torrez, Dwight Evans, Wade Boggs, and Nomar Garciaparra. But the only one I got a lot of grief from was Nomar.

DL: *Who are some of the others who have complained, and what are some of the stories?*

CS: Twice I had Roger Clemens ask me to change calls . . . and both times he wanted me to change errors to hits that wound up costing him earned runs late in seasons in which he was battling for the ERA championship. [He went on to win the ERA title both times, anyway.] Clemens is one of only two players I've ever had ask me to change rulings that damaged his own stats. "It was a tough play," he would tell me. "It should be a hit." I may have disagreed, but how can you argue with someone who knows he won't benefit from a scoring change? Johnny Damon asked me this year to change a double to an error after he dropped a ball that he ran a long way for, leaped to catch at The Wall, and couldn't handle.

DL: *I understand you have a good Jim Rice story.*

CS: A couple of years ago, when Jim Rice was the hitting coach for the Red Sox, he called me after a game and asked me to change a call that would give John Valentin a hit. I immediately told him I would. "Don't you want to know the reason I'm asking?" he asked. "No," I replied, "and I'll tell you why. I was the official scorer here during the last 11 years of your career, and not once in those 11 years did you ever ask me to change a call. There are always balls that are in gray areas, and many nights I came down here expecting that would be the night you'd ask me to change my call, and you never did." "That's right. I never did, did I?" he chuckled. "You never did," I said, "So you have a lot of credibility in the bank with me. So if you think that's a hit, it's a hit."

Later, it occurred to me that if Rice had asked me to change one or two calls a year during those 11 years, and I had done so, he would have hit .300 lifetime instead of .298. Those two points might have made the difference in whether or not he gets into the Hall of Fame.

DL: *How about players from visiting teams?*

CS: Somewhere around 1980, I think, Toronto's Dave Stieb and Baltimore's Mike Boddicker were dueling for the ERA title. Stieb was ahead when he made his final start of the year in Fenway. He pitched something like five scoreless innings, then gave up six of the ugliest runs you'd ever want to see in the sixth. The Red Sox did not hit a ball out of the infield, and they were all choppers and rollers with a walk or two thrown in. But there were no errors, and all the runs were earned. Stieb called the press box after the game, furious that none of the balls had been errors. I didn't change anything, and Boddicker wound up winning the ERA title.

DL: *Any others you can share?*

CS: A year or two ago, I called an error on Anaheim third baseman Troy Glaus, who called after the game to tell me the ball hit the lip of the grass and took an unnatural hop before it got to him. I reviewed the play on videotape, saw that he was right, and changed the call to a hit. Glaus was grateful . . . for 15 minutes. Then he called me back when he realized the hit had cost his pitcher two earned runs and asked me to change it back to an error. I had to laugh. He got me to change a bad call to the right one, and then wanted the bad one back. Couldn't do it, of course. He should have thought of the consequences before he asked me to review it.

DL: *What are the biggest controversies you've been involved with?*

CS: The most infamous was in 1992, Wade Boggs' last year with the Red Sox and his most miserable year as a hitter, when he batted only .259. Late in that season, Detroit's Tony Phillips, a switch-hitter batting left-handed against Clemens, slapped a ball toward third base that was mishandled by Boggs and ruled an error. After the game, Boggs asked me to change it to a hit. I thought the request was rather strange. The Red Sox were in last place, and he was having a brutal year. But Clemens was going for the ERA title, and changing it to a hit would make two unearned runs earned. But it wasn't my duty to tell him that; he, like the aforementioned Glaus, should have known and just eaten the error. I asked him why I should change it, and he said he couldn't pick up the ball initially because he lost it in the white shirts of the Saturday afternoon crowd. I had not seen the play all that clearly myself, the TV replay had been useless, and now Boggs had given me a compelling reason to change the call. So I did, even though I suspected it would ignite a firestorm. For the next two days, that's all anyone talked about. Clemens was furious, though not with me. He knew I was just doing my job. And I already knew, as explained previously, that whether the runs were earned or unearned was irrelevant to Clemens. He was only upset by Boggs' selfishness, and the rest of the team sided with him. ESPN had a good time ridiculing me for the next few days. They had some stock footage of me in the press box, and every time on SportsCenter that there was a play that was remotely controversial, they'd show that clip and ask "Is it a hit, or is it an error?"

And for some reason, almost 20 years later, the wild pitch charged to Bob Stanley in Game 6 of the 1986 World Series remains controversial. A lot of people believe Rich Gedman should have been charged with a passed ball. I still get grief about that, although I can't understand why it's a big deal. The ball got by the catcher, and a run scored. Why does it really matter if it was a wild pitch or a passed ball? All I can say is that I was one of three official scorers working that World Series, and it was unanimous among all three of us that it was a wild pitch. There wasn't even any discussion among us before we made the ruling.

DL: *I've heard that a player once threw a beer at you. Tell us about that.*

CS: Jerry Remy hit a ground ball with the infield back and a runner on third, and the first baseman threw the ball home anyway, instead of taking the obvious out at first. He threw the ball away, and I charged an error. Remy thought he should have gotten a hit because the first baseman couldn't have gotten him anyway, which may have been true, but I ruled a good throw would have gotten the runner, who wasn't running hard, at the plate. He threw a can of beer past me that hit the clubhouse wall. [I really don't think he was trying to hit me.] He apologized the next day, and we've always gotten along since then. He likes to joke that my scoring decisions kept him from getting 3,000 hits and into the Hall of Fame. Darned if I can figure out how I cost him 1,774 hits, though.

DL: *Who has most surprised you by questioning a call, and why?*

CS: Clemens, of course, as outlined above. But a couple other incidents come immediately to mind. Two nights after the Boggs–Clemens incident, Danny Darwin was pitching for the Red Sox, called the press box after the first inning, and asked to speak with me. I told the PR person that I did not talk to players while a game was in progress and that I'd see him afterward, although I couldn't figure out why. A ground ball had sneaked through the infield that I had called a hit, but no runs had scored. After the game, I went to see Darwin, and he stunned me by giving me grief about the Boggs error/hit that had cost Clemens two earned runs on Saturday. He was furious and grabbed the sleeve of my shirt [the only time I've ever had a player get physical with me]. I listened to his diatribe and, because of the ambush, determined that he had forfeited all future right to discuss scoring decisions with me. Butch Hobson, the manager, found out about it and said he would have Darwin apologize to me. But Darwin never did.

DL: *These are great. Any more?*

CS: Another one was more humorous. Between games of a day–night doubleheader with the Royals, Mike Greenwell called me down and asked me to change an error [not his] that would give Kevin Seitzer of the Royals a hit. I asked why, and he said that Seitzer was a good friend of his and that he, Seitzer, thought it should be a hit. I told Greenwell I would talk with the principals involved. I did and wound up changing it to a hit. The kicker was the Red Sox were playing in K.C. a few days later, a city where the scoring was notoriously bad, and Greenwell hit a ball that should have been a hit and was egregiously ruled an error. After the Red Sox returned home from the trip, I asked Greenwell if he had asked Seitzer to intercede with the scorer on his behalf the way Greenwell had interceded with me. "Yeah, I asked him. The so-and-so wouldn't do it!" Greenwell griped. I think that was the end of a beautiful friendship.

DL: *Again, any others?*

CS: Another incident I recall was Red Sox reliever Tom Burgmeier, who had impeccable control, asking me why I had charged him with an earned run when a batter he had intentionally walked had scored. "The rule book says to treat an intentional walk as an unintentional one for scoring purposes," I explained. "That's ridiculous," he said. "You know I wouldn't have walked that guy if I hadn't been ordered to." I shrugged. "I know that, and you know that. But that's the way the rulebook says to score it." "That rule is stupid," he complained.

DL: *Switching from players to the plays, what are some of the oddest ones you've seen from a scorer's perspective?*

CS: Fortunately for me, by the time players reach the Majors they have been pretty well schooled to avoid making bonehead plays. I have seen plenty of unfathomable plays in the minors, however, that I wouldn't begin to know how to rule on them. Official scoring is a thankless task at that level. The aforementioned Remy play was one of the few dumb plays I've seen in the Majors. Probably the most confusing play I had to rule on was one I had seen in highlights [or lowlights] from other ballparks but never happened in Fenway until 2003. That's when Trot Nixon forgot how many outs there were and tossed the ball into the stands after making a catch while two Anaheim players ran around the bases. I initially ruled it a two-run sacrifice fly, because, to me, it was obviously more of a mental than a physical error. But before the end of the game, Seymour had overruled me and said it should be an error. And I guess he was right, since the umpires treated it as an overthrow. But there was nothing in the rulebook that dealt specifically with what is becoming a common event.

This one wasn't especially odd, but it illustrates how scorers and players can sometimes be handcuffed by the rules. A few years ago in a game against Oakland, the Athletics' left fielder scooped up a single and tried to throw out a Red Sox runner at the plate. The throw was perfect, but the ball and the runner arrived at the plate at the same time, and the runner took catcher Brent Mayne out of the play while the ball went to the backstop. Because another runner went from second to third while the ball was being retrieved, and the rules require that I account for every base, I had to charge an error and gave it to Mayne. The next day I was told that Mayne wanted to see me. "How can you give me an error on that play?" he complained. "I had no chance to catch the ball." "I absolutely agree," I told him. "But I have to give an error to somebody, and it's gotta be either you or the left fielder. Was the throw good?" "Yes, it was perfect," Mayne said. "Well, then, neither you nor the left fielder deserve the error, but one of you has to get it. That's the rule. If you want to talk it over between the two of you and decide that the left fielder should get the error, I'll change it. But the reason I gave it to you is that while neither of you is really to blame, I feel it's the catcher's primary job to catch the ball first, even if it means stepping away from the plate." Mayne said he would eat the error, however unfair. And he thanked me for coming down to talk about it with him.

There has been some discussion for several years about giving team errors to deal with situations that involve giving unfair errors to players [such as balls hitting seams on artificial turf and taking a crazy bounce, or pop flies falling between fielders]. I don't think it's a good idea. I think official scorers would use it as a crutch and a copout to avoid giving tough errors to individuals. Yes, some errors in baseball are unfair. But the very nature of the game is unfair.

DL: *Joe Castiglione likes to talk about a play in Detroit where two runners came into home plate, one right after the other. Rich Gedman tags out the first on a close play, and an instant later the second barrels into him, sending everyone, including the home plate umpire, flying. Mistaking a ball that fell from the home plate umpire's pouch as the game ball, the first base umpire calls the second runner safe [he should have been ruled out]. My question is: assuming that an error isn't charged on the play, would you credit the batter with an RBI?*

CS: Although I wasn't at that game, I saw the play on TV and remember it reasonably well. Kirk Gibson, one of the fastest men in the game, was the second runner and was running right up the shirttail of the runner in front of him. [I think he may even have hit the ball and was trying for an inside-the-park homer.] Indeed, Gedman got the ball in time to tag both runners and should have been credited with one of the most unusual double plays in baseball history had the umpire not been upended and become confused by the loose ball from his bag. Nowadays, as we saw in Game 6 of the ALCS, the umpires probably would have huddled and overturned the plate ump. But umpires were reluctant to challenge each other in those days. As for scoring such a play, this one isn't covered specifically in the rules. I would credit the batter with an RBI.

DL: *What can you tell a fan about official scoring that he [or she] probably doesn't know?*

CS: The Official Baseball Rules are divided into 10 major rules that cover a total of 97 pages in the rulebook. The first 9 rules govern how the game is played, and how umpires should call plays is covered in 72 pages, or an average of eight pages per rule. Rule X, the rules of official scoring, need 25 pages to be explained. More than one-quarter of the pages in the rulebook are devoted to official scoring. The scoring rules can be highly complicated.

DL: *What are some of the oddest things you've seen in your job—not on the field, but in the press box?*

CS: How about two writers getting in a fistfight in the press box after a game in Cincinnati during the 1975 World Series? I also saw *Record-American* columnist Larry Claflin throw a notebook belonging to a writer from the *Boston Phoenix* out of the press box onto the screen in the middle of a game because he didn't like a question the reporter had asked. One time, a foul ball came screaming back into the old press box and struck the computer a shocked Peter Gammons was typing furiously on. The word "error" flashed on his computer screen. Usually, the media is well-behaved, but there have been a lot of funny lines thrown around that none of us would dare put in the paper. You might know that cheering in the press box is strictly forbidden, although ripping ballplayers is not. The only time I ever saw the cheering rule universally ignored was after Fisk won Game 6 of the 1975 World Series with that 12th-inning homer. Almost every writer in the press box got to his feet and gave both teams a standing ovation because it was—and to many of us still is—the most dramatic ball game we had ever seen.

DL: *What are the most memorable moments and events in your career as an official scorer?*

CS: One I've never had is scoring a no-hitter. I thought for sure I had scored a perfect game a couple of years back when Mike Mussina was pitching for the Yankees and was one strike away. Carl Everett ruined it with a pinch single. That's the only time I've even scored a potential no-hitter into the ninth inning. Roger Clemens' first 20-strikeout game in 1986 is the most memorable game I've scored. I've never been much for collecting memorabilia, but I kept the lineup cards from that game [one of only four sets that could possibly be in existence], had Clemens autograph them, and have them framed and hanging on a wall in my house. Pop Quiz: Who was the Seattle second baseman that night? [Answer later.] I also scored the 1,000th game of Cal Ripken's playing streak and planned to have him autograph those lineup cards. But I asked him first if he wanted them for a keepsake, and he did, so I gave them to him. [Scorers don't even get copies of the official lineup cards anymore.] Scoring three All-Star games and getting rings for them has also been a thrill, particularly the 1999 game in Boston. I also scored the 1982 All-Star game in Montreal [the words on the ring are in French] and the 2000 All-Star game in Atlanta.

Pop Quiz Answer: Danny Tartabull.

DL: *Last one: Along with being a sportswriter and official scorer, what are some of the other things you've done in your career?*

CS: I'm proud that I got to serve as national president of the Baseball Writers Association of America in 2000 and to speak at the Hall of Fame inductions in Cooperstown that summer. I've written a book on the history of minor league baseball in Lowell [*Bricks and Bats*] and am currently working on another book about the Red Sox that is scheduled to be published in the spring of 2006. I've also done play-by-play and analysis on radio for Lowell Spinners games and learned I might have been able to make a career out of that had I started at a younger age. [My partner and I were semifinalists from a field of 160 applicants for the Pawtucket radio job a couple of years ago, and one of the broadcasters who got that job is already in the Majors, doing radio for the Giants.] I enjoy doing radio more than I do writing these days. But I hope to keep official-scoring long after I've retired from the media because it's also something I enjoy, I'm proud to do, and even though a lot of people don't agree, I know I'm good at it.

JOE SHEEHAN

JOE SHEEHAN IS A CO-FOUNDER AND WRITER FOR *BASEBALL PROSPECTUS*. A NATIVE OF NEW YORK, SHEEHAN WRITES A REGULAR COLUMN FOR *BASEBALL PROSPECTUS* AND IS A CO-AUTHOR OF *MIND GAME: HOW THE BOSTON RED SOX GOT SMART, WON A WORLD SERIES, AND CREATED A NEW BLUEPRINT FOR WINNING*. THIS INTERVIEW TOOK PLACE IN SEPTEMBER 2005.

David Laurila: *What is the history behind* Baseball Prospectus, *and what is its mission statement?*

Joe Sheehan: Back in 1995, we started as a group of guys who wanted to write the book we wanted to read. Clay Davenport had been publishing his translations on Usenet for years, and Gary Huckabay had his Vladimir projections system. They invited Rany Jazayerli, Chris Kahrl, and myself in to help write the first book that fall. It was an arduous process, and we sold 170 copies out of my bedroom. The miracle of the first book is that we got to do a second.

The Web site launched in the summer of 1996, back when the Web was still mostly unknown. We've benefited along the way from great relationships with *ESPN.com*, by impressing people within the game—which brought us credibility—and mostly, from having an unbelievable amount of talent write under the banner. People like Keith Woolner and the late Doug Pappas would come in and bring their enormous talents to *BP*, and that just made us better.

We don't talk in terms of mission statements, but I guess I'd say that our mission is to provide high-quality baseball content across all mediums.

DL: *What is the history behind Joe Sheehan, and what is his mission statement?*

JS: I'm 34, grew up in New York City a 10-minute cab ride from Yankee Stadium. I went to the University of Southern California, got a bachelor's in journalism, and ended up settling in L.A. I'm awfully lucky; I'm not one of the 50 most talented analysts out there, but I guess I can write a little. I love baseball, and with a lot of breaks along the way, I get to leverage those things into a fun job.

DL: *What is PECOTA, and what kind of career has it had so far?*

JS: PECOTA is Nate Silver's projection system, and he can tell you a lot more about it than I could. It utilizes a lot of information that other systems don't, such as a player's height and weight, as well as a lot of Nate's research into various career paths and the way in which skills interact in player development.

We've used it for three years now, and I think it's a strong system, with the caveat that almost all systems are operating within a fairly small range of accuracy. It seems adept at finding changes in player performance, which was a strength of Gary's Vladimir system.

DL: *What does the future portend for Kevin Youkilis?*

JS: A trade, one would hope. Youkilis isn't going to be a star, as he won't have the gaudy power or RBI totals that attract attention. He will be an underrated player, a .290/.390/.450 guy with average defense at third; the kind of hitter who pushes a team towards a championship. I do not think the power he showed at Pawtucket this year will translate to the Majors. Think Kevin Seitzer with a better glove, maybe, or Bill Mueller with both his knees.

DL: *How would you compare and project David Ortiz and Manny Ramirez?*

JS: They've become similar hitters now, although Ramirez was at 23 what it took Ortiz another four years to become. Ortiz is four years younger and has a little better handle of the strike zone at the moment. Ramirez is exiting the back end of his peak, and while still a great hitter, isn't the same one who was an MVP candidate from 1999 to 2002. Neither player has any defensive value or speed.

On a year-to-year basis, I'd rather have Ortiz, who should sustain his peak and be a better hitter than Ramirez in 2005 and 2006, at least. His body type makes me think he could have a rapid decline, along the lines of what Mo Vaughn and Kent Hrbek experienced. Ramirez could shift into Edgar Martinez mode, especially if he were to become a DH in a few years, where he just hits .300/.400/.500 until he can't physically run the bases any longer. I wouldn't be surprised to see him retire after Ortiz, even given the age difference. Loosely speaking, David Ortiz is a good hitter who's had an MVP peak. Ramirez is a Hall of Famer, maybe an inner-circle one.

DL: *How do you project Dustin Pedroia, and is Marcus Giles a better comparison for him than David Eckstein?*

JS: With just a season and change as a professional under his belt, Pedroia presents a challenge to any projection system. [One of the areas in which smart people like Clay Davenport are working is in looking at the value of using college stats in projection systems, but we're not there yet.] PECOTA loved him after '04, but that was off of 200 or so professional plate appearances.

A year later, Pedroia has shown that he's someone you can be optimistic about, having done very well in a tough environment at Portland. He's a different player than Eckstein, and while that's a convenient comparison—college middle infielders of small size drafted by the Red Sox—I think Pedroia has more going for him. He's got power Eckstein didn't, and that looks like it'll carry forward to the pros. He's also advancing much more rapidly through the system.

I think the bump in the road Pedroia hit at Pawtucket is likely the best thing that could have happened to him. Having him start 2006 at Triple A, rather than rushing him to the Majors, will give him an opportunity to do something he hasn't had to do yet: make adjustments.

DL: *Mark Bellhorn was a big disappointment for the Red Sox this year, and Tony Graffanino has been a godsend since replacing him at second base. How surprised should we be at either's performance, and can Graffanino be expected to play at the same level next year, keeping Pedroia in Triple A?*

JS: Bellhorn has had stretches like this in his career, and as a high-variance player, is prone to a stretch like what cost him the job. Even had he not been injured, I think he was in trouble. Graffanino is a good utility infielder hitting a little bit over his head as a Red Sox player. I wouldn't want to go into a season with him as my regular 2B; a platoon with Cora might not be the worst idea in the world if the idea is to give Pedroia two months in Triple A and then have him up by the middle of June.

DL: *What happens if Hanley Ramirez is the Red Sox center fielder next year instead of Johnny Damon?*

JS: I don't think that's a good situation for the Red Sox. Ramirez isn't ready to hit at the Major League level, isn't all that close, and he's certainly not ready to play a difficult center field, like the one at Fenway, on a regular basis.

The other factor—and this applies to Pedroia, as well—is that present-day Boston is probably not the best place to break in young players. There are sky-high expectations that don't mesh well with the patience required for effective player development. If the Sox are going to commit to a young player in a key role, they would be well-served to wait until that player is more than ready to contribute to a winning team. This isn't the Royals; the Nation, the media, and the front office fully expect to win, and that's not the easiest way to let a rookie come in and go .265/.310/.365, which is about what I'd expect Ramirez to hit with Fenway as his home park in 2006.

DL: *Last year, Ichiro Suzuki had 262 hits and scored 101 runs. In 1996, Rickey Henderson had 112 hits and scored 110 runs. Are either of these records, and which is more of a departure from the norm?*

JS: I don't even know how you'd measure what you're looking for. Ratio of hits to runs? The difference between the two? Barry Bonds has had some recent seasons along the lines of what Rickey did [93/91 in 1999; 135/129 last year], and I'm sure there are others.

I cheated and asked Keith Woolner. Ichiro set the record for difference between hits and runs, but a lot of other guys have had higher ratios. Henderson's 1996 is edged out by Max Bishop's 1930 when he had more runs scored than hits.

Of course, what you've really done is illustrated the inadequacy of those two numbers. Ichiro batted a million times and never walked, while Rickey Henderson drew a ton of walks. You always want as much information as possible when making evaluations or just messing with trivia.

DL: *Statistically, how does swinging at the first pitch impact OBP, and why are "So-and-so hits .330 on the first pitch," statements often misleading?*

JS: Well, you can't strike out on the first pitch, which is the main difference. Foul balls or misses aren't factored in, only outcomes that end the plate appearance. Performance when an outcome is reached on the first pitch isn't far from performance on all plate appearances if you knock out walks and strikeouts, or more to the point, performance in even counts when you do the same. There's no study showing that performance on the first pitch is a skill separate from performance as a hitter, period.

DL: *Pitchers with high ground ball ratios give up fewer home runs than fly ball pitchers, for obvious reasons. Is there also a difference in base hits allowed, and if so, why?*

JS: Well, it's complicated, and . . . hey, look over there, isn't that Theo? Theo!

Didn't work, huh? OK . . . ground ball pitchers give up a higher BABIP, in general, than do fly ball pitchers. From a performance standpoint, this is cancelled out by the higher slugging allowed on balls in play by the latter.

Voros McCracken's work on defense-independent pitching statistics continues to be one of the most-debated topics in performance analysis.

DL: *Is the value of players allowing themselves to be hit by pitches—think Ron Hunt or Don Baylor—worth much, or is it statistically insignificant?*

JS: Only at the extremes, guys like the ones you mention, or Jason Kendall or Craig Biggio. HBPs are walks, performance-wise, so yeah, if you have some kind of skill that adds 20 walks and 35 points of OBP a year, that means something. It is not really something to worry about in evaluating, except that minor leaguers who get hit a lot may become injury-prone Major Leaguers. See Johnson, Nick.

DL: *Teams leading after 8 innings won 95 percent of the time last year. What does that tell us about the importance of closers, and, more specifically, the closer-by-committee theory?*

JS: Closers, as a class, are terrifically overrated. Virtually all relievers effective enough to be used in high-leverage situations before the ninth are capable of becoming closers, and the difference between closers and other relievers is pretty much entirely usage patterns. We've invented this entire construct around the last three outs of the game that simply didn't exist before the 1980s, and we've managed to convince the people who play the game there's a difference.

You tell me what's more difficult: Papi, Manny, and Trot Nixon in the eighth, or Jason Varitek, Kevin Millar, and Bill Mueller in the ninth?

There's probably some value in regular roles, but even that smacks of over-thinking. For all the talk about how starting pitchers are babied these days, I think the game has done a much worse job in turning relief pitchers into these hothouse flowers. The good ones should pitch more innings and higher-leverage innings.

DL: *How important are strikeout rates for closers, and do you see any similarities in the Keith Foulke/Billy Koch and Danny Kolb/Jose Capellan trades?*

JS: Well, I don't think "closer" should be a position. If we use the term "high-leverage reliever," I think it's a bit more important than for a starter because you expect a guy throwing 30 pitches an outing to have more ability to miss bats than a guy throwing 100–110. Beyond that, a high strikeout rate should reduce variance, as it keeps balls out of play. That last is speculation.

The only similarity I see in the two deals is that the GM acquiring the guy who'd just saved a lot of games—Kenny Williams and John Schuerholz, respectively—overrated a statistic that reflects opportunity more than ability, and inferred from that statistic not only ability, but certain character traits. Looking for character in a stat line is a terrible idea, but we see it all the time when it comes to saves and runs batted in.

DL: *In an interview last year, we asked Bill James about the impact of having a running threat on first base, and how much added value there is to getting a hitter more fastballs while disrupting the pitcher's rhythm. James answered: "The impact of having a running threat at first base, on many teams, is negative, not positive." What's your opinion?*

JS: I'm not sure what Bill might be saying today—he's reversed field on any number of things he wrote in the 1980s—but it has been proven that the performance of a hitter at the plate during a stolen-base attempt is less than what it is otherwise. That makes sense without thinking about the numbers; when there's a stolen-base attempt, we know that there's no outcome on the first pitch [and therefore at least some chance of a strikeout], and often the hitter falls behind [to provide an opportunity to steal] or makes a weak swing to "protect" the runner. Whatever benefit there may be from a "distracted" pitcher does not show up in the performance lines.

Thinking back to my limited playing days, I always preferred to have a slow runner on base ahead of me. Virtually all runners get held, anyway, and as a left-handed batter, I liked having the hole on the right side. I think having the defense adjusted to the runner on first, but not having him steal, is optimal.

DL: *Ted Williams hit 521 home runs in his career; Mel Ott 511. What are the numbers if Williams plays in the Polo Grounds and Ott in Fenway Park?*

JS: 655 and 427. Really, I don't know. This is one of the areas where I think we make things a little too simple, where just grafting home-run rates onto new parks may not catch enough of the nuances. Williams would likely be helped more than Ott would be hurt, but to what extent is impossible to say.

DL: *Last one: In your opinion, who are the most underappreciated players today, and in MLB history?*

JS: Today, I'd look to maybe Jim Edmonds, who no one thinks of as a Hall of Famer but who already has more career value than a bunch of Hall of Fame center fielders. Jeff Kent, whose defense at its peak was much better than people gave him credit for, is another player with a similar profile.

Historically...[Early] Wynn certainly, and as long as Ron Santo and Bert Blyleven aren't in the Hall of Fame, I'll consider them "underappreciated." John McGraw is so much better known as a manager that I don't think people realize how good a player he was.

GLENN STOUT

GLENN STOUT IS THE CO-AUTHOR, WITH DICK JOHNSON, OF *RED SOX CENTURY: THE DEFINITIVE HISTORY OF BASEBALL'S MOST STORIED FRANCHISE.* THIS INTERVIEW TOOK PLACE IN MARCH 2004.

David Laurila: *Since* Red Sox Century *was first published in 2000, much has happened with the Olde Towne team. Can you explain why a revised edition is coming out now—did anything serve as a catalyst, or has a 2004 update been in the works for some time?*

Glenn Stout: When Richard Johnson and I first conceived of *Red Sox Century,* our intention was to create a book that could and would be updated periodically as events merited—we want this book to remain as the standard history for as long as possible. In regard to this franchise in particular, that meant one of three things had to happen to stimulate an update—a world championship, a new ballpark, or new ownership. Obviously, that forces me to keep close track of what's going on all the time, just in case. The decision to update was made by our publisher quite early during last season, before any of us knew [except, perhaps, in emotional DNA] what would happen. Then, as the season wound down, I had to keep waiting to see how the story ended. When it ended the way it did, that determined the last half of the new chapter. I think Game 7 rendered what had been a remarkable regular season rather insignificant in the larger scheme of things, just as the playoff failure in 1999 similarly wiped out the 1999 regular season.

DL: *In the new edition, you question whether last October's Game 7 loss might have been the worst in team history. Grady Little was subsequently quoted as saying there were players on the team who feared "being Bill Buckner" [which was ironic, because he had himself become Buckner in the eyes of many]. Whether you believe in curses or not, has any team ever had more to overcome? Or ghosts to exorcise?*

GS: I really think fans of most teams, in most sports, can probably recite their own unique litany of failure and pain—Red Sox fans aren't that special. What is unique is that since 1986 that precise emotional vibe has been exploited and marketed to make money. And too many Sox fans [and way, way too many casual fans here and elsewhere, and an absolutely obscene number of know-nothing broadcasters] have gobbled it up because it goes down quick and easy and seems to explain everything. It's instant Red Sox history, antiseptic, without having to deal with the real nasty stuff, like racism and incompetence.

DL: *So any perceived "curse" is both fairly recent and media-driven?*

GS: You can look it up, as I have, but before 1986, when George Vecsey of the *New York Times* first wrote about it, the entire notion that the Red Sox were "cursed" did not exist—you'll find no mention of it after '67, '75, or '78—none, zero, zilch. In last year's HBO documentary, for example, Denis Leary was talking about how much he hated the name "Nanette," as a child. Well, he was making up a memory, because when Denis was a kid absolutely no one was yammering about the [false] Ruth/Nanette thing. If I'm proud of anything, it is that *Red Sox Century* gave reasons for why the Red Sox have won and why they have lost without feeding such false notions or exploiting the fans. That and the way the book caused everyone, finally, to take a close look at the Yawkey era.

But at this point, it's too late, almost—a kind of historic expectation of loss has permeated both the fans and the organization, a willing desire to believe in the worst just so you can feel part of something larger. Even new ownership is affected. When they bought the club, they were essentially ignorant of club history, apart from the "curse" nonsense. And any psychologist will tell you that negative thoughts can lead to negative consequences, so in a sense it has become a self-fulfilling prophecy—it flows back and forth between fans and media, and by osmosis even reaches the players, who are usually so narcissistic they aren't affected by anything.

But that is why it is so hard for this team to win and why I think Game 7 was so disastrous. If you look at the history of this team, excruciating losses have always affected the organization for years—the ripples take forever to dissipate. I think firing Grady Little, putting Manny on waivers, and trying to trade Nomar proves this is already happening.

DL: *You also make note of the team painting the 2003 World Series logo on the field at Fenway Park before the deciding game versus the Yankees. The following day, the Boston Herald's Jeff Horrigan wrote that the logo "lay beneath a blue tarp like a corpse covered with a sheet." Countless Red Sox fans know that there is no such thing as a done deal with this team—ever. Can anyone explain how this was allowed to happen?*

GS: It's called arrogance and hubris, with a touch of the sense of entitlement that comes from being ungodly wealthy. And I think that's the most dangerous thing in the entire new group, a top-to-bottom tendency to pat itself on the back before it is time to do so. The first rule you ever learn in sports is win first, then celebrate. If you do it backwards, well, you deserve what you get. It reminded me of when Dusty Baker took Russ Ortiz out of Game 6 in the Series two years ago and gave him the ball to keep as a souvenir. You could see the bad karma.

DL: *There was reportedly some disagreement between the team's leadership—John Henry, Tom Werner, and Larry Lucchino—in the weeks following that loss, centering on Grady Little. There had been similar discord in the days when Jean Yawkey, Haywood Sullivan, and Buddy LeRoux shared power. Those times were often fraught with turbulence—is current ownership positioned to fare any better than that earlier troika?*

GS: Troikas do worry me, for the exact reason cited, and I really can't think of any successful ownership by committee. I don't think these guys are positioned any better—two-to-one votes always piss someone off. In the end, one person always takes control. I think in many ways, John Henry already has. Werner and Lucchino are redundant. Epstein has become the public face. Francona is impotent compared to the usual manager's role. Henry wields the real power, and he is beginning to use it. He wanted to fire Little before midseason but was talked out of it. From here on, he won't be very patient.

And this is a side comment, but one I find curious industry-wide. As much as MLB and ownership always bitch about player salaries, in the one area where ownership has total control over what they pay—in the front office—the salaries have escalated right along with player salaries. Larry Lucchino reportedly makes in the mid-seven figures annually, and many GMs are above the million mark. Why? I just don't get it. Wouldn't that money have been better spent on some players? I mean, for what the Red Sox pay Lucchino they could have closed the A-Rod deal. Who would you rather have?

DL: *The team suffered through some difficult seasons during the John Harrington/Dan Duquette era, both on and off the field. What do you see as the predominant reasons behind those disappointing years?*

GS: That question is sort of too large to address here [I do so in Chapter 20 of *Red Sox Century*], but in a nutshell I think Harrington was a toady for interests other than winning, namely serving Bud Selig and acting as if the Sox were a small-market team to keep in Bud's good graces because he appeared to like feeling important and having influence. He also held fast to this grotesque, moldy notion of the "Yawkey tradition," as something worth preserving. He certainly did that well enough.

Then, while the team was raking in dough and Fenway was falling apart, Harrington chose not to spend it until he made the decision to sell. Then, he tried to buy a going-away present, going into debt and leaving the club in the awkward contractual situation it is in now. Duquette was hired with the directive to win cheap and build from below, but when they unexpectedly snuck into the playoffs his first season, I think it put him in a spot where he couldn't start from scratch, so they got into a cycle of patching holes to remain "competitive" rather than building. Duquette was also unfairly made the franchise's public face, which he clearly wasn't equipped for. In the long run, I think Harrington abused the franchise and the fans. People were ripped off. The Sox pulled a bait-and-switch.

DL: *Despite all that went wrong with Duquette at the helm, there were also positives. Among them were huge strides made in integrating the team, long a sorry part of Red Sox history. Does he deserve most of the credit for that, or were others just as responsible?*

GS: Well, I think he deserves a great deal of credit for it, although there were certainly others in the past, such as Dick O'Connell, who did their part, but under Duquette's watch the most onerous aspects of that repugnant tradition were put to rest—hopefully for good [but racism, like alcoholism, requires constant vigilance]. That's not a small accomplishment. You know, I grew up in the Midwest and didn't come to Boston until 1981. Coming from elsewhere, the racism in Boston was palpable and unmistakable from the first day. I mean, I eventually worked for the city and had bosses try to stop me from hiring minorities, then tell me with a straight face they weren't racists. And I sat in the bleachers about 30 times a year in the early to mid-eighties and was absolutely stunned by what I would hear people yell at Jim Rice, and no one, [myself included, I'm ashamed to say] would ever tell them to knock it off. Later, when I started writing for *Boston Magazine* and other places, many of my first stories were about African-American athletes from Boston's past—Sam Langford, Will Jackman, Lou Montgomery, Louise Stokes. Why? Because in this town they had been totally overlooked [and I'm sure most readers of this will have no clue who they are, even now]. As Howard Bryant points out in his book *Shut Out,* the local press played a role in ignoring race as an ongoing story in regard to this franchise.

DL: *It has been written that the team had an opportunity to sign both Jackie Robinson and Willie Mays, but declined due to their skin color. Is it fair to label Tom Yawkey a racist, or would it be more accurate to say that he was simply adhering to the social norms of his times?*

GS: I think it is interesting that the entire question of racism and the Red Sox is so often distilled down to the question of whether or not Yawkey was a bigot. It is as if people think the answer to that question also answers the entire question of racism and the Red Sox. That kind of thinking searches for some kind of "smoking gun," a statement or a piece of paper in which Yawkey said something overtly racist. The logic goes, "Well, if he did, then the problem is his, and his alone, not the ballclub's." And if there is not, "Well, that provides absolution to both Yawkey and the Red Sox because they were just a product of the times." I reject that. The question of Yawkey's personal racism isn't irrelevant—after all, the buck always stops at the top—but it is not all-encompassing, either.

DL: *So, does a smoking gun exist?*

GS: Of course, there is no smoking gun as described above—most bigots are too cowardly to leave behind evidence like that. My father was a "product of the times" in regard to his attitudes, but he didn't leave behind any kind of "smoking gun" evidence like that either, and on an individual basis he was fine with African Americans, as was Yawkey. But one must also remember that Yawkey was a willing participant in all the back-room meetings MLB owners had after World War II to try to block Branch Rickey—they didn't take minutes of those meetings, either, and there's a reason for that.

But I think there is a smoking gun, one much more powerful and definitive, and always was. All anyone ever had to do was look on the field while every other team in baseball integrated, even ball clubs like the Phillies and Cardinals who had been aggressively racist, but there were no African Americans wearing a Red Sox uniform. That was the evidence, the smoking gun, the irrefutable statement, and it was there for years, for every one of 154 or 162 games a year, and hardly anyone ever, ever mentioned of it. It was the elephant in the corner of the room that no one talked about. It is not just the individual instances of racism in the history of this franchise that is troubling—the fact the Sox didn't sign Robinson, or waited until 1959 to bring up Pumpsie Green, or didn't make a trade for a black player from 1947 to 1960 [Willie Tasby]. It is the enduring pattern, the fact that the Red Sox continued to have problems for five decades—even after Yawkey's death—from the Elks' Club all the way up to Thomas Sneed. The Yawkey tradition, from the top down, created an institutional culture that not only allowed racism to remain in place, but didn't easily admit its existence when it was uncovered and frankly didn't consider the issue very important. It was not surprising to us at all that when *Red Sox Century* was published, the ballclub—John Harrington, specifically—went on the attack about that issue. Personally, Tom Yawkey was rarely confronted about this during his lifetime. Because of his wealth, he had the whole town cowed. Even the most basic facts of his biography were never reported until our book [as an aside, I find it interesting that John Henry has been here two years now and like Yawkey, has faced no scrutiny at all].

DL: *It sounds like you're saying Yawkey liked to keep the whole thing swept under the rug and out of sight.*

GS: Clearly, the entire issue just wasn't very important to Yawkey, except to dodge the question and dodge his personal culpability. The racial story of the Red Sox was a hard, hard part of the book to write, because we knew if we weren't careful, readers would reject conclusions before we made our case—how do you tell people their favorite team has a rotten spot that shouldn't be ignored any longer? Well, we did it by laying out the facts, the evidence. That's why we avoided making the question of Yawkey's personal bigotry the central question—it was the wrong question to ask. If anything, at the time I think we may have been too soft and cautious on the issue. That's why I was happy Howard Bryant's book, *Shut Out,* was being done, to carry the story further. History is cumulative, and I think *RSC* moved the discussion forward in a very substantive and useful way.

DL: *What about the societal aspect?*

GS: Was Yawkey adhering to norms of his time? Of course, he was— but he was adhering to the norms of bigots and racists, who were in the majority. Listen, there were plenty of men and women of courage and conviction during Yawkey's reign, and much farther back, who didn't "adhere to social norms," but followed moral truth. Yawkey simply didn't have that kind of courage. But I don't think you can give anyone a total pass because "those were the times." Tom Yawkey was rich enough that he didn't have to adhere to any social norm if he didn't want to or if he didn't believe it. As a result, Red Sox fans got screwed— totally screwed—by this policy. No one should ever yammer about 1918 without thinking that, if not for racism, that season probably wouldn't even matter. And for the record, another question that is often asked in follow-up, the argument Will McDonough always tried to make, was "What about the Yankees and race?" Well, I address the Yankees and racism in *Yankees Century* and they don't get a pass on the subject either, but that's another story. That the Yankees were racist, too, doesn't justify what the Red Sox did, or make it better.

DL: *Is there anything you want to add regarding Robinson or Mays?*

GS: In the waning days of the 1967 season, Jackie Robinson was asked which American League team he wanted to win the pennant. Even though Dick Williams had been his teammate, he said anybody but the Red Sox, because "Tom Yawkey is one of the most bigoted men in baseball." Robinson didn't throw charges like that around lightly.

And Tom Yawkey is in the Hall of Fame. For what? He didn't win and he was behind the curve on every issue baseball faced during the time he owned the team. Well, once I asked someone who worked at the Hall that very question. And they said it was because he contributed a lot of money, and that's a fact. For him to be the first man inducted solely for being a team owner is repugnant.

DL: *The sale of the team was by no means a simple undertaking, with innuendoes of back-room dealings running rampant. Among the perceptions was that there were groups Harrington did not want to sell to, and money wasn't the only issue. What are your views on this?*

GS: Money is never the only issue in the sale of a Major League Baseball franchise. It is a private club that gets to choose who to let in. John Henry had paid his dues, buying a small piece of the Yankees to give the other MLB owners and officials time to get to know him and feel comfortable, then buying the Marlins, then helping to facilitate the bailout of Jeffrey Loria in Montreal. He was the guy MLB wanted, and Harrington always did what MLB wanted. Personally, I find it interesting that John Hancock's Dave D'Allesandro reportedly bought a small piece of the Red Sox recently, which makes me wonder if he's beginning the same process, you know, getting to know the other MLB owners so he can buy a team one day—he's a big Yankee fan and Steinbrenner isn't getting younger.

DL: *Since the current ownership came on board, much work has been done to create a more "fan-friendly" atmosphere. These improvements have been greeted with open arms by a fan base long deserving of such treatment. Why did previous administrations do so little in this regard?*

GS: Because under Harrington, they didn't care about making fans feel comfortable or appreciated, because they could make money anyway, and they wanted the building to deteriorate past the point of renovation so they could squeeze money from the state and city for a new park. Back in 1987, I wrote a story for the Red Sox yearbook that mentioned that when Fenway was built the foundation was designed to support a second deck, and that when Yawkey renovated the park that foundation was reinforced—the Red Sox were not happy that information was included. I've always thought they added the 600 Club solely to prevent the addition of a second deck, because they wanted the park to become obsolete and adding the 600 Club made it impossible to add a complete second deck. Remember, too, that before 1986 there wasn't the constant attendance pressure that today makes Fenway's worst aspects stand out in terms of comfort. The best years I spent in Fenway were 1982 to 1985, years where the crowds were small and for $3 you could get a bleacher seat, put your feet on the bench in front of you, lean back on the bench behind you and watch the game like sitting in a recliner. Perfect. I was broke but for about 10 bucks, I could see a game and drink beer about 30 times a year.

DL: *Whether or not the team stays in Fenway Park or builds a new home is a huge question for ownership. You comment in the updated edition of* Red Sox Century *that the current regime has distanced itself from the Yawkey era, and Fenway is in many ways representative of the past. Although there seem to be indications that they want to stay in Fenway, do you see it as being a feasible long-term commitment?*

GS: When I decided to move about a year after I got out of college, I was torn between going to Chicago because of Wrigley Field or Boston because of Fenway—but I was determined to come to a city with an old ballpark. I had more friends in Boston, so that's where I went. But personally, at this point I think Fenway may make it harder for the team to win. I'm not sure that it's a coincidence that the two teams in the two oldest dead-ball-era ballparks have both been shut out from championships since the lively ball. Fenway, in particular, is very demanding—huge in right, small in left, and far too tempting to tailor a team to the ballpark, one with right-handed power and left-handed hitters who can go the other way, both of which don't translate as well on the road. I think staying in Fenway is feasible financially—people will pay any price now that Fenway has morphed into a tourist destination like a museum, despite the fact that it is horribly uncomfortable and hard to take little kids or the elderly to—but it may not be feasible in terms of the larger goal, which presumably is to win.

DL: *Over the last 50 years, which Red Sox team do you feel was the most talented?*

GS: I think it's the 1986 team. Although the 1975 Sox had a better line-up and batting order, they didn't have the pitching of the '86 team. It seems that every time the Sox have a really talented team, so does someone else. And when there really is no dominant team, the Sox haven't been able to take advantage. For some reason, this team always stops a player or two short. Last years' club reminded me a lot of the Sox of '46 or '48, a club that was the equal of any for the first 19 or 20 spots on the roster, built to win over the long haul or a regular season, but one that didn't have the full roster needed to win the close games in the postseason, when everyone has to contribute. I mean, Little was afraid to use guys like Sauerbeck and Suppan at the bottom of the roster. The Yankees played with 25 men, the Sox played with 20. The Yankees' final at-bat went to Aaron Boone, and they still had a stud on the mound. The Sox last at-bat went to Doug Mirabelli, and they were forced to use a starter, Wakefield, at the end of the game. It never should have come down to that.

DL: *If you owned the team, whose numbers would be added to those retired on the façade in right field?*

GS: In some way, and this is before they wore numbers, I think you need to recognize the most successful manager in the history of the franchise, Bill Carrigan, the club's first manager/GM and greatest third baseman, Jimmie Collins, and pitcher Cy Young. Then, you put up Jimmie Foxx's number, and Tony C's because of the tragedy and his local ties, and then Johnny Pesky for the lifetime achievement of being a human being. I'm against arbitrary rules that determine who can and who can't get his number retired, particularly since they rigged it for Fisk. It's more of a feel thing. Rice probably makes it someday, as do Tiant and Evans. And like it or not, eventually Boggs and Clemens have to be there or their absence will become an even bigger story. But I would paint over the Morse code on the scoreboard.

DL: *The team has been covered by an outstanding array of journalists. That said, these knights of the keyboard have not always been on the best of terms with the men they cover. How do the Dave Egans of yesterday compare with the writers covering the team today?*

GS: In this instance, the times do make a difference, because their roles have changed so much that it is really impossible to compare eras. And because of my role as series editor of the *Best American Sports Writing* series, it really isn't appropriate for me to get too specific about the guys writing today. But I will say that as far as I'm concerned, the golden era of Boston baseball writing was from the turn of the century to about 1920—there were eight or nine daily papers in town, plus *Baseball Magazine,* which was published here. Boston had the best baseball writing and reporting in the country then— Tim Murnane, Walter Barnes, Shannon, a guy named Frederic O'Connell who died young, and others—even Ring Lardner was here for a while. But in the 1920s, the New York writers were the best of the group—Broun, Runyon, Kieran, etc., then later Red Smith, Dick Young, and others. The best writing was in New York from the 1920s into the 1970s. During that same time period, sports writing in Boston was very parochial. Guys like Harold Kaese were ahead of their time—he kept incredible stats—but most of the columnists, like Bill Cunningham and Austen Lake, weren't stylish writers. They were entertaining if you lived here, but almost impenetrable from the outside, obsessed with their own role. I think some of that self-obsession still exists. In general, Boston spends far too much time looking inward, reporting on itself, with the media looking at the mirror and making itself the story. In the 1970s, with Gammons and Montville, plus Collins and others, the *Globe* obviously made great strides and became relevant again, as did the *Herald* behind people like Tim Horgan and Charlie Pierce, who, like George Kimball, came from the alternative press. Thank God it's still a two-paper town, particularly now that the *Times* owns part of the Sox. Many Boston writers of that era became national figures not so much because of their ability, but simply because there were former Boston people in places of authority at *Sports Illustrated* and ESPN—they had the connections, and to some degree that's still true today. But I think it is also significant that there's room enough for other Boston-centric writers not completely dependent on the newspapers—and still enough left unwritten to write about, and obviously a sizable enough market, to keep guys like myself, Charlie Pierce, Bill Littlefield, Bill Simmons, and some others busy.

DL: *Although Egan was well-known for his feuds with Ted Williams, you wrote in* Impossible Dreams *of how he also had a side many aren't aware of—a more compassionate one that was sympathetic to Ted and championed the integration of the game. Can you tell us a little about that?*

GS: Egan, like Harry Frazee, is always vilified by people who simply don't know the facts and don't care to check. In Egan's case, it's primarily because of Ted Williams' ghostwritten and error-filled *My Turn at Bat*, which throws a lot of blame Egan's way for "mistreating" Ted. Well, I've actually read Egan and spoken to people who knew him, and that portrait is incomplete. Like all the other writers of the time, Egan was usually positive, but with six or seven newspapers being published at the time someone was always blasting Ted. Egan was probably the best pure writer in the sports pages of his era, so his words got remembered. He made many of his contemporaries jealous, but sadly, he was also something of a troubled guy, an alcoholic. But he steered the ship, and the other writers wrote in his wake. Ted, really, was one of the guys the local media most protected, but he couldn't stand a single word of criticism. If they had written all that they could have, they could have destroyed Ted—he wasn't a particularly nice or good guy all the time— today, he'd never survive it. Egan's criticisms stuck because they were the most pointed.

But Egan was also fearless, with an extraordinary moral sense for the time. He didn't care what people thought of him. In 1945, he started taking baseball on in regard to integration and pointing the finger at Tom Yawkey—no one else in Boston did. The NAACP even honored him for his efforts in this area. I'm convinced that's one reason why Egan's reputation suffered the way it did later. He pissed off powerful people, so after he died they trashed him.

DL: *Last question: Can we expect to see another edition of* Red Sox Century *next year if we win the Series in 2004? And after that chapter has been added, will it ever be necessary to write more?*

GS: If it happens, you will—but I don't think it will happen. There are, by my count, seven books already in the works about either the Sox/Yankees rivalry or this season. That's the kiss of death, like painting the logo on the field. But there's always more to write. Always.

ERIC M. VAN

ERIC M. VAN IS A SABERMETRICIAN WHOSE WORK HAS APPEARED ON USENET [1999–2002] AND ON THE SONS OF SAM HORN WEB SITE [2003–PRESENT]. A NATIVE OF NATICK, MASSACHUSETTS, AND A GRADUATE OF HARVARD UNIVERSITY, VAN WAS HIRED AS A STATISTICAL CONSULTANT BY THE RED SOX IN 2005. THIS INTERVIEW TOOK PLACE IN FEBRUARY 2006.

David Laurila: *How do you—a renowned number-cruncher—view the relationship between traditional scouting and statistical analysis?*

Eric M. Van: I strongly endorse the consensus that they are complementary. As Theo Epstein has often put it, they are two different lenses to view players through. But I'll go further and say that the best statistical analysis includes information that is not numeric and hence borrows some attitudes from scouting. Furthermore, my latest thinking is that statistics and scouting can actually be *synergistic.*

There are two different questions that we ask about a ballplayer. First, how good has he been, on the field? How valuable has his actual performance been? Once you've answered that, what we really want to know, nearly all of the time, is *how good he'll be in the future.* The relationship of statistics to scouting is very different, depending on which question you're asking.

When assessing how good an MLB player has been on the field—not the whys and hows of the goodness, but a simple assessment of value—I think the best approach is something like 97 percent statistical analysis and 3 percent scouting. [That's strictly my opinion. With the Red Sox, my involvement in player assessment is currently limited to tossing them any numbers I discover and find interesting. I provide some data, but I'm not involved at all in the final assessment.] At this point, we've got numbers for just about everything.

DL: *How do you project future performance?*

EMV: It's a two-part process. First, we need to *understand* the past performance in order to project the future. And that's where the relationship between statistics and scouting gets very interesting. Second, you want to know if there's any reason to expect the player in the future to be fundamentally different from the player in the past—different from the guy we understand—and that's largely a task for scouting.

When we seek to understand past performance, we are starting with a set of data that is our best assessment of it, month by month, year by year. There's almost always some variation in that data that requires explanation, if we want to understand the player's career to date. And depending on the nature of that data, I see four separate ways that statistics and scouting can mix in order to reach an understanding of the variation. There are sets of data that are relatively easy to make sense of, where you don't need scouting. There are other times when the numbers make perfect sense, if and only if you go beyond them and consider information that isn't numeric, which is to say the stat-head needs to cross the border and think like a scout. There are sets of numbers that are even tougher, where the statistics are suggestive but not conclusive, and generate questions that scouts can investigate. And finally, there are sets of numbers that are basically inexplicable, where all the understanding has to come from the scouting side.

DL: *Can you give us a few examples?*

EMV: Sure. Let's start with the "relatively easy" case. There's a pitcher, who shall remain nameless, whose ERA the last three seasons has varied by 2.00 runs. I'm sure there were scouting reports filed this winter that went into great detail to explain why he's been so up and down. But has he really been that inconsistent? One of the things we analysts do is build master spreadsheets that attempt to remove every confounding factor we can think of in order to generate a set of numbers that represents true performance. According to my spreadsheet's 73rd column [when I said "relatively easy," I didn't say relative to what], this pitcher's "true ERA" has varied not by 2.00 runs, but by *0.07* over the last three seasons. So that's an example of understanding the numbers via pure statistics. There's no need to ask a scout how and why he's pitched differently, because he actually hasn't.

Next, you sometimes do need to go beyond the numbers and consider other sorts of information. Looking beyond the numbers is anathema for a subset of analysts I've dubbed the Statistically Correct, but I think it's a crucial analytical method. The perfect example is Johnny Damon's career with the Red Sox. His first half-season here [2002], he hit exactly as he did in K.C. [1999–2000], and he returned to exactly that level in the second half of his second year. [I'm leaving out his rough year in Oakland in 2001 from this short version, but it's amenable to the same sort of logic]. For the two half-seasons in between, the end of '02 and the start of '03, he was pretty awful. Now, if you were reading the papers, you gathered that the awful stretch started around the time his marriage broke up. Most folks in the saber community were projecting Damon's 2004 to be like his 2001, 2002, and 2003—that is, they thought these three seasons had established a new, lesser performance level. But why would his true skill level suddenly *decline* at age 27? And why had each of his two seasons in Boston divided so neatly between his old skill level and a dramatically worse one? What were the odds of that happening by sheer chance? I thought the most parsimonious explanation of the numbers was that his K.C. and early-2002, late-2003 performance represented his true level, that the divorce had caused the intervening awfulness, and that his 2004 numbers should look like his K.C. numbers. And they did.

Next, there are many cases where the numbers form a suggestive pattern, but the analyst doesn't have enough information to solve the puzzle. Sometimes, there are patterns in the numbers that do point to a specific hypothesis. There's a guy whose ERA has varied by 2.80 the last three seasons who still has a 1.80 variation in my "relatively easy" spreadsheet. A closer look at his numbers shows that he has run out of gas after 75 pitches in his bad years, but not in his good ones, and that he has consistently pitched best in April and gone steadily downhill the rest of the season, with the decline being worse in his bad years. It's easy to hypothesize that he's been out of shape in his bad years and in better shape in his good ones. But you would absolutely need a scout to verify that. Other times, all you have is a pattern in the numbers that seems meaningful, but no ready explanation. If Damon's marital problems had not been public knowledge, I would have been left arguing that something seemed to have happened to him in mid-2003 that ruined his performance for a year. It's not hard to generate a list of possible problems, but only a scout could find the answer.

And finally, there are cases where the numbers just won't speak no matter how hard you prod them. I can't find anything in the numbers to suggest why Mike Lowell collapsed last year. Now, it's not unhelpful to run analyses on past collapse years and find out how much value a player usually recovers. But that knowledge pales in its usefulness, compared to a scout's insight about what caused the collapse.

So that's a [not very] short outline of the way scouting can complement sabermetrics when we try to understand past performance in order to predict the future. There are times when the analyst can use readily available scouting-style information to make sense of the numbers, à la Damon. There are times when the analyst can figure out what things a scout might want to look at. And there are times when all the analyst can say is, we need a scout to make sense of this.

DL: *What did you mean when you said that statistics and scouting can be not just complementary, but synergistic?*

EMV: By synergistic, I mean that the two approaches can be *played off each other,* so that the sum is greater than the parts.

There are places where the numbers appear to contradict the seemingly evident observational truths of the game, places where sabermetrics and scouting appear to be in conflict rather than in concert. Perhaps the best-known example is a pitcher's batting average on balls in play [BABIP or BPA for Ball in Play Average, which fits better atop a spreadsheet column!]. The year-to-year correlation for this stat for pitchers who don't change teams and have a minimum 650 BFP is about .175. That's very low: K/BFP is about .780, BB/BFP about .715, and HR per contact about .410. But though it's low, it's still immensely significant: we have 811 pairs of pitcher seasons from 1985 to 2004, and the odds against getting the correlation by chance are 567,439 to 1 [$p = .0000018$, if you know that lingo]. Nor does it follow that the range in a pitcher's true BPA must be small. The average BPA is .290, and it commonly ranges from .250 to .330; the weak year-to-year correlation does not mean that the true range is .285 to .295 with the rest of the observed variation being noise. In fact, the strength of a year-to-year correlation tells you nothing at all about the true range of the data [more on that later]. But what the weak correlation does tell you is that the stat does not have much predictive value. Even given the same home ballpark and most of the same defenders, a pitcher who is particularly good at getting easy outs one year [like Bronson Arroyo in 2005] or particularly bad at it [like Curt Schilling, same year] is likely to have a much less extreme performance the year after. If you wanted to make the best set of BPA predictions for a group of pitchers, you'd take 17 percent to 22 percent of each guy's BPA and add it to some constant [.220 to .240]. This is known in statistics as "regression to the mean." You virtually always see it when you try to make the best set of predictions for a group, but this is a particularly extreme example. If we were projecting strikeout rates, for instance, you'd take 80 percent of a pitcher's K rate in the first year and add a small constant in order to predict his K rate the year after.

Now, this sabermetric insight—that getting easy outs is not a phenomenon that can be relied on to happen from year to year, and that getting hit hard is not generally a persistent problem—pretty much goes against the grain of observational baseball wisdom. We see [or think we see] that good pitchers get easy outs and bad pitchers get hit hard. The standard sabermetric take on this is that the observation must be wrong. But why not trust that both points of view are correct? And then ask: What further things would need to be true in order to reconcile this apparent conflict? Those further things may turn out to be new and potentially valuable insights into the game of baseball. That's what I mean by synergy.

DL: *Have you actually done that with BPA? Reconciled the conflict?*

EMV: I think so, at least in some small but important part. If you look at BPA relative to team over the course of a career, you immediately notice that BPA skyrockets when guys are hurting. Curt Schilling last year, Carl Pavano in '01 and '02, and there are many, many more examples. There was actually some interesting discussion of Curt's BPA last year; some folks were saying, you know, he's actually pitching quite well, he's just having awful luck on balls in play [since luck indeed plays a huge role in BPA variations]; and others were pointing out that if you had actually watched the games, you noticed they were hitting line drives off him left and right. So it wasn't luck. I think that when guys are off their game physically, it's BPA that takes the first and hardest hit, rather than K and BB rates. And that's a big reason why the stat correlates worse from year to year than the other pitching rates, because in any given year a certain number of guys are nursing injuries, and, whomp!, there goes your correlation, shot to hell. And I think you can make good sense of the relationship of health to BPA from a scouting point of view. It has something to do, I think, with the frequency of mistake pitches, of loss of control within the strike zone. I can't articulate it completely, but it makes sense to me intuitively. I think I could spend an hour with Curt discussing his '05 season and come to a very good understanding of why a pitcher's physical problems manifest themselves much more in his BPA than in his K and BB rates.

DL: *Bill James once said something like: "Lack of evidence of an effect is not evidence of a lack of an effect." What was he talking about?*

EMV: The fact that a signal of *any size* can be obscured by sufficient noise. If all you can see or hear is noise, it doesn't follow that there must be no signal! I hear a huge cacophony of noise, jackhammers in the street outside and airplanes passing overhead; I can't conclude that my neighbor is not practicing the violin.

When Voros McCracken first published his finding that there was no correlation of pitchers' BPA from year to year, he went on to assert that therefore there were no differences in pitchers' actual BPA levels. But that conclusion doesn't follow from the finding. The lack of correlation just tells you that the noise is vastly larger than the signal; it tells you nothing about the size of the signal.

I recently made this point on SoSH, via the following thought experiment: imagine that the true range of BPA is from .250 to .350. Now, construct two defensive teams, one composed of Little League fielders and the other composed of the ghosts of the greatest defensive players in MLB history. Play two seasons with the pitchers randomly reassigned between teams. How large a BPA correlation do you expect to see? Almost none, because the variation in defense swamps the variation in pitching.

[As it turned out, even Voros' initial premise was incorrect. I believe I was the first person to find a significant year-to-year BPA correlation [in posts to *rec.sport.baseball* in December of 2000 and January of 2001], and some other work which I posted to the newsgroup covers some territory which, I think, hasn't been explored since. Perhaps the most interesting work concerned the large impact that managers have on the stat. This is not, by the way, meant to denigrate Voros' work—the discovery that BPA correlated so weakly has proven to be one of the great sabermetric breakthroughs of all time. And I think it's not unusual for someone making such a radical discovery to end up overstating his case.]

DL: *Production-wise, players have ebbs and flows within individual seasons, and often from season to season. What do you feel tells you more about the player's talent level: his peaks, his valleys, or the entire landscape?*

EMV: A peak sustained for a sufficient length of time may often represent an upside that the player is capable of sustaining in the future, especially if it happens more than once, especially if the down periods are dramatically different, and most especially if you have an explanation for the difference. The classic example is Big Papi. Back in Minnesota, he was pretty much already the Big Papi we know and love [minus the postseason heroics]—whenever he was healthy. Which was just not very often. He had numerous brutal slumps, but with one exception they were all clearly caused by injuries. [Ironically, the only inexplicable slump of his career came just before we signed him: the last five weeks and postseason of 2002, but of course that could have been caused by an injury that never made the papers.]

At the very least, if you have a guy who blows hot and cold dramatically, you can hope that better coaching can lengthen the hot streaks and shorten the cold ones. The study of streakiness is in its infancy [no one, in fact, has really proven it exists, but I'm not a skeptic].

A second principle to keep in mind is that what's happened most recently may be particularly important. Ironically, the perfect example is another big 1B that we picked up after he had finished a season badly and was waived or released—Tony Clark. I loved that signing and opined that he might be a "monster" in a Sox uni. [Well, it did turn out to be terrifying!] I was chagrined to go back a year later and notice, for the first time, his collapse the previous August and September with the Tigers. The guy had a .406 OBP and .537 SA at the end of July, then missed four games with a bad back and had a .280 OBP and .327 SA the last two months before shutting it down a week early with a wrist injury. Now, if we all knew that he'd been hampered by injuries at the end of the year, why didn't we foresee his collapse the next year?

There were two factors at play, I think. First, very few people realized just how awful his August and September numbers were. He had finished with an 855 OPS, and most people could not tell you how badly a guy needs to hit in two injury-shortened months to drag an OPS down from 943 to 855. But more importantly, his career OPS coming into the season was 857. Among the Statistically Correct, it is an absolute article of faith that if a guy puts up the same numbers that he always does, he had the same season, regardless of what splits you can find that say otherwise. The alternative hypothesis, that for four months he was legitimately a somewhat better hitter than previously, and then for two months was truly a different and awful hitter, and that the combined results just happened to match his career averages—well, the Statistically Correct regard that sort of thinking as downright silly. Once I noticed the splits, though, I ran my favorite toy, the chi-square, which tells you the odds of getting any particular streak or slump in an essentially random simulation like Diamond Mind. And it confirmed what anyone's baseball sense should be telling them, looking at splits that dramatic [if you knew what they were]: there was no way that slump was random. You just don't go from a 943 OPS to a 607 because you've stopped getting the breaks. Something was different, and it should have been a huge red flag.

One more example, because it's my favorite. Bill Mueller was hitting .295/.403/.448 in May of 2001 when he busted up his knee playing for the Cubs. He had a second surgery the next winter, missed all of spring training and five weeks of the season, then hit a so-so .262/.350/.393, well below his career numbers [especially after park adjustments]. Now, I'd been campaigning online for the Sox to pick up Mueller virtually from the day John Valentin wrecked *his* knee in 2000, so I dove into those numbers to see if there was a potential explanation for the mediocrity. It wasn't hard to find. He had hit .214/.267/.310 his first seven weeks back—after missing spring training, remember—and then hit *.294/.401/.448* the rest of the way. Déjà vu all over again. That's an overall .370 OBP, and chi-square tells us that the odds against a .370 guy randomly posting a .267 OBP in a specified seven-week stretch and a .402 OBP otherwise are 505 to 1. So I confidently concluded that the injury had wrecked an otherwise terrific season, and when the Sox signed him soon afterwards I predicted great things for him [it's the subject of my very first post on SoSH], especially since he seemed to be born to hit in Fenway.

DL: *Is there a best way to evaluate trades and free agent signings?*

EMV: Well, to start with, you can't evaluate player transactions only in terms of the results. When judging a trade [or the overall performance of a front office], you look first and foremost at how good things looked at the time, according to the best possible analysis. Then you make a separate assessment of how good the results were, relative to what could have been expected. The first assessment will tell you the soundness of the sabermetric thinking that went into the move. The second assessment will tell you how good the scouting was, and/or how lucky the team was. There's a lot of luck involved, so it's difficult for an outsider to judge the quality of the scouting in an individual trade. But I think that over enough time, the wisdom of the scouts accumulates, so you can look at a front office and know how well they've scouted.

Here we are again, back where we started. You need sabermetricians, and especially sabermetricians who understand that the players are human beings who need to be professionally watched! And you need scouts, and especially scouts who respect the numbers and are eager to evaluate the players with respect to that starting point. Any front office that has both is going to do very, very well.

CHUCK WASELESKI
"THE MANIACAL ONE"

CHUCK WASELESKI IS A STATISTICIAN AND LONG-TIME CONTRIBU-
TOR TO THE *BOSTON GLOBE'S* SUNDAY BASEBALL COLUMN. A
RESIDENT OF MILLERS FALLS, MASSACHUSETTS, WASELESKI IS
PROBABLY BETTER KNOWN AS "THE MANIACAL ONE." THIS INTER-
VIEW TOOK PLACE IN OCTOBER 2005.

David Laurila: *When, and how, did you become "The Maniacal One"?*

Chuck Waseleski: Bill James, in his 1982 *Baseball Abstract,* mentioned
that there was a lot of information that he would like to have that was
not available from box scores. Even simple data like batting average
with runners in scoring position wasn't generally available. Well, I had
always kept score sheets when I watched a game, and I watched a lot of
games. I also had one of those newfangled VCRs, so, if the information
had some value, I knew I could assemble a complete set of score sheets
for the upcoming season. I wrote to Bill, and after the 1982 season, he
had a couple of questions for me. It's hard to imagine now, but how
many stolen bases occurred when Dennis Eckersley was pitching was a
generally unavailable number back then.

When Bill included my data in the 1983 *Abstract,* he got my name
wrong. So, in 1984, when he used a lot more information, he apologized
profusely and printed my name all in capitals about 20 times. A friend
who graduated from my alma mater a few years before I did saw the
Abstract and called to ask if that was me. I didn't know that he was
going to share the material with Peter Gammons and Al Nipper, who
was always very interested in analyzing his own performance. I provid-
ed a lot of material to Peter for the rest of the time he was at the *Globe,*
and ever since then I've had my own little obscure corner on Sundays.

Maniacality officially evaded me, though, until 1990, when Dan
Shaughnessy named me in a profile he did for the *Globe.*

DL: *Have you done any work with James, beyond what you just mentioned?*

CW: After the first couple of years when Bill used my material, I did the
"pitching boxes" for his *Abstract* for the next three or four years. They

were pretty simple, just home/road breakdowns and run support, but even run support was not something that was available back then.

When Bill was looking to hire his first assistant, we talked about it, but it just wouldn't have been a workable situation. Bill went on to hire some very talented individuals, and I stayed in my little Boston niche.

DL: *Have the Red Sox ever approached you about working for them, and have you ever contributed your findings to players or their agents?*

CW: I've never done any work directly for the Red Sox, but if there's ever anything that I've compiled that they would find useful, of course, it would be my pleasure to provide it.

I've done quite a bit with agents in preparation for salary arbitration and some other contract negotiations. Steve Lyons was the first who told me that the material could be useful at contract time.

In 1985, I made my first Red Sox–related road trip to Oakland and Seattle. In Oakland, I ran into Marty Barrett, who I knew was arbitration-eligible after the season. Oddly enough, it was Marty who approached me. The second time we were on the same hotel shuttle bus, curiosity got the best of him. He had seen me at the hotel talking with some of his teammates, and the newspaper and radio guys. He just had to know, so he asked, "Are you with the team or something?" I introduced myself and told him that I was hoping we'd meet. His response was, "You mean you know who I am?" My response: "Sure, you're Jim Rice, aren't you?" I'll treasure that look on his face forever.

Marty was interested in some specific numbers, which I told him I'd be happy to run for him. That December, he called me to ask if I minded if he turned some of the material over to his agent. As it turned out, his agent was looking for me, too, since he also represented Wade Boggs, and he had seen my work in the *Abstract*. He had nine cases he was working on that winter, three of which went to hearings, and we won all three, including, fortunately, Marty's and Wade's.

After that season, that same agent talked to a local reporter who gave me the best and funniest compliment I'll ever get. He told the reporter, "He thinks Al Nipper is the greatest pitcher who ever lived, and I'm afraid he could prove it."

DL: *Boggs put up some fascinating numbers when he was with the Red Sox. Looking at the more esoteric ones, what are among the more notable?*

CW: Here are some of my favorite Wade numbers:

- In 1985, Wade hit .390 after the count went to 0-2.
- In 1986, he became the seventh batter in Major League history to win the batting title and lead the league in walks [Ruth, Hornsby, Arky Vaughan, Ted Williams (4 times), Ashburn, and Yastrzemski (2 times)] had accomplished the feat before Wade.
- In Wade's first 1,000 at bats, he had 352 hits, the fourth highest total at the time, bested only by Joe Jackson [389], Chuck Klein [360], and Paul Waner [358].
- Over the 1985 and 1986 seasons, Wade popped out to an infielder a total of 7 times.
- In 1986, Boggs faced 3,059 pitches. He swung 990 times and missed 46 times.

DL: *What are some of your favorites for players not named Wade Boggs?*

CW: The Wade numbers will probably always be my favorites. In some ways, it was Wade's performance that made me necessary. He was doing so many extraordinary things that weren't part of the official statistics. It's a shame that, at the time, I could count them, but there was no way of getting comparable numbers for other players.

Among the current numbers, though, there's one that's pretty astounding. I'd guess most Red Sox fans wouldn't know that the last season where the Red Sox hit more home runs at Fenway than on the road was 1996. In 2005, the Red Sox hit 107 home runs on the road and 92 at Fenway Park. In 2004, they hit 111 on the road and 111 at Fenway Park. And in every year from 1997 to 2003, they hit more home runs on the road.

DL: *A common refrain of Red Sox fans is, "I can't believe so-and-so swung at the first pitch again!" Edgar Renteria is among the players who have received criticism for doing that. What did Renteria hit on first pitches this year?*

CW: Edgar Renteria hit .359 on the first pitch this season, but that's not unusual. The first pitch is definitely a hitter's pitch. Over the last 10 years, the Red Sox as a team have hit .340 on the first pitch. Opponents have also hit .340.

DL: *What did the team hit when they put first pitches in play this year, and who were some of best performers in this category?*

CW: Boston's batting average on the first pitch in 2005 was .378. The top performers on the first pitch were Tony Graffanino [.588], Jason Varitek [.444], David Ortiz [.443], and Johnny Damon [.432].

DL: *What was the ERA of Red Sox starting pitchers in games we won this year, and what was it when we lost?*

CW: Red Sox starting pitchers combined for a 2.94 ERA in games the Red Sox won, 7.36 in losses.

DL: *As a team, how many runs have we allowed in each of the past few years, and how many were unearned?*

CW: The Red Sox allowed 805 runs in 2005, 11th in the league. They allowed 768 in 2004, which was good enough for fourth. In 2003, they allowed more than this year, 809, but that was good enough for eighth. In 2002, they allowed only 665, third in the league.

The Red Sox allowed 37 more runs in 2005 than in 2004, but 41 fewer unearned runs.

DL: *Tim Wakefield has been invaluable with, among other things, his ability to eat innings. How deep into games did he go this year compared to other pitchers in the league, and how much run support did he receive?*

CW: Tim Wakefield averaged 6.83 innings per start, which was eighth in the American League among pitchers with 10 or more starts. Bronson Arroyo averaged 6.29 innings, Curt Schilling 6.27, and David Wells 6.13.

Wakefield ranked 42nd in the American League in run support [4.79 runs per start]. Schilling and Wells were first and second in the league, respectively, and Matt Clement was seventh, so there was quite a difference. Some of that difference is probably attributable to Doug Mirabelli replacing Jason Varitek in the lineup, but Trot Nixon only hit .239 in Wakefield's games, and Edgar Renteria only hit .218.

DL: *Mirabelli catches most of Wakefield's games. How much do the results differ when Varitek is behind the plate when Wakefield pitches?*

CW: This year, there was a huge difference depending on who was catching. Wakefield was 16-8, 3.66 with Doug Mirabelli catching; 0-4, 8.86 with Jason Varitek. In his career, he is 50-32, 3.95 with Mirabelli and 27-25, 4.59 with Varitek.

DL: *Some baseball statistics are more important than others. Which do you place the most value in?*

CW: The obvious answer, of course, is runs scored and runs allowed, since, after all, those are the only stats that matter in the long run. But I really don't think one specific performance statistic is clearly more important than another.

Even a statistic as simple and pervasive as batting average with runners in scoring position has its limits. The Red Sox hit .291 as a team with runners in scoring position in 2005. But out of 438 hits with runners in scoring position, 98 of them didn't drive in a run. Obviously, that's distorted a lot by the unique dimensions of Fenway Park, but that's more than one hit out of every five that doesn't directly score a run.

What the stats really do show is just how simple the game of baseball is. To prevent runs, get a first-pitch strike and get the leadoff batter out.

DL: *The Red Sox scored 910 runs this year. How many of those were scored by batters who got on base to lead off an inning, including those who homered?*

CW: 286 of the 910 runs [31 percent] were scored either by the leadoff batter in an inning or by the batter who replaced him on the bases by a fielder's choice. Even more impressive: over two-thirds of the runs were scored in innings where the leadoff batter reached base. The Red Sox scored 613 runs in 514 innings where the leadoff hitter reached, and 297 runs in 906 innings where the leadoff batter was retired.

DL: *Getting ahead of the hitter contributes greatly to a pitcher's success. Who on the staff did the best and worst job of throwing first-pitch strikes?*

CW: Chad Bradford had the highest percentage of first-pitch strikes. He threw a first-pitch strike to 73 of the 103 batters he faced [70.9 percent]. Curt Schilling was right behind him: 295 of 418 batters [70.6 percent].

But in Schilling's case, opposing batters hit .310 against him when he threw a first-pitch strike, including batters who put the first pitch in play. In 2004, they hit .225 against him.

DL: *Which Red Sox hitters swung at the highest and lowest percentage of first pitches this season? Also, did those same hitters have similar numbers last year?*

CW: The Red Sox didn't really have any first-pitch swingers in 2005. Among the regulars, David Ortiz was the most frequent first-pitch swinger at 31 percent, followed by Manny Ramirez at 30 percent. In 2004, Ortiz swung at 30 percent and Manny 37 percent. Honorable mention has to go to Jay Payton at 41 percent in 2005.

On the low end, Jason Varitek swung at the first pitch 21 percent of the time [down from 30 percent in 2004], and John Olerud swung at only 17 percent of first pitches.

DL: *The Red Sox' offense features a two-headed monster named "Manny Ortiz." What were some of the scary numbers he put up this season?*

CW:
- 32 of Manny Ramirez's 45 home runs came with runners on base.
- 93 of his 144 RBI came on home runs.
- Manny Ramirez hit .354 with 6 home runs and 16 RBI when he was the first batter to face a relief pitcher.
- David Ortiz hit .443 with 9 home runs on the first pitch.
- David Ortiz hit .410 with two or more runners on base.
- David Ortiz had 48 RBI that either tied the game or put the Red Sox ahead, 16 from the seventh inning on. He had 21 game-winning RBI, 8 from the seventh inning on.
- 19 of David Ortiz's 47 home runs and 50 of his 148 RBI came from the seventh inning on.
- David Ortiz had 74 RBI at Fenway Park and 74 RBI on the road.
- On the first pitch with runners in scoring position, David Ortiz hit .533 [16 for 30].
- David Ortiz hit .407 against left-handed pitchers with runners in scoring position.
- David Ortiz hit .368 with two outs and runners in scoring position.
- David Ortiz reached base by hit, walk, or hit by pitch in 144 of his 158 games. He reached base three times or more in 81 games.

• When the Red Sox trailed by one to three runs and runners were in scoring position, David Ortiz hit .517 [15 for 29].

DL: *What were Ortiz's numbers this year with Manny hitting behind him, and vice-versa? Also, what did each hit when the other was out of the lineup?*

CW: When David Ortiz hit third and Manny Ramirez hit fourth [111 games], Ortiz hit .310 with 36 home runs and 117 RBI, and Ramirez hit .307 with 35 home runs and 109 RBI. When Ramirez hit third and Ortiz hit fourth [32 games], Ramirez hit .274 with 8 home runs and 30 RBI; Ortiz hit .274 with 8 home runs and 20 RBI.

Ortiz started 13 games that Ramirez did not, in which he hit .286 with 3 home runs and 11 RBI. Ramirez started 5 games that Ortiz did not, in which he hit .250 with 2 home runs and 4 RBI.

DL: *Which Red Sox players hit the most balls off and over the Green Monster this season?*

CW: Kevin Millar and Manny Ramirez each had 20 hits off or over the Green Monster. And Millar had 25 fewer at-bats at Fenway than Ramirez. Millar was the leader in 2004, too, with 28, ahead of Ramirez's 20.

DL: *Led by Big Papi, the Red Sox have had a number of come-from-behind wins. Exactly how many have there been, and how does that compare to the rest of the league?*

CW: The Red Sox came from behind to win 46 times in 2005, which led the Major Leagues, one ahead of Minnesota and Cincinnati. They won 46 of 113 games in which they trailed at some point, also the best percentage in the Majors.

They actually had more come-from-behind wins in 2004 [47], but the Yankees set a Major League record with 61.

DL: *How many games did the Red Sox win in their final at-bat each of the last three years?*

CW: The Red Sox have won 61 games in their final at-bat over the last three seasons, 21 in 2005, 17 in 2004, and 23 in 2003. They are 39-10 in games decided in the final at-bat at Fenway Park, 22-32 on the road.

DL: *Batters who draw a walk to lead off an inning come around to score a large percentage of the time—or so it seems. Statistically, how often does that actually happen?*

CW: They don't score anywhere near as often as broadcasters would have you believe. I hear figures like 75 or 80 percent fairly often. But the truth is, they score much less frequently. For the last 11 seasons, which I'm using since that just happens to be what's stored on my computer at the moment, Red Sox batters who walk to lead off an inning score 42 percent of the time. And their opponents score 41 percent of the time.

DL: *Which Boston hitters had the highest and lowest strikeouts and walks per plate appearance?*

CW: Kevin Youkilis walked in 14.7 percent of his plate appearances, followed by Mark Bellhorn at 14.6 percent, and David Ortiz at 14.3 percent. On the low end, Gabe Kapler walked in 2.9 percent of his plate appearances, with Tony Graffanino at 4.5 percent, and Johnny Damon at 7.7 percent.

Mark Bellhorn struck out in 32.5 percent of his plate appearances, followed by Doug Mirabelli at 31.6 percent, and Jason Varitek at 21.7 percent. The least frequent batters to strike out were Johnny Damon [10.0 percent], John Olerud [10.4 percent], and Alex Cora [10.4 percent].

DL: *To close, tell us about your history as a baseball fan, including what October of 2004 meant to you.*

CW: Like so many Red Sox fans, there's only one beginning: 1967. Besides the daily drama, that was also the season when a friend's mother taught me how to keep a scorecard. I think I learned too well.

My fan journey really isn't very different than the rest of the Nation, except that the emotions are probably a little more tempered. Baseball to me is like a good serial or soap opera. One game flows into and affects the next game, probably more than in any other sport. I've just had the opportunity to occasionally interact with the characters, and my copy has had some pretty good DVD extras.

Of course, 2004 was sweet. Obviously, it was the chapter with the happiest ending. And the best part is that the story continues.

Shorter Views

DICK BEVERAGE

DICK BEVERAGE IS THE PRESIDENT OF THE SOCIETY FOR AMERICAN BASEBALL RESEARCH [SABR]. FOUNDED IN 1971, SABR'S STATED PURPOSE IS TO FOSTER THE RESEARCH AND DISSEMINATION OF THE HISTORY AND RECORD OF BASEBALL. THIS IS AN EXCERPT FROM AN INTERVIEW THAT TOOK PLACE IN MARCH 2005.

David Laurila: *A lot of people equate SABR to sabermetrics and stathead baseball. How accurate is that perception?*

Dick Beverage: Although our Statistical Analysis Committee is our largest committee and much statistical research is performed, the great majority of our membership is composed of historians, and that covers many aspects of the game. Very little that has gone on in baseball has not been affected by SABR research. Player records are compiled, league histories are researched, the Negro Leagues, biographical and demographic research, the rules of the game—that is just a sample of what SABR members are interested in. Naturally, statistics are an important part of the game, but by no stretch of the imagination is SABR confined to them.

DL: *What is SABR's mission statement and how has that differed over the years?*

DB: SABR's objectives have remained virtually unchanged over the years. We wish to foster the study of baseball as a significant American institution. We do that so that an accurate historical account of the game through the years is established, and we disseminate our findings to the general public and interested parties. All of this leads us to stimulate the best interest of baseball as our national pastime.

DL: *Tell us about SABR's ongoing Bio Project.*

DB: The Bio Project is an example of SABR members "thinking big." Three years ago, Mark Armour, one of our brightest members, brought the idea of writing a biography of every man who played in the Major Leagues to the attention of the Executive Board. His thinking was that such a project would attract interest from all areas of SABR and bond the participants in the project more closely to SABR. It's a Herculean task. Over 16,000 have played in the Majors, and many of them appeared in just a few games. The bios would be 1,500–2,000 words long and would be electronically published. There was much skepticism when the project was announced, but through the efforts of Mark and several other dedicated researchers the project is well under way with over 200 bios online and several hundred more in various stages.

DL: *How would you compare the popularity and importance of today's game, relative to previous eras? And is there such a thing as a "golden age" of baseball?*

DB: In some circles, the game is as popular today as it has ever been, if not more so. I doubt that there has ever been greater interest in baseball than there was in Boston last summer. But overall, it might not be as popular as it was when there was much less competition for the entertainment dollar. Young people do not appear quite so interested as I was when I was a boy. But most ballparks are very full day-in and day-out. Are they there because of the game itself? For many, probably not. But their very presence indicates a pretty strong interest.

As far as a golden age of baseball existing, I think it is always the era that is going on at the time the question is asked. For those of us who are devoted, the present time is always the best. And it can't be any other way.

DL: *What is your history as a baseball fan?*

DB: I was born and raised in Nebraska and first became interested in the game when I was nine. My best friend's father went to the World Series that year and came back with a scorecard or two, a hat, things like that. My interest was piqued. I started to read the sports page, and before long I was hooked. I discovered *The Sporting News* the next year and couldn't wait to read it. A whole new world unfolded before my eyes. I began to read everything I could find about baseball. I remember a Christmas when I was 12. I received a gift of $10 from one of my uncles. The very next day I went to a bookstore in downtown Omaha, all by myself, and bought two baseball books—*The Pittsburgh Pirates* by Fred Lieb, and *The Boston Braves* by Harold Kaese. They cost $3 each, thus taking a good portion of my Christmas present. When I got home, my mother was very critical of my decision to buy those books. She said I had wasted my money. But I read those books, and guess what? I still have them to this very day.

DL: *Any closing thoughts?*

DB: I don't think my experience in finding baseball was much different than that of most boys. What is probably more distinctive is that I stayed with it when others acquired new interests. I did so, as well, but never lost my obsession with baseball and probably never will. It is a definite part of my life.

JEFF IDELSON

Jeff Idelson is the vice president of communications and education at the National Baseball Hall of Fame. A native of West Newton, Massachusetts, Idelson began his professional career as an intern with the Red Sox in 1986. This interview took place in February 2005.

David Laurila: *The Red Sox winning the World Series was a historic event for the sport. In what ways might that impact the Baseball Hall of Fame?*

Jeff Idelson: The World Series is a great fan experience, which is what the Baseball Hall of Fame strives to be. Where a team fits into history is important to fans. People have always been fans of players, and the Red Sox will now be thought of more in the context of a team since they won the World Series. I'm a native New Englander, so I understand both the euphoria and the historical impact. It is something that will only benefit the Hall of Fame.

DL: *What are some of the items from the 2004 postseason that are now or will be on display in Cooperstown?*

JI: Well, "the bloody sock" is on its way as we speak. Curt Schilling was kind enough to agree to let us display it. We already have his specially designed spikes, which are what allowed him to pitch with the injury—that along with a lot of grit and guile. By placing "K-ALS" on the side of the spike, he is also relating to two of our Hall of Fame members who passed away from ALS, Catfish Hunter and Lou Gehrig. We have bats used by Manny Ramirez and Johnny Damon, along with jerseys worn by David Ortiz and Derek Lowe. There are also items from Pedro Martinez, Keith Foulke, Orlando Cabrera, and many others.

DL: *How many Red Sox players are in the Hall of Fame, and what are historically the most popular Red Sox–related destinations at the Hall?*

JI: There are 28 players enshrined who have worn a Red Sox uniform, and the Plaque Gallery is always a big draw. We have several Ted Williams items, including a bat from the season he hit .406—that is actually on loan from my friend Bob Breitbardt at the San Diego Hall of Champions. We have the ball from the final out of the 1903 World Series—Bill Dineen struck out Honus Wagner with it to end the game. We have a ball from the 1860s that was used by the Tri-Mountain Baseball Club, the first team in the city of Boston. There's even a gun that Gene Autry gave Carl Yastrzemski. There are many others. Those are just a few.

DL: *The Red Sox will be playing the Tigers in the 59th annual Hall of Fame game on May 23rd. What can you tell us about that?*

JI: It's played here in Cooperstown at Doubleday Field, which was built in 1920 and seats 10,000. As you said, it's been a tradition for a number of years. The crowds aren't as big as they are for the induction ceremony, but the game is very popular. This year's is drawing even more attention than usual, especially with baseball at such a fever pitch in New England.

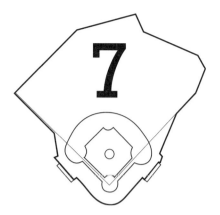

Scribes and Authors

HARVEY ARATON

HARVEY ARATON IS A SPORTSWRITER FOR THE *NEW YORK TIMES*.
A NATIVE OF NEW YORK CITY, ARATON HAS BEEN WITH THE *TIMES*
SINCE 1991. THIS INTERVIEW TOOK PLACE IN DECEMBER 2004.

David Laurila: *Knowing the importance of tradition and mystique, was
2004 good for the game of baseball, or was it actually bad?*

Harvey Araton: 2004 was not only good for the game, it was historic
and may one day be viewed as what reminded fans what makes baseball
worth looking past the horrors the game does unto itself—the latest
being the steroid scandal. I would venture to say even lifelong Yankee
fans—at least those whose passions are born of the right stuff and not
the misplaced anger and acting-out that is too often mistaken for love of
the game—would have to admit that the sight of the Red Sox celebrating on the field in St. Louis was a moment like few others in modern
sports. Tom Verducci's recent *Sports Illustrated* story on the Red Sox'
fans is a classic and a treatise on why we care so much in the first place.

DL: *Fifty years from now, when historians are rating the greatest events in baseball history, how will the 2004 postseason stack up?*

HA: I believe, from a team-performance perspective, the Sox' rallying to beat the Yankees the way they did—down 0-3, facing Rivera in the ninth, winning two mind-blowing, sudden-death marathons, sending the wounded Schilling out in Game 6, winning 7 in Yankee Stadium—ranks as the most spellbinding series in my lifetime, though I will admit that I am not that good when it comes to taking inventory of these things. I say this because of the circumstances, not only what was at stake, what was accomplished by the Sox but by everything that led into it: The blown Game 7 of 2003, the A-Rod saga, the fierce regular-season games, the Yanks-are-my-daddy September preliminary. Stephen King would have had difficulty making this stuff up.

DL: *From a national perspective, have the Red Sox lost their charm and become just another large-market team to be despised? Or is that an oversimplified and possibly inaccurate premise?*

HA: On the night the Red Sox won the Series, I did write that they will no longer represent, nationally speaking, the kind of compelling drama that 86 years' worth of frustration had built (and was immediately bombarded by e-mails from all over the country, and even the world, accusing me of underestimating the breadth of Red Sox Nation). My point wasn't to suggest there weren't Red Sox fans everywhere. It was that the Sox—and this was supported by the heightened television ratings for the Cubs the previous season and Red Sox in 2003 and 2004—were compelling theater for casual fans, for people who only become emotionally involved in sports (and will stay up to ungodly hours on work nights) when the event reaches their heart, or when a once-in-a-lifetime individual (Michael Jordan) becomes too irresistible to miss. I believe the Sox will be bigger than ever in New England, but the cachet of breaking a curse (or however we classify 86 years of frustration) can only happen once.

DL: *Putting on your sports psychologist hat for a moment, how will 2004 affect the fans of Boston and New York? How much of the respective inferiority complex and arrogance will remain, and what about the animosity from both sides?*

HA: Very simply: Yankee fans have been knocked off their smarmy pedestal. Any chant they manufacture will be met by 2004. Red Sox fans are no longer the world's most persecuted lot.

DL: *The Yankees are without a World Series title since 2000, have a number of question marks on their roster, and their farm system is regarded poorly. Is it time for them to re-evaluate their modus operandi, or will it just continue to be business as usual for the S.S. Steinbrenner?*

HA: The Yankees are in a precarious position, not necessarily in terms of wins and losses, but because Steinbrenner is now operating his business in a manner that demands a World Series championship in order to maintain the sense of the Yankees as the brand name in baseball. His investment in the YES network hinges on his team remaining high-demand programming, to continue its uneasy relationship with cable distributors who have balked at carrying YES on their basic tiers when all it really has to offer are the 130 or so Yankee games not shown on free TV. The longer the Yankees do not win, the more Steinbrenner operates as he did in the 1980s—impulsively—and the closer the team gets to implosion.

DL: *How would you compare Theo Epstein and Brian Cashman? Are there more similarities or differences in the approach they take to their jobs? And what reputation does each currently have within the game?*

HA: Both Theo Epstein—whose reputation couldn't be better right now, although let's be honest, he did stumble somewhat into it, after the A-Rod deal fell apart—and Cashman are obviously part of the whiz-kid general manager society. Both are bright, likeable guys, and clearly live and breathe baseball but it's difficult to anoint them as geniuses when they are working with the kind of financial advantages they have. True, the Red Sox payroll isn't $180 million, but $120 million is still double that of many other teams.

DL: *Deserved or not, the "Curse of A-Rod" theory has begun to work itself into baseball vernacular. What are your thoughts on this?*

HA: The curse of A-Rod sounds a bit premature to me. The bigger question, left unanswered in 2004, is whether A-Rod is a player who ultimately grades out to be less than the sum of his parts—or the opposite of his good buddy, Jeter. Most baseball people I have spoken to about A-Rod seem to offer a more pragmatic point of view when discussing his failures after Game 3 of the ALCS and his poor performance with runners in scoring position during the regular season. They say that while he undoubtedly is a great talent and will invariably put up great numbers as he goes along, the upshot is that top-of-the-line pitchers demonstrated this year that A-Rod can be pitched to in tight spots, that he does not possess the intangible quality that cannot be quantified. We shall see, but one thing is sure: There will be no more Texas-like seasons when from games 50 to 162 he is playing with no pressure.

DL: *What do you see as the best destination for Pedro Martinez? With the health of his arm—and his effectiveness—in mind, would he be better off in a warm-weather city, or should he simply stay in Boston—or go to New York?*

HA: It would be sad for Pedro to leave Boston, where he will never have to defend his legitimacy again. Despite his head-hunting and other peculiarities, I've always felt Pedro took too much grief, especially in New York. It wasn't his fault Grady Little failed in his capacity as a decision-maker. Pedro got his team into the eighth inning with a three-run lead, with a hot bullpen in October 2003. How many Yankee starters since 1996 have been immortalized for going six innings? Pedro is a Hall of Famer who had to carry around Boston's institutional baggage until he went out in Game 3 in St. Louis and proved his greatness once and for all. It would be a shame if he didn't go back to celebrate with his teammates.

DL: *Red Sox ownership continues to renovate and enhance Fenway Park, seemingly committed to stay rather than replace it with a modern facility. Knowing the importance of history and tradition to the game's character, what does this mean for baseball?*

HA: The Sox have done a nice job enhancing the profitability of Fenway without changing the essential nature and character of the facility. It is my fervent hope that the Yankees and the Red Sox will continue in their present ballparks, that they will realize their historic and familiar settings are appealing to people, especially in these perilous times of global uncertainty. A wider concourse and a sushi bar are nice, but that's not what most true Yankee and Red Sox fans go to the games for.

Howard Bryant

Howard Bryant is the author of *Juicing the Game: Drugs, Power, and the Fight for the Soul of Major League Baseball*, a book Peter Gammons has said "explains how the steroid era evolved and puts it in its context." Currently a reporter for the Washington Post, Bryant is a native of Boston and former Red Sox beat writer for the Boston Herald. This interview took place in October 2005.

David Laurila: *In an interview last year, Leigh Montville said of Ted Williams: "People say, 'Well, Ted never would have taken steroids.' He would have taken them in a minute! The biggest pills he could find!" What are your thoughts on that: the idea that players will do anything in their power to improve their performance?*

Howard Bryant: The first thing to do, regardless, is to think about what you know. Ted is dead. Leigh Montville knew Ted Williams; I never met him, so it would be impossible for me to guess how he would have reacted. In this project, I tried to narrow down the anecdotal and emotional from the factual; I parsed. This was a research book, not one that dealt in the hypothetical. Something I find frustrating in the whole steroids story is the need people have to extrapolate on things they don't know. Would Ted have used heroin if he thought it would help him? We don't know that.

On one hand, players have always been able to do everything they could to perform at their best. As a player, you want to compete. That is what it boils down to. It's not so much being the best player as it is not allowing yourself to be put at a disadvantage. I think everybody would stop in a heartbeat if everyone else stopped. It's all about getting your piece. It's a domino effect. Maybe you don't want to use something, but what if it's the difference between playing Major League baseball and selling washing machines?

DL: *Referring to the steroid era's emphasis on offense and power production, Sandy Alderson was quoted in the book as saying, "The Luis Aparicios of the world wouldn't be playing today." Has the game truly evolved to where a Hall of Famer from a previous era no longer would have the skill-set to make an MLB lineup?*

HB: To me, that was probably the most underrated chapter in the book. That transition began in the mid-nineties, and it evolved into a fundamental change in approach, one that favored players who could hit with power. A deliberate attempt to find a new type of player emerged, and it wasn't a great defensive shortstop like Aparicio. I remember talking with Billy Beane during spring training a few years ago and asking him if there was a position where defense came first. Of course, this is someone who had Scott Spiezio, who weighed over 200 pounds, playing second base. Billy talked about production per money spent and how he's in a position where he has to choose the tools he can afford to buy. Defense wasn't one of them. Power per at-bat was more valuable, which made players like Spiezio and Jeremy Giambi suddenly more desirable.

DL: *Brady Anderson did something in 1996 that Williams—or Aaron or Killebrew or Schmidt—never accomplished: he hit over 50 home runs in a season. What did that signify?*

HB: The first red flag of the decade. It also pointed to recognition by the players that this is how you'll be compensated the most. Home run hitters were getting the big contracts, because that's what teams were looking for more and more. Think about position players who were earning at the top of the scale. The only two I can think of that weren't 50-home-run threats were Derek Jeter and Bernie Williams. The trends had already been changing, but the separation was now becoming bigger, money-wise. A lot of it was being handed out, and where was all of the money coming from? The game was now doing well financially. Neither side wanted to rock the boat.

DL: *What you're saying is that . . . ?*

HB: That this is an economic story at its core. From the owners' standpoint, people liked the product, which meant increased revenues. They were also coming off of the strike and knew that the fans wouldn't stand for a scandal. There was no way, less than a year later, they would start questioning Anderson. Home runs helped put people in the seats, so why would they do anything that could change that? The owners wanted home runs. More than half of the teams were even providing creatine to their players in '97 and '98. And they barely even knew what it was.

DL: *The Dietary Supplements Health and Education Act [DSHEA] was signed into law in 1994, facilitating the use of creatine and similar substances. In your opinion, is Congress subpoenaing baseball players 11 years later if DSHEA doesn't happen?*

HB: Yes and no. You didn't need it to find anabolic steroids, but it did help create murkiness in what's legal and what's not. It was basically a Republican gift to the pharmaceutical industry, and what it did in the long term was undermine the credibility of people like Tom Davis and Henry Waxman. These guys helped pass DSHEA unanimously, and now they're mad because it wasn't policed by baseball? This is hypocritical, because they were equally complicit—everybody rode along at some point, including Congress. What they did, if you think about it, was help create original sin. As it became clear that this scandal had far-reaching implications, it seems like members of Congress forgot how much they helped shape it.

DL: *How long have anabolic steroids been a part of baseball?*

HB: Since the 1970s, but a better question is when did the economic mindset come into play—when did players begin to believe they needed them to make it? The answer would be the nineties. Prior to that, everyone had suspected Oakland, San Diego, the Mets, and Phillies, but it was post-strike when it became "Holy Toledo." When you walk into a clubhouse, your IQ is equivalent to your batting average and home run total. That is a reality that prevents more players from having a voice. It's all alpha-male, like in the seventh grade. The big dogs rule the roost in the clubhouse, and even if you think it's wrong, peer pressure says otherwise. There has always been a silent majority—marginal players like A.J. Hinch—but that's all they've been. For some, it's probably cost them a career. They've become the guys selling washing machines.

DL: *Does Jose Canseco have much credibility?*

HB: Of course, he has credibility. He was in the room. Everyone is afraid of him, because he wore a uniform. People like Sandy Alderson, who have also spoken out, didn't—so you know he didn't see anything.

That would be like smoking a joint in front of the principal. I have to give Canseco credit. He's nuts, but he has the guts to say things. His initial message—the umbrella message of his book—is that players were using, and he helped. Is there anyone following this story who doesn't buy that? A lot of people don't want to believe things they don't like the sound of, but that doesn't change what's been happening. You have to get past that. To much of the public, this has been a story of subterfuge. You can try to compare Ted Williams to now, but the real issue is that baseball has had a drug problem and has been paralyzed by its value system and handcuffed leadership.

DL: *In* Juicing the Game, *you wrote that in the days following the release of Canseco's book, "... Selig argues loudly with Peter Gammons, who asks him if baseball would be in this position had Fay Vincent, or Bart Giamatti, still been commissioner." Elaborate on that.*

HB: It was another hammer-blow to Bud, because it was coming from someone with an influence-shaping platform—it wasn't just guys in the press box playing cards and talking. That cut to the core of Bud Selig, because he's a history major and knows that history will outlive him. That's why he has religion on this; he's a legacy guy. Bud doesn't want to be known as the commissioner who presided over the steroid era. He called me after I talked about the issue on *60 Minutes.* People will listen to Jose and me, which had Bud thinking that he had to go on the offensive. He said he feels the people are behind his position, but I don't think he understands they don't believe he's done what he can. He actually believes that he's a crusader, but that he's been thwarted by the union. But what does Peter have to do with Paul? It's Bud versus Don [Fehr], but when you look at his proposals over the years, that doesn't mean he's done anything to solve the problem. I do believe that he understands the depth of the situation now, but he was late getting there. His vision was always shaped by pressure—from the press, Canseco, the federal government—not moral certitude. He changed his position far too many times to gain the trust he needed. He's had control, yet never advocated more than a 15-game penalty until he was forced to do so. Had Congress not jumped in, would there even be a policy in place now?

DL: *Given the politics involved, does Selig wield enough power to give a Barry Bonds a lengthy suspension if he so desired—assuming, of course, that he had proof to back up that decision?*

HB: Proof is obviously a huge problem, but of course he does. The networks wouldn't like it, but the owners would love it. It would devastate the union's bargaining position. Baseball—plain and simple—is not a game. It is two entrenched positions, no different than industry. The sides don't simply dislike each other. They hate each other. And they've been trying to destroy each other. Bud and the owners are trying to force a position down the union's throat. That is the reason there is a problem. It's all about power.

DL: *Rafael Palmeiro tested positive for steroids after testifying before Congress. What reason could you possibly surmise for his allowing that to happen?*

HB: One-word answer: Arrogance. Do you remember what his first quote was when he was subpoenaed? He said, "March 17 is my wife's birthday. That's where I'll be." Some of these guys look at themselves as untouchables. They're almost like the Mafia in believing that they can't be held accountable. This was the government subpoenaing Palmeiro, not the Kiwanis Club. It's arrogance, plain and simple.

DL: *In* Juicing the Game, *you write that Tony LaRussa and others have seemingly been aware of steroid use for some time but have chosen to cover it up. Do you feel these people should be held as accountable as the players themselves?*

HB: Absolutely. They all do. LaRussa is one of the reasons why this story is wrong. He's a disgrace. You can't tell the story without indicting yourself, so you are confronted with a clear, unambiguous question. You can protect the code or you can tell the truth. He tried to do both, and he tried to intimidate people in doing so. Being articulate doesn't mean that you're smart. Schilling has also tried to do both. It doesn't work that way. Either you're honest, or you're not.

DL: *There are a lot of bad guys in this story. Are there any good guys?*

HB: Along with the true crusaders—the doctors involved—I think Alderson comes out looking okay. Tony Gwynn was remarkable. Reggie Jackson is another. The game is their lives, and you can tell they've been thinking about it seriously. Frank Thomas is one of the few current players who have spoken out. He's said that everyone should be tested, because he doesn't want the perception that everyone has always been cheating. Unfortunately, the union hasn't agreed with him, and Bud Selig hasn't done anything, so there's been little progress. The price of this paralysis is the reputation of the decade.

JIM CALLIS

JIM CALLIS IS THE EXECUTIVE EDITOR OF *BASEBALL AMERICA*. *BASEBALL AMERICA* IS THE FOREMOST AUTHORITY WHEN IT COMES TO THE MINOR LEAGUES, AND CALLIS IS ITS RESIDENT PROSPECT GURU. THIS INTERVIEW TOOK PLACE IN JANUARY 2006.

David Laurila: *Fans tend to overrate their team's prospects, and Red Sox Nation certainly has high expectations for the players on top of this year's list. Objectively, just how do Jonathan Papelbon, Jon Lester, and Andy Marte compare to the "big three" on other teams?*

Jim Callis: It would be hard to overrate those three. I put them in this order—Marte, Lester, Papelbon—and I think you could make a case for putting them in any order. On my personal overall prospect list in the *Prospect Handbook*, I had Marte at number 13 (third-best third baseman), Lester at number 16 (second-best left-handed pitcher), and Papelbon at number 22 (fourth-best right-handed pitcher). They'll all move down one notch after Justin Upton signed, but it's hard to argue with three prospects in the top 23. The only team I had with three prospects better than that is the Diamondbacks (Justin Upton, Stephen Drew, Conor Jackson, and Carlos Quentin). Other clubs that would be comparable would be the Angels (Brandon Wood, Howie Kendrick,

Erick Aybar, Jered Weaver, Kendry Morales), Marlins (Jeremy Hermida, Hanley Ramirez, Anibal Sanchez, Scott Olsen), and Dodgers (Chad Billingsley, Adam LaRoche, Joel Guzman, Russell Martin, Scott Elbert), but I'd take Boston's top three over those.

DL: *Was there much debate, or do most people in the* BA *office agree with how the top half of the order was ranked?*

JC: I wouldn't say there was a lot of debate, but you really can make the case for rating Marte, Lester, and Papelbon in just about any order. Papelbon has accomplished more at a higher level than the other two, obviously, while Lester has a shorter track record of really standing out. Some guys have cooled on Marte a little bit, which I don't understand. He was just 21 last year, and the only thing he hasn't done is hit well in the Majors—in 57 at-bats.

DL: *Going beyond the top prospects, how would you rate the overall depth in the Red Sox farm system?*

JC: I really liked their depth before they gave up two blue-chip prospects and two power arms for Josh Beckett, Mike Lowell, and Guillermo Mota, though I can't fault that trade. I'd say Boston's depth is slightly above average. Our prospect list (and our ranking of the Boston system) could look a lot different a year from now if Marte, Lester, Papelbon, Craig Hansen, and Dustin Pedroia all play so much in the Majors that they no longer qualify. Four of the six spots at 6–11 on our list are taken up by 2005 first-rounders (Jacoby Ellsbury, Jed Lowrie, Clay Buchholz, Michael Bowden), and after a few more familiar names (David Murphy, Luis Soto, Brandon Moss, Edgar Martinez), it starts to thin out pretty quick.

DL: *Had they not gone to Florida in the Josh Beckett deal, where would Hanley Ramirez and Anibal Sanchez have been ranked?*

JC: My top five would have been Marte, Lester, Papelbon, Ramirez, Sanchez, in that order. Ramirez is number 30 on my overall top 50, Sanchez number 33. Again, that's before the Upton signing. I do have some reservations about Ramirez. It's been long enough for his tools to start to translate into megaproduction. We may look back and realize that Boston sold high on him.

DL: *Last year, the Red Sox had five shortstops on the list, four of them among the top 12. Now, due to trades and position switches, that depth is no longer there. What are your thoughts on that, including the futures of Dustin Pedroia, Jed Lowrie, and Christian Lara?*

JC: That is a concern, especially with no obvious shortstop at the big league level. Pedroia could have stayed at shortstop if he wasn't playing alongside Ramirez at the start of 2005, and he may get a look at short in big league camp. I think he'd be adequate defensively there, but he wouldn't stand out with his glove. Second base is a better fit for him. Lowrie surprised some people with how good he looked at shortstop in his pro debut last summer, but when all is said and done, I bet he's a second baseman. Lara can be a good glove man at short, but he has a lot to prove with his bat. It's hard to project him as a big league regular until he does.

DL: *Luis Soto dropped to 13 on the list this year after being number 7 in 2005. Did his move from shortstop to the outfield lessen his value, or were there other reasons for him sliding?*

JC: His value did decrease with the move, because shortstops are harder to find than right fielders. The move did make sense, though, because he probably was going to outgrow shortstop and the Red Sox wanted to expedite the value of his bat, which is his ticket to the Majors. Obviously, he's going to have to hit more as a right fielder than he would have had to as a shortstop to be a big league regular, though he has the bat to do it. He didn't adapt well to low Class A Greenville, so he took a hit for that as well, though he played well after a demotion to short-season Lowell.

DL: *Brandon Moss fell from number 2 last year all the way to number 14. Why?*

JC: In retrospect, I overrated him somewhat a year earlier. He had a great year at a young age in Class A, but there were scouts who questioned how well he projected as a corner outfielder. His power is a question for a corner guy, and while he held his own in Double A this year, he didn't overwhelm anyone and didn't make many adjustments. Right now, he looks like more of a fourth outfielder to me.

DL: *Infielder Jeff Natale posted an eye-opening 1.007 OPS in Greenville after being taken in the 32nd round of last year's draft. Was that likely an aberration, or are we possibly looking at a diamond in the rough along the lines of a David Eckstein?*

JC: Maybe some of each, but I'd caution getting over-excited about a 32nd-round college senior tearing up low Class A. Natale, a consistent .400 hitter at Trinity (Conn.), where he also played hockey, has tremendous hand–eye coordination and can really hit. He'll obviously have to continue to prove that at higher levels. He's not a very good defender at second base, so finding a position could be a problem. I don't know if he has enough power to fit in at a lesser position. Good sleeper to watch, and we'll learn more about him in 2006. He would have ranked in the 31–35 range if our list went that deep.

DL: *Jeff Corsaletti was taken in the sixth round, and despite hitting .357 in Greenville seems to be getting relatively little attention. Why do you think that is?*

JC: He's not as much of an unknown like Natale, but Corsaletti was a college senior coming from an upper-echelon program (Florida). Those kind of guys should be able to hit in low Class A. Also, few scouts think he can really handle playing center field in the Majors. If he's a left fielder, a guy who hits for some average with some line-drive power isn't real exciting. Corsaletti has a chance, but let's see how he does at higher levels.

DL: *How quickly do you see Jacoby Ellsbury moving through the system, and which facet of his game needs the most work?*

JC: Ellsbury is pretty polished and should move quickly. He could be ready to take over center field in Boston after just two years in the minors. He doesn't have a glaring flaw. He knows what kind of player he is—a lefty line-drive hitter with some gap power and good speed—and plays to his strengths. He's a solid center fielder. The main thing he needs is 1,000 or so minor league at-bats against quality pro pitching.

DL: *Of David Murphy and Adam Stern, which is closer to MLB-ready and which has the better long-term potential?*

JC: I'd say Murphy on both counts. Stern didn't play a whole lot last year, so both really have only proved themselves in Double A. Murphy is a better hitter and a better defender. If he can learn to hit for more power, I can see him being a big league regular. Stern looks like more of an extra outfielder to me.

DL: *How do you rate the potential of young outfielders Willy Mota and Reid Engel?*

JC: Those guys are two very young, very toolsy outfielders who are still very raw. Neither made the top-30 list, but both could jump on there in 2006. Guys to keep an eye on, very easy to dream on their potential. But they have a long way to go.

DL: *Mickey Hall and Ian Bladergroen battled injuries last year, hindering their development. What is their status, and which do you see as having the brightest future?*

JC: They both should be healthy in 2006, which the Red Sox hope will translate into improved production. Bladergroen is a slightly better prospect in my book, though not by a lot. This is a big year for both of them.

DL: *After a forgettable 2004 season, Chris Turner seemingly reestablished himself as a legitimate prospect last summer. Does he have enough talent to take his game to a higher level?*

JC: He does. Turner is one of the better all-around athletes in the system. He didn't make the top 30, but he was close and just needs to keep showing he can get the job done at higher levels.

DL: *John Otness added a catcher's mitt to his résumé while hitting .331 in Greenville last year. How much might that added versatility mean for the 2004 non-drafted free agent?*

JC: I'm not sure Otness is really a big league catcher. But if he can pull that off, that's huge. He had a great year, but he's still a marginal prospect. If he can catch and have that extra versatility, that could be the difference in eventually reaching the Majors.

DL: *Is Kelly Shoppach ready to be a solid contributor in the Major Leagues?*

JC: I think Shoppach could start for more than a few teams right now. If he played every day, I could see him hitting .250–.260 with 12–15 homers and some walks and good defense as a rookie. He'll never hit for much average, but he has power, a good eye, and defensive and leadership skills. He may be more valuable as trade bait than as a backup, though.

DL: *The Red Sox took a catcher, Jon Egan, in the second round of last year's draft. What are your thoughts on him?*

JC: Egan was supposed to be a primarily offensive player, but he struggled at the plate while showing more than expected defensively in his pro debut. If he can stay behind the plate and his bat improves, he could be pretty interesting. He did get arrested for a DUI this off-season, during which police found traces of cocaine in his wallet, so that was alarming. The Red Sox believe it was a one-time slipup and don't think it will be a long-term concern, though I believe he's receiving some counseling.

DL: *Edgar Martinez was a good story last year, enjoying success as a hard-throwing reliever after beginning his career as a catcher. What can we expect from the next chapter of "El Guapo Jr.'s" conversion to the mound?*

JC: As soon as he gains consistency with a second pitch, I think you'll see him in Boston pretty quickly. Martinez has a plus fastball and commands it well, to the point where he had a lot of success last year with just one consistently reliable pitch.

DL: *With a more consistent offspeed pitch, Craig Hansen could potentially be a dominant starting pitcher in the Major Leagues. Do you think his future value is higher as a closer or as a starter?*

JC: I think almost every pitcher's value is higher as a starter if he can pull it off. Hansen possibly could, but I think the Red Sox will groom him as a closer. His slider is a knockout pitch, but it wasn't at its best last summer after his long layoff and subsequent tired arm. He definitely has two plus pitches, maybe two plus-plus pitches. If he doesn't make the opening-day roster, I don't think he'll spend much time in the minors.

DL: *Two pitching prospects the Red Sox have acquired this offseason are Jermaine Van Buren and James Vermilyea. What can you tell us about each?*

JC: Bullpen fodder, could be sixth- or seventh-inning guys, maybe better in time. Van Buren made the top 30 in the bottom half, while Vermilyea just missed. They have solid but not overwhelming stuff and compete well. The Blue Jays tried to use Vermilyea as a starter last year, which didn't work out well. The Red Sox took him in the Rule 5 draft based more on what they had seen in previous years.

DL: *Alexandro Machado had a good year in Pawtucket and earned a late season call-up to Boston. What kept the versatile 23-year-old switch-hitter off the list?*

JC: He could have made the list, but I see him as more of a utility guy at best. The Red Sox have had middle-infield holes arise and haven't shown much interest in promoting him. He's a safer bet than some of the guys at the end of the list, but I went with players with higher ceilings.

DL: *Cla Meredith came out of nowhere last year and almost as quickly fell back below the radar. What happens next for the colorful sinkerballer?*

JC: Meredith lost his confidence after giving up a grand slam to Richie Sexson in his first big league appearance. He just needs to get back to being the fearless guy who throws nasty sinkers rather than trying to invent new ways to get hitters out. I expect he'll get back on track in 2006.

DL: *Left-hander Randy Beam has quietly impressed out of the bullpen since being drafted in 2004. Is he one of the real sleepers in the organization?*

JC: Another guy who just missed the top 30. Beam isn't overpowering by any means, but he has a quality change-up and no fear, and keeps getting hitters out. We may see him in Boston this year.

DL: *Left-handers Mike Rozier and Ryan Phillips both had solid first seasons, yet Phillips didn't make the list and Rozier was a somewhat disappointing 24th. What are your thoughts on each?*

JC: Rozier has a higher ceiling, though he didn't prepare well for his first pro season and his stuff was markedly down from where it was in high school. Phillips hasn't shown the quality of stuff Rozier has in the past but pitched well at Lowell. Rozier needs to show more in 2006. If Phillips repeats his success, he'll make the top 30 next year.

DL: *Sticking with lefties, do Lenny DiNardo and Abe Alvarez currently project better as starters or relievers?*

JC: Relievers. I don't think either has close to enough stuff to fool Major League hitters two or three times through the lineup. Looks like DiNardo is the frontrunner to be the lefty reliever in Boston at the start of the season.

DL: *The often-overlooked David Pauley made a notable climb from 26th on last year's list to 16 this year. What was behind his climb in the rankings?*

JC: I actually wouldn't call it that notable. There's not a huge difference in those spots on the bottom of the top 30 rankings, especially when you consider the attrition through trades, injuries, or lack of performance. Pauley has a chance to be a back-of-the-rotation starter, solid but not spectacular, and at that point of the list I thought he stood out more than anyone else.

DL: *Michael Bowden and Clay Buchholz both look to have good futures, although Bowden had some minor health issues last year while Buchholz's velocity in Lowell was less than advertised. Is either a concern, or are we likely to see them near the top of the list in the next few years?*

JC: Neither is a concern. Bowden was more a case of just taking it easy with a high school arm. I don't know of any real health concerns. A converted position player, Buchholz had pitched more innings in 2005 than ever before in his life. At Angelina [Texas] JC, he tended to build velocity as his outings went on, often throwing harder late in games than he did early. At Lowell, he pitched mostly in two-inning stints and thus didn't light up the radar guns as much. I like both of them a lot and bet you see them in the middle of the top 10 a year from now.

DL: *Last one: While the Red Sox farm system has greatly improved over the past few years, uncertainty remains in the post-Theo front office— Ben Cherington's move from farm director to co-GM being a notable change. What lies ahead for the Red Sox player development machine?*

JC: They're going to graduate some significant players to the Majors over the next two years, and they're going to need to replenish that talent. Scouting director Jason McLeod is going to have four extra draft picks to play with in 2006, which will help. There's no reason Boston can't continue to find talent. The Red Sox have the money to sign whomever they want, and I think everyone in the front office is working on the same page. They're much more organized and detail-oriented than they were in the past. People know about Cherington now because he's co-GM, but he quietly did an excellent job as farm director. Obviously, the co-GM believes in the importance of the farm system. I also think McLeod is doing a nice job, though he tends to fly under the radar when it comes to getting press.

BOB HOHLER

BOB HOHLER HAS WORKED AS A REPORTER FOR THE BOSTON GLOBE SINCE 1987. A NATIVE OF BOSTON, HOHLER COVERED THE RED SOX AS A BEAT WRITER FROM 2000 THROUGH THE 2004 WORLD SERIES. THIS INTERVIEW TOOK PLACE IN FEBRUARY 2005.

David Laurila: *Most fans know what a beat writer does, but do they really understand what goes into the job? Tell us about that.*

Bob Hohler: Before I started on the Sox beat in 2000, I learned something about deadline pressure covering events from the Challenger disaster to presidential debates to the Clinton impeachment saga. I also had made a few trips to Fenway to write Sox stories while I was covering sports for the *Concord Monitor* in New Hampshire in the 1980s. But nothing prepared me for the nightly grind on the Sox beat, one of the most demanding and competitive in the business. Here's a summary of a typical day:

For a game at 7 p.m., the job requires reporting to Fenway (or the park in a road city) by 3:30 p.m. to gather material for the first-edition Sox notebook. The manager usually meets with writers about 4 p.m., and the players generally are available for another hour before batting practice. The Sox notebook needs to be as informative, entertaining, and comprehensive as possible because it conveys much of the day's news and is competing with other papers, mainly the *Herald*. The objective is to file the first-edition notebook before the first pitch, although I rarely filed it before the third inning because of the extra time I spent to make sure I wasn't missing anything, the nightly pregame segment the *Globe* beat writer needs to do for NESN, and a quick dinner break.

Once the game begins, the beat writer is expected to record every play—and every pitch—in his scorebook while performing the rest of his duties. After the first-edition notebook is finished, the next task is producing a large chunk of "running" copy for the first-edition game story. The running copy typically covers the action through the first six or seven innings: how the runs were scored and how the starting pitcher fared, among other developments. That needs to be filed no later than the seventh inning and forms the bottom portion of the first-edition game story.

The next challenge is writing the top of the first-edition story, hopefully with a touch that will make it interesting to readers in northern New England and other outlying areas who receive the first edition but probably already know the score when they pick up the paper in the morning. The top must be filed the instant the game ends, which can make the final innings the most nerve-wracking of the beat. I can't tell you how many times Jeff Horrigan, the *Herald* beat writer, and I felt as if we were on the verge of heart attacks as we scrambled to rewrite the top of our stories as the score changed multiple times in the final innings. Extra-inning games get dicier because once the first-edition deadline approaches (about 10:30 p.m. for the *Globe*), we need to file "wooden" leads that the copy desk can finesse.

Then once the game ends, we need to file "flash" leads so editors can replate if the press run already has begun. It requires having two separate leads ready to file: one if the Sox win, the other if they lose. Once the game ends, we need to scramble to the clubhouse and gather reaction from the manager and players in time for the next deadline. The tension escalates if key figures in the game—players who had the winning hit or made the crucial error, for example—are not available because they are receiving medical treatment, lifting weights, or simply choosing not to make themselves available, as sometimes happens. By 12:15 a.m., we need to have rewritten our game story to include the reactions, and provide more explanation and analysis of the night's events. We also need to rewrite or update the Sox notebook by the same deadline. If we miss the 12:15 deadline, we miss delivering the news to the overwhelming majority of our readers. The deadline for the final edition is about 1:45 a.m., but that edition goes to only a small percentage of the total readership.

Considering the demands, the beat writer sometimes struggles to actually watch the game. I'm exaggerating only slightly when I say I covered two no-hitters (Nomo's and Lowe's) and hardly saw them because I was so busy writing, tracking plays, and pitch counts, fielding calls from the office, etc. The beat writer's night usually ends between 12:30 and 1 a.m. after he packs up and checks for questions from the copy desk. Then it's time to start gearing up for the next game, usually the next night. The Sox play about 215 games a year between spring training, the regular season, and the playoffs.

DL: *Do you think that being so connected to the team on a day-to-day basis can cause a writer to lose perspective or even be unable to enjoy the game from an aesthetic point of view?*

BH: I think the best beat writers either adhere to bedrock standards of fairness or evaluate themselves regularly to make sure they don't lose perspective. It's easy to develop friends or foes when you spend several hours a day with the people you cover, as baseball writers do with players from the first day of spring training in February to the last game in October. Writers may harbor personal feelings about the people or institutions they cover, but the good ones avoid any bias when they begin typing. As for enjoying the aesthetics of the game, baseball is so wonderfully complex that you can learn something new almost every day, even if you played it a lot as a kid, as I did. In that sense, I gained a greater appreciation of the game the more I covered it. I also felt like I was learning something every day about the people who play and manage the game, which made the job more enjoyable.

DL: *Following up on that, Howard Bryant recently spoke about being relatively unmoved by the World Series win, as covering the team didn't allow him to be a fan in the truest sense. What are your thoughts on that?*

BH: As someone who grew up within walking distance of Fenway as a huge Sox fan, I have often been asked how much fun it was to cover them, especially when they won the World Series. I refer you in part to my earlier comments about missing the no-hitters by Nomo and Lowe because of the workload and deadline pressures. Serving as a beat writer for the *Globe* and other larger dailies is work—lots of it. Several friends have mentioned seeing me when a FOX camera zoomed in on the press box in the final game of the World Series in St. Louis. I was hunched over my laptop, feverishly trying to make deadline writing about a monumental event in Boston sports. I was trying to write the first draft of history while running on fumes and sick. Baseball beat-writing is a marathon, and we were running the final mile. I was in the midst of working 32 straight days while traveling from Boston to Tampa to Baltimore to Oakland to Boston to New York to Boston to New York to Boston to St. Louis to Boston, often with four hours of sleep or less. While Horrigan downed energy drinks and candy to try to keep going, I was on a steady diet of antibiotics, ibuprofen, and pseudoephedrine. It was an honor and a privilege to cover the historic event, but I can't say it was a lot of fun at the time. It was more fun later when I could relax, watch the DVDs, and reflect on being a witness to one of my greatest childhood dreams.

DL: *Chris Snow is stepping into your shoes and already looks like he'll be a success. How does one learn to be a good beat writer, and how does an editor recognize who can excel at the job?*

BH: You learn while doing it, but you also bring to the job your ability as a writer and reporter. The *Globe* places a high premium on both writing and reporting. That said, it takes time to form the relationships with players, agents, general managers, clubhouse workers, parking lot attendants, ushers, and everyone else in the game who will help you become a better beat writer. It took me nearly two years to feel comfortable in the job. It's not easy, and it helps if you have someone to support you, as I did and as Chris will in Gordon Edes, one of the nation's best baseball writers. As for how an editor recognizes who can excel at the job, I can't speak for the editors. They trusted me to do the job, and they trust Chris, as well. In addition to being a solid writer and reporter, Chris is young and eager. That certainly will help. He's going to be very successful. Remember, Peter Gammons, Bob Ryan, Dan Shaughnessy, John Powers, and many other great sportswriters were about the same age as Chris when they began their careers at the *Globe* or other major dailies.

DL: *What advice have you given Chris, and what's the best advice you received when you started?*

BH: The advice I remember receiving was, "Don't do it." Dan Shaughnessy and others warned me how taxing and competitive the job was, but it was a chance to do something I had dreamed of since I was a kid writing school papers about why Ted Williams was the greatest man on earth. My advice to Chris basically was to be himself, do his best, and ignore the slights and the potshots. There may be players who hardly will give him the time of day for awhile. There will be writers in the press box who believe they could do a better job—and should have gotten the job. And there will be amateur media critics on the Internet and radio passing judgment, however biased and uninformed. I advised him to ignore them all. He's got a job to do. They don't.

DL: *Who were your role models and mentors when you started out, and whom do you most admire in the business now?*

BH: Two of the sports writers I admired most growing up were the *Globe*'s Ray Fitzgerald and Leigh Montville, gifted writers and good people who never seemed to grow jaded doing a very demanding job. Since I joined the paper in 1987, I have received valuable guidance from many great editors and reporters, including Matt Storin, Helen Donovan, Tom Mulvoy, David Shribman, Walter Robinson, Ben Bradlee, Jr., John Burke, David Nyhan, Mark Morrow, Don Skwar, Joe Sullivan, Reid Laymance, and Gordon Edes. I recently returned from the Super Bowl, which I covered with many *Globe* sportswriters who rank among the best in the business. I can't tell you how proud I am to work with them. Also, the editors on the sports copy desk at the *Globe* are world-class. They have been incredibly helpful to me and many others.

DL: *In the past, sportswriters tended to "protect" players, not reporting off-the-field activities such as drinking and womanizing. That is, for the most part, no longer the case. What are your thoughts on this?*

BH: It's true both in politics and sports. President Kennedy and Mickey Mantle, for example, generally seem to have received the same deferential treatment. Since then, there clearly has been a cultural shift, with magazines like *People* replacing forerunners like *Look* and putting much more emphasis on the private lives of public figures to feed the public's appetite for that kind of stuff. In my view, though, baseball writers are not in the business of prying into the private lives of players. I don't think you see that kind of stuff in the Boston papers. Yes, we reported that Manny met socially with Enrique Wilson the night he was too sick to play against the Yankees, but I would argue that it was relevant enough to warrant mentioning in a story about Manny's inability to play. Otherwise, I don't think you see much written by baseball writers about the private doings of players unless the players bring it up (Johnny Damon and Derek Lowe, for example, each volunteered their reactions to allegations about their night life). Yes, gossip writers zero in on players after hours, but I'll let them explain themselves.

DL: *While tabloids are often accused of compromising ethical standards in order to sell more newspapers, the* Globe *has a reputation for integrity. Have you ever been in a situation where you let someone else break a story because you, or your employer, felt it improper to do so?*

BH: A couple of *Globe* reporters, including me, received a copy last season of Curt Schilling's post in a Sons of Sam Horn chat room about his medical options for dealing with his injured ankle. We believed it was best to report an issue like that only after first speaking directly to Schilling or the team medical staff, which is what we did. I'm not sure how other papers handled it. I also know there have been times where there has been information, for example, about the personal lives of public figures that a paper like the *Globe* would not publish without fully reporting it. Although I wasn't involved in it, the story last year about John Kerry allegedly having been romantically involved with a former staffer comes to mind. Many responsible papers knew about the allegation and withheld it because they did the reporting and proved it was wrong or were unable to substantiate it. I believe some less responsible news outlets ran with it, and by all indications it was a false allegation.

DL: *Many people covering professional athletes once dreamed of being on the other side of the microphone or notebook. Did you ever have such aspirations?*

BH: I grew up wanting to hit like Ted Williams, but by the time I batted against a big league prospect in high school—and got over-matched—I was comfortably resigned to the fact that Ted's records were safe from me. As for being on the other side of the notebook, I have some experience in that because of my role in two episodes. As the reporter who covered Christa McAuliffe most closely, I wrote a book about her and the Challenger disaster and did countless interviews about it across the country. I also was involved in a relatively high-profile case in Maine in which I refused to testify against a murder suspect and was put on trial for criminal contempt (and convicted). In both episodes, I learned valuable lessons about how vulnerable people feel when they have no choice but to trust strangers to convey their stories to the public.

DL: *Last question: One could make an argument that covering the Red Sox is the most important newspaper job in Boston. Your thoughts?*

BH: When I was working for the *Globe* in Washington five years ago and weighing whether to apply for the Sox job, Mark Morrow, then the national editor, urged me to give it a shot. He said covering the Sox for the *Globe* would be like covering the Kennedy White House for the paper. I think there is a measure of truth to that.

⚾

STEWART O'NAN

STEWART O'NAN IS THE CO-AUTHOR, WITH STEPHEN KING, OF *FAITHFUL*, WHICH TAKES US THROUGH THE 2004 SEASON IN THE EYES OF TWO SELF-PROCLAIMED RED SOX FANATICS. A NATIVE OF PITTSBURGH, O'NAN LIVES IN CONNECTICUT AND IS THE AUTHOR OF SEVERAL NOVELS. THIS INTERVIEW TOOK PLACE IN DECEMBER 2004.

David Laurila: *How did* Faithful *come to be, and did the project have as many ups and downs as the baseball season itself?*

Stewart O'Nan: *Faithful* came out of last year's [2003] stretch run. The Sox got hot, and Steve and I both got excited and ended up e-mailing back and forth nearly every day, picking game situations apart.

The project itself was a steady effort. When the team was going good, there was a lot to talk about (like Bellhorn stepping up in April and May); and when the team was going bad, there was even more to talk about (June and July). Plus, this year there were so many storylines. The difficult thing was limiting ourselves. We're talking 30 preseason, 162 regular season and 14 postseason games in 400 pages, with two of us writing. Trying to stay concise without losing that loose, informal feel of a conversation was a challenge.

DL: *You grew up a Pirates fan, yet your devotion to the Red Sox seems as intense as any "lifers." How can you explain this?*

SO: I think any Sox fan who's with the team for more than, say, 15 years, naturally takes on our past, our tradition and identity, which goes all the way back. And that's true for the Pirates, too. As a kid, I learned to appreciate what Honus Wagner and Arky Vaughan and the Waner brothers meant to the team and to the city. As a Sox fan, I'm a Johnny Pesky fan, and a George Scott fan, and a Bernie Carbo fan, even if I wasn't around then.

DL: *It is well known that Stephen King is a Sox fanatic. How did your friendship evolve—specifically from a baseball standpoint—and how would you describe the differences and similarities in the way the two of you view the team and the game?*

SO: As writers, we had a long-distance professional relationship, but as fans we sit elbow to elbow and riff off each other, buy each other Sports Bars, point out a change in the out-of-town scores to each other. We share a huge pool of pop culture, so we're a good comedy duo, or a drive-time radio team, always topping each other's last crack. The biggest difference in the way we see the game is geographical. Steve, being a lifelong New Englander, is always waiting for the worst to happen, where I, coming from the land of Maz and Clemente, always see the possibility of the best. But, paradoxically, he's way more volatile, as if, once he's finally got his hopes up, he's mad that he's been let down. I'm a little steadier, a little sunnier, though that's not true when it comes to umpiring. Steve's much nicer to Blue, while my standards may be inhuman.

DL: *Early in the book, Stephen muses that, "I'm a Red Sox junkie . . . and if [they] win the World Series this year, this forty-year obsession of mine may break like a long-term malarial fever." Prediction?*

SO: No way. The guy's hooked.

DL: *And yourself—does anything change?*

SO: The biggest change will probably be how packed spring training's gonna be, and how tough it'll be to get into Fenway. And I'm not talking just '05, I'm talking 10, 20 years down the line.

DL: *In the book, you talk about your fishing net and how many balls you captured in batting practice last year. Tell us about that, and then explain how you're really just a normal person who likes baseball.*

SO: I get bored easily, and I like to be involved in what's going on. If I'm going to be at the game, I want to do anything I can to be part of it as well as pass the time pleasantly. Shagging BP adds a little challenge and excitement to being at the park. Anyone who's been on the Monster for BP can tell you it's a blast, but I actually get more balls right down on the field, reaching over the low wall down along the left-field line. That's the beauty of Fenway: you're so close that you can snag grounders. I even got one from Tony Clark in fair territory. You just can't do that in other parks. Over the season I picked about 120. What can I say? I'm compulsive.

DL: *Your all-time favorite Red Sox players—you can pick three.*

SO: Jim Rice, Mo Vaughn, David Ortiz (with honorable mentions to Pedro, Manny, and Johnny).

DL: *Most Valuable Player on the 2004 Red Sox.*

SO: Hands down, Manny. Without him, El Jefe just doesn't see the same pitches. From the first day of spring training, Manny led our exercises. Every game, he was the first guy out of the dugout. Always goofing, always smiling. Don't let him fool you: He works his ass off to make it all look offhand. And just a genius of a hitter. Hall of Famer, no doubt.

DL: *What did you think last winter when we put Manny on waivers?— tell the truth.*

SO: I thought it was disrespectful. Manny and Papi carried us last year, too. Sure, it's a monster contract, but it's not like we're Baltimore looking at Albert Belle or the Mets looking at Mo. Manny's always produced, even when opponents swear they won't let him beat them.

DL: *You get to be Theo for a day, and Oakland offers you either Tim Hudson or Barry Zito for Bronson Arroyo, Hanley Ramirez, and a mid-level prospect. You say . . .*

SO: We'll take Hudson. And: Sorry, Bronson. Hanley's a slick glove but he's not knocking the stuffing out of the ball in Double A.

DL: *Back to* Faithful *for a minute. You opined early in the season that "Daubach's our Lou [Merloni] now." Talk about that.*

SO: Lou was always trying to crack the starting lineup, doing anything he could to help the team, only to get sent to Pawtucket. Dauber had to battle Tony Clark and then Jeremy Giambi for the spot he'd basically earned. He earned it again, only to get dissed. Likewise, this year he made the club with a solid spring and was batting fifth as late as June, only to end up buried in Pawtucket and buried even deeper when we picked up Mientkiewicz. You've got to respect Dauber busting his hump to be on this team. He could have gone anywhere else and made the roster (okay, not the Yankees), but he came back here and did his best.

DL: *You also wrote that Mark Bellhorn was "the guy they hoped Jeremy Giambi would be." What is your opinion on the team's second base position?*

SO: Obviously, Bellhorn did a great job, despite his 177 Ks. His runs and RBIs from the position were the best in the league, and while he's no Pokey, he made plays that Todd Walker wouldn't have had a chance at. He also filled that number two slot that Billy Mueller somehow can't wrap his head around. So big props to Marky Mark, and screw the boo-birds.

DL: *Speaking of Giambis, what are your thoughts on his more famous older brother's current situation?*

SO: I'm glad that he's gotten off the stuff. It's the right way to go, even if it means he'll never be the player he was. Ken Caminiti died at age 41, and that's just too young. The other players who are still on the juice had better wise up. It ain't worth it. And it would be nice if MLB went the way of the NCAA and took away all the wins of teams with juiced players. Meaning that, yes, we'd rightfully be the 2003 AL champs. And the AL East champs at least three years running. Take it from Slappy A-Rod: Cheaters never win.

DL: *Do you think Nomar ever juiced? And now that he's gone [and has recently re-signed with the Cubbies], is he really better than Jeter?*

SO: I've never thought of Nomar as being involved with that type of cheating. When he was healthy, he was as good as Jeter, and because Jeter's been surrounded by so much more talent, Nomar always had to carry more weight. In that sense, he was more valuable (and therefore better in that way) than Jeter. In the same way, Papi is so much more valuable than Sheffield because if Papi doesn't step up big, we have to rely on our 5 through 9 guys. We didn't really have a number 5 guy this year, while the Yanks had Matsui and Bernie back there to mop up. This meant that Sheffield could take walks or swing at his leisure, while Papi couldn't.

DL: *You wrote that "It's amazing how loud you have to yell at the TV in order for the players to hear you." Is this indicative of what it's like in your household, and do you look at this ruefully or as a badge of honor?*

SO: That's me. I get a little worked up and forget I'm not at the park. It's embarrassing sometimes, especially if I rush the set as if I can get closer to the action and let loose a blast of swearing. But when Millar drops a fricking pop-up, what am I supposed to do, just sit there? As a fan, you're part of the game, even if you're by yourself listening to it on the radio. When Joe says something, he's saying it to you, so it's just natural that you'd say something back.

DL: *You often sport a PawSox cap. How often do you see Pawtucket play, and do you ever catch a Sea Dogs game with Stephen King?*

SO: I only see the PawSox once or twice a summer at McCoy. I catch a lot of the Twins' Double A New Britain Rock Cats' games and always take in three or four with the Sea Dogs, but with my son Steph, not Steve.

DL: *We just experienced the most exhilarating and draining postseason ever. How hard was it to write your book entries on little sleep, with the adrenaline flowing?*

SO: Easy, because everything was burned into my brain. Indelible.

DL: *How many of the postseason games were you at, and what are your favorite memories—and stories—from them?*

SO: I made it to all our home games plus Game 7 at Yankee Stadium. My favorite memories are Papi's three walk-offs. My favorite playoff storyline is definitely Mark Bellhorn's, who made the boo-birds shut the hell up. And Derek Lowe turning his whole half-assed season around in four amazing games.

DL: *Stephen writes in* Faithful *about how superstitious he is about baseball. Does that mean he'll be suggesting a sequel in 2005, and could you afford to say "no" if he does?*

SO: No, no sequel, but I bet he wears that Youkilis shirt till it's in tatters.

DL: *Two more: If you and Stephen played for the Sox, which positions would you play? And why?*

SO: Steve would be a first baseman—a big target and a big stick. I'd be where I've been since I was 10—third base. Good reactions, decent glove, strong arm.

DL: *Last one: What do you want for Christmas?*

SO: Okay, this is embarrassing, but I want a WEEI "We Always Believed" button. I've got the "We Believe" and the "We Still Believe," but I must have been inside the park by the time they were handing out the last one before the World Series home games.

Oh yeah, and an "Idiots Rule" poster from WBCN. I'm a sucker for that freebie stuff.

Thanks, and SIGN TEK!

Bob Ryan

Bob Ryan is a sports reporter for the *Boston Globe* and the author of several books, including *When Boston Won the World Series*. A graduate of Trinity College, the London School of Economics and Boston College Law School, Ryan has been with the *Globe* since 1968. This interview took place in October 2004, after the World Series.

David Laurila: *You've been covering the Boston sports scene for more than 30 years. Where would you place the Red Sox' 2004 World Series championship from a historical perspective?*

Bob Ryan: Since I began covering in 1969, we have had five Celtics' titles, two Stanley Cups and two Super Bowls. I was also in town for the 1965, 1966, 1968, and 1969 Celtics' championships. Nothing measures up to the Boston Red Sox winning the World Series, for reasons almost everyone reading this already knows.

The ongoing futility of the Red Sox was always an interesting story, but it took on a significantly larger import following the events of 1978 and 1986. Increased media coverage created a fandom that became fixated on the inability of the team to win it all, and the whole "curse" thing took on a new life of its own when Dan Shaughnessy wrote his book 14 years ago. Let's get something straight. He did not come up with the idea. He appropriated it. No one knows where it came from. It's like those dirty jokes that are supposed to get their start in prison. No one has a clue where they come from; they just appear. I first heard of a phenomenon called "the curse of the Bambino" in 1983. I heard it from a friend of a friend with whom I had become acquainted. His name is Darrell Berger, and at the time he was a functioning Unitarian–Universalist minister practicing in Scituate, Mass. As he explained what he had heard, the selling of Babe Ruth to the Yankees in January of 1920 was "an original sin from which there could be no redemption." I was in e-mail contact with him about six or eight weeks ago. He now lives in Connecticut. I asked him if he could recall where he had first heard it, and he could not. Nor can anyone else.

Just to set the record straight. When the Red Sox lost the Series in 1967, there was no talk of a curse. Nor was there curse talk when they lost to the Reds in the great 1975 World Series. However much it was hanging out there, it was only a minor part of the story until Dan's book. The idea of the Red Sox being peculiarly "cursed" probably took on its present form with the events of the 10th inning in Shea. Things heated up in 2003 with the Grady/Pedro contretemps. Aaron Boone being such a minor part of the Yankee things exacerbated it further. I think people could have accepted that ending a wee bit better if Derek or Bernie or Jorge hit the HR. Anyway, the whole thing had grown to enormous heights. It had dominated the Red Sox dialogue for years, even though any rational person knows there was no such thing as a curse.

So the 86-year business was one thing. The second thing making this the biggest story in our town's sports history is the general love affair this region has had with baseball, dating from the 1870s. As the nation switched from a baseball country to a football country, Boston kept the faith, even with a pair of Super Bowls serving as a nice distraction. Baseball matters here. People enjoy seeing it played well, and winning the World Series simply had more resonance than winning any other of the three titles, because so many people here appreciate the nuances of the best sport there has ever been. Baseball is the greatest game ever to spring from the mind of mortal man. Never forget that.

Thirdly, there is this tremendous generational thing. My great-grandfather, grandfather, father, uncle, great-grandmother, grandmother, mother, aunt, etc., etc., etc. With no other sport, in no other locale, is there anything to match the generational baseball torch that has been passed along by so many in New England. Add it all up, and you get this championship being the best sports story, and perhaps even the best (positive) New England/Boston story, since the Boston Tea Party in 1775.

DL: *Was this the most talented Red Sox team you've seen, or did it win because of intangibles that others didn't possess? Why were they able to do what the '46, '67, '75, '78, '86, and '03 teams couldn't?*

BR: I'm not sure if this a better hitting team, in or out of league and other context, than the 1978 squad. There have been equal or better defensive teams. But the reason this team got the job done was a pitching staff none of the others could match. The '86 1-2-3 of Clemens-Hurst-Oil Can matches up pretty well, but Al Nipper versus Wake? I don't think so. Calvin Schiraldi versus Foulke? I don't think so. The other '86 middle guys versus Timlin-Embree-Myers-Arroyo? I don't think so. I also like this team's bench, starting with Doug Mirabelli, the best backup catcher in the league, if not all of baseball. And no other Sox team had Dave Roberts. Top to bottom, this team is the best I've seen in 40 years of watching Red Sox baseball.

DL: *The 86-year quest for a title—"the curse"—was a big part of the team's appeal, especially from a national perspective. Now that we've won, how will fans across the country view the Red Sox in years to come?*

BR: Fans across the country have framed the Red Sox in terms of the C-word; there is no doubt. So that will change. Now they will be regarded by many as a Have with the number-two payroll. Forget about any cuddly stuff. The Red Sox will be viewed as a behemoth, the 1-A Yankees. So?

DL: *What about here in Red Sox Nation? Will we retain a core of diehard fans, but lose the interest of many casual followers? Should ownership and businesses that depend on the baseball dollar be concerned?*

BR: There has long been a theory hanging out there that the worst thing that could ever happen to the Red Sox is for them to win, because their fans would then lose their *raison d'être,* which is to feel sorry for themselves. Bullshit! What two-cent philosophical drivel. I think most people prefer winning to almost winning. I think that another title will please people immensely. I think these core fans will be just as capable of becoming smug as any Yankee fan if the Red Sox go on a championship roll. I think auxiliary businesses will boom.

DL: *Did Theo, Francona, and the ownership just win a free pass, or will people still call for their heads when the team loses four straight? And is there any chance that the team can now safely cut some costs and rebuild through the farm system?*

BR: There are rumors of a (somewhat) reduced payroll, which I cannot verify personally. They are rebuilding the farm system, by the way. You're asking me to predict how people will react if things get a bit rocky next year. We're in new territory now. I would guess people will cut them some slack. Just a guess.

DL: *One-word question: Steinbrenner.*

BR: The Boss' number-one thing is winning. The Boss' number-two thing is doing all he can to prevent the Red Sox (read Lucchino, primarily) from winning. He must be livid. The Red Sox have won on what I'm sure he regarded as his watch, and I'm sure he's furious. Look out.

DL: *Of all the players you've seen in a Red Sox uniform, which would you have most liked to see be a part of a championship team?*

BR: Bob Stanley. He should have been Foulke, receiving the congrats. Yaz, I suppose. He put his heart and soul into it for 23 years. Ted, it goes without saying. But, for me, Bob Stanley is number one. He was Everyman with a bowling ball sinker.

DL: *Who did you think of when the final out of the Series was recorded?*

BR: Lou Gorman. A wonderful guy from Rhode Island who built a championship team that was one strike short.

DL: *Putting aside your journalist's hat for a moment, what did Bob Ryan, the fan, think about when it ended? What did you do?*

BR: I am well-known in the business for having a strong fan sensibility. I had Celtics season tickets for 22 years, and I've had four in Section 19 since 1991. So what can I say? I was immensely pleased.

DL: *Beating the Yankees was, by itself, a huge moment in Red Sox history. What would the reaction have been had we lost to the Cardinals? Would Red Sox Nation have gone into the off-season satisfied or with an empty feeling?*

BR: This one bugs me. I know there was a minority of fans who would have been satisfied with just beating the Yankees, but this is idiotic. The object is to win the World Series. I do not have the requisite hate-N.Y. DNA that produces such a ludicrous thought process.

DL: *Could A-Rod knocking the ball out of Bronson Arroyo's glove become symbolic of a "new world order" in Red Sox versus Yankees? Could that play remain frozen in time as a defining moment in the rivalry?*

BR: Very likely.

DL: *What happens if A-Rod is in a Boston uniform, and Manny is in Texas? Or what if the Nomar trade never happens? Do you have any thoughts on either "what if"?*

BR: No title. That's pretty obvious. I was happy to see Manny go at the time. I wrote that. I also didn't know what the baseball feeling was concerning A-Rod. Now I do. The Red Sox were phenomenally lucky to have things turn out as they did.

DL: *It's always seemed as though a Red Sox championship would result in a statue being erected in Faneuil Hall (Dave Henderson in '86?). Who gets immortalized now that it's happened?*

BR: Well, let's see. Schilling? There's one. D-Lowe? Ortiz? And there should be a bust, at the very least, of Dave Roberts. Pedro gets something for seven years of meritorious service. Oh, and Theo, of course.

DL: *Could you draw parallels between any of the 2004 Red Sox and players who have worn the uniform previously?*

BR: Schilling is Cy Young. Varitek is Pudge. Actually, Varitek is closer to Jimmy Collins, because he, too, could be a legit player-manager—right now. Ortiz is somewhere between Ted and Jimmie Foxx. D-Lowe in the '04 playoffs was Lonborg in '67. Mueller is Pesky. Manny is absolutely sui generis. Damon? Piersall, with more power, but not quite the arm (admittedly, something of a reach). Millar? Dick Stuart's running buddy. Pedro is Smokey Joe, but it's really more the Pedro of '98–00 and the Smokey Joe of '12 than it is the current Pedro.

DL: *It's the end of the world as we know it for Red Sox Nation, and perhaps the local sports scene as a whole. But what about the Boston sports media? What are some of the changes you foresee going forward?*

BR: Most of us will be fine. Nothing will change. But one of us must now confront a world in which his fundamental assumptions have now changed forever. Guess who.

DL: *Last question: With apologies to Bobby Thomson, what are your thoughts on "The Shot (of Jack Daniels) Heard 'Round the World?"*

BR: I envision a ceremonial passing of a cup, nothing more. If that was the case. Bravo!

ROBERT SULLIVAN

ROBERT SULLIVAN IS DEPUTY MANAGING EDITOR OF *LIFE* MAGA-
ZINE AND EDITORIAL DIRECTOR OF *LIFE* BOOKS. A ONE-TIME
WRITER FOR *SPORTS ILLUSTRATED*, SULLIVAN IS ALSO THE
AUTHOR OF SEVERAL BOOKS, INCLUDING *OUR RED SOX*, A MEM-
OIR OF ONE FAN'S—AND HIS FAMILY'S—LOVE AFFAIR WITH THE
TEAM. THIS INTERVIEW TOOK PLACE IN MAY 2005.

David Laurila: *Let's start with one of the memorable stories in the book— the foul ball incident at LaLacheur Park in Lowell. What happened, and why were you there?*

Robert Sullivan: Well, we were there to introduce our older daughter, Caroline, to baseball. She was three-and-a-half in the spring of 2001, and I felt it was time to take her to the ballpark. I thought of Fenway, of course, but figured the sensory overload of a big league game might be a bit much for her. Let's start quieter, more pastoral. Plus, with all the fun things the minor leagues do for kids now—the contests, the mascots roaming around—that seemed to be the way to go. My wife, Lucille, and I are both from Chelmsford, though we now live in Westchester County, outside New York City. So we thought we'd bring Caroline back home, to the Merrimack Valley, and start teaching her the reasons for the BoSox. I scored tickets to the Lowell Spinners, the Sox' Single A short-season team in that beautiful new ballpark they built by a bend in the Merrimack. Everything was perfect: warm Friday night, Caroline all excited, Lucille and I just as proud and happy as can be. And then, yes, she's out in the play area with her mom, and Caroline gets whacked in the side of the head by a 310-foot foul ball that faded over the short left-field fence. Goes down like a shot. She and I spent the night in Saints Memorial Hospital, after the CT scan and all the other tests showed negative. Her first sports concussion—if she takes after her dad, the first of too many. She's fine now, and still a diehard Sox fan. Some good came out of it: The Spinners put up netting in left so foul balls can't get into the kids' play area any more. The Spinners fans of Lowell are safe, thanks to Caroline.

DL: *Tell us about growing up in the Chelmsford/Lowell area and your indoctrination into Red Sox Nation.*

RS: When my brother, sister, and I grew up in Chelmsford, it was much more rural, much more of a farm town than it is today. The folks from Chelmsford, like my dad, went in to Lowell to earn their wage. Now, most of them go in toward Boston or 128. My brother and I, when the family lived in West Chelmsford, enjoyed what I remember as Huck Finn summers: fishing down by the Red House on Stony Brook, home run derbies in the middle of the street, lots of poison ivy. It's funny how the memories came back once I got into writing the book. I hadn't thought about the Earl Wilson no-hitter for years. But once I was into this stream-of-consciousness thing with the book, it was like 1962 was yesterday: I heard the mosquitoes buzzing, heard the screen-door slam, heard my dad call Kevin and me over to the radio to listen to the final outs. Same for that first game at Fenway, when Dad took us to see Ted Williams play before Ted retired. It was very much like Gammons recalling in his foreword [to *Our Red Sox*] when he first went to Fenway. All the sounds and smells come back instantly. It was funny, when Gammons' foreword came in, to see how so much of what he recalled from growing up as a Sox fan down the road in Groton was similar to what I remembered from Chelmsford. That's part of what's behind the book: This Rashomon quality of being a Sox fan and seeing it all the same, but also individually and different. *Our Red Sox* is only one version of millions.

DL: *You now live in Yankees territory. When driving north to attend games at Fenway, are you (to use a baseball metaphor) going home—or escaping?*

RS: Both, no question. And in that order. Going home to Chelmsford, Lowell, Boston is more important to me than escaping New York. The Yankees excepted, I really do like most everything else about life down here. Lucille and I both left New England around 1980, so we've been New York–centric, living in the city and now outside it, for a long while now—more than a quarter century. But our extended families are still back up there, and we love to go back. As far as traveling back, you can do that physically or mentally. We visit, and it's always terrific. That's physically. But I listen to the Sox game from TIC in Hartford, and I'm back up there, even if I'm weeding or raking or playing catch with Jack in the backyard. When Joe and Jerry tell me Foulke just gave up a two-run shot in Texas and it's now 6-5, I'm back listening in Chelmsford with my dad, even though it's really Jack listening with his dad in Westchester County, and my dad's listening from Heaven. This make any sense?

The book was another way of going home. Every morning and evening between Halloween and Christmas, working on the book, I was back up in New England. And 9-to-5, I was very much in New York. When the publisher offered me a chance to try this thing, I found this aspect of the work irresistible. To revisit it all. And also, I figured he had given me an opportunity to do something that I could hand to our three kids, so they might know a bit more about a grandfather they won't get to know, and also a bit more about where their parents are from. Our heritage.

You know what it is? It's the narrative that I wish I had from my own dad from 1946, when he, fresh from the Army, was going to Fenway almost every night with Mom to watch Ted Williams lead that great team to the Series. The publisher gave me a chance to do that for Caroline, Mary Grace, and Jack.

DL: *Perspective gets pretty clouded when it's Red Sox versus Yankees. Can you imagine watching without prejudice—or malice—when the two rivals do battle? And what would it mean if you could?*

RS: I can't imagine watching without prejudice but I do know what it's like to watch without malice. When the book takes a little turn there after the middle, and we're about to head into the 2003 and then '04 ALCSs, I took a step back to try to figure out what this Sox–Yanks thing had become. I mean, we burn cars and riot in Kenmore these days. What's that about? This is the section where I fess up that, as a kid, I used to root for the Mick. I'd root for him to hit a homer in the top half of the inning and for Yaz to answer with one in the bottom. My dad couldn't figure out my thinking, but . . . well, Mickey Mantle, right? The Mick.

And also, even these days: It's sometimes difficult to properly hate a Torre-managed team. I do hate them, of course, but it's sometimes hard. It's a bit easier now with Sheffield and Giambi and A-Rod and Randy than it was a few years back when it was right-down-the-lineup class—Jeter, Tino, Mariano, O'Neill, Bernie, Georgie. They've made it easier, but until the Boss cans Joe—any day now?—it'll always be a little bit tough. A little bit.

DL: *In the book, you write about not waking your young daughter, as promised, after Game 7 in 2003. You say that "She has plenty of time to be a Red Sox fan." What impact might the 2004 championship have on both the generational bonding and mystique we've long experienced as New Englanders?*

RS: I can't tell you how easy it is to be a young New England fan right now. My daughter Caroline's an absolute villain in her second-grade class at Westorchard School, as are Mary Grace and Jack at Jennie's School for Little Children. Caroline's seven, and she's got a World Series win and three Super Bowls in her pocket. Lucille and I tell the kids how long we've waited, and they just don't get it. To them, we're nothing but winners, eternal champions.

Jack's experience is instructive. Last summer, he's four, so he's hearing from all the other boys about the Yankees, and he sees the Evil Empire insignia everywhere. He sometimes has trouble putting on his B-hat. He could do without the grief. And being four, he of course wants to tease his dad. So sometimes he's telling me with a grin, "Daddy, I'm a Yankeeees fan." And I joke about how he has to move out of the house, and then we go on to whatever's next.

But in the fall, when it's Sox–Yanks again in the ALCS, Jack senses sometime more consequential is going on, and he's firmly with the Sox—especially when, down 3–zip, Daddy's so bummed out. He showed great forbearance and sympathy at that point, and I don't think it was just because he'd get a major time-out if he gave me any Yankees static just then. Then, when we win and I give the kids that little lecture about not gloating at school—not rubbing it in—Jack is hooked for life. He's sitting there, B-hat on, T-shirt on, big smile, ready to hit Jennie's School and let 'em know the news.

You see, Lucille and I are dedicated to the proposition that we can raise New Englanders in New York State. It's kind of a sociological experiment, and that's a big underlying theme in the book. We may be right, we may be wrong. Time will tell. But I'll tell you, the Sox and Yanks and this whole passion-play they've been enacting recently are making it a helluva lot easier. The lines are clearly drawn. It's us and them.

DL: *Many of us agree that radio baseball is great. Why do you think that is?*

RS: I think it's the pace of the game and the shape of the field. When Joe or Jerry—or Ned, Ken, Curt—gives you the situation, you have time to picture it. That can't be done with hockey or basketball. And then you put it in a setting, preferably Fenway. I can listen to football in the car and, between plays, I can figure out that Troy is split and Tom's in a shotgun and we need eight. But it's more of an equation than a picture. A football field's a football field. It's a grid. Fenway sits there in your mind, and when Joe says the ball has been released, you're actually watching the whole field. On TV, you'd just be seeing the batter. You know when it's best? When Wakefield's pitching. It takes so awfully long for the ball to reach the plate, it's delicious.

DL: *Your father loved players with good character. Who were some of his favorites, and who are yours—both past and present?*

RS: His favorite was Ted. Stuff like being surly and spitting at the fans, those were small things for Dad, inconsequential. What mattered was: war hero, raised millions for kids with cancer. I remember when Cramer's bio of Joe DiMaggio came out, Dad called me and said, "See! Our guy was classier than their guy, after all!" Image meant nothing to Dad. Deeds counted. He thought, for instance, that Jim Lonborg was classy. He heard Radatz was a good guy, and so always rooted for Radatz. Earl Wilson helping the retirees—Dad heard about that, and so he was glad that, long ago, he had been in Wilson's camp. "I was glad he did so well in Detroit," he told me once, reminiscing about Wilson. Dad enjoyed our "characters"—the Hawks, Oil Cans, and Spacemen of Red Sox history. He was amused by them. But it was the classy guys he supported.

For me? I had a great seat at Yankee Stadium two years ago, right by the Sox dugout. It was Dr. Charles' box for the night, in fact. Dick Durrell and Jay Emmett set it up; I was in pretty good company that night. Doesn't happen often. Anyway, before the game, two Sox are down at our end of the dugout, reaching around and signing autographs for the kids. Only two. Any guesses? Manny and Papi. It's not hard, of course, but I've been firmly in their corner ever since. Stan goads me that Manny won't run out pop-ups, or is a terrible fielder, and I ask him whether Sheffield signs for the kids. In fact, Manny I get a double kick out of: He amuses me as a character, and of course it's pretty easy to root for him as a game-breaker.

My favorite is Wakefield. There's a bit about this in the book, and some more in a piece I posted on *time.com* after the Fenway opener and then the Patriots Day game this year. It's called "Our Red Sox, Still?"—in case your readers want a free taste—and it's about whether the team, as world champs, is turning into a national team. You know: "Fever Pitch," Johnny Media Superstar—all that stuff. Or is it still New England's team? Anyway, we all know about Wake's charity work. But there was some interesting stuff about the high regard that Torre has for him, and how Torre called him in the clubhouse after Game 7 of last year's ALCS. If the enemy feels that way about you, you're special. And just the guts it takes to throw another knuckler after someone's just sent one 500 feet. I mean, that's character.

DL: *Your book begins with a passage by Herman Melville and a foreword by Peter Gammons. Tell us about each.*

RS: Well, I thought the Melville quote was kind of a miracle: I figured it meant that he was a Sox fan. All of that suffering, and coming 'round again to where we were as boys, and staying constant, and all that. But, of course, he predated not only King Kelly but Cartwright, so that's unlikely. But I felt that it set a nice tone up front, not least because, I hoped, it would be taken humorously—from *Moby-Dick,* a book about Massachusetts and mission. My editor tried to talk me out of it, but I said, oh, let's leave it in. I thought it started things off okay. Who knows? My editor might've been right.

Peter was an early friend in this trade, but I hadn't seen him in years. When I started this particular piece of writing, I remembered distinctly an essay that Peter had written in 1986 after the Sox had lost. I was convinced, in that recall, that Peter, revisiting those emotions, was just right to lead off this book—if he would agree. He agreed in one minute, and it was nice to get back in touch. It was very nice to exchange copies with him after opening day—that great opening day—in Fenway. He was down on the field getting ready to do his ESPN report, and it was nice to see him again and think about the old days at the Eliot Lounge.

DL: *To close, you're passing on the torch to your own children. Tell us how baseball—winning, losing and how you play the game—can be used as a teaching tool. You touched on that a bit earlier. Does the game truly mirror life?*

RS: I'm not sure. What I'm sure of is this: Sports can help as metaphor, and also as boundaries. It's odd to end this interview with a quote from a different sport, but I was once doing a piece on Ray Floyd. And he told me that he brought up his kids, in life and in golf, with this adage: "Live your life by the rules of the game." That's right. The rules say, play fair, don't cheat, don't lie, don't gloat, don't brag, call 'em right, close calls go to your opponent (well, that's tennis), be polite, be competitive, be energetic, concentrate, shake hands. That, in 2005, is the way one family of Red Sox fans in Westchester County is trying to proceed.

Shorter Views

JOHN MANUEL

JOHN MANUEL IS THE EDITOR-IN-CHIEF OF *BASEBALL AMERICA*. CONSIDERED THE FOREMOST AUTHORITY ON AMATEUR BASEBALL AND THE MINOR LEAGUES, *BASEBALL AMERICA* IS AVAILABLE IN PRINT AND ONLINE, AND ALSO PUBLISHES SEVERAL BOOKS ANNUALLY. THIS IS AN EXCERPT FROM AN INTERVIEW THAT TOOK PLACE IN JANUARY 2006.

David Laurila: *What is* Baseball America's *mission statement?*

John Manuel: Ha! Mission statement . . . Jerry McGuire would call it more of a memo. We don't have an official one, but here's what I tell prospective employees/interns: *BA* covers baseball at all levels from a player-development point of view. When we're judging high school and college players, we're doing it with that in mind. In fact, our college coverage is the only time we even care who wins the games, outside of the Major Leagues.

DL: *How would you describe your target audience?*

JM: Our target audience is anyone who follows baseball as their favorite sport. We are cognizant of the fact that we're considered by most in the baseball industry as the de facto publication of record. We try to live up to that responsibility.

DL: *How much has the focus of your coverage changed over the years, specifically the amount given to the Major Leagues and amateur baseball?*

JM: Our Major League coverage waxes and wanes. Our amateur coverage just keeps growing, and I'd say is the area where we've had the most growth. Think of it this way: five *BA* staffers have worked there for nine years or more: Jim Callis, Will Lingo, Alan Schwarz, myself (nine years), then Allan Simpson. Three of us, Jim, Alan, and I, have covered college baseball extensively. For me, it was almost exclusively my beat for six seasons. *BA* is even more of a leader in college baseball coverage than we are in minor league coverage, and our coverage of the draft—which is essentially an amateur exercise—well, we invented baseball draft coverage and remain the leader in that regard. If we're not, then I've failed, and I hope that's not the case.

DL: Baseball America *has a reputation of greatly favoring tools over performance when putting together its annual player rankings. How accurate is that belief, and has the* Moneyball *approach had much impact on those assessments?*

JM: (A) *BA* is not a monolith. We have many different writers who contribute to the *Handbook* and our prospect rankings, and each one brings subtle differences in approach. (B) If one person guides our rankings the most, it is Jim Callis—that's been true since Jim's return to *BA* in 1999. Jim can't say "blend" enough. He has statistical savvy and knows the bat is the most important tool. Jim does a great job of making sure we incorporate statistical analysis into our prospect rankings. To say we "greatly favor" tools over performance is wrong. It may have been true, say, 10–15 years ago, but we were making adjustments long before *Moneyball*.

DL: *Your ratings and player profiles are put together with input from scouts and organizational staff. With the number of prospects you cover, that makes for a lot of conversations. What can you tell us about that process, including just how much information, and from how many sources, you typically get for each prospect?*

JM: It just takes a lot of time. This year, I did four organizations. I had input from at least four in-house sources for each organization, and at least two from outside each organization. For some, I had to go more to scouts outside the organization. That helps in some ways—scouts outside an organization usually have 1 or 2 mph less on their guns than the organization might, if it's trying to give you the sunny side on a player. But they also have a harder time getting to know makeup. The best source is an in-house source who isn't afraid to say, "No, that guy is not a player." The worst is like one farm director this fall told me, when I asked what made a player a good defender. He replied, "Wow, who wants to know that?"

DL: *Tell us a little about your background and John Manuel the baseball fan.*

JM: Quick bio: Born and raised in North Carolina, son of Greek immigrants (dismayed by the way Greeks are represented by one Major League owner), married, father of one, Red Sox fan since I was three, able to let it go some after 2004 and pull back a bit. Also a University of North Carolina alum, so in 2004–05, I had a son, the Red Sox World Series, North Carolina's national title, and a promotion to editor-in-chief. I had about as good a year as I could hope for.

JAYSON STARK

JAYSON STARK IS A SENIOR WRITER AT ESPN AND FREQUENT CONTRIBUTOR TO SPORTSCENTER AND BASEBALL TONIGHT. WITH THE PHILADELPHIA INQUIRER BEFORE JOINING ESPN, STARK ONCE COVERED THE RED SOX FOR THE PROVIDENCE JOURNAL. THIS IS AN EXCERPT FROM AN INTERVIEW THAT TOOK PLACE IN JANUARY 2005.

David Laurila: *Let's start with your thoughts on Pedro Martinez. Why did he ultimately sign with the Mets, and at what point did he decide to leave Boston?*

Jayson Stark: You can sum up why Pedro signed with the Mets in one word: $$$$$. Hmmm, is that a word? In my column at the time, I essentially accused Pedro of using the Red Sox to cajole the Mets into overpaying—and of leading them on with no apparent sincerity. But I now believe he'd have stayed had they matched the Mets' offer. On that Saturday night in December, when the Red Sox agreed to meet virtually all his demands, they thought he was staying. Instead, he took their offer back to the Mets and used it to parlay another year—and another $12.5 million—out of Omar. I don't think Pedro knew he was leaving until the Mets went to the fourth year—and the Red Sox then balked at that. But staying sure wasn't a big priority for him, either, obviously.

DL: *Beyond the negotiation ploys, what was Pedro's interest in the Yankees? And did either George Steinbrenner or Brian Cashman want him in pinstripes?*

JS: It was a ploy all the way. It was all about driving up the price, because he had to know the Yankees weren't interested. *He's* the one (or at least Fernando Cuza was the one) who asked to meet with the Yankees—not George. George only agreed to do it because it helped drive up the price for the Red Sox or Mets, whichever signed him. And George loves seeing those teams overspend. I never heard one member of the Yankees' baseball operation express any interest in Pedro. Not one.

DL: *Jason Varitek inked a four-year, $40 million contract, while A.J. Pierzynski was released and only recently signed a one-year deal for $2.25 million with the White Sox. How do people in the game view their respective leadership qualities, and how much does that outweigh their hitting and receiving skills? Does either get more credit, or criticism, than is warranted?*

JS: Just taped a "Sunday Conversation" with Curt Schilling, and when Varitek came up, Schilling said: "If Jason had left, we'd have had no chance to repeat. None." So does that answer that question? Varitek is the most prepared catcher in the league. I like A.J. personally, but his lack of preparation killed his chances of staying in San Francisco. I don't think people overrate catchers who relate to and inspire their pitchers. If anything, that's underrated.

DL: *How many more players can we expect to be implicated in the BALCO scandal?*

JS: It depends on what you mean by "implicated." We already know the names. The guys who were subpoenaed are the only players who have been linked to the case. And none of those players was indicted. So most are just names on the witness list. But Barry and Giambi are different, and possibly Sheffield. Barry was the inspiration for the case, the object of most of the leaks and a prosecution target in many ways. BALCO is his worst nightmare. He'll be damaged by BALCO. The only question now is how seriously. But he has more than his reputation to worry about. Those prosecutors intimated strongly in their grand-jury inquisition that they believed he was perjuring himself by claiming he didn't know what he was taking. So a perjury charge is not out of the question. Sheffield could be in the same boat, since he also claimed he didn't know. Or they may use him to get Barry. Giambi has probably avoided being implicated legally by being so extensive and truthful in his testimony. But his career and his reputation are down the tubes forever now. How can this guy possibly play out his contract? He isn't going away, because he isn't forfeiting the money. But who would want to be him? Not me.

DL: *Last one: What did your Hall of Fame ballot look like? Was Ryne Sandberg a no-brainer, and is either Jim Rice or Bruce Sutter worthy of induction?*

JS: Here's my ballot: Boggs, Sandberg, Bruce Sutter, Andre Dawson, Jim Rice, Jack Morris, Dale Murphy. As I've written, I voted for Rice for the first time. I've never thought it was fair—or even humane—to force these guys to spend 15 years on the ballot. But over time, the candidacies of other players—and the perspective I gained from looking back on Rice's career from a distance—helped give me a different take on his career. All these players from the late seventies and the eighties are getting screwed by the voters in some way because their numbers look so wimpy compared to the stats players put up today. So I've become more determined than ever to judge them against their peers. If that's the case, how could I possibly not vote for Rice, when he was by far the dominant hitter in his league for 12 years? And six top-five finishes in the MVP voting—that finally put me over the top. Not sure if he'll ever make it. But next year is a big, big opening for him or one of these perennial near-miss candidates to get in—because I don't see Orel Hershiser or Albert Belle sailing in there on the first ballot. Maybe Albert will actually help Rice—because he was kind of the Jim Rice of his generation. Then again, some voters might decide that's not good.

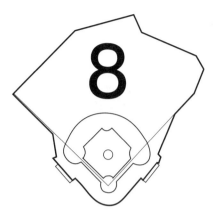

Fans and Family

KELLY BARONS

KELLY BARONS IS A RED SOX BALL ATTENDANT AND FENWAY PARK AMBASSADOR. A NATIVE OF LEXINGTON, MASSACHUSETTS, BARONS WORKS FOR THE NEW ENGLAND SPORTS NETWORK AND IS STUDYING BROADCAST JOURNALISM AT BOSTON UNIVERSITY. THIS INTERVIEW TOOK PLACE IN FEBRUARY 2006.

David Laurila: *Let's start with your history as a Red Sox fan. What can you tell us about that?*

Kelly Barons: In a way, it started as soon as I was born. My dad is a huge Sox fan, and when I was a baby he'd whisper the '67 lineup into my ear to get me to stop crying. Ever since, I've always been a very, very dedicated fan. Troy O'Leary was my first favorite player. Later it was Nomar, and when I was a freshman in high school my friend Noah and I stole a box of ballots once and voted for him 2,000 times at a game. We were sitting up in section 3 when we did that. When I was 16, I went to the hitting camp Nomar had with Mo Vaughn. I was probably a little old for it, but I didn't care. To have him walk by and say, "nice cut" was pretty amazing.

DL: *Did you play baseball growing up?*

KB: I played baseball and then switched to softball when I was 13. There were three girls in the league when I played baseball—me and two of my best friends.

DL: *Which position did you play, and what kind of hitter were you?*

KB: In baseball, they moved us around a lot, but I wanted to be a short-stop. I'm left-handed, though, which didn't exactly help my cause! In softball, I was a catcher in high school and the one year I played at Regis College. As a hitter, maybe I'd compare myself to a Bill Mueller—not the greatest for power, but I got hits when I had to.

DL: *How did you end up working for the Red Sox?*

KB: My senior year of high school, Noah applied for an open call they were having for Fenway ambassadors. He was selected to attend but couldn't go, so I took his spot. I think 3,500 people tried out, and from there they cut back until they got down to 25. I was lucky enough to get picked, and it's been a really fun job. It's been great to interact with the fans, especially when we were bringing the World Series trophy everywhere.

DL: *How did you become a ball attendant, and what do you remember about your first game?*

KB: I remember being terrified, absolutely terrified. Not that I'd get hurt, but that I'd screw up. Part of the job is catching the ceremonial first pitch, and on my first day a kid threw the ball over my head and up against the screen. That wasn't my fault, but it was still embarrassing. I think I only had one ball hit to me that game, and it was a pretty easy one. How I got the job . . . they just asked me at a yearly meeting. They had also asked a few girls who had played at Tufts and BU—they were the ball attendants before me. I guess they knew we'd be OK because we had softball training—we wouldn't get killed.

DL: *I understand that you were injured by a foul ball once.*

KB: That was one of the most traumatic moments of my life! Ken Griffey, Jr., lined a ball foul, and it caromed off the side wall, right into my face. I thought my face was broken! I remember stumbling and then crouching down. Jim Rowe, the trainer, came running out, and I've never heard Fenway that quiet. Then the organist started playing something. I think it was "Happy Together," which was kind of ironic.

DL: *How badly were you hurt?*

KB: It wasn't really that bad. I did have a big scrape on my chin, but probably the worst part was being embarrassed in front of 34,000 people! I guess after the at-bat, Griffey came out of the visiting clubhouse, asking if I was OK. The next day, Dan Shaughnessy brought him over to me during batting practice. I remember him and Adam Dunn standing there, towering over me. Griffey apologized for what had happened. Then he said, "You gotta remember to get your glove up on those."

DL: *Tell us about "the catch that made Kelly famous."*

KB: That was in June of my first year, about a month after I started. We were playing the Dodgers, and Dave Roberts hit the ball—I guess you could say it was "soundly struck"—and I leaped up and caught it. Apparently it was heading right at a little girl I had been talking to earlier. Her name was Siobhan—Siobhan with the Irish spelling—and she was about five years old. She was really cute. She had made a little Red Sox flag out of some paper and colored it in. I gave her the ball, and her dad has told me that it still means a lot to her. That actually happens quite a bit. Kids will come up to me and say that I gave them a ball once. Getting a ball means so much to them. They're so wide-eyed, and love being there more than anybody.

DL: *Can you share any interesting conversations you've had with adults?*

KB: Bob Kraft [New England Patriots owner] came down by third base once. I had missed a ball, so I went up to him and asked if he could keep his hand down, because the glare off the diamonds of his Super Bowl rings had distracted me. I think I surprised him, because he reacted like I was serious. He said, "Sorry, hon," or some term of endearment like that. I had to tell him I was just kidding!

DL: *Who are some of the other celebrities you've met on the job?*

KB: I got to meet Kenny Chesney, the country singer, who I love. He was on the field taking batting practice, and I was standing near the cage waiting for a chance to meet him. I was really nervous and apparently even shaking. When he was walking over, Tim Wakefield came by and said, "Kelly, you look pretty nervous. Are you OK?"

DL: *You have a good story about going to St. Louis for the 2004 World Series. What happened?*

KB: There was no way I was going to miss it, so Drew—he's another ambassador—and I found a flight out of New Hampshire on Southwest. We had an early flight, around 8:30 in the morning, and overslept. I woke up panicking and started shoving stuff into a bag. We started racing up I-93 at 95 mph, but there was no way we could make it in time. We had non-refundable tickets but somehow managed to sweet-talk them into getting us on another flight—one that was leaving in 10 minutes. We would have made it, but going through security I was randomly selected to be screened. I told them, "You have to be kidding." They said, "No, ma'am, please step over here." So we missed that one, too, and all I could think was, "This is horrible! We'll never get there."

DL: *What happened next?*

KB: They found us another flight, but it wasn't direct—we had to go via Orlando. We took it—we had to get there somehow—but then we found out that the stadium in St. Louis is an hour from the airport. That was a problem, because we didn't have enough cash to take a cab that far. We ended up getting a ride from a guy—a perfect stranger—who heard us talking about it on the plane and said he'd drive us. We didn't have tickets for the game, either, but were able to come up with some when we got there. We made it to our seats just in time for the first pitch. That was Game 3.

DL: *How would you describe what you experienced at Game 4?*

KB: It was just amazing. We all had a good feeling going in, but when Johnny homered to lead off the game we absolutely flipped! We were sitting way up in the nosebleed section, but in the ninth inning I decided I absolutely had to go down to the field. Ever since I was eight years old, I knew I had to be on the field when it finally happened. So right after Foulke underhanded the ball to first, I climbed over the wall. As soon as I did, I burst into tears—I was so happy that I couldn't control myself. Tek, Damon, Kapler, and David Ortiz all came over and gave me hugs. After Ortiz hugged me, he said, "Girl, why are you crying? We just won the World Series!"

DL: *What's in Kelly Barons' future?*

KB: I'll still be ball-girling as much as I can, but not as much as I have the last two years. I think I worked 75 games last season, but I'm a lot busier now. I transferred from Regis to Boston University this year to study broadcast journalism, and I've applied for an internship at ESPN. I've been interested in broadcasting as a career ever since I was asked to host *Baseball Tonight* after getting all the publicity for catching the ball Roberts hit. That was an amazing experience. Just sitting in the pre-game meeting with Peter Gammons and Karl Ravech was amazing.

DL: *Do you have any final thoughts we can close with?*

KB: My time spent working with the Red Sox has been one of the best experiences of my life. I'm so glad I will be able to look back on this period of Red Sox history and say, "I was there. I was a part of something special."

KEN CASEY

KEN CASEY IS A MEMBER OF THE DROPKICK MURPHYS, THE BOSTON-BASED IRISH PUNK BAND THAT REMADE "TESSIE." ORIGINALLY SUNG AT RED SOX GAMES IN THE EARLY 1900S, "TESSIE" BECAME THE TEAM'S RALLYING CRY AS THEY WON THEIR FIRST CHAMPIONSHIP IN 86 YEARS. THIS INTERVIEW TOOK PLACE IN OCTOBER 2004.

David Laurila: *Before we get to the band and "Tessie," let's start with your own history as a fan.*

Ken Casey: I've been coming since the seventies. My grandfather brought me to Fenway and the Garden when I was a kid—the 1975 World Series is one of my first recollections. When I was six or seven, I got to run around on the field after games because my grandfather knew Johnny

Pesky; he knew everybody. I got to meet players and get balls auto-graphed, but then I'd get in trouble because I'd play with them and the ink would smear! Later on, when I was a teenager I used to sneak into the park. I came to all of the postseason games in '86 that way. I've been a fan my whole life.

DL: *Now you're in a band that's filmed a video at Fenway and played there prior to games. What has that meant to you?*

KC: I've almost been speechless. When we were shooting the video in July, I remember standing back and thinking: "Look at what we're doing!" In many ways, that was the most special of the times we've played there. But the others were, too, including the fan-rally when we played on the dugout. It's been incredible.

DL: *Besides Fenway Park, what are the most exciting venues the band has played?*

KC: Boy, good question. We played at the kick-off of a Glasgow Celtic game, the only fan base I've seen that rivals Boston's. We play a song called "The Fields of Athenry," which is their club anthem, so playing there was pretty exciting. We've also played music festivals in Europe with tens of thousands of people. And from a very different perspective, playing at places like The Rat when we were just starting out was mem-orable, too.

DL: *How about notable bands you've played with?*

KC: The Sex Pistols are one. We played with them at a one-off in London several years ago, in front of 30,000 people at Crystal Palace. Johnny Lydon and the band couldn't have been nicer to us. But then we played with them again on the reunion tour last year, and it didn't go as well. He didn't seem nearly as friendly or happy, although it didn't seem to have anything to do with us. At one point, Steve Jones' guitar broke, and we let him use one of ours—they didn't even thank us. Sometimes it's best not to meet your idols.

DL: You've played with the Pogues and Shane MacGowan. What can you tell us about him?

KC: He sings on our *Sing Loud, Sing Proud* album, and there are a few good stories. He was doing a show at The Harp, down by the Fleet

Center, so we called him from Philadelphia, where we were on tour. He was familiar with the band and agreed to meet us in New York City the next day—we did the vocal tracks in a studio there. I was doing the production work, which meant I had to be the bad guy and have him do retakes. He wasn't crazy about that, especially on a old Irish tune like "Wild Rover"—something he's probably sung a thousand times. And every time his lines were coming up, I'd have to reach over and snatch the cigarette out of his mouth! He was pretty hammered, and for some reason thought our manager was Bruce Springsteen—I'm not sure if I can explain why. And then, a few years later, I got an urgent message to call him. I did, and he asked if we still needed him to sing on the album. I told him that he already had, and he sounded confused and hung up.

DL: *Tell us about "Tessie."*

KC: I had been talking to Jeff Horrigan of the *Herald* and said to him, "Everyone thinks we're just hockey fans—probably because we've played at a Bruins game—but I'd love to be involved with the Red Sox, too." Soon after that, he overheard Charles Steinberg [the Red Sox executive vice president of public affairs] saying he'd like to have "Tessie" remade. Jeff told him that he had just the band to do it, so we gave it a shot.

DL: *And how did that go?*

KC: When we first heard the song, it was barely audible and awful. You have to remember it's an old show tune from around 1900. The other guys in the band didn't want anything to do with it, but I was gung-ho about the idea and talked them into doing it. I also suggested to Jeff that he rewrite the lyrics to be about the team and the rabid fans of that era, which he did a great job on. Another thing is that the song is in B-flat, the only key that bagpipes play in. I took that as a sign we were meant to do it.

DL: *Talk about recording the song, including Johnny Damon, Bronson Arroyo, and Lenny DiNardo contributing background vocals.*

KC: We had already recorded the basic tracks and were finishing it at Woolly Mammoth studio across the street from Fenway. Jeff Horrigan walked over to the park to get the guys who wanted to pitch in, and they came over to sing backup. Charles Steinberg did, too. Pokey Reese was supposed to, but didn't make it.

DL: *How was it working with them?*

KC: They were totally cool, really good-spirited. I had already met Arroyo and DiNardo. Bronson is a big music fan. Damon was hilarious. He had no fear doing the vocals, even though he had cameras in his face the whole time. I guess you can't have fear, playing center field for the Red Sox!

DL: *You did the lead vocals, even though you're not the primary vocalist for the band. Why?*

KC: I'm the primary baseball guy, so it seemed natural for me to sing it. I'd say that five of the seven guys in the band are big sports fans, but I tend to take it to another level!

DL: *When did you first play "Tessie" live?*

KC: Interestingly, it was at a festival in Denmark. We wanted to try it out before we got back to Boston, and it went over well. We explained the song before we did it and got a big cheer. The crowd understood the underdog factor—everyone does. And then the second time was in Fenway, during the "brawl game" with the Yankees.

DL: *What are some of the other notable performances?*

KC: The three we've played before games at Fenway were all great, and every one was won with a last at-bat home run! Mueller hit one off Rivera the first time, and then Ortiz did against Anaheim in the first round of the playoffs. Both were walk-offs, and then we played at the first game of the World Series, and Bellhorn hit the foul-pole in the bottom of the eighth!

DL: *You played at Peter Gammons'* Hot Stove Cool Music. *Tell us about that.*

KC: That was fun. It was a charity, which makes it a great show to play. And it was interesting because we hadn't really played a show before without our fan base—the event was sold out before we were announced to play. You have to be better when you're playing for people who don't know your music as well. We're spoiled that our fan base is so loyal—almost like the Red Sox—and they almost make the show for us, they're so into it that it always inspires us to play better. Our crossover is better now, that's for sure. A lot more Red Sox fans are familiar with the band than there were at last year's Hot Stove event.

DL: *Talk about baseball and touring, how the two come together.*

KC: When we go to New York, I'll wear my "Yankee Hater" T-shirt, or a Bruins shirt in Montreal. Sometimes the rest of the band wants to hide, so they don't get hit by flying bottles, but it's all in good fun. Playing in front of 3,000 people in New York can be a hornet's nest. It takes more balls than wearing a "Yankees Suck" shirt at Fenway!

DL: *The band is touring Japan later this month. What can you tell us about that?*

KC: We're going next week, and we're getting a great response on the Red Sox victory and the whole "Tessie" project. A lot of e-mails are coming from Japan, in part because they're so big into baseball over there. We've played there four or five times, and I'd love to go to a Japanese League game some day when we're over.

DL: *Let's jump over to the other sport the Dropkick Murphys are known for: Hockey. Are you an "old-time hockey" guy?*

KC: Absolutely. Baseball and hockey are my two big sports. I loved the Larry Bird Celtics but don't watch much basketball any more. With the Red Sox and Bruins, maybe it's been something about not winning and trying not to get jaded. And I definitely like the "old-time hockey" thing. Intimidation is a big part of the game—it's like Pedro coming inside and establishing what's his on the baseball field.

DL: *Do you know any of the Bruins?*

KC: I'm friendly with some of the players, yes, in part because I have friends from around here that went pro. I actually went to Game 2 of the World Series with P.J. Stock, who played for the Bruins. We also had Irish Mickey Ward [the boxer] with us. Jeff Horrigan called us "the undisputed toughest row in the park!"

DL: *The Red Sox captured the Series with "Tessie" as their official theme song. What was your opinion of "Cowboy Up" last year?*

KC: We're not cowboys here! So anything is better than "Cowboy Up." That said, I know some people don't like our song, either, or the idea of a punk-rock band playing it. But one thing they should remember is that it's for charity. Even if you don't believe in curses or our music, the cause is still there. I think that's important.

EDITOR'S NOTE: Proceeds of the recording go to the Red Sox Foundation.

DL: *Let's close with this year's team and the postseason. What were your experiences watching the Red Sox capture the World Series?*

KC: To be honest, for most of the season I wasn't as enamored as I was last year. There weren't all the come-from-behind wins, but in the play-offs we saw that all over again. I don't know if it's possible to describe what winning it all meant to me.

DL: *You were at most of the postseason games?*

KC: All but the first two in Anaheim. After that I was there for every one, including the road games, thanks mostly to Charles Steinberg—currently one of my favorite people in the world! To be in Yankee Stadium for Game 7 and seeing them put in their place was an incredible experience. In the first game, as soon as I sat in my seat, Schilling gave up two runs and this guy started taunting me. He had this voodoo doll that looked like "Chucky," with a big 1918 sign on it. He was waving it in my face, and I had to hold back the urge to go after him. Then, as luck would have it, after Game 7 I see him coming up the aisle, right in front of me. He's got the doll hanging by his side, bouncing off the floor, and he looks like he wants to cry. That was a happy moment, man—a happy moment.

ERIC CHRISTENSEN

ERIC CHRISTENSEN, A.K.A. "LANTERNJAW," IS THE FOUNDER OF THE SONS OF SAM HORN [SOSH] WEB SITE. THE GOLD-STANDARD INTERNET COMMUNITY OF RED SOX NATION, SOSH IS NAMED AFTER ONE-TIME BOSTON SLUGGER SAM HORN. THIS INTERVIEW TOOK PLACE IN MARCH 2005.

David Laurila: *Let's start with a brief history. What's the story behind SoSH?*

Eric Christensen: SoSH itself was started in February of 2000, but the story goes back a little further. Around 1997 or '98, the Internet was growing in popularity and baseball message boards began popping up. One of them was *Fastball.com*, a site which doesn't exist anymore. Several longtime denizens of Red Sox message boards posted there—Maalox, StillCursingBucky, DieHard3, MikeF, SpokaneSoxFan, and BosoxNut, to name a few. But the site started to get too big, and the signal-to-noise ratio too high. Most of the better posters left and eventually found each other in the cozy confines of *DickieThon.com*. They had a relatively hidden set of MLB forums that produced some great baseball talk. As it turned out, a few years later the site crashed and I set up SoSH in a pinch. It was really meant as a temporary holding-ground until *DickieThon.com* got back up and running—I didn't want to lose that great core group—but that ended up taking six months and we never went back.

DL: *Where did the Sons of Sam Horn name come from?*

EC: It was somewhat random—a bit of a play on the Dickie Thon—and something we figured only diehard Red Sox fans would recognize. I'd say a dozen of us moved over from *DickieThon.com*. CumberlandBlues, one of the current SoSH moderators, was one. Of course, back then he went by StillCursingBucky.

DL: *Have you always been Lanternjaw?*

EC: Yes, that's what I've always gone by. In college, I read a good translation of Don Quixote, and apparently "lanternjaw" is a Spanish slang term for "thug." I've always liked words, and "lanternjaw" is a pretty fun term.

DL: *Now, five years later, you're hosting the World Series trophy and prestigious guests at a fancy hotel, and are known worldwide. When you think back to the early days, does this even seem real to you?*

EC: You know, it's interesting, because we've never done anything to promote ourselves. For a while we grew slowly, and that's really how we wanted it. Members would pass on the link to like-minded folks, and in that way we were even more elitist than we often get accused of now. We've never wanted loudmouths or people who don't know what they're talking about. We wanted people who knew their baseball. For instance, Art Martone of the *Providence Journal* was one of the early people we invited. Bill Simmons was another. But then Bill posted a link on his own site, and suddenly we had hundreds of people registering every day. Back then it was open—anyone could register—and we felt we had to do something.

DL: *And you reacted by . . .*

EC: We wanted to keep things under control, so we started staggering memberships and instituted a registration process. We didn't let everyone in at once—it was done incrementally—and we began requiring that people apply for membership, explaining why they wanted to join. It was all about keeping quality standards and making sure we didn't get too big for our own good.

DL: *What did you require from applicants?*

EC: Basically, a well-written explanation. Simply saying, "I've been a season ticket holder for 20 years" didn't tell us much. Just because you follow the team doesn't make you an asset to the site. Nor does talking a good game if you can't convey your ideas effectively in print. We're a message board, so you need to be able to communicate well in that fashion.

DL: *Along with the Simmons link, what are some of the landmark events that have brought SoSH to where it is now?*

EC: Curt Schilling posting on the site is the obvious one. That began around Thanksgiving of 2003, right before he joined the team. We had already drawn a lot of attention, though. We'd had chats with Theo Epstein, which Steve Silva of Boston Dirt Dogs helped set up. Gordon Edes and Jim Callis had done chats with us. John Henry had posted a few times. But Schilling, and the AP mentioning us in a few articles, has had the biggest impact on our notoriety.

DL: *How much traffic do you get in an average day?*

EC: More than any other Red Sox board, to my knowledge. We get around 100,000 visits per day, of which about 75 percent is lurker traffic. To me, that says we're doing something right as far as the signal-to-noise ratio goes. Even if they can't post, people are interested in what's being said on the site.

DL: *How many applications for membership do you currently receive?*

EC: At least 20 a day. Right now, there are about 10,000 applicants in the actual pool, and that doesn't include all the people who've actually e-mailed an "application" before registering on the site. It's a little overwhelming.

DL: *You mentioned how SoSH has been accused of being elitist. Can you comment on that?*

EC: An analogy I like to use is this: If you put 10 M.I.T. rocket scientists in a room, you'll get great discourse on the matter at hand. But what happens if you bring in 10,000? That would simply be too many voices, and it would overwhelm the quality of discussion. There are a lot of great Red Sox fans out there, with a lot to say, but it would detract too much from what we are to let all of them in. We're not elitist, per se, but we have an obligation to maintain the standards that have made the site a success. We allow new members in at a rate that won't disrupt the flow of discussion.

DL: *Most people know that Curt Schilling and John Henry are occasional contributors to your site. Are you at liberty to tell us who some of the other notables are?*

EC: Most of the people with names you'd recognize just use their own. There are 6 or 10 who use pseudonyms, but that's for a reason. So, no, I can't really say. Quite a few members of the local media, though.

DL: *SoSH includes a private forum, which only members can access. A year ago, posts made by Curt Schilling in that forum were reported by the media. What were your thoughts on that?*

EC: I wasn't too crazy about it, obviously. We set up that forum so members would have a place to talk among themselves. You don't always want everything you say to be public. Curt enjoys talking to fans, and it was reasonable enough for him not to want the media to report his every word. His feelings were that the media can ask him questions every day, and there's a time and place for them to do that.

DL: *Have you had offers from larger entities, wanting to buy into, or take over, SoSH?*

EC: We get offers like that every other month or so. I suppose if someone made an offer that couldn't be refused . . . we'd have to think about it. But we don't want anyone else in control and dictating our standards. We're really not interested in being anything other than what we are.

DL: *What is your current relationship with Sam Horn, and what do you see as the future of SoSH?*

EC: I became partners with Sam last summer. To some extent, the party with the World Series trophy was a launch of that partnership— our first commercial venture. We'll be doing similar things in the future, probably half a dozen smaller scale events this year. But beyond SoSH realizing an offline community, the hopes are that nothing will really ever change about the site. We're just a group of fans who like to get together and talk about the Red Sox.

⚾

KAY HANLEY

KAY HANLEY IS A SOLO ARTIST AND THE FORMER LEAD SINGER OF THE BAND LETTERS TO CLEO. A NATIVE OF DORCHESTER, MASSA-CHUSETTS, HANLEY NOW LIVES IN LOS ANGELES AND IS A REGULAR PERFORMER AT THE *HOT STOVE COOL MUSIC* BENEFIT CONCERT. THIS INTERVIEW TOOK PLACE IN NOVEMBER 2005.

David Laurila: *I understand you have a good story about going to a Cincinnati Reds spring training game in 1996. What happened?*

Kay Hanley: We were on tour, and Michael [Hanley's husband and gui-tar player] and I were shooting a spot for *Baseball Tonight* that Peter Gammons had asked us to do. Jeff Horrigan was working as a Reds beat writer at the time, and he introduced us to some of the players. One of them was Ray Knight. We were taking some photos, and someone asked if we wanted our picture taken with him. I said that would be fine, but I did mention that my father would die if he knew I was getting my picture taken with the guy who crossed home plate after the ball went through Buckner's legs in '86. Upon hearing that, Ray immediately went and got his World Series ring—to torture us, I'm sure—although it was all in good fun. We never did have the picture taken.

DL: *It sounds like your father is a pretty big Red Sox fan, too.*

KH: He swears that he hates them with the heat of a thousand suns, but he watches every game. He's like a lot of Red Sox fans that way, I guess.

DL: *What's it like following the Red Sox while living in L.A.?*

KH: The biggest hurdles are the time difference and not being able to watch the games on TV. We could buy the MLB package, but that's expensive and not something we can justify right now, so we listen to a lot of games on the computer. We don't mind that though, because we like listening to Joe Castiglione. And you wouldn't believe how many Red Sox fans there are out here. There's even a Red Sox bar, Sonny McLean's, which Michael has been to. My main writing partner, Michelle Lewis, is actually a big Yankee fan. Friends Despite Baseball was the name of our first EP—the band we have together is called The Dilettantes. We were together every day for the rollercoaster ride of the playoffs in October of '04, which was kind of hard on us, as you might expect.

DL: *On October 17, 2004, we were down three games to none against the Yankees in the ALCS. That night, as Game 4 was being played, you wrote on your Web site: ". . . if anything poetic or heroic is going to happen, it will be in favor of the Yankees."*

KH: Yes, I'm wrong a lot, and I couldn't have been more wrong there. Gosh, it was just amazing, wasn't it? Are you a lifelong fan too? Do you remember how you were feeling at zero-hour? It was so surreal and so dramatic. When I wrote that, we had been listening to the game on the radio—that's our power center—but Michael had just turned on the TV. I couldn't watch, so I started typing. I was hoping to change the team's power center by doing that. And it was unthinkable that we were going to win three more, but somehow we did.

DL: *What are your thoughts on Theo Epstein resigning as Red Sox GM, and rumors that he could end up with the Dodgers?*

KH: I'd be all right with that. It would be a lot harder if he went to another American League team. If it was here, I could root and not feel guilty. And not that I'd ever give up the Red Sox, but being a part-time Dodger fan would be OK. As for what happened, I feel horrible for the Red Sox and sad for Theo. But it's such a pressure cooker there. This might sound unpopular, but I wonder if maybe he was just the tiniest bit over his head. I'm saying that kind of from a mother's point of view. Maybe he could have used another 10 years of life-experience before he got into it? But I guess I'm a girl when it comes to how I look at sports. Sometimes I even feel bad for the opposing pitcher when he's getting killed. So maybe it would be good if Theo came to L.A. The Dodger situation would be a lot less tenable, and he could build more from the ground up. And what if he brought Johnny with him, too? That would be even better! But I'm being selfish with thoughts like that, aren't I?

DL: *If you were named Red Sox GM, what would be your biggest priorities?*

KH: I'd try to get the team back to basics. I wouldn't want just a bunch of sluggers. I'd want more scrappy little guys like David Eckstein. But first of all, I'd build up a young, malleable pitching staff at Pawtucket. That's what we need more than anything.

DL: *What if you played for the Red Sox? Which position do you see your-self at, and what kind of player would you be?*

KH: I'd love to get on base a lot—hit a lot of singles and doubles. I wouldn't be home run, home run, home run. I'd be a simple player. I think on-base percentage is really important. As for what position— that's a good question. I'd never be a first baseman. Catching would kill my knees. Pitching is too stressful. You know what? I'd be a shortstop. It's an exciting position, and you don't have to be tall to play there. I'm only 5'2".

DL: *To close, what is it like singing the national anthem at Fenway Park?*

KH: I?ve done it six or seven times, including a few Yankee games, and I'm so happy just to be on the field. It was terrifying the first time. What's weird is that they have you tape it, because the sound system is old and they want to eliminate any possible problems. But even without that to worry about, it's still a little scary in a way. After all, I'm singing for my team.

SHEILA PAPELBON

SHEILA PAPELBON IS THE MOTHER OF RED SOX PITCHER JONATHAN PAPELBON. A RESIDENT OF JACKSONVILLE, FLORIDA, AND A FORMER STUDENT-ATHLETE AT LSU, PAPELBON WORKS FOR THE BANK OF NEW YORK. THIS INTERVIEW TOOK PLACE IN FEBRUARY 2005.

David Laurila: *Along with Jon, you have two other sons playing base-ball. Tell us about them.*

Sheila Papelbon: They're twins, and each is pitching at the University of North Florida for Dusty Rhodes. Jeremy is a left-handed starter, Josh a right-handed submariner and their closer. They're redshirt sophomores, so they'll be eligible for the draft this year. Josh actually joined the team as a walk-on, and he's been a poster-boy for success. He hadn't pitched a lot, but really became successful when Dusty had him start throwing as a submariner two years ago. Jeremy is the more natural one and has been pitching the longest. He dominated in high school here in Florida, and is healthy again after having a knee injury and then almost dying because of a bleeding ulcer caused by Vioxx.

DL: *With Jeremy a lefty, and Josh a submariner, is Jon the "normal" one?*

SP: Well, Jonathan's told me that I should have tied his right arm behind his back when he was young, so he'd have been forced to be a left-hander. I'm not sure if that's normal, or not. All three are extremely competitive. Of the twins, Jeremy is more reserved, like his father. Josh is more outgoing, like me, more of a social butterfly. Jonathan is probably somewhere in between.

DL: *Last year, I wrote a story about Jon winning a cow-milking contest and being a fun-loving guy off the field. Was that an accurate portrayal?*

SP: I think so. While the twins are more detail-oriented, Jonathan can light the candle at both ends. He's very carefree and doesn't over-think or worry too much. That's actually a good thing, as there's a lot of pressure in the game of baseball. He has the right personality to not let things get to him too much.

DL: *But on the field he's competitive?*

SP: When he crosses the white line, it's like Jekyll and Hyde. He won't even talk to anyone before the game on days he's pitching. He's very serious about the game.

DL: *How would you describe yourself as a fan, especially when your sons are on the mound? Can you sit back calmly, or are you yelling, "Kill the umpire"?*

SP: I definitely can't sit quietly! Even at the office, I can't wait to go to the ballpark. My adrenaline gets worked up, and when I get there you can hardly talk to me, either! I'm into the game, and I live and breathe every pitch.

DL: *Prior to becoming "mom Papelbon," you pitched on LSU's first women's fast-pitch softball team. When you watch your sons' games, do you think along with their pitching patterns and have opinions on what they should throw?*

SP: Oh, yes! I'm right in their mind with them. Sometimes I'll think, "Take a deep breath," or "Throw high-heat on this pitch." It can be nerve-wracking. And I can usually tell if a pitch is going to be a strike during their wind-up or when the ball is coming out of their hand. I know their motions and release-points, and I can tell if they're in sync or not.

DL: *What was your personality on the mound at LSU, and were you a power pitcher like Jon?*

SP: I was like Jonathan to some extent—or like Joshua. I'm outgoing and competitive, and I was when I pitched. And I was a power pitcher, yes. I learned in fourth grade, growing up in California. When I moved to Louisiana in 11th grade, it was actually culture shock as far as competitiveness on the softball field goes. It was much more serious in California.

DL: *Jon pitched in Sarasota last year. How many games did you see, and what are your plans for this summer?*

SP: Once the twins' games ended in June, we saw most of the ones he pitched. It was a four-hour drive, and we listened on the Internet when we couldn't make it down. It will be different this year, especially because it looks like Jonathan will be in Portland. We plan to fly up for opening day, and then in June on vacation. That's what we did when he pitched in Lowell—took our vacation there.

DL: *How do baseball organizations accommodate the families of players? When you want to see Jon play, what do you do?*

SP: There's a "player's list," and every day they put names on it if they have someone coming. We just pick up our tickets at the gate when we come in. In Sarasota, there was hardly anyone there, so we could sit anywhere we wanted. In Lowell, our seats would usually be several rows above the dugout. The families would be grouped together.

DL: *How many family members of other players do you typically see at games, and is there a fraternal bonding that takes place with them?*

SP: There tend to be more wives and girlfriends than parents. I have met some parents, like Matt Murton's and Brian Marshall's. You become friends with some, but I think there's less camaraderie than there is in the college game. In the pros, there's a feeling of "team," and wanting to win, but it's different. Here, everyone's big goal is to make the Major Leagues. That doesn't mean people aren't nice to each other, but there's a different feel to it.

DL: *Talk about your interactions with fans and what they ask you, knowing that your son is a player.*

SP: They usually want to know all about them—Jonathan, for instance. And I don't mind talking to people—as long as he's not pitching! If he is, I'm too much into the game. As a matter of fact, I have a funny story about a game in Lowell. I got to talking with someone who had seats in the first row, right above the visitors' dugout, and I went down to sit with him for a few innings. The Vermont Expos were playing, and I was yelling at Jonathan, "Strike this guy out," or "Come on, let's get this guy!" After the inning ended, the Vermont manager comes out of the dugout and looks up at me. He said, "You must be Mrs. Papelbon!" That was really funny and kind of embarrassing. And it turns out that he knew my twins, through Dusty Rhodes, because he coaches in the off-season in Florida. He hadn't even known they had an older brother playing pro ball.

DL: *How hard is it to accept that booing and catcalls are a part of the game, and sometimes it's directed at your son[s]?*

SP: You don't want to hear it. It hurts. But you have to learn to have thick skin—otherwise it can really get to you. It's not like you can walk over and slug somebody, so you have to take it with clenched teeth sometimes.

DL: *What about newspapers and Internet message boards? How do you deal with criticism and rumors—which aren't always accurate—from each?*

SP: That's hard, too. And when the speculation or criticism is wrong, it's even more difficult. But in some respects, you realize that because it's Boston there's going to be more interest. And with more interest, there's going to be a wider variety of opinions and rumors. There's a temptation to always answer back, but often it's best not to. You know the truth—they don't—and you have to take things with a grain of salt. Jonathan understands this, and he tells me that all the time.

DL: *All parents offer their children perspective and advice, even after they become adults themselves. With your sons pursuing Major League careers, what role are you currently playing in this regard?*

SP: Keeping them grounded. We've never put them out there as stars, and we'd be disappointed if they developed big egos. I think I'd put them in their place if they did. No matter how good they become, there will always be more important things in life than baseball—things like God and family. I think they all understand that.

DL: *Who was more nervous on the day Jon was drafted—him or you?*

SP: I'd say it was him. We all knew it was going to happen, we just didn't know the exact round or the team. We knew it would be around the third or fourth, and Jonathan didn't really care who it would be. Every time his cell phone rang, he'd jump up. We all did, to be honest. And when the call came from the Red Sox, we were definitely surprised. There were other scouts who seemed more interested, and when he got off the phone he said, "You're not going to believe who that was." We guessed, "Arizona? The Mets?" He said, "No, the Red Sox!" All we could say was, "Wow"—I don't think we'd even talked to their scout. Of course, then we all started jumping up and down!

DL: *Talk about what it was like leading up to the draft, including visits and calls from scouts and agents.*

SP: There wasn't much from agents, because Coach Polk at Mississippi State had advised Jonathan not to hire one. He felt Jonathan could handle that on his own, and once they learned that they quit calling. Jonathan knew what a fair offer was and didn't want to quibble over a few thousand dollars. He just wanted to get his career started. As for scouts, we met many of them at games, but they mostly called for Jonathan directly. I know that they had him fill out a lot of questionnaires and personality tests. Teams wanted to know about a lot of things, including whether his family had college educations, or if they played sports themselves. They seemed particularly interested in things like genetic makeup and value systems. The Red Sox definitely seemed to put a lot of value on those.

DL: *Let's look into the future. Jon is on the mound for the Red Sox, and pitching against him, for the Yankees, is Josh or Jeremy. Are you at the game or too nervous to watch?*

SP: Oh, boy! I'm at the game for sure—I wouldn't miss it—but it would be hard. I guess that what I'd do is cheer for them, and not the teams. You can get a loss and still perform well, so the outcome wouldn't matter as much as them giving it their all and pitching good games. I'd want them both to do well. I'm competitive, but I'm still a mother.

DL: *Last one: Can you share a good story about Jon?*

SP: I think I can get away with this one. In high school, he was going to be taking the ACTs on a Saturday morning, so we told him he couldn't go out on Friday night. Around nine o'clock, we realized he was gone and had actually left a note on his bed. It said, "I snuck out, but don't worry—I'll be back soon." So we closed and locked all the windows and doors, except for the front door. When he got home a few hours later, he had to come in that way, and we were on the couch waiting for him. I think he'll remember that one pretty well—we weren't exactly happy!

ANNE QUINN

ANNE QUINN IS AMONG THE LONGEST-STANDING SEASON TICKET HOLDERS AT FENWAY PARK. EIGHTY YEARS YOUNG, QUINN HAS OCCUPIED THE SAME SEATS, IN THE BLEACHERS, SINCE 1964. THIS INTERVIEW TOOK PLACE IN SEPTEMBER 2004.

David Laurila: *Let's start with this season—how many games did you miss?*

Anne Quinn: Only the one on Easter Sunday, when there was a family get-together I had to attend. But I was able to follow the game on television and the radio while I was there.

DL: *You started coming to every game in 1964. Why that year?*

AQ: My husband, Jerry, and I lived in Worcester until then. He had been at the newspaper there for 20 years—he worked in printing and as a proofreader—but the company went on strike and he lost his job. We decided to come to Boston, and he ended up working at the *Globe* for 25 years. And we started going to Fenway Park together.

DL: *And you always sat in the same seats?*

AQ: Yes. We'd come in when the gates opened and take them. You couldn't get season tickets in the bleachers back then—that didn't happen until 1980—but we always got there early enough to claim our spot. And once they did become available, well, we bought them and have had them ever since.

DL: *You lost your husband last summer.*

AQ: Yes, Jerry passed away last June 30th. He had to quit coming to most games two years ago because of his health and didn't come to day games for several years before that—the doctor didn't want him sitting in the sun all afternoon.

DL: *So now your daughter is with you for most games.*

AQ: Anne Marie comes and quite often her husband. You see, we actually have three seats. That's what we had originally, but she got married and moved to Florida for a few years, so we gave up the one. Now we have it back.

DL: *How often have you sat in other seats?*

AQ: We had to sit in section 36 for the 1975 World Series, but that's the only time we've been moved. I did sit in the Monster seats once last year—it was the day before my birthday, and someone offered me the ticket. And I've sat in a few other places over the years, but it's only been a couple of times.

DL: *Had you been to Fenway Park prior to 1964?*

AQ: Oh, yes. My parents took me when I was young, but I don't remember the first time or anything like that. I know that Jerry took me in 1949—that was before we were married—I do remember that. We didn't start sitting in section 41 until we moved here, though.

DL: *Were you already a fan when he took you in 1949?*

AQ: I sure was. When Jerry came to the house, my mom told him, "You don't have to tell her anything about baseball. She knows."

DL: *Thinking about those earlier years, who were some of your favorite players?*

AQ: I liked Ted [Williams], although I didn't see him very much. He could do everything, but didn't do more than he had to in the outfield. Dom [DiMaggio] would stand sideways out there, turned toward Ted so he could cover for him. Dom should be in the Hall of Fame. He was such a wonderful player, especially on defense. Jim Rice is another one who should be in the Hall. He put up numbers that nobody else did, but he didn't get along with the media—that probably costs him. It's like Albert Belle not winning the MVP award that one year. He probably should have, but some guys didn't want to vote for him because they didn't like him.

DL: *What are your thoughts on "the wave?"*

AQ: I don't like it very much. It would be OK if it was just once a game, but they keep trying to do it over and over. Beach balls, too—what's the point? I want to yell, "Take it to the beach!" Why come to the game if you don't want to watch? When there are fights in the stands, everybody gets up and forgets about the game. Not me—the heck with that.

DL: *How about the recent Fenway Park tradition of singing along with Neil Diamond's "Sweet Caroline" in the eighth inning?*

AQ: Oh, that's enjoyable. I sing along, too, just like with "Take Me Out to the Ball Game." And I have a tape—I hope I haven't lost it—of me singing along with the national anthem. That's from Channel 3 News interviewing me in 1989. I think that's what year it was.

DL: *How has the atmosphere in the bleachers changed over the years?*

AQ: Well, there are definitely more beach balls. I remember how Bob Stanley used to pop them with a rake, but there are even more now. And it's not too bad where I sit, but up higher they drink too much and chant. I don't like the "Yankees suck" stuff. It sounds dumb and just fires up the competition.

DL: *What is your opinion of the Yankees, and do you hope we get another shot at them in the playoffs?*

AQ: In a way I do, but mostly I just want them to lose. I don't hate their players, but I do hate the system. Steinbrenner wants to run everything, and he has too much power. Like the A-Rod deal, and all that stuff about restructuring his contract. The league wouldn't let it happen when we wanted him, but the next thing you knew, the Yankees had him and there didn't seem to be the same rules for them. And with Contreras the year before, Steinbrenner sent 11 men down to negotiate with him, and told them they'd all get fired if they didn't bring him back.

DL: *You've had a lot of interaction with the players over the years. Who have you met this year?*

AQ: I met Pokey [Reese] at a BoSox Club luncheon. I go to all of those. He said, "You have to root for me now."

DL: *Anyone else?*

AQ: Oh, sure. I met David Ortiz and David McCarty. And the third base coach, what's his name? . . . oh, yes, [Dale] Sveum. And Papa Jack [Ron Jackson], too. I saw Jim Rice earlier this year at the park, and he hugged me and asked, "Where have you been?" And, of course, I talk to Jason Varitek all the time.

DL: *Tell us about that.*

AQ: I go down to see him in the bullpen before every game—he's so friendly to me and such a nice guy. It's a little different when Schilling is pitching, though, because he warms up the longest. That means there's less time for Varitek to sign autographs or talk. And I call his home runs, too. He told Johnny Damon about that once at a baseball writers' dinner. He said, "This is the lady who calls my home runs." And another time, he said to me, "Better call one quick, I haven't hit one in a while."

DL: *Does he top your list of players we should re-sign after the season?*

AQ: I hope we keep him, yes. But we need to re-sign Pedro, too. If we don't, the Yankees will get him in a minute.

DL: *Who are some of the other players you've talked to over the years?*

AQ: Oh, there are many. Yaz [Carl Yastrzemski] always says, "Hello." I remember once in spring training, in Winter Haven, I saw Mike Boddicker. I said to him, "I know someone who didn't shave this morning." He answered back, "It was either that or ten more minutes of rest, and I thought it was better to get the rest."

DL: *Can you share a few more?*

AQ: Ellis Burks used to always wave to me when he came out to center field—that was when he was here the first time. Now, it's Johnny Damon and Mike Timlin who wave. And I helped Bruce Hurst once. I don't remember the year, but he started out 1-7. I went down to the bullpen before a game and said, "I think I know what's wrong with you." He came over and asked, "What?" I told him that he wasn't following through completely—he wasn't wrapping his arm around his back like he did the year before. Well, he started winning, and later he was on the radio saying, "A fan helped me turn my season around."

DL: *Let's switch from players to broadcasters. I assume you've had favorites over the years.*

AQ: Ken Coleman was wonderful, and so was Curt Gowdy. I liked Rico Petrocelli when he was broadcasting. Joe [Castiglione] and Jerry [Trupiano] are good, too. I've always listened to all of the games, even the ones on the West Coast. Sometimes my husband would go to bed before the late games ended, but I've always stayed up until the end.

DL: *Have you had any interactions with Joe or Jerry?*

AQ: Oh, yes. Once I told Jerry that he needs to change the way he announces. We'll have the bases loaded and he'll say, "All it will take is a single," and it ends up being a double-play instead. Or the other team will have them loaded and he'll say, "All we don't need now is a single," and that's what will happen. Or somebody from the other team is up and he'll say, "This guy hasn't had a home run for a long time," and then he hits one. I told him that he jinxes us when he says things like that.

DL: *Along with always keeping score, you bring a portable radio to the ballpark, but never a walkman. Why is that?*

AQ: I don't like earphones, because you can't hear the people in the stands. I like to enjoy the sounds around me.

DL: *Do many people come up to talk to you?*

AQ: Yes, a lot of people are nice. I remember some helping me in 1990 when I took sick at the park—my husband wasn't with me that day. It was a rainy Sunday and I had a lot on my mind. I had just celebrated my 40th anniversary and had been bowling about four times a week. I had other things going on, too, and ended up having a minor hemorrhage—my right arm went completely numb. I couldn't figure out what had happened, so the first thing I did was put the pencil in my left hand and tried to keep score that way. But after a while, I realized that I needed help and people got the medics for me. They got me to the hospital, and fortunately it wasn't too serious and I didn't miss too many games.

DL: *Let's jump over to managers—who have your favorites been over the years?*

AQ: I loved Joe Morgan. Dick Williams was good, too—he was tougher—but Morgan always had hunches, and they worked. Did you know that I made out a lineup for him once?

DL: *Tell us about that.*

AQ: He was on *The Joe Morgan Show* one Sunday night with John Dennis, and I had a chance to go. Afterwards, I told him that he had Jody Reed hitting in the wrong spot, and that Ellis Burks should hit in front of Dwight Evans. He had me explain why, and I wrote out a lineup for him. He used it the following night.

DL: *What are your thoughts on Terry Francona?*

AQ: He's OK, but I blame him for a lot of the losses, especially when it comes to pitching decisions. He never seems to know when to take a pitcher out, and he really cost Derek Lowe this year when he changed the rotation and made him sit for 10 days. He should have just kept things the way they were.

DL: *What is your opinion of Lowe?*

AQ: He's not what he was. I think the trade rumors bother him, and so does getting squeezed by the umpires. Pedro, too—he really gets squeezed. But I like Lowe. He threw a ball up to me from the bullpen this summer. And the next night, a batting practice home run bounced right to me—that's the first time that ever happened. Reid Nichols threw a ball to me once, too, on my 33rd anniversary. After that, he stopped me in Kenmore Square once and showed me his new baby. He was such a nice guy.

DL: *What is your opinion of Fenway Park being replaced some day?*

AQ: I'd hate to see it. We'd lose a lot of our home field advantage, just like the Celtics and Bruins did when they replaced the Garden. I like the improvements they've made to the park, though. The only thing I don't like is the prices.

DL: *With the playoffs coming up, what are your thoughts on some of the team's most tragic disappointments?*

AQ: In some ways, 1986 was the worst. But 1978 was bad, too, because the playoff shouldn't have even happened—that was when we blew the big lead. And everybody remembers Bucky Dent's home run, but it was Reggie Jackson's that really won the game for them. Nobody expected Dent's, though, which is why he gets so much of the credit. And a lot of people think Mickey Rivers gave him a corked bat, too. I guess we'll never know. And then, after the game ended, a police horse stepped on my foot outside the park and broke one of my toes.

DL: *Last question: What will happen if the Red Sox win the World Series this year?*

AQ: Oh, God. I just hope people don't start smashing things—that's so stupid. We've come close so many times, and it will be exciting when we win. Maybe this will finally be the year. I certainly hope so. I've been waiting a long time.

⚾

SHONDA SCHILLING

SHONDA SCHILLING IS THE WIFE OF RED SOX PITCHER CURT
SCHILLING. A GRADUATE OF TOWSON STATE UNIVERSITY,
SCHILLING IS AN ACTIVE SUPPORTER OF SEVERAL CHARITIES,
INCLUDING THE FIGHTS AGAINST ALS [LOU GEHRIG'S DISEASE]
AND MELANOMA. THIS INTERVIEW TOOK PLACE IN JUNE 2004.

David Laurila: *Let's start by talking about a great event you're involved
with. Tell us about Picnic in the Park.*

Shonda Schilling: It's to benefit some wonderful causes: Jane Doe Inc.,
the Massachusetts Coalition against Sexual Assault and Domestic
Violence, and the Red Sox Foundation. It's being held on the field at
Fenway Park, and it includes picnic food from great local chefs, a raffle,
a live auction, and a VIP reception.

DL: *Talk about what it means to be involved in an event like this.*

SS: Any time you can help people, it's a good feeling. I really believe that
Curt and I get more out of events like this than we give. Making the quality of someone's life better is worth more than the time we put into it.

DL: *Let's talk about your life around the game of baseball. What was
your interest and involvement in it prior to marrying Curt?*

SS: I used to work at a television station in Baltimore that covered the
Orioles, so I was very involved. I went to a lot of games growing up, too.
My dad and mom used to bring me, and we'd sit in the bleachers.

DL: *You were an Orioles fan growing up?*

SS: I was. They had good teams back then and were fun to watch. I liked
Brooks Robinson, and then later Cal Ripken and Rick Dempsey. One of
my favorite memories as a fan was being at the game where Cal broke
Lou Gehrig's consecutive-games record. It was in my home town, and I
had our oldest son, Gehrig, with me. He was six months old at the time.

DL: *Did you participate in sports when you were growing up?*

SS: Quite a bit. I played fast-pitch softball in high school and for one year in college. I was a catcher. I also played basketball and field hockey, and was even voted female athlete of the year.

DL: *Being a catcher made you a perfect match for Curt. Maybe that was the attraction.*

SS: I never thought of it that way. It's funny, though, because we used to play catch and long-toss together. After we got married, we stopped. He didn't want to do it anymore. I was OK catching him as long as he wasn't throwing curves.

DL: *Do you still find time for athletic endeavors?*

SS: I just started playing field hockey again, believe it or not. I had really missed being part of a team. Sports teach you what can be accomplished as a team, and I missed the camaraderie. The wives' group is like that, in a way. We're all working together for a common goal, and we support each other.

DL: *I've heard that you're planning to run the Boston Marathon next year.*

SS: I am. It will be my first time, and I'm excited about it. I've always been a runner, and after being diagnosed with melanoma I felt like it had been taken away from me. Running the marathon is, in a way, like taking my life back.

DL: *Talk about some of the wives you've gotten to know on this year's team.*

SS: This is our first year here, so I'm just getting to know a lot of them. Now that school is out, I'm really looking forward to doing just that— getting to know them better.

DL: *Do you think baseball wives are stereotyped?*

SS: I think so, but maybe a little less than years ago. A lot more of us are college-educated, and people are coming to learn that. There will always be some perception of the high school sweetheart marrying the jock, but I don't let that bother me any more. We come from so many different backgrounds and experiences. People who get to know us find out who we are.

DL: *What is the most frustrating part of being a baseball wife?*

SS: Probably the single-mom part of it. Curt's a great father, but he's obviously away a lot. Having to go to events and school functions by myself is frustrating in many ways. I've certainly gained a great admiration for single mothers.

DL: *How often do you make it to Fenway to see Curt pitch?*

SS: We actually go to most of the home games, and now that school's out it's easier. We like to be at the park, and it's good to see him when the game ends.

DL: *How often do you travel to games in other cities?*

SS: I try to go as much as I can, maybe one city each road trip. A lot of the wives do. We're all from somewhere, and often there's a team in our hometown. I'm from Baltimore, so I like to go when we play there. My best friend lives in Chicago, so that's another trip I look forward to. When Curt and I were in Arizona, it was pretty easy to travel to San Diego, which is a great city for kids.

DL: *What's the best advice you've received from another wife involved with baseball?*

SS: It was from Graig Nettles' wife. She said you'll only have one or two really close friends in the game, and you should be careful who you trust when it comes to money.

DL: *The money part is pretty obvious. Can you say a little more about the friendships?*

SS: You meet a lot of people in the game, and you make a lot of friends. The names and faces change, though, and you can only be close to so many of them. Peggy Morandini and Lisa Johnson are the ones I've been closest to over the years. You do feel a connection with the other wives, though. It's hard to truly understand what someone's life is like unless you're in their shoes, and you need someone to talk to about it. A lot of us are close in that way.

DL: *Let's talk about Curt for a minute. How does he differ from the public's perception of him?*

SS: He doesn't talk as much. He's used to talking all day, and people sticking microphones in his face, but when he comes home it's a different story. I've been taking care of four kids all day and haven't spoken to an adult, and when he gets in from a game I want to talk to him—and often he doesn't have anything to say!

DL: *Are we going to get you in trouble if we include this in the interview?*

SS: No—he knows it. I love him, anyway.

DL: *Tell us a story that shows what Curt is like out of uniform.*

SS: He coached Gehrig's baseball team last year, and I really admired how he went about it. He was very patient with the kids and did more than teach organization and fundamentals—he taught them to respect the game. I was proud of how he stressed the right values to them.

DL: *Talk about raising children. Do you think you're forced to approach it differently than you would if Curt were in a different profession?*

SS: In some ways, yes, but in most ways, no. We try to be as normal as possible. The kids are used to their lives as they are and know that Dad is a baseball player. If I ever heard one of them brag to someone: "Do you know who I am?" they'd find themselves getting punished.

DL: *Talk about dealing with packing up and moving when your husband changes teams. Do you have any horror stories?*

SS: I remember when Curt got traded from Houston to Philadelphia. That was in the days before everyone had cell phones, and I actually heard about it on the radio. I was driving back from spring training—we had a caravan of Nancy Caminiti, Patty Biggio, and myself—and I almost crashed when I heard the news. It stunned me. We all pulled over to the side of the road, and I remember all of us being in shock about it. Patty and I were crying.

DL: *I assume it was a little easier coming to Boston.*

SS: Of course. We had plenty of time to make the decision, so there were no surprises.

DL: *What are your thoughts, and Curt's, on living and playing here?*

SS: There's no other place that appreciates baseball as much as Boston. You walk down the street, and every other kid has on a Red Sox jersey. I grew up in a city with a great baseball tradition, and it's even more baseball-savvy here. People really understand the game, and they don't need a message board telling them when to cheer—they know what's going on. I can hardly imagine what it would be like to win it all here.

DL: *One more question: Who is your second favorite player on the team?*

SS: I love to watch David Ortiz hit. He's got great power, and like most fans I enjoy home runs—as long as they're not against my husband! David is such a happy person, too, and his wife is so nice. And their daughter is the friendliest little three-year-old you'll ever see. I like a lot of the players, but I guess I'd pick him. After number 38, of course.

DL: *Thanks for taking the time, Shonda. Let Curt know that Red Sox Nation wants to find out what it would be like to win it all. And good luck with Picnic in the Park.*

SS: You're welcome. I know Curt wants it as badly as anyone. I hope to see a lot of you on the field for the picnic. Stop by and say hi to the Schillings.

HANNU TOIVONEN

HANNU TOIVONEN IS A GOALIE FOR THE BOSTON BRUINS. A 21-YEAR-OLD NATIVE OF KALVOLA, FINLAND, TOIVONEN WAS THE BRUINS' FIRST PICK IN THE 2002 NHL ENTRY DRAFT. THIS INTERVIEW TOOK PLACE IN FEBRUARY 2006.

David Laurila: *You grew up in Finland. Is baseball played there?*

Hannu Toivonen: A little, but mostly it's a game called *pesäpallo*. The basics are the same, but a few of the rules are different and the pitcher tosses the ball higher in the air. It's pretty popular in school gym classes and is actually the national game, although I don't know all of the history behind it. I do know that a guy saw baseball played in the U.S. a long time ago and developed it when he returned to Finland.

DL: *Did you know much about American baseball, and the Red Sox, growing up?*

HT: My parents had a satellite dish, so at times I'd see it on TV. I was kind of interested in the game, but I didn't know a lot about it. I did know that it was big—that all of the pro sports in this city were big—but not to the extent that they actually are. It's kind of hard to describe, but just being around it . . . there's a lot of passion.

DL: *Have you been to Fenway Park yet?*

HT: I have, but not to a game. Just being there, you can feel the tradition. And seeing what it's like on TV, I couldn't believe what it would be like to play there—over 30,000 people standing up and cheering the whole game. It would be incredible, especially when they were playing New York.

DL: *What would you consider the biggest rivalry in Finland?*

HT: Definitely Sweden. It would be kind of like Yankees against Red Sox . . . maybe. I'm good friends with most of the Swedes I know, but put us in uniforms and out on the ice and it changes. Then you want to beat them. That's the way it is. I guess it's a part of history, with Finland once being ruled by Sweden. It's a similar type of feeling against the Russians, but not as much as it is with the Swedes.

DL: *Where were you when the Red Sox won the World Series?*

HT: I was playing with the Providence Bruins at the time, so I was there watching with some friends. They were all from the area, so they were really excited about it. My emotional background with the team wasn't the same as theirs, but I was happy for them. Of course, I'm rooting for the Red Sox to win, too.

DL: *Besides hockey, which teams and sports are important to you?*

HT: I'm a huge, huge soccer fan. I played my whole childhood and absolutely love it. Besides Finland, my favorite nationally is Spain. I just love the skill, enthusiasm, and passion they have. I also followed Liverpool growing up, even before Sami Hyypia and Jari Litmanen played for them.

DL: *Who were your favorite hockey players growing up?*

HT: I watched the goalies all the time. I have always liked the guys who would help their teams win, no matter what they had to do. Everyone has their style, and you want to watch them to maybe pick things up for your own game, but what matters most is their passion. Guys like Martin Brodeur and Patrick Roy just hate to lose, which is what makes them so good.

DL: *It sounds like you mean they have* sisu.

HT: That's it. They have lots of *sisu*. That's the big thing for me. My point of view is that it comes together when you work hard and refuse to lose. That is what matters most.

EDITOR'S NOTE: *Sisu* is a Finnish word that does not translate directly into English but has been described as "Biting off more than you can chew, and then chewing it."

DL: *Before you came to the U.S., you played for HPK Hameenlinna in the Finnish Elite League. Why did you play with HPK?*

HT: I grew up nearby and played juniors there. My parents live 10 minutes away from Hameenlinna, which is not so far from Helsinki. Before I knew it, I was in the Elite League. They told me one day, "You'll be with the big boys tonight." That's when I kind of realized I could do it, that playing was more than just for fun. Then, of course, I came over here to play in 2003.

DL: *Tell us about your NHL debut, earlier this season.*

HT: It was totally sporting competition. I gave up some goals but we won 7-6, and that's what was important. It was really emotional for me. After the game, you realize, "This is it. I'm in the NHL . . . just what I've always dreamed about." To play here for such a great organization, in a great city, is really special.

DL: *You gave up goals to Mario Lemieux, a Hall of Famer, and Sidney Crosby, expected to be the game's next superstar. When you think about it, that's a pretty memorable debut.*

HT: I guess it was, but it didn't make me feel so good to give up the goals, regardless of who scored them. But goals come and go in hockey, and the reality is that you'll give some up. I didn't like it at the time, but maybe it will be something to laugh at later on. It was Crosby's first NHL goal, so maybe I'll be on a lot of history tapes someday!

DL: *What do you like to do when you're off the ice?*

HT: I love golf. I picked it up a couple of years ago, and in a way it's like playing goalie. You're kind of like an individual within a team sport, almost like a pitcher in baseball. It's the same kind of approach. Of course, some people say that pitchers and goalies are both different, and maybe they're right. You have to be different to handle the pressure and actually enjoy it.

DL: *How about outside of sport—what do you enjoy?*

HT: You're always working with your body in sports, so I try to find time to relax and get my mind off of hockey. I always have my music on at home, and I enjoy reading. I have my parents send me things so I can read in Finnish—it is nice to read in my native language when I can. When I go home in the off-season, I mostly try to recharge my batteries. We have a nice summer place, with a sauna, near a lake. Finland is very nice in the summer.

ED VALAUSKAS

ED VALAUSKAS PLAYS BASS IN JULIANA HATFIELD'S BAND AND IS ALSO A MEMBER OF THE GRAVEL PIT AND THE GENTLEMEN. A NATIVE OF GUILFORD, CONNECTICUT, VALAUSKAS HELPS RUN THE Q-DIVISION RECORDING STUDIOS AND IS AN ORGANIZER AND PERFORMER AT THE HOT STOVE COOL MUSIC BENEFIT CONCERT. THIS INTERVIEW TOOK PLACE IN OCTOBER 2005.

David Laurila: *You're involved with Hot Stove Cool Music, as is Peter Gammons. What is your history with Peter?*

Ed Valauskas: My fascination with the Red Sox began when I was eight, so I had known who Peter Gammons was for a while. One day, a number of years ago, I picked up the *Sunday Globe* and saw Gravel Pit song titles in his column. That was mind-blowing. I called the guys in the band and said, "Did you see that?" Later, I got involved with Hot Stove Cool Music, which, of course, he's a big part of. The first year, he didn't play, and I didn't even know that he did. Then, when he decided to start performing at Hot Stove, he asked if the Gentlemen would be his backing band. I had no idea he could sing as well as he does. He sounds just like Big Al Anderson of NRBQ.

DL: *What is it like playing with Gammons?*

EV: We usually only have time for one or two rehearsals, but he picks the songs ahead of time and we generally learn things really quickly. And this year he brought in one of his own. I think he's been working on it for a while now, probably changing the lyrics on it for 10 years. I think it's called, "She Fell from Heaven [and Landed on her Face]." It's a pretty good song; a real slap to right-wingers. Anyway, he brought it in and we arranged it. He picks up changes very well. Something interesting about Peter is that in learning songs, rather than telling you the chords, he explains parts by reciting the lyrics and actually going as far as to explain them. That's unique, but maybe it shouldn't seem that odd. He's obviously a word guy.

DL: *What are Hot Stove Cool Music rehearsal conversations like when the subject turns to baseball?*

EV: It depends on whether Bill Janovitz [Buffalo Tom] is in the room. I try not to ask too much, but between songs Bill will turn to Theo and ask things like, "So, what's up with the Millar/Mientkiewicz situation?" or "So, are we going to re-sign Pedro or not?" As you might guess, Theo is fairly close to the vest on this stuff. But it's kind of cool to see the off-the-field personas of guys like Theo and Peter—both what you would think; both really smart and funny guys who know as much about music as they do baseball. Peter is such a polite, articulate, and intelligent guy. It sounds funny to hear him say what a great f-ing guy, and player, Ortiz is!

DL: *Do you have any good stories about baseball and touring?*

EV: The Gravel Pit had the good fortune of hitting spring training in 1997 on our way to the SXSW Music Festival. That year, our friend Jeff Horrigan [Hot Stove organizer/*Boston Herald* sportswriter] worked for a Cincinnati daily at the time and got us into a bunch of Reds games and a few Red Sox ones. We got to meet George Foster, who was the Reds' hitting coach at the time, as well as meeting a young shortstop by the name of Pokey Reese. Somewhere we have an autographed ball from Pokey to the Gravel Pit.

DL: *Have you played much baseball?*

EV: I played ball in Connecticut growing up from the time I was nine, until college, mostly short and second. I got my first hit off Rob Dibble when I was nine. I had a partial scholarship to play college ball at Southern Connecticut State University. I decided not to play for fear of injuring my hands and not being able to play bass. Good career move, huh? I'm an idiot. I can't imagine I would have even been close to a prospect—good glove, good speed, OK arm, lame bat. Drummer/pitcher Pete Caldes actually probably could have played pro ball. He blew his arm out in high school, needed Tommy John surgery, and opted not to have it. He gave up a few home runs to Jeff Bagwell back in the day.

DL: *Do you have any thoughts on the 2005 Red Sox pitching staff?*

EV: I hate to be the guy who states the obvious, but the pitching just wasn't the same. I never felt like we had a number one this year. Was it Wells? Maybe. Was it Wake? Maybe. Clement was really good the first half, but down the stretch he was a mess. Maybe he was gun-shy after being hit by the line-drive. Maybe shaving the worst baseball beard in history would have helped.

DL: *Do you, or either of your bands, have any favorite players?*

EV: None of us know him, but we kind of had a fascination with Mark Bellhorn. Pete Caldes even had a Bellhorn cap made, and later I bought an 8 × 10 photo of him, kind of as a joke. We were playing a show at the Paradise right after Bellhorn got traded, and I put the photo on Juliana's amp while we were setting up. At one point, she asked for a moment of silence for him during the show. Some people in the crowd actually booed, not grasping the concept of "moment of silence." It always seemed like Bellhorn was on someone's shit-list, mostly for the Ks. I could relate. I was Bellhorn my first year of Little League. I either walked or struck out. I had one hit. There's something really likeable about the guy—probably because he's the type of player who reminds you of you. He's not a star.

Shorter Views

SHAUN KELLY

SHAUN KELLY, POSTING AS "JACKLAMABE65," STARTED THE NOW-LEGENDARY THREAD ON THE SONS OF SAM HORN WEB SITE ENTITLED "WIN IT FOR." A NATIVE OF WELLESLEY, MASSACHUSETTS, KELLY TEACHES ENGLISH AND AMERICAN HISTORY IN GREENWICH, CONNECTICUT. THIS INTERVIEW TOOK PLACE IN MARCH 2005.

David Laurila: *Let's start with your personal history. You post as "jack-lamabe65." Tell us about that.*

Shaun Kelly: Jack Lamabe was a very respectable Major League pitcher who served as both a starter and reliever for the Red Sox in the early sixties. He was traded along with Dick Stuart from the Pirates and played in Boston for three years. By 1967, he was pitching for the Cardinals against the Red Sox in the World Series. From 1973 to 1977, Jack Lamabe served as both my coach and mentor at Jacksonville University. I found him to be an absolute sweetheart of a guy. He was incredibly supportive and intelligent—a great role model for those of us lucky enough to play for him. Coach Lamabe's nickname, "the Old Tomato," was given to him by Johnny Pesky because of Coach's infatuation with pizza. By the way, the "65" part of my poster name has to do with the fact that by the time I was 10 in 1965, I knew that the Red Sox would be an integral part of my life from then on. Most posters on SoSH call me "Jack." Coach Lamabe, who is retired and residing in Baton Rouge, Louisiana, still finds it very amusing that I am using his name as my Red Sox Internet identity!

DL: *Tell us about how the "Win it For" thread came about.*

SK: It all started because of a word that had been long used in countless threads begun over at SoSH. The word, of course, was "mojo." Mojo, according to Webster's Dictionary, is a noun with a fascinating denotation: "A magic power or supernatural spell." I had no idea, however, that there would be anything supernatural associated with the thread. I had actually started a similar thread right before the start of Game 7 of the 2003 ALCS. As we all know too well, Aaron Boone hit the home run later that evening, we lost once again to New York, and the first "Win it For" posts eventually disappeared into the mist of cyberspace. Because of the way the 2004 Series had almost surreally spun itself out, I once again decided to summon some palpable magic in all of us at SoSH that could provide a little impetus that would somehow enable us to beat the hated Yankees.

With only eight hours left before the deciding game of the 2004 ALCS, I sat down at my teacher's desk during a free period and began pounding away on my computer keyboard. The original post took only about 15 minutes to compose. At a little before noon on that day, I submitted the first of what would be over a thousand entries to the thread.

DL: *At the end of your initial post, you wrote: "Most of all, win it for James Lawrence Kelly, 1913–1986. This one's for you, Daddy. You always told me that loyalty and perseverance go hand in hand. Thanks for sharing the best part of you with me." Tell us about your father and the connection you shared through baseball.*

SK: He was born and raised in northern New York and was actually a New York Giants fan growing up! He attended many games at both the Polo Grounds and Ebbets Field when he lived in Brooklyn for a spell. He even saw Babe Ruth hit a home run in the right-field bleachers at Fenway in 1933! However, when he moved to Boston after college, he soon began to follow the Braves. Eventually, he and Mom secured season tickets to the Braves until they moved to Milwaukee before the 1953 season. It took the '67 Impossible Dream Red Sox to bring him on board, but Dad remained loyal and faithful to the Sox until the day he died. Like many fathers and sons, we spent our best times together watching and rooting for "the Boston nine"—as he used to say in his antiquated vernacular. You see, my father experienced a living hell in places like Iwo Jima, Okinawa, and Leyte Gulf. Baseball became an invaluable vehicle for him to connect with his sons on a daily basis. I am so very proud that Daddy's picture is the first one to be featured in our book. That is my last gift to him.

DL: *Do you have a particular favorite posting within the 55 pages of the thread?*

SK: Actually, I do. An unknown lurker sent me an ezboard message, which ended with the following words:

"Some morning next week, in the hours just after dawn, the cemeteries all over Red Sox Nation will be filled with middle-aged men, standing by ancestral graves marked [whatever the headstone] with the same bronze veterans' plaques at the foot—First Sergeant, Staff Sergeant, PFC, served some range of years beginning with a high school graduation and ending with 1945. We will be reading aloud from tear-stained newspapers, sharing our first too-early libation of the day. [A Gansett? A Ballantine Ale?] We will be drinking to Cabrera's defense, Foulke's grit, Damon's grace, Ortiz's incredible sense of timing. Maybe we'll even have a reason to toast Manny. We will be waving the bloody sock—thanking God and Theo for sending us Schilling, on whom all our hopes rested and did not rest in vain. Remembering all those who came so close but did not get there, like Yaz and Lonborg and Boomer and Rico and Hawk and Tiant and Dewey and Jim Ed and Fisk and Mo and even Nomar. Remembering all those who did not live to see us get there, like Ted and Tony C and my Grampa Dan. The clock will be unwinding, the pages will be flying off the calendar, the earth will tilt slightly on its axis. I will be there. My brothers will be there. Get there early. It's going to be crowded."

Appendix

RED SOX MINOR LEAGUE AFFILIATES

This material is adapted from "A Look into the Future: Red Sox Minor League Report" by Brandon Magee, originally published in the *Maple Street Press 2006 Red Sox Annual*. © 2006 Maple Street Press LLC. All Rights Reserved.

Pawtucket Red Sox (Triple A, International League)
AAA has two types of players: 1) the most advanced prospects and 2) players who are able to shuttle quickly to the major league team in case of emergencies (so-called AAAA players)

Portland Sea Dogs (Double A, Eastern League)
AA is the last level where the majority of players can be considered prospects. The best prospects may jump from this level directly to the major league level.

Wilmington Blue Rocks (High Class A, Carolina League)
At this level, the most advanced second-year players will make their full season debuts. The rest of the roster is filled with slower advancing prospects. The Red Sox moved their high Class-A affiliate from Sarasota to Wilmington prior to the 2005 season

Greenville Drive (Low Class A, South Atlantic League)

Most of the previous season's rookies will make their full season debuts at this level. Certain first year players will also make their debuts here. The Red Sox moved their low Class-A affiliate from Augusta to Greenville prior to the 2005 season. The name of the team was changed from the Capital City Bombers to the Greenville Drive prior to the 2006 season.

Lowell Spinners (Advanced Rookie, New York-Penn League)

Short Season League that starts after the June draft. College draftees often debut at this level. Some advanced international signees will also make their US debuts here, and.some younger second-year players will also play here.

GCL Red Sox (Rookie League, Gulf Coast League)

Short Season League which starts after the June draft. High School Draftees and Undrafted Free Agents often debut here. Most international signees make their US debut at this level.

Index